3

RECENT AMERICAN FICTION

Some Critical Views

Recent
American Fiction

SOME CRITICAL VIEWS

EDITED BY

Joseph J. Waldmeir
Michigan State University

HOUGHTON MIFFLIN COMPANY · BOSTON

For John Christian

PREFACE

THE BODY OF CRITICAL WRITING devoted to American novelists who have come to prominence since the end of World War II is extensive and constantly growing. It appears in periodicals of all sorts, from *Life* and *Time* to the *Evergreen Review* to professional academic journals. Though the range of its quality is equally wide, much of it is of genuine assistance to the reader's pursuit of meaning in the contemporary novel. My purpose here has been to make conveniently available some of the best of this criticism.

In order to achieve, despite the brevity of this book, a breadth and depth of mature critical judgment, I have passed over reviews, and even review articles, in favor of more extensive treatments of the novelists and their work. And, since most of the novelists are still producing books, I have given preference, all else being equal, to later rather than earlier essays about them.

"Breadth" and "depth" are terms which describe well enough the organization of the essays here presented. The collection is in two parts. Part One begins with some general statements concerning contemporary American fiction as a whole, its meaning, aims, and directions. Favorable and unfavorable criticisms have been juxtaposed here. Part One ends with three essays, still of a general nature, which consider three distinct segments or elements of the literature — Jewish, Existentialist, and Beat.

Part Two comprises a dozen essays, each concerned in depth with a single novelist. The arrangement here is simply alphabetical, from an essay on Saul Bellow to one on William Styron; it reflects in no way a judgment either of the essays or of the authors who are their subjects.

Obviously, it has been impossible to include more than a small fraction of the excellent criticism that is available. I have tried to compensate in some degree for this inevitable incompleteness by making the bibliography more than usually comprehensive, and by annotating many of its entries.

I would like to express here my gratitude to the essayists themselves, who have been cooperative in a variety of ways, and to colleagues who have lent a willing ear to the alternating worries and enthusiasms attendant upon the preparation of the book. In particular I record my gratitude for a Michigan State All-University Research Grant which made funds available for carrying out the project; and to Russel Nye, Robert Reilly, and Virginia Rock, whose assistance and advice have substantially strengthened the book.

JOSEPH J. WALDMEIR

CONTENTS

Part I. SOME OVERVIEWS

Part II. ON SOME INDIVIDUAL NOVELISTS

x CONTENTS

PART I

SOME
OVERVIEWS

PART I

SOME OVERVIEWS

✺ IRVING HOWE

Mass Society and Post-Modern Fiction

RASKOLNIKOV is lying on his bed: feverish, hungry, despondent. The servant Nastasya has told him that the landlady plans to have him evicted. He has received a letter from his mother in which she writes that for the sake of money his sister Dounia is to marry an elderly man she does not love. And he has already visited the old pawnbroker and measured the possibility of murdering her.

There seems no way out, no way but the liquidation of the miserly hunchback whose disappearance from the earth would cause no one any grief. Tempted by the notion that the strong, simply because they are strong, may impose their will upon the weak, Raskolnikov lies there, staring moodily at the ceiling. It must be done: so he tells himself and so he resolves.

Suddenly — but here I diverge a little from the text — the doorbell rings. A letter. Raskolnikov tears it open:

> Dear Sir,
> It is my pleasure to inform you, on behalf of the Guggenheim Foundation, that you have been awarded a fellowship for the study of color imagery in Pushkin's poetry and its relation to the myths of the ancient Muscovites. If you will be kind enough to visit our offices, at Nevsky Prospect and Q Street, arrangements can be made for commencing your stipend immediately.
> (signed) Moevsky

Trembling with joy, Raskolnikov sinks to his knees and bows his head in gratitude. The terrible deed he had contemplated can now be forgotten; he need no longer put his theories to the test; the way ahead, he tells himself, is clear.

But Dostoevsky: is the way now clear for him? May not Raskolnikov's salvation prove to be Dostoevsky's undoing? For Dostoevsky must now ask himself: how, if the old pawnbroker need no longer be destroyed, can Raskolnikov's pride be brought to a visible dramatic climax? The theme remains, for we may imagine that Raskol-

Reprinted from *Partisan Review,* XXVI (Summer, 1959), 420–436, by permission of the author.

nikov will still be drawn to notions about the rights of superior individuals; but a new way of realizing this theme will now have to be found.

It is a common assumption of modern criticism that Dostoevsky's ultimate concern was not with presenting a picture of society, nor merely with showing us the difficulties faced by an impoverished young intellectual in Czarist Russia. He was concerned with the question of what a human being, acting in the name of his freedom or disenchantment, may take upon himself. Yet we cannot help noticing that the social setting of his novel "happens" to fit quite exactly the requirements of his theme: it is the situation in which Raskolnikov finds himself that embodies the moral and metaphysical problems which, as we like to say, form Dostoevsky's deepest interest.

The sudden removal of Raskolnikov's poverty, as I have imagined it a moment ago, does not necessarily dissolve the temptation to test his will through killing another human being; but it does eliminate the immediate cause for committing the murder. Gliding from fellowship to fellowship, Raskolnikov may now end his life as a sober Professor of Literature. Like the rest of us, he will occasionally notice in himself those dim urges and quavers that speak for hidden powers beyond the assuagement of reason. He may remember that once, unlikely as it has now come to seem, he was even tempted to murder an old woman. But again like the rest of us, he will dismiss these feelings as unworthy of a civilized man.

The case is not hopeless for Dostoevsky: it never is for a writer of his stature. He can now invent other ways of dramatizing the problem that had concerned him in the novel as it was to be, the novel before Moevsky's letter arrived; but it is questionable whether even he could imagine circumstances — imagine circumstances, as distinct from expressing sentiments — which would lead so persuasively, so inexorably to a revelation of Raskolnikov's moral heresy as do those in what I am tempted to call the unimproved version of *Crime and Punishment*.

From which it will not be concluded, I hope, that a drop in our standard of living is needed in order to provide novelists with extreme or vivid situations. I am merely trying to suggest that in reading contemporary fiction one sometimes feels that the writers find themselves in situations like the one I have here fancied for Dostoevsky.

II

Let us assume for a moment that we have reached the end of one of those recurrent periods of cultural unrest, innovation and excitement that we call "modern." Whether we really have no one can say with assurance, and there are strong arguments to be marshalled against such a claim. But if one wishes to reflect upon some — the interesting minority — of the novels written in America during the past 15 years, there is a decided advantage in regarding them as "post-modern," significantly different from the kind of writing we usually call modern. Doing this helps one to notice the distinctive qualities of recent novels: what makes them new. It tunes the ear to their distinctive failures. And it lures one into patience and charity.

That modern novelists — those, say, who began writing after the early work of Henry James — have been committed to a peculiarly anxious and persistent search for values, everyone knows. By now this search for values has become not only a familiar but an expected element in modern fiction; that is, a tradition has been established in which it conspicuously figures, and readers have come, somewhat unhistorically, to regard it as a necessary component of the novel. It has been a major cause for that reaching, sometimes a straining, toward moral surprise, for that inclination to transform the art of narrative into an act of cognitive discovery, which sets modern fiction apart from a large number of 18th and even 19th century novels.

Not so frequently noticed, however, is the fact that long after the modern novelist had come to suspect and even assault traditional values there was still available to him — I would say, until about the Second World War — a cluster of stable assumptions as to the nature of our society. If the question "How shall we live?" agitated the novelists without rest, there was a remarkable consensus in their answers to the question "How do we live?" — a consensus not so much in explicit opinion as in a widely shared feeling about Western society.

Indeed, the turn from the realistic social novel among many of the modern writers would have been most unlikely had there not been available such a similarity of response to the familiar social world. At least some of the novelists who abandoned realism seem to have felt that modern society had been exhaustively, perhaps even excessively portrayed (so D. H. Lawrence suggests in one of his letters) and that the task of the novelist was now to explore a chaotic multiplicity of meanings rather than to continue representing the surfaces of common experience.

No matter what their social bias, and regardless of whether they were aware of having any, the modern novelists tended to assume that the social relations of men in the world of capitalism were established, familiar, knowable. If Joyce could write of Stephen Dedalus that "his destiny was to be elusive of social or religious orders," that was partly because he knew and supposed his readers to know what these orders were. If Lawrence in his later works could write a new kind of novel that paid as little attention to the external phenomena of the social world as to the fixed conventions of novelistic "character," that was partly because he had already registered both of these — the social world and the recognizable solid characters — in *Sons and Lovers*. The observations of class relationships in the earlier novels are not discarded by Lawrence in the later ones; they are tacitly absorbed to become a basis for a new mode of vision.

Values, as everyone now laments, were in flux; but society, it might be remembered, was still there: hard, tangible, ruled by a calculus of gain. One might not know what to make of this world, but at least one knew what was happening in it. Every criticism that novelists might direct against society had behind it enormous pressures of evidence, enormous accumulations of sentiment; and this, one might remark of those literary people who bemoan the absence of "tradition," this is the tradition that has been available to and has so enriched modern fiction. A novelist like F. Scott Fitzgerald, whose gifts for conceptual thought were rather meager, could draw to great advantage upon the social criticism that for over a century had preceded him, the whole lengthy and bitter assault upon bourgeois norms that had been launched by the spokesmen for culture. That Fitzgerald may have known little more than the names of these spokesmen, that he drew upon their work with only a minimum of intellectual awareness, serves merely to confirm my point. The rapidity with which such criticism was accumulated during the nineteenth century, whether by Marx or Carlyle, Nietzsche or Mill, enabled the modern novelists to feel they did not need to repeat the work of Flaubert and Dickens, Balzac and Zola: they could go beyond them.

Between radical and conservative writers, as between both of these and the bulk of non-political ones, there were many bonds of shared feeling — a kinship they themselves were often unable to notice but which hindsight permits us to see. The sense of the banality of middle class existence, of its sensuous and spiritual meanness, is quite the same among the conservative as the radical writers, and their ideas about the costs and possibilities of rising in the bourgeois world are not so very different either.

If one compares two American novelists so different in formal opinion, social background and literary method as Theodore Dreiser and Edith Wharton, it becomes clear that in such works as *Sister Carrie* and *The House of Mirth* both are relying upon the same crucial assumption: that values, whether traditional or modernist, desirable or false, can be tested in a novel by dramatizing the relationships between mobile characters and fixed social groups. Neither writer felt any need to question, neither would do so much as think to question, the presence or impact of these social groups as they formed part of the examined structure of class society. In both novels "the heart of fools is in the house of mirth," the heartbreak house of the modern city;

and as Carrie Meeber and Lily Bart make their way up and down the social hierarchy, their stories take on enormous weights of implication because we are ready to assume *some* relationship — surely not the one officially proclaimed by society, nor a mere inversion of it, but still some complex and significant relationship — between the observed scale of social place and the evolving measure of moral value. It is this assumption that has been a major resource of modern novelists; for without some such assumption there could not occur the symbolic compression of incident, the readiness to assume that X stands for Y, which is a prerequisite for the very existence of the novel.

Beset though they might be by moral uncertainties, the modern novelists could yet work through to a relative assurance in their treatment of the social world; and one reason for this assurance was that by the early years of our century the effort to grasp this world conceptually was very far advanced. The novelists may not have been aware of the various theories concerning capitalism, the city and modern industrial society; it does not matter. These ideas had so thoroughly penetrated the consciousness of thinking men, and even the folklore of the masses, that the novelists could count on them without necessarily being able to specify or elaborate them. In general, when critics "find" ideas in novels, they are transposing to a state of abstraction those assumptions which had become so familiar to novelists that they were able to seize them as sentiments.

Part of what I have been saying runs counter to the influential view that writers of prose fiction in America have written romances and not novels because, in words of Lionel Trilling that echo a more famous complaint of Henry James, there has been in this country "no sufficiency of means for the display of a variety of manners, no opportunity for the novelist to do his job of searching out reality, not enough complication of appearance to make the job interesting." I am not sure that this was ever true of American fiction — the encounter between Ishmael and Queequeg tells us as much about manners (American manners), and through manners about the moral condition of humanity, as we are likely to find in a novel by Jane Austen or Balzac. But even if it is granted that the absence of clearcut distinctions of class made it impossible in the nineteenth century to write novels about American society and encouraged, instead, a species of philosophical romance, this surely ceased to be true by about 1880. Since then, at least, there has been "enough complication of appearance to make the job interesting."

Nor am I saying — what seems to me much more dubious — that the presumed absence in recent years of a fixed, stratified society or of what one critic, with enviable naiveté, calls "an agreed picture of the universe" makes it impossible to study closely our social life, or to develop (outside of the South) human personalities rooted in a sense of tradition, or to write good novels dealing with social manners and relationships. That all of these things can be done we know, simply because they have been done. I wish merely to suggest that certain assumptions concerning modern society, which have long provided novelists with symbolic economies and dramatic conveniences, are no longer quite so available as they were a few decades ago. To say this is not to assert that we no longer have recognizable social classes in the United States, or that distinctions in manners have ceased to be significant. It is to suggest that the modern theories about society — theories which for novelists have usually been present as tacit assumptions — have partly broken down; and that this presents a great many new difficulties for the younger writers. New difficulties, which is also to say: new possibilities.

III

In the last two decades there has occurred a series of changes in American life, the extent, durability and significance of which no one has yet measured. No one can. We speak of the growth of a "mass society," a term I shall try to define in a moment; but at best this is merely a useful hypothesis, not an accredited description. It is a notion that lacks common consent, for it does not yet merit common consent. Still, one can say with some assurance that the more sensitive among the younger writers, those who feel that at whatever peril to their work and careers they must grapple with something new in contemporary experience, even if, like everyone else, they find it extremely hard to say what that "newness" consists of — such writers recognize that the once familiar social categories and place-marks have now become as uncertain and elusive as the moral imperatives of the nineteenth century seemed to novelists of fifty years ago. And the something new which they notice or stumble against is, I would suggest, the mass society.

By the mass society we mean a relatively comfortable, half welfare and half garrison society in which the population grows passive, indifferent and atomized; in which traditional loyalties, ties and associations become lax or dissolve entirely; in which coherent publics based on definite interests and opinions gradually fall apart; and in which man becomes a consumer, himself mass-produced like the products, diversions and values that he absorbs.

No social scientist has yet come up with a theory of mass society that is entirely satisfying; no novelist has quite captured its still amorphous symptoms — a peculiar blend of frenzy and sluggishness, amiability and meanness. I would venture the guess that a novelist unaware of the changes in our experience to which the theory of mass society points, is a novelist unable to deal successfully with recent American life; while one who focussed only upon those changes would be unable to give his work an adequate sense of historical depth.

This bare description of the mass society can be extended by noting a few traits or symptoms:

1) Social classes continue to exist, and the society cannot be understood without reference to them; yet the visible tokens of class are less obvious than in earlier decades and the correlations between class status and personal condition, assumed both by the older sociologists and the older novelists, become elusive and problematic — which is not, however, to say that such correlations no longer exist.

2) Traditional centers of authority, like the family, tend to lose some of their binding-power upon human beings; vast numbers of people now float through life with a burden of freedom they can neither sustain nor legitimately abandon to social or religious groups.

3) Traditional ceremonies that have previously marked moments of crisis and transition in human life, thereby helping men to accept such moments, are now either neglected or debased into mere occasions for public display.

4) Passivity becomes a widespread social attitude: the feeling that life is a drift over which one has little control and that even when men do have shared autonomous opinions they cannot act them out in common.

5) As perhaps never before, opinion is manufactured systematically and "scientifically."

6) Opinion tends to flow unilaterally, from the top down, in measured quantities: it becomes a market commodity.

7) Disagreement, controversy, polemic are felt to be in bad taste; issues are "ironed out" or "smoothed away"; reflection upon the nature of society is replaced by observation of its mechanics.

8) The era of "causes," good or bad, comes to an end; strong beliefs seem anachronistic; and as a result, agnostics have even been known to feel a certain nostalgia for the rigors of belief.

9) Direct and first-hand experience seems to evade human beings, though the quantity of busy-ness keeps increasing and the number of events multiplies with bewildering speed.

10) The pressure of material need visibly decreases, yet there follows neither a sense of social release nor a feeling of personal joy; instead, people become increasingly aware of their social dependence and powerlessness.

Now this is a social cartoon and not a description of American society; but it is a cartoon that isolates an aspect of our experience with a suggestiveness that no other mode of analysis is likely to match. Nor does it matter that no actual society may ever reach the extreme condition of a "pure" mass society; the value of the theory lies in bringing to our attention a major historical drift.

If there is any truth at all in these speculations, they should help illuminate the problems faced by the novelists whose work began to appear shortly after the Second World War. They had to confront not merely the chronic confusion of values which has gripped our civilization for decades. In a sense they were quite prepared for that — the whole of modern literature taught them to expect little else. But they had also to face a problem which, in actually composing a novel, must have been still more troublesome: our society no longer lent itself to assured definition, one could no longer assume as quickly as in the recent past that a spiritual or moral difficulty could find a precise embodiment in a social conflict. Raskolnikov, fellowship in hand, might still be troubled by the metaphysical question of what a human being can allow himself; but Raskolnikov as a graduate student with an anxious young wife and a two-year-old baby — what was the novelist to make of him? Something fresh and valuable, no doubt; but only if he were aware that this new Raskolnikov had to be seen in ways significantly different from those of the traditional modern novelists.

How to give shape to a world increasingly shapeless and an experience increasingly fluid; how to reclaim the central assumption of the novel that telling relationships can be discovered between a style of social behavior and a code of moral judgment, or if that proves impossible, to find ways of imaginatively projecting the code in its own right — these were the difficulties that faced the young novelists. It was as if the guidelines of both our social thought and literary conventions were being erased. Or as a young German writer has recently remarked:

> There's no longer a society to write about. In former years you knew where you stood: the peasants read the Bible; the maniacs read *Mein Kampf*. Now people no longer have any opinions; they have refrigerators. Instead of illusions we have television, instead of tradition, the Volkswagen. The only way to catch the spirit of the times is to write a handbook on home appliances.

Taken literally, this is close to absurd; taken as half-comic hyperbole, it reaches a genuine problem.

The problem, in part, is the relationship between the writer and his materials. Some years ago Van Wyck Brooks had spoken of the conflict between the life of the spirit and the life of commerce, and had called upon American writers to make their choice. Most of them did. Almost every important writer in twentieth century America, whether or not he read Brooks, implicitly accepted his statement as the truth and chose, with whatever lapses or qualifications, to speak for the life of the Spirit.

But was the conflict between spirit and commerce, between culture and society still so acute during the postwar years? Was not a continued belief in this conflict a stale and profitless hangover from the ideologies of the Thirties? Might there not be ground for feeling, among the visible signs of our careless postwar prosperity, that a new and more moderate vision of society should inform the work of our novelists? It hardly matters which answers individual writers gave to these questions; the mere fact that they were now being seriously raised had a profound impact upon their work.

Those few who favored a bluntly "positive" approach to American society found it hard to embody their sentiments in vibrant — or even credible — fictional situations. The values of accommodation were there for the asking, but they seemed, perversely, to resist creative use. For almost two decades now there has been an outpouring of "affirmative" novels about American businessmen — Executive Suites in various shades; but I do not know of a single serious critic who finds these books anything but dull and mediocre. At least in our time, the novel seems to lend itself irrevocably to the spirit of criticism; as Camus has remarked, it "is born simultaneously with the spirit of rebellion and expresses, on the esthetic plane, the same ambition."

But what has been so remarkable and disconcerting is that those writers who wished to preserve the spirit of rebellion also found it extremely hard to realize their sentiments in novels dealing with contemporary life. Most of them were unable, or perhaps too shrewd, to deal with the postwar experience directly; they preferred tangents of suggestion to frontal representation; they could express their passionate, though often amorphous, criticism of American life not through realistic portraiture but through fable, picaresque, prophecy and nostalgia.

Morally the young novelists were often more secure than their predecessors. Few of them were as susceptible to money and glitter as Fitzgerald; few had Hemingway's weakness for bravado and swagger; few succumbed to hallucinatory rhetoric in the manner of Faulkner. Yet, as novelists, they were less happily "placed" than the writers who began to publish in the Twenties and early Thirties. They lacked the pressure of inevitable subjects as these take shape in situations and locales. They lacked equivalents of Fitzgerald's absorption with social distinctions, Hemingway's identification with expatriates, Faulkner's mourning over the old South. Sentiments they had in abundance and often fine ones; but to twist a remark of Gertrude Stein's, literature is not made of sentiments.

Literature is not made of sentiments; yet a good portion of what is most fresh in recent American fiction derives from sentiments. Better than any other group of literate Americans, our novelists resisted the mood of facile self-congratulation which came upon us during the postwar years. To be novelists at all, they had to look upon our life without ideological delusions; and they saw — *often better than they could say* — the hovering sickness of soul, the despairing contentment, the prosperous malaise. They were not, be it said to their credit, taken in. Yet the problem remained: how can one represent malaise, which by its nature is vague and without shape? It can be done, we know. But to do it one needs to be Chekhov; and that is hard.

My point, let me hasten to add, is not that novelists need social theories or philosophical systems. They do, however, need to live in an environment about which they can make economical assumptions that, in some ultimate way, are related to the ideas of speculative thinkers. Let me borrow a useful distinction that C. Wright Mills makes between troubles and issues. Troubles signify a strong but unfocussed sense of disturbance and pain, while issues refer to troubles that have been articulated as general statements. Novelists, as a rule, concern themselves with troubles, not issues. But to write with assurance and economy about troubles, they need to be working in a milieu where there is at least some awareness of issues. And in the troubled years after the Second World War it was precisely this awareness that was often lacking.

A few serious writers did try to fix in their novels the amorphous "troubledness" of postwar American experience. In *The Violated,* an enormous realistic narrative about some ordinary people who reach adulthood during the war, Vance Bourjaily seemed consciously to be dramatizing a view of American society quite similar to the one I have sketched here. He chose to write one of those full-scale narratives composed of parallel strands of plot — a technique which assumes that society is distinctly articulated, that its classes are both sharply visible and intrinsically interesting, and that a novelist can arrange a conflict between members of these classes which will be dramatic in its own right and emblematic of larger issues. But for the material Bourjaily chose — the lives of bewildered yet not uncharacteristic drifters during the past two decades — these assumptions could not operate with sufficient force; and as his characters, in the sameness of their misery, melted into one another, so the strands of his narrative, also having no inevitable reason for separate existence, collapsed into one another.

Norman Mailer, trying in *The Deer Park* to compose a novel about the malaise of our years, avoided the cumbersomeness of the traditional social novel but could find no other structure that would give coherence to his perceptions. Mailer tried to embody his keen if unstable vision in a narrative about people whose extreme dislocation of experience and feeling would, by the very fact of their extreme dislocation, come to seem significant. But in its effort to portray our drifting and boredom full-face, in its fierce loyalty to the terms of its own conception, *The Deer Park* tended to become a claustrophobic work, driving attention inward, toward its own tonal peculiarities, rather than outward, as an extending parable. Throughout the novel Mailer had to fall back upon his protagonist, through whom he tried to say that which he found hard to show.

IV

A whole group of novelists, among the best of recent years, has found itself responding to immediate American experience by choosing subjects and locales that are apparently far removed from that experience yet, through their inner quality, very close to it. These writers are sensitive to the moods and tones of postwar American life; they know that something new, different and extremely hard to describe has been happening to us. Yet they do not usually write about postwar experience *per se:* they do not confront it as much as they try to ambush it. The film critic Stanley Kaufmann has noted a similar phenomenon:

> When Vittorio de Sica was asked why so many of his films deal with adultery, he is said to have replied, "But if you take adultery out of the lives of the bourgeoisie, what drama is left?" It is perhaps this belief that has impelled Tennessee Williams into the areas that his art inhabits. He has recognized that most of contemporary life offers limited dramatic opportunities . . . so he has left "normal" life to investigate the highly neurotic, the violent and the grimy. It is the continuing problem of the contemporary writer who looks for great emotional issues to move him greatly. The anguish of the advertising executive struggling to keep his job is anguish indeed, but its possibilities in art are not large-scale. The writer who wants to "let go" has figuratively to leave the urban and suburban and either go abroad, go into the past, or go into those few pockets of elemental emotional life left in this country.

Abroad, the past, or the few pockets of elemental emotional life: — many of our best writers have pursued exactly these strategies in order to suggest their attitudes toward contemporary experience. In *The Assistant* Bernard Malamud has written a somber story about a Jewish family during the Depression years, yet it soon becomes clear that one of his impelling motives is a wish to recapture intensities of feeling we have apparently lost but take to be characteristic of an earlier decade. Herbert Gold's *The Man Who Was Not With It* is an account of marginal figures in a circus as they teeter on the edge of *lumpen* life; but soon one realizes that he means his story to indicate possibilities for personal survival in a world increasingly compressed. The precocious and bewildered boy in J. D. Salinger's *The Catcher in the Rye* expresses something of the moral condition of adolescents to-day — or so they tell us; but clearly his troubles are not meant to refer to his generation alone. In *A Walk on the Wild Side* Nelson Algren turns to down-and-outers characteristic of an earlier social moment, but if we look to the psychic pressures breaking through the novel we see that he is really searching for a perspective for estrangement that will be relevant to our day. In *The Field of Vision* Wright Morris moves not backward in time but sideways in space: he contrives to bring a dreary Nebraskan middle-class family to a Mexican bull-fight so that the excitement of the blood and ritual will stir it to self-awareness. And while, on the face of it, Saul Bellow's *The Adventures of Augie March* is a picaresque tale about a cocky Jewish boy moving almost magically past the barriers in American society, it is also a kind of paean to the idea of personal freedom in hostile circumstances. Bellow's most recent novel, *Henderson the Rain King,* seems an even wilder tale about an American millionaire venturing into deepest Africa, in part, the deepest Africa of boy's books; but when he writes that men need a shattering experience to "wake the spirit's sleep" we soon realize that this ultimate reference is to America, where many spirits sleep.

Though vastly different in quality, these novels have in common a certain obliqueness of approach. They do not represent directly the postwar American experience, yet refer to it constantly. They tell us rather little about the surface tone, the manners, the social patterns of recent American life, yet are constantly projecting moral criticisms of its essential quality. They approach that experience on the sly, yet are colored and shaped by it throughout. And they gain from it their true subject: the recurrent search — in America, almost a national obsession — for personal identity and freedom. In their distance from fixed social categories and their concern with the metaphysical implications of that distance, these novels constitute what I would call "post-modern" fiction.

But the theme of personal identity, if it is to take on fictional substance, needs some kind of placement, a setting in the world of practical affairs. And it is here that the "post-modern" novelists run into serious troubles: the connection between subject and setting cannot always be made, and the "individual" of their novels, because he lacks social definition and is sometimes a creature of literary or even ideological fiat, tends to be not very individualized. Some of the best postwar novels, like *The Invisible Man* and *The Adventures of Augie March*, are deeply concerned with the fate of freedom in a mass society; but the assertiveness of idea and vanity of style which creep into such books are the result, I think, of willing a subject onto a novel rather than allowing it to grow out of a sure sense of a particular moment and place. These novels merit admiration for defending the uniqueness of man's life, but they suffer from having to improvise the terms of this uniqueness. It is a difficulty that seems, at the moment, unavoidable and I have no wish to disparage writers who face it courageously. Still, it had better be said that the proclamation of personal identity in recent American fiction tends, if I may use a fashionable phrase, to be more a product of the will than of the imagination.

It may help strengthen my point — critics ought not to strengthen such points too much — if I turn for a moment to the two most-discussed literary groups of the last few years: the "angry young men" in England and the "beat generation" writers of San Francisco.

Partly because they write in and about England, Kingsley Amis, John Braine and John Wain are blessed with something utterly precious to a writer: a subject urgently, relentlessly imposing itself upon their imaginations. They have earned the scorn of a good many American critics — notable, of course, for asceticism — who point out that it is not clear whether it is a better or just a bigger share of the material and cultural goods in contemporary England that these writers want. But while you can feel righteous or even hostile toward Amis and Braine, you can hardly deny that in their novels one finds something of the focussed desire, the quick apprehension and notation of contemporary life which, for reasons I have tried to suggest, has become somewhat rare in serious American fiction. These English writers face a predicament of the welfare state: it rouses legitimate desires in people of the "lower orders"; it partly satisfies these desires; but it satisfies them only to the point of arousing new demands beyond its power of meeting. For society this may be irksome; for writers it is exhilarating. Gripes can be transformed into causes, ambitions cloaked as ideals. And the "angry young men" are particularly fortunate in that their complaints lead them to deal with some of the traditional materials of the novel: frustrated ambition, frozen snobbery, fake culture, decaying gentility. Through comedy they are able to *structure* their complaints. Their work touches upon sore spots in English life, hurting some people and delighting others. It threatens the Establishment, perhaps its survival, more likely its present leaders. It creates tension, opposition, a dialectic of interests. All of which is to say: it rests upon an articulated, coherent though limited vision of English social relations.

By contrast, the young men in San Francisco seem largely a reflex of the circumstances of mass society. They are suffering from psychic and social disturbance: and as far as that goes, they are right — there is much in American life to give one a pain. But they have no clear sense of why or how they are troubled, and some of them seem opposed in principle to a clear sense of anything. The "angry young men" in England, even if their protest will prove to be entirely opportunistic and momentary, can say what it is that hurts. The San Francisco writers fail to understand, as Paul Goodman has remarked, that

> It is necessary to have some contact with institutions and people in order to be frustrated and angry. They [the San Francisco writers] have the theory that to be affectless, not to care, is the ultimate rebellion, but this is a fantasy; for right under the surface is burning shame, hurt feelings, fear of impotence, speechless and powerless tantrum, cowering before papa, being rebuffed by mama; and it is these anxieties that dictate their behavior in every crisis.

These writers, I would contend, illustrate the painful, though not inevitable, predicament of rebellion in a mass society: they are the other side of the American hollow. In their contempt for mind, they are at one with the middle class suburbia they think they scorn. In their incoherence of feeling and statement, they mirror the incoherent society that clings to them like a mocking shadow. In their yearning to keep "cool," they sing out an eternal fantasy of the shopkeeper. Feeling themselves lonely and estranged, they huddle together in gangs, create a Brook Farm of Know-Nothings, and send back ecstatic reports to the squares: Having a Wonderful Time, Having Wonderful Kicks! But alas, all the while it is clear that they are terribly lost, and what is more pitiable, that they don't even have the capacity for improvising vivid fantasies. As they race meaninglessly back and forth across the continent, veritable mimics of the American tourist, they do not have a Wonderful Time. They do not get happily drunk, many of them preferring milk shakes and tea; and their sexual revelations, particularly in Kerouac's *The Subterraneans,* are as sad as they are unintentional. They can't, that is, dream themselves out of the shapeless nightmare of California; and for that, perhaps, we should not blame them, since it is not certain that anyone can.

No wonder, then, that in Kerouac's novels one is vaguely aware that somewhere, in the unmapped beyond, a society does exist: a society with forms, requirements, burdens, injustices, duties and pleasures; but that in the space of the novels themselves we can only find a series of distraught and compulsive motions. The themes of what

I have called "post-modern" fiction are reflected in the San Francisco writers as caricature and symptom; for if you shun consciousness as if it were a plague, then a predicament may ravage you but you cannot cope with it.

Where finally does this leave us? In the midst, I hope, of the promise and confusion of American writing today. No settled ending is possible here, because the tendencies I have been noticing are still in flux, still open to many pressures and possibilities. But it may not be too rash to say that the more serious of the "post-modern" novelists — those who grapple with problems rather than merely betraying their effects — have begun to envisage that we may be on the threshold of enormous changes in human history. These changes, merely glanced by the idea of the "mass society," fill our novelists with a sense of foreboding; and through the strategy of obliqueness, they bring to bear a barrage of moral criticisms, reminders of human potentiality, and tacit exhortations.

The possibilities that appear to them are those which struck at T. E. Lawrence when he returned from Arabia and discovered that he did not know how or why to live. One such possibility is that we are moving toward a quiet desert of moderation where men will forget the passion of moral and spiritual restlessness that has characterized Western society. That the human creature, no longer a Quixote or a Faust, will become a docile attendant to an automated civilization. That the "aura of the human" will be replaced by the nihilism of satiety. That the main question will no longer be the conditions of existence but existence itself. That high culture as we understand it will become increasingly problematical and perhaps reach some point of obsolescence.

But before such prospects — they form the bad dreams of thoughtful men, the nightmares our "post-modern" novelists are trying to exorcise — the mind grows dizzy and recalcitrant. It begins to solace itself with rumblings about eternal truths, and like the exacerbated judge in Faulkner's *The Hamlet,* cries out, "I can't stand no more. . . . This case is adjourned!"

❧ ALFRED KAZIN

The Alone Generation

THE other day a prominent American publisher advertised a book of stories by a Continental writer who died some time ago: "These stories, never before published in English, could only have been written by a great writer who flourished before World War II. They are stamped by that unobtrusive assurance, perfect sympathy with their subjects, and resonant tone which have become, it would seem, lost secrets in almost all the fiction of the immediate present." Not very encouraging, what? Yet I must admit that while I see a host of brilliantly talented writers all around me, I don't often get a very profound satisfaction out of the novels they write.

I am tired of reading for compassion instead of pleasure. In novel after novel, I am presented with people who are so soft, so wheedling, so importunate, that the actions in which they are involved are too indecisive to be interesting or to develop those implications which are the life-blood of narrative. The age of "psychological man," of the herd of aloners, has finally proved the truth of Tocqueville's observation that in modern times the average man is absorbed in a very puny object, himself, to the point of satiety. The whole interest of the reader seems to be summoned toward "understanding" and tolerance of the leading characters. We get an imaginative universe limited to the self and its detractors. The old-fashioned novel of sensitive souls, say Somerset Maugham's *Of Human Bondage* or even Sinclair Lewis's *Main Street,* showed a vulnerable hero or heroine battling it out (a) for principles which he identified with himself and (b) against social enemies who were honestly opposed to the protagonist's demand of unlimited freedom. Now we get novels in which society is merely a backdrop to the aloneness of the hero. People are not shown in actions that would at least get us to see the conditions of their personal struggle. Carson McCullers's beautiful first novel, *The Heart Is a Lonely Hunter,* characterized a stagnant society in the silent relationship between two mutes; in her third novel, *The Member of the Wedding,* the adolescent loneliness of Frankie fills up the scene, becomes the undramatic interest

Reprinted from *Harper's Magazine*, CCXIX (October, 1959), 127–131, by permission of the author.

of the book, to the point where the reader feels not that he is witnessing a drama but that he is being asked to respond to a situation.

American society is remarkable for the degree of loneliness (not solitude) in which the individual can find himself. In our mass age, the individual's lack of privacy, his unlimited demand for self-satisfaction, his primary concern with his own health and well-being have actually thrown him back on himself more than before. Our culture is stupefyingly without support from tradition, and has become both secular and progressive in its articulation of every discontent and ambition; the individual now questions himself constantly because his own progress — measured in terms of the social norms — is his fundamental interest. The kind of person who in the nineteenth-century novel was a "character" now regards himself in twentieth-century novels as a problem; the novel becomes not a series of actions which he initiates because of *who* he is, but a series of disclosures, as at a psychoanalyst's, designed to afford him the knowledge that may heal him. It is astonishing how many novels concerned with homosexuality, on the order of Truman Capote's *Other Voices, Other Rooms,* are apologies for abnormality, designed to make us sympathize with the twig as it is bent the wrong way.

I would suspect that it is the intention of extracting "understanding" that accounts for the extraordinary number of children and adolescents in American fiction: at least in the imaginative society of fiction they can always be objects of concern. Even in a good writer like Capote, to say nothing of a bad writer like Gore Vidal, the movement of the book comes to a standstill in the grinding machinery of sensibility. As in James Baldwin's *Giovanni's Room,* sympathetic justice is always accorded homosexuals. No Vautrin as in Balzac, no Charlus as in Proust, no honest homosexual villains! The immediate result is the immobilization of narrative, the fashionable mistiness of prose; first the hero is cherished to the point of suffocation, then the style. *Other Voices, Other Rooms* is a brilliant effort of will, but it is unmoving rather than slow, retrospective rather than searching. In the past, the movement of fiction was more energetic than life; now fiction becomes vaguer, dimmer, an "exercise" in "craft."

This demand on our compassion is not limited to the quivering novels of sensibility by over-conscious stylists; it is the very essence of the deliberately churned-up novels of the Beat Generation. I mention Jack Kerouac here only because his novels, in which he has increasingly developed the trick of impersonating spontaneity by bombarding the reader with a mass of deliberately confused impressions, depend on a naked and unashamed plea for "love," understanding, fellowship, and are read and enjoyed only because this pleading so answers to our psychological interest in fiction that we indulge Kerouac without knowing why we do. Nothing human is now alien to us; after all, the fellow's problem could be our problem! It is ridiculous that novels can now be sent off as quickly as they are written and published immediately afterwards in order to satisfy the hopped-up taste of people who, when they open a novel, want to feel that they are not missing a thing. The sluttishness of a society whose mass ideal seems to be unlimited consumption of all possible goods and services is the reason for the "success" of writers whose literary strategy is to paint America as an unlimited supply of sex, travel, liquor — and lonely yearners. The individual who is concerned entirely wtih his aloneness will inevitably try to invade society, "the other" in his universe, by writing stormily, angrily, lashing the reader with a froth of words. But we are at fault in allowing the addict quality of such books to stand for "intensity" in fiction. More and more we judge novels by their emotional authenticity, not their creative achievement; we read them as the individual testifying for himself in a confused and troubling time. But the testimony is so self-concerned that we equate this glibness of feeling with recklessness of style. And here I come to another complaint, the increasing slovenliness, carelessness, and plain cowardice of style in fiction today.

We were wrong when we thought that the ghost of Henry James had put his too, too careful hand on our young 'uns. It is true that some of the new professor-novelists, Benjamin DeMott in *The Body's Cage* or Monroe Engel in *The Visions of Nicholas Solon,* like Capote himself in his first book and his stories, can remind us of the rage of style in the fiction of the 'forties. So talented a writer as Jean Stafford has of late years often seemed to bury herself in fine phrases. It is a rare professor-novelist, Robie Macauley in *The Disguises of Love,* who can escape the ostentatious carefulness, the jogging of the reader: *Please don't lose sight of my arm as I put together this beautiful edifice of words.* But actually, the increasing fussiness of our social ideals and the plain boredom of a period in which writers so often feel incapable of imagining decisive roles for their characters have led to the opposite quality. John Wain recently wrote:

"At the moment, the literary mind of the West seems to be swamped in one of its periodic waves of what George Orwell once called 'sluttish antinomianism,' which he defined as 'lying in bed drinking Pernod.' "

What we get now is not the style of pretended fineness — the *New Yorker* ladies with every tuck in place — but the imitation of anger, the leer of the desperado. You can't fool us with your genteel learning, we're young American men who have been around and who have a punch! So I read in an article on fiction, by Herbert Gold, that something-or-other is like kissing a girl with spinach on her teeth. Wow, bang, and slam. Kerouac and whoever it is who follows *him* are "wild" in the hope of getting out of themselves, in finding some person, thing, or cause to latch onto. Gold is slovenly in the hope of sounding "cool"; he is understandably alarmed by the softness that threatens young novelists in so self-pitying an age as this. In England the young men are angry because still made to feel inferior; in America, young novelists get angry because they hope to sound belligerent and positive, *alive,* against the doldrums of the Eisenhower age.

One root of their difficulty is the irresistible example of Saul Bellow's *The Adventures of Augie March.* Anyone who has read his first two novels, *Dangling Man* and *The Victim,* knows that Bellow began with an almost excessive nobility of style, that the open and comically pretentious style in which Augie talks is a *tour de force.* Bellow has always been fascinated by characters who, in the deep Existentialist sense, are conscious of being *de trop,* excessive of themselves and their society, insatiable in their demands on life. All his representative men, in the phrase of Henderson the rain king, cry, *"I want! I want!"* This excess of human possibility over social goals, of the problem, man, over his intended satisfactions, led to a prose in *Augie* which is rapturously, not whiningly, faithful to all the signs and opportunities of experience. "If you've seen a winter London open thundering mouth in its awful last minutes of river light or have come with cold clanks from the Alps into Torino in December white steam then you've known like greatness of place." In *Augie,* Bellow attained a rosy deliverance from the grip of his past, he discovered himself equal to the excitement of the American experience, he shook himself all over and let himself go. "I am an American, Chicago born — Chicago, that somber city — and go at things as I have taught myself, free-style, and will make the record in my own way. . . ."

But just as no poet should attempt free verse who has not performed in traditional forms and meters, so no novelist should identify toughness with "free-style":

> He brought his hand with the horny nail of his index finger in a wide circle, swinging an invisible lassoo, looping their belly-eyed gaze and taking it at his eye. They were caught first at the spongy wart on his nose and then in his eyes, working it for themselves now like the flies caught wriggling in sticky-paper. That wart made a still flop when he tossed his head in beckon and hitch toward the pungent foot-darkened sawdust at the door of Grack's Zoo, a gobble of cajolery up from his throat and the swollen Adam's apple.

This is from Gold's most admired book, *The Man Who Was Not With It,* and makes me think of what was once scrawled on a student paper at Harvard by ancient Dean Briggs: "falsely robust." I think I understand where such worked-up militancy of phrase comes from:

from the novelist's honest need, in the spirit of Henry James, to have language do the work of characterization. There is so much for a novelist to put together before he can invite people into the world of his imagination; there are so many things to say about human beings who, in the absence of public beliefs, appear arbitrary to themselves and to everyone else. The novelist feels he has to work ten times harder than he used to, falls into despair, and tries to ram it all home. Things aren't as clear as they used to be, and there's no kidding ourselves that they are. The true novelist wants only to set the stage, to get people going, to tell his story, but as Augie March says, "You do all you can to humanize and familiarize the world, and suddenly it becomes stranger than ever." The sense of that strangeness is vivid despite the murky powers of contemporary novelists; no wonder, having to make language work all the time for them, that they often escape into an assumed violence and negligence of tone.

Sometimes the language of violence fits. Ralph Ellison's *Invisible Man* is a series of episodes, but the screaming crescendo on which the book opens — the hero in his Harlem cellar, all the stolen lights ablaze, collaring the reader and forcing him to notice and to hear — is an unforgettably powerful expression, at the extreme of racial experience, of the absurdity, the feeling of millions that the world is always just out of their reach. I don't care for novelists who ignore what H. G. Wells himself called the "queerness" that has come into contemporary life since the bomb. The ways of escape from this queerness are legion, but let me name some who don't try to escape it. Paul Bowles doesn't, although his values are so skittery that he sometimes seems to escape from horror into a Fitzpatrick travelogue. The American writer is so likely to see more of the world, and to experience it more openly, that, like Hemingway at the end of *Death in the Afternoon,* he always wants to get in after the bell all the sensuous travel notes he hadn't been able to fit into his book. Bowles tends to fall into this sophisticated romanticism; sometimes he reports North Africa and Asia instead of setting his imagination in them. On the other hand, the landscape in *The Sheltering Sky* itself represents the inhumanity of people who can no longer communicate with one another, the coldness of a world that now seems to put man off. What minimizes the symbolic values in *The Sheltering Sky* and deprives us of the "resonance" we used to get in fiction is the aloneness of people who are concerned entirely with the search for their own sexual satisfaction. The slightly depressing atmosphere of anxiety that hangs over Bowles's novel is characteristic of the effort to find an identity for oneself in sexual relationships. Norman Mailer, a writer with so much more native power than Bowles, with so much more ability to confront American life directly than he seems to acknowledge, has created in *The Deer Park* the same essential atmosphere of paralysis, of the numbness that results when people feel themselves to be lost in the pursuit of compulsions.

Mailer's novels, at least for me, personify the dilemma of novelists who are deeply concerned with history but dangerously oversimplify it; if they seem consumed by their interest in sex it is because they are always seeking some solution for "the times." In many ways Mailer seems to me the most forceful and oddly objective novelist of his age, objective in the sense that he is most capable of imagining objects to which a reader can give himself. You see this, despite the obvious debts to older writers, in *The Naked and the Dead* and in the satire behind the wonderful exchanges between the producer and his son-in-law in *The Deer Park.* Yet Mailer's interest in the external world has dwindled to the point where the theme of sexual power and delight — which Mailer feels to be a lost secret in contemporary life — has become a labyrinthine world in itself. Mailer now seems bent on becoming the American Marquis de Sade, where once he seemed to be another Dos Passos. Yet the energy, the often unconscious yet meticulous wit, above all the eery and totally unexpected power of concrete visualization are curious because Mailer is able to make more of a world out of his obsessions than other writers are able to make out of the given materials of our common social world.

Here I come to the heart of my complaint. I complain of the dimness, the shadowiness, the flatness, the paltriness, in so many reputable novelists. I confess that I have never been able to get very much from Wright Morris, though he is admired by influential judges. In reading Morris's *The Field of Vision,* I thought of George Santayana's complaint that contemporary poets often give the reader the mere suggestion of a poem and expect him to finish the poem for them. Morris's many symbols, his showy intentions, his pointed and hinted significance, seem to me a distinct example of the literary novel which professors like to teach and would like to write: solemnly meaningful in every intention, but without the breath or extension of life.

There are many writers, like J. D. Salinger, who lack strength, but who are competent and interesting. He identifies himself too fussily with the spiritual aches and pains of his characters; in some of his recent stories, notably "Zooey" and "Seymour: An Introduction," he has overextended his line, thinned it out, in an effort to get the fullest possible significance out of his material. Salinger's work is a perfect example of the lean reserves of the American writer who is reduced to "personality," even to the "mystery of personality," instead of the drama of our social existence. It is the waveriness, the effort at control, that trouble me in Salinger; the professional hand is there, the ability to create an imaginative world, plus almost too much awareness of what he can and can't do. Only, it *is* thin, and peculiarly heart-breaking at times; Salinger identifies the effort he puts out with the vaguely spiritual "quest" on which his characters are engaged, which reminds me of Kierkegaard's saying that we have become "pitiful," like the lace-makers whose work is so flimsy. The delicate balances in Salinger's work, the anxious striving, inevitably result in beautiful work that is rather too obviously touching, and put together on a frame presented to it by the *New Yorker*.

But I must admit that the great majority of stories I read in magazines seem only stitchings and joinings and colorings of some original model. No wonder that in so much contemporary fiction we are excited by the intention and tolerate the achievement. We are so hungry for something new in fiction that the intention, marked early in the handling of a story, will often please us as if it were the dramatic emotion accomplished by the story; the intuition of hidden significance that usually waits for us at the end of a Salinger story is both a reward to the reader and the self-cherished significance of the story to the writer himself.

Salinger's characters are incomparably larger and more human than those of John Cheever, but Cheever has a gift for being more detached and at the same time more open to what *is* — to the ever-present danger and the half-felt queerness of contemporary existence. It is a pity in a way — I am thinking here of Cheever's stories, not his novel — that contemporary American fiction must derive so much of its strength from the perishable value of social information. James Jones wrote a really extraordinary documentary novel in *From Here to Eternity,* and ever since, like so many Americans who wrote extraordinary first novels directly out of experience, he has had the look of someone trying to invent things that once were conferred on him. So Cheever, in the *New Yorker* style, sometimes takes such easy refuge in the details of gardens, baby-sitters, parks, dinners, apartment houses, clothes that he goes to the opposite extreme of the Beat writers (who present the sheer emptiness of life when human beings are not attached to a particular environment): he falls into mechanical habits of documentation, becomes a slyer John O'Hara. It is as if he were trying to get back to the social reportage and satire that worked in our fiction so long as the people writing these stories, like Sinclair Lewis or Scott Fitzgerald, knew what values they could oppose to the "rich." As one can see from O'Hara's novels, which get more pointless as they get bigger and sexier, it is impossible to remain an old-fashioned "realist" unless you can portray a class or an individual opposed to the dominant majority. (James Gould Cozzens was able to do exactly this in *Guard of Honor* but not in *By Love Possessed,* which is more of an aggrieved complaint against the destruction of values.) O'Hara's *Appointment in Samarra* was an exciting book because it involved the real conflict of classes in America; *From the Terrace* suggests that the transformation of our society has proceeded beyond the power of a commonplace mind to describe it deeply. For depth of description demands that the writer identify himself with a social force to which he can give symbolic significance, that he can discern a pattern in history, that he can not only plot his way through it but recognize himself to be a figure in it.

This social intelligence is now lacking to our novelists — except to those brilliant Southern writers, like William Styron and Flannery O'Connor, who can find the present meaningful because they find the past so. But other Southern writers run the risk of being as confused as anyone else once they get off that safe subject, the betrayal of the past, which has been Faulkner's great theme. The bigger, richer, and more anxious the country becomes, the more writers in the traditional mode, like O'Hara, or writers who are now formidably "hip," like Mailer, find themselves trying to find in sex as individual appetite the drama of society in which they can see themselves as partisans and judges. This lack of breadth and extent and dimension I have been complaining of: what is it but the uncertainty of these writers about their connection with that part of reality which other novelists include in their work simply because they are always aware of it — not because they have strained to know it? What many writers feel today is that reality is not much more than what *they* say it is. This is a happy discovery only for genius. For most writers today, the moral order is created, step by step, only through the clarifications achieved by art and, step by step, they refuse to trust beyond the compass of the created work. There has probably never been a time when the social nature of the novel was so much at odds with the felt lack of order in the world about us. In the absence of what used to be *given,* the novelist must create a wholly imaginary world — or else he must have the courage, in an age when personal willfulness rules in every sphere, to say that we are *not* alone, that the individual does not have to invent human values but only to rediscover them. The novel as a form will always demand a common-sense respect for life and interest in society.

Whatever my complaints, I never despair of the novel. As someone said, it is more than a form, it is a literature. I hope never to overlook the positive heroism of those writers who believe in the novel and in the open representation of experience that is its passion and delight — who refuse to believe that there can be an alternative to it for an age like ours. And it does seem to me that the tangibility, the felt reverberations of life that one finds in a writer like Bernard Malamud, spring from his belief that any imaginative "world," no matter how local or strange, *is* the world, and that for the imaginative writer values must be considered truths, not subjective fancies. It is really a kind of faith that accounts for Malamud's "perfect sympathy" with *his* characters in *The Assistant* and *The Magic Barrel*. Though it is difficult for the alone to sympathize with each other, it is a fact that fiction can elicit and prove the world we share, that it can display the unforeseen possibilities of the human — even when everything seems dead set against it.

❦ IHAB H. HASSAN

The Character of Post-War Fiction in America

CONTEMPORARY American fiction is sometimes noted to be dismissed by critics who seem to have lost their youth in the golden age of Faulkner and Hemingway. At other times, it is noticed merely to document the sociological imagination of our time, as if literature were a nice footnote to our mass culture. People somehow expect the fad to pass, the dust to settle, so that the objects of our critical admiration may be finally certified, so that our judgments may escape the sin of error. Why take a chance on a fleeting fashion? As if fashions did not hold the enigma of our time!

My first statement, obviously, is a judgment and a plea. The contemporary novel — and it is of the novel that I mainly speak — has energy and persuasion. It deserves from us a response equally patient and passionate. It deserves, above all, to be read.

There was a moment, I think, right after the Second World War when everyone sensed a bracing quality in the climate of literature. There was a promise of intensity, a new and troubled kind of awareness, a feeling that a new world had been born in catastrophe and that it required to be expressed in ways unlike the old ways. The old ways, to be sure, had been radical in their formal experiments, in the freedom writers took with time and space, consciousness and metaphor. But the experiments of one generation can become the pieties of the next. Language had been stretched to its limit — as in *Finnegans Wake*. It was now time not to retrench but to discover characters or styles, a new vision, to describe the new experience. The dislocation of time, after all, may not be the most radical thing in a world where science, with the approval of the State, does so every hour!

The intensity which people discerned in fiction after the last war — particularly in "war novels" — has not entirely vanished; it has been merely threatened by a powerful cliché. This is the cliché that our literature is a literature of conformity. It is not. Our literature is a literature of *opposition*. America is still, as Van Wyck Brooks claimed fifty years ago, "a vast Sargasso Sea," and there are all manners of living

Reprinted from the *English Journal,* LI (January, 1962), 1–8, by permission of the author and the National Council of Teachers of English.

27

things drifting in it. Nor is heresy, as one might be led to believe, the privilege of few critics alone. Heresy and heterodoxy make vital a great part of our fiction. Where others see conformity, I sense protest unto anarchy.

For one thing, naturalism and symbolism, comedy and tragedy, picaresque and romance, even surrealism, crowd into the form of the recent novel. They jostle and jangle in Styron's *Lie Down in Darkness,* Swados' *Out Went the Candle,* Ellison's *Invisible Man,* Salinger's *The Catcher in the Rye,* Bellow's *Henderson the Rain King,* Purdy's *Malcolm,* and Hawkes' *The Lime Twig.* The fusion of modes in contemporary fiction — a subject to which I must later return — does not prove that ours is a generation of cool or silent writers. Fusion does not always mean confusion.

It is also misleading, I think, to speak in obituary tones of the death of manners in the novel. Henry James, to be sure, is no longer with us except as a rare spirit, and Jane Austen, who never immigrated to America anyway, has been laid to rest for some years. But the crucial fact about manners in recent fiction is that in becoming more diverse, they have also become more fragmentary. This is not to say that manners — the way gestures body forth the hum or buzz or whatever sound implications are reputed to make in a culture — have disappeared. (It would be more accurate to claim that society itself has vanished.) This is rather to say that the Jewish society of Bernard Malamud may be as incomprehensible to the Southern characters of Flannery O'Connor as the hipster gang of Jack Kerouac may be bewildering to the Yankee protagonists of John Cheever. Better then to say that manners and gestures have not died but that they are there to betoken the death of a coherent society.

There are, we see, pockets of resistance in American culture, and Bible, hibachi, and marijuana belts of manners in it too. America, despite our cars, fashion models, and supermarkets, is not entirely the septic, air-conditioned dream Europeans dream it is. It is still possible, for instance, to draw some distinctions between the wide agrarian valleys of the South and the dense industrial cities of the North. The two most active centers of contemporary fiction in America are situated in the Gentile rural South of Carson McCullers, Flannery O'Connor, Truman Capote, and William Styron, and the Jewish urban North of Saul Bellow, J. D. Salinger, Bernard Malamud, Harvey Swados, and Philip Roth. It may very well be that the Southern novelist and the Jewish writer have both emerged from the tragic underground of our culture as the true spokesmen of mid-century America.

The most meaningful expression of diversity in our culture, however, is encountered in the huge discrepancy between its dominant and opposing images. Compare — if you can! — the cellophane world

implied by the Miss America contests in Atlantic City with the nightmare of junk and homosexuality which emerges, say, from William
Burroughs' *The Naked Lunch.* Yet it is this dialectic between the
normative and dissenting selves of our society, irrespective of mode,
manners, or locale, that gives our literature its particular character.

The normative image of our culture can be projected in a series
of preposterous or unctuous clichés. It is the image of an organization
man who forgoes the ulcerous rewards of executive suite, pottering
about a house with a cracked picture window looking into the crack
of another picture window, and viewing with apathy the coming caesars
of our imperial state, the hidden persuaders and clowns of commerce
of Madison Avenue, and the exploding metropolis on whose far fringes
our Quiet American has found his corner of Shangri-La. In this other-
directed paradise, where everyone is another to someone else and
nothing to himself, the American Adam obviously can have no knowledge of evil, except perhaps that which is vicariously rendered on his
stereophonic set by Eartha Kitt: "I wanna be evil — I wanna be bad,"
thus fulfilling his manifest destiny in the republic of consumers united
under God.

In this orgiastic technological phantasy in which our lives are led
for us, it is all too easy to assume that basic human needs are altered
or radically modified. Culture itself retreats from the unreality of
its surface image, and literature, which plumbs the depths of culture,
recognizes at least two other levels on which basic needs can be acknowledged or realized.

The first level of reaction against the normative image of culture
harbors values still powerless to be born. It is the level on which the
temporary and temporizing search for privacy and disaffiliation is
conducted. Richard Frede's inadequate novel of college life, *Entry E,*
Sloan Wilson's best-seller, *The Man in the Grey Flannel Suit,* express
and criticize the impulse to affirm a kind of passive or epicurean
sanity in a world of insane bustle. The reaction of privacy, however,
has proven too mawkish for our most serious writers. Disaffiliation,
these writers conclude, is simply not enough. Crime, or that saintliness
which is the other face of crime, is perhaps the only way to keep up
with the Joneses in these days of affluence and obsolescence.

Dissent from the ballyhoo and lunacies of a mass society finds, in
consequence, a more compelling means of expression on a second and
more fundamental level of responses to culture. On that level, the
search for *love* and for *freedom* continues with radical intensity. The
search for love brings men to the threshold of religious experience —
Zen or Buddhist thought, Christian mysticism, the I-Thou encounter
so vividly explored by Martin Buber — and the search for freedom
ends, sometimes, in crime or anarchy, the burden of the hipster, the

plight of the "White Negro" which Mailer expounded with eloquence and vigor. The two quests start from different points — they often meet in the idea of the holy-goof, the criminal-lover, the rebel-victim.

So far, I have overemphasized, perhaps, the diversity in the background and underground of contemporary fiction. Diversity, however, is for the radical mind akin to disorder. Our quest for order requires that we discover some controlling image of recent fiction in America. I find such an image in the figure of the hero of fiction, or rather, its typical anti-hero.

The central and controlling image of recent fiction is that of the rebel-victim. He is an actor but also a sufferer. Almost always, he is an outsider, an initiate never confirmed in his initiation, an anarchist and clown, a Faust and Christ compounded in grotesque or ironic measures. The poles of crime and sainthood define the range of his particular fate, which is his character. Nihilism, frenzied self-affirmation, psychopathy constitute the limit towards which one type of hero tends. Martyrdom, immolation, defeat constitute the other limit which a different type of hero approaches. More often, however, both elements of rebellion and victimization are conjoined in the quixotic figure of what R. W. B. Lewis has called the picaresque saint: Bellow's Henderson, Salinger's Caulfield, Capote's Holly Golightly, Purdy's Malcolm. They are conjoined, too, in the figure of the grotesque who is perhaps the true, ironic symbol of man in this century: Flannery O'Connor's Haze Mote, in *Wise Blood,* Carson McCullers' Miss Amelia, in *The Ballad of the Sad Café,* or even Ralph Ellison's Invisible Man in the novel by that name. For in the grotesque, the distortion of physical forms corresponds to that perversion of mental states which is the malady of the age. Of this, the Mugwumps of Burroughs' *The Naked Lunch* are the ghoulish example.

The figure of the rebel-victim, we see, incarnates the eternal dialectic between the primary Yes and everlasting No. He is man's answer that he conform or abolish himself. There is, perhaps, a mixture of Prometheus, Job, and Sisyphus in him. Compounding the ambiguities of initiation prefigured in *The Adventures of Huckleberry Finn* with the spiteful dissent of Dostoyevsky's *Notes from the Underground,* the new hero mediates the contradictions of American culture by offering himself, in passive or demonic fashion, as scapegoat. His function is to create those values whose absence from our society is the cause of his predicament and ours. It is fatuous, therefore, to say that recent fiction is devoid of values. The "ethic" which the new hero projects is inductive; it is defined existentially by his actions and even more by his passions. This accounts for the shifts and evasions, the ironies and ambiguities, the self-made quality, of his morality. Still, in a post-individual era, the rebel-victim is perhaps one of the last exemplars of a vanishing conception of man. A grotesque effigy to the rule of chaos, this half-demonic and half-quixotic creature still placates darkness with the light of human pride, agony, or derision. In this, he does not differ greatly from the ancient heroes and scapegoats of myth. His true design, however, is to fashion some unity where none can obtain save in the momentary repose of artifice. Art, we see, seems to persist in its romantic role as ironic redeemer of life. Yet our age is also a post-romantic age, and the emergent role of art may be an aspiration to complex silence. When the new will of literature finally becomes clear, we may discover it to be a religious will, born under the shadow of nihilism, yet dedicated to some mode of life, earthly or utopian, that transcends the facts of our existence.

I may have given the impression that the rebel-victim, in our time, is indeed the hero with a thousand faces. I should now like to view some of the particular faces — or are they grimaces? — which he presents in fiction. The novels I shall cite as examples are, I believe, among the remarkable works of the last two decades.

First: The hero as a child who may stand for truth or Edenic innocence, and is victimized, as in Jean Stafford's *The Mountain Lion,* or Truman Capote's *Other Voices, Other Rooms,* or James Purdy's *63 Dream Place,* by an ideal that society can never sanction or recognize. Innocence, it seems, can only reveal its face in perverse guises, and childhood recalls the demon world as few adults can safely remember.

Second: The lonely adolescent or youth, exposing the corrupt adult world, as in Salinger's *The Catcher in the Rye* and Purdy's *Malcolm;* or destroyed by a regressive search for an Oedipal relation, as in Styron's *Lie Down in Darkness* or Swados' *Out Went the Candle.* In no case is full initiation granted. Even in Jean Stafford's *Boston Adventure,* Carson McCullers' *The Member of the Wedding,* or Herlihy's *All Fall Down,* dramatic emphasis is on loss, the pain and bitterness of growth, the fall from uneasy grace.

Third: The lover caught in the impossible web woven by instincts and institutions around him. Adultery is usually the focus of the action, as in Nemerov's *Federigo,* Buechner's *A Long Day's Dying,* or Macauley's *The Disguises of Love.* A more desperate version of the lover is the homosexual, as seen in Vidal's *The City and the Pillar* or Baldwin's *Giovanni's Room.* In time of organization, Eros is utterly disorganized.

Fourth: The Negro in search of the eternal, elusive identity which white men refuse to grant him or themselves, shadow boxing with shadows, as in Ellison's *Invisible Man* or Baldwin's *Go Tell It on the Mountain.* The cellar to which Ellison's hero repairs is the very underground of our culture where issues can be seen finally starkly, unembellished by reason or piety.

Fifth: The Jew engaged with Gentiles in a harrowing dialogue of reciprocal guilt and ironic self-betrayals, as in Bellow's *The Victim* and Malamud's *The Assistant*. The limits of responsibility, the dignity of suffering, the price of failure — these define the ironic meaning of redemption.

Sixth: The grotesque, sometimes a hellbent seeker of godliness, as in O'Connor's *Wise Blood* and *The Violent Bear It Away,* sometimes a freakish and crippled saint, as in McCullers' *The Heart Is a Lonely Hunter*.

Seventh: The underdog, most often a hapless soldier, victim of the awesome powers of regimentation in war or peace, as in Mailer's *The Naked and the Dead,* Jones' *From Here to Eternity,* and George Garrett's *Which Ones Are the Enemy?*

Eighth: The disinherited American, uprooted from his civilization yet finding no roots in the primitive African setting which witnesses, in Bowles' *The Sheltering Sky* and *Let It Come Down,* his violent end with cosmic indifference.

Ninth: The comic picaro, traveling through a crowded life with verve, and sustained by a gift of hope, but never finding for himself a home, except in the mythical territory ahead. Bellow's *The Adventures of Augie March* and Capote's *Breakfast at Tiffany's* are examples of this, and so is Joseph Heller's "hilarious" *Catch-22*.

Tenth and last: The hipster, the holy-goof, in search of kicks and revelation, gunning his cars into the American night or straining for an apocalyptic orgasm at a tea party, as in Kerouac's *On the Road,* or Holmes' *Go*. Variations of the hipster may be found in Donleavy's *The Ginger Man,* the "carnies" of Gold's *The Man Who Was Not With It,* and of course in William Burroughs' shocking book, *The Naked Lunch*. What the heroes of all these works share is the condition of extreme alienation, the status of the marginal man.

These are a few, twisted faces of the contemporary hero. The mask he wears, however, is usually frozen into the same grimace, which is neither comic nor exactly tragic.

Masks are a kind of form, and it is appropriate for us to ask: Given the character of the rebel-victim, what form does his destiny assume in the novel? The form of fiction is the pattern of the hero's existential encounter with experience. The encounter, as we have seen, tends to be destructive. It is delimited by outrage and defiance. Its true nature, however, can be most accurately described by referring to the assumptions neither of comedy nor of tragedy, nor yet of romance, but to those of irony.

In his *Anatomy of Criticism,* Northrop Frye has elucidated these assumptions in a way pertinent to recent fiction. Irony selects from the tragic situation the element of absurdity, the demonic vision, the sense of isolation; it takes from comedy the unlawful or quixotic motive, the savagery which is the other face of play, and the grotesque scapegoat rituals of comic expiation; and from romance it adopts the quest motif, turning it into a study of self-deception, and the dream of wish-fulfilment, transforming it into a nightmare. Irony, the mythos of winter, is the form to which other literary forms tend when disintegration overtakes them. It is, nevertheless, preeminently suited to the needs of the present situation. Irony, in fact, is the basic principle of the form which dominates our fiction. It is the literary correlative of the existential ethic; it implies distance, ambiguity, the interplay of views. It is the form of containment, a self-created pattern of contradictions, the union of the terrible and the ludicrous. Irony is all the certainty we can allow ourselves where uncertainties prevail. Yet irony also commits itself to that which it criticizes. It is, at bottom, not the form of negation but rather the stark shape of hope when death and absurdity are finally recognized. A good many structural and stylistic elements — the function of time, the handling of point of view, the nature of imagery in the contemporary novel — derive from these general assumptions of irony. "Comic" novels like Cheever's *The Wapshot Chronicle* or Nabokov's *Lolita,* tragic books like Styron's *Lie Down in Darkness* or Hawkes' *The Lime Twig,* "picaresques" like Salinger's *The Catcher in the Rye* or Bellow's *Henderson the Rain King,* "romances" like Capote's *The Grass Harp* or Kerouac's *The Dharma Bums,* "gothic" tales like McCullers' *The Ballad of the Sad Café* or O'Connor's *Wise Blood,* "allegories" like Mailer's *Barbary Shore* or Buechner's *A Long Day's Dying* or Hawkes' *The Cannibal,* "satiric fantasies" like Terry Southern's *The Magic Christian,* and "morality novels" like John Updike's *Rabbit, Run,* all share an ironic sense of dreadfulness, and manifest that fusion of genres and modes, that ambiguity of tone and attitude, which is characteristic of the age.

Forms may outlast the ravages of time, but critics really have no business with eternity. It is, after all, the confluence of gifted authors at a particular moment that gives the moment its character. The literary stock market, to be sure, vacillates from day to day, and the crystal ball in which future reputations are revealed remains a blank, lucent space for me. Still, there are novelists whose achievement has engaged our interest over the years; their impact on the contemporary scene, I feel, has force, promise, and magnitude. I should like to mention ten of these. Five have been inclined to explore tighter and more nervous fictional forms. Their works, in fact, have tended to be compact. The other five make fuller use of the mixed resources of the novel. Their books have tended to be crowded and long. Each in his particular way remains unique.

Carson McCullers is perhaps the oldest novelist in the first group. Her conception of grotesques seeking to transcend their spiritual isolation in love — witness her best work, *The Ballad of the Sad Café* — is one of the central facts of our time. With her, the Southern tradition of the Gothic novel is refined into a poetic sensibility which has not escaped either imitation or misuse.

Truman Capote, though he does not like to be labelled a Southerner, has moved from the haunted dream of *Other Voices, Other Rooms* to the daylight romance of *The Grass Harp,* and, most recently, to the zany story of Holly, in *Breakfast at Tiffany's.* The precision of his idiom should not prejudice us against the stubbornness with which he defends the complex and infrangible values of the imagination. For Capote remains, above all, a devotee of the *word,* and it is that devotion which permits him to roam the fabulous underside of consciousness with steady tread.

Bernard Malamud has a tough, sardonic, and deeply compassionate vision. The obscurities which mar his first novel, *The Natural,* are absent from his second book, *The Assistant.* Few writers can transform pain into responsibility with the quiet, steady glow Malamud can give to language. The refuge he sometimes takes in Jewish irony defines his basic commitment — and limits its scope.

Salinger's *The Catcher in the Rye* is perhaps the classic of post-war fiction. It is both mature and adolescent in the best manner of the American tradition. A virtuoso of the short story too — "For Esmé, With Love and Squalor" — Salinger penetrates in his prose to the elusive center where love and squalor silently meet. His latest novelettes, "Zooey" and "Seymour: An Introduction," make an attempt to break down the form, recreating it in the shape of parody and autobiography. His Glass family has become a myth by which the actualities of American life may be gauged, criticized, and — as few critics seem to realize — even upheld.

The last novelist in this arbitrary group is one who has been much neglected. John Hawkes has written five novels to date, bringing satire and surrealism to bear on the shocking realities of our time. *The Cannibal* may be the most profound novel written about the last war. And *The Lime Twig* reveals a nightmare world of evil that is mitigated only by a unique style that reclaims man from the absurdity of his condition.

In the second group, Ralph Ellison, like Salinger, rests his high reputation on a single novel, *Invisible Man.* It is a rich, passionate, and original book, and it shows an energy of *mind* comparable only to Bellow's. The shifting perspective in which Ellison reveals the Negro is unparalleled even by Faulkner.

William Styron, another Southerner who does not like to limit himself to the assumptions of Southern fiction, has written a brilliant and powerful first novel, *Lie Down in Darkness.* His novelette about the Marine Corps, *The Long March,* is notable, and his most recent book, *Set This House on Fire,* reminds us that existential fiction has become as indigenous to America as it is to Europe.

The most extreme and ambitious talent of our time is perhaps Norman Mailer. It is a mistake, I think, to define his achievement by his first novel, *The Naked and the Dead*. His essay, "The White Negro," gives to anger the dignity of a metaphysical principle. And the lurid imperfections of *Barbary Shore* and *The Deer Park* are the source, I feel, of the controlled violence in *Advertisements for Myself*. Power, demonic, instinctual, and human, is the crucible into which Mailer's values are cast, burnt out of their dross, and re-fashioned.

Saul Bellow, no doubt, seems to many the most impressive novelist since the war. He writes in the great intelligent tradition of fiction, concerning himself with freedom — the way things are and the way they can be — in its irreducible forms and manifold disguises. His versatility is evident in the difference between such earlier novels as *Dangling Man* and *The Victim* and the torrential narratives of *Augie March* and *Henderson the Rain King*. But it may well be that his finest work is a novelette, *Seize the Day*.

Finally, there is Vladimir Nabokov, who writes in three languages with an antic and subversive disposition, pressing language to create illusions and subvert realities, and pressing it again to strike at the cunning core of reality. *Pnin, Invitation to a Beheading,* and *Laughter in the Dark* are not as widely known as the notorious *Lolita*. Yet all writhe into life under the touch of grim or ironic comedy, and they show that in our time language may parody itself into some form of metaphysical play, leaving the mirror of art unblemished by any image.

The names and titles I have been dropping freely are an admission that, in the end, the best thing a critic can do is point back to such literary works as call attention to themselves. The spectacle before us is not a bland or shabby spectacle. There are novelists — Flannery O'Connor, James Purdy, John Updike, Philip Roth, James Baldwin, Frederick Buechner, William Burroughs, Terry Southern — who deserve more attention than I have been able to give them in this hurried profile of our fiction. No summary is possible without a fiat of the critical will.

In conclusion, however, I take my cue from a dark, rich, and exasperating book, Lawrence's *Studies in Classic American Literature*. Lawrence claims that the American, the "homunculus of the new era," is nothing but a sort of "recreant European." Perhaps one had better say that the "recreant European" is the rebel-victim of American literature, the Man from Underground in the soul of Huck Finn, a figure unique and indigenous, radical and innocent, troubled with memory and haunted by hope. The figure is acquainted with anarchy; it insists on the extreme imperatives of the Self; it acknowledges neither death nor the end of man. Hence the energy of the contemporary novel which is the energy of opposition.

❧ HERBERT GOLD

Fiction of the Fifties

1. The Writer as Metaphysician

INDEED it is difficult not to live cautiously these days. There is so much to gain (car, house, rank); there is so much to lose (rank, house, car). And yet, what we are sure of gaining and sure of losing remains the same. We are sure of losing our lives. We are sure of the chances at gaining our lives. The ceremonial observances of passion and joy, regret and renewal, continue as always. Parents die, children are born, lovers meet and cling to each other, "their arms round the griefs of the ages." Days pass. Age comes. Mortality decides much and yet gives us many choices: *What are we to make of our lives?* Each step of the way, bound to instinct and accident, controlled by the past and by those others who surround us, involves a new decision: *In what direction the next step?* We are left with this peculiar good news in the shape of a question; by asking it we earn the right of eminent domain. In spite of the way of the world, we utter our hopes, we challenge our fears, we take our chances: *What next? When? Where? How? Why?*

These ultimate questions are contained within every act a man or a woman performs; they have always been contained within the act of creation which is the writing of a story. This has been true for ever and ever, and was true during the decade of the Fifties.

A fly in the metaphysics has been growing, however, until it has near reached the size of a bounding Australian kangaroo. Is it *we* who decide? Who decides under the humid breath of the mass media, psychologizing preachers, statesmen of clay and lanolin made — under that interior whisper to belong, conform, and R.I.P.? Who decides about modern war, atomic fission, mass murder? We are in the shoes of the man poised on the edge of the cliff, deciding about life and mortality, who finally sighs and turns away, resolute against suicide. He will live! There is only one chance for a man, and it is here on earth! . . . At that moment he is shot in the chest by a mad sniper.

Therefore the writer, that exemplary figure, that scapegoat with a diet of tin and hope, scampering first in the lead and then in the rear of society, must accept a complicated mission. He must bounce along with the busy-rumped kangaroo. He must celebrate and value experience. He must see clearly. He must relish what he sees. He must make sense. *And he must not forget the snipers.* Sir Graspinghands who chased the grail had no harder task. Only his armor weighed him down — no publishing fads, anonymous reviews, girls asking "Are you happy?", cocktail therapy. He had his horse, his mission, his box of See-rations; "Go!" He went.

In order to balance the impossible burden of this mid-century on his back and head, the writer must be possessed by what is called style. Style is a notion much worried these and all days. It has to do with controlled strength — the control of the nervous juggler, the strength of the very strong man. It means everything is kept in the air at once, and coherent, and ordered, and eloquent, and also actually *there* in the mind. It is not a scampering trick, a minor felicity, a small device sandpapered into life. An illustration of the power of style is that carnival game which asks you to hammer a nail into a board in three strokes in order to win the prize. The stylist does not bang the board all about; he does not splay his thumb; he hits the nail neatly and swiftly and accurately. Of course, there may be hidden obstructions in the board which deflect the nail; the nail itself may not bear the burden of his stroke; but he fails with dignity and clear sight and a sense of purposeful, directed energy. Also, with good luck in an honest show, he carries off the prize doll.

Style in a writer is a policy about life, not a stunt. It is the personal cabinet of the man who is President of Himself (or at least First Tenor of Egosdale-on-Avon). It is the package containing sealed orders, and when far at sea or in the jungle we open it, we read these terrible words: *Think about cardinal matters!* It is both the map to treasure and the treasure itself.

Aiming at the truth about life on earth, possessed of his style, what has been the special mission of the writer of fiction during the decade of the 1950's? Not absolutely different from the mission of the writer of any time, of course. One role did not leave off in 1949 when automobiles were just beginning to grow their postwar tumors and television aerials sprouted like wild asparagus on the roof tops of America. But a special kind of light has been focused, a direction marked out, and when we look at the contemporary writers who mean much to us at this end of the decade, we may see how they have responded as a group to the particular disasters and challenges of our time.

We may be made uncomfortable by looking. If we are interested in fiction, we usually want only to embrace it; we hate to see too clearly

— it's like examining the piece of spinach on the teeth of the loved one whom we are about to kiss. So let's look quickly, have it over with, and be ready for the kissing. Now here is the spinach:

Writers of fiction have been taking on the role traditionally played by religious leaders, philosophers, metaphysicians. They have returned in deep need to the most primitive poetic purpose: *to know;* to try to know even when they know not; to invoke knowledge; to ransom the god within by peeling off their skin. They have been driven to asking the ultimate questions. And those who love fiction must nowadays love it partly because it concerns itself with final matters.

Where? Whither? Why?

For whom do I live?

For whom?

For what?

What is the relation between freedom and isolation? When am I free and when am I merely isolated? When am I alone and independent? When am I responsible? When am I groupy, togethered into socialized isolation? When am I selfished into insignificance, savaged into incoherence?

What is the connection between love and weakness, love and strength?

Why do I live, struggle, love, defy age and history?

Why must I die and for what?

Who am I?

This question is the spinach on all our teeth and it stinks up our breath when we utter it. It's not, either, that these concerns are unique to our time — the spinach is still visible on Dostoyevsky's teeth, and Tolstoy filled his mouth with green. The great writer always explores both his inner space and that other world outside his head, and bridges the air between. *There must be coherence,* he insists. But an aching personal concern with meaning is the exceptional by-product of our age. Where can we find the truth amid the lies which surround us? There is lassitude in our bones and an aching hope in our loins. This is not ordinary spinach; this is Spinach-90.

Naturally the other kinds of writers and readers still exist. Family novels, fat historical romances, suspense and mystery stories, and various partial talebearers still have their audiences, and why not? Spinach, harsh and gritty, is not necessarily good for us, and some make no demand for it. The impulse toward metaphysics and prophecy is not universal, and why should it be? Also religious leaders, political thinkers, philosophers, psychoanalysts, columnists in *Look,* fortunetellers, revivalists, and drug-sellers all marshal their happy (unhappy) throngs. These citizens have little need to look for thought in fiction and usually have little need of fiction at all, except for the fiction of self-help.

Having eliminated these good citizens, we are left with you and me and perhaps some cowboy in Butte, Montana, waiting in a library while his MG is repaired. We like to read, you and I and that cowboy. (He is also the child in the second balcony whom the violinist plays for.) We read. We see no way of justifying the ways of men to men except by imaginative examination of life on earth. We have looked for the strong sense of personality (mysteries, style); we have found dilemmas and problems (unsolved, unsolvable); we have found resolutions (impossible, essential); we have occasionally been wrung by that strong response which tells us, in literature and in love, in ourselves or in others, I feel! I am alive! I think; therefore I exist.

All this is not to argue that the storyteller is a mere systematic philosopher, conducting a streetcar named Reality, heading home toward the Truth after a hard day. No, no. The car barn is empty; the streetcars have all been sold to Mexico City; futile to look to tropical paradises of tequila and bee-stung lips, or to Rome, or to Moscow, or to any perfect answer in the fancy heavens of archaic simplicity. The bee-stung pair of lips or the various appointments with ritual are answers to something — to a need for rest — but not to our questions, and these questions are what count. It is not so easy. We must also beware of the lofty question-answering fury in a writer. For the crime of *hubris* — that mad pride which leads a mortal to compare himself with Aldous Huxley or William Saroyan — he should be trampled into submission by ten thousand of the top editors of *Time*, all wearing wet galoshes. The writer may be looking for Reality (abstract), but he can find it only in Real Life (concrete). That is, the abstract essence is contained only within the facts of life. The Idea of Woman can never replace the way Sally scratches her head. The Celestial Milkman can only be surmised from that clinking, clanking chap who comes to the door with a brilliant smile, a doctored bill, a teamster's button in his cap, and an opinion about Brigitte Bardot. The Ultimate Meaning of coconuts and milk remains elusive despite coconut cream pie, camembert, butter, and that bump on the head when you fall asleep under the palm tree. When the writer eats a meal for the FBI and finds God, what he really finds is the roast beef pearled with droplets of blood, the golden sweet potatoes, the stray pea in the succotash, the salad tossed with crisp moral lettuce and determined erotic vinegar. That is, he finds God. That is, he finds food and love in time of hunger.

He is not sure of anything. He is absolutely certain about everything.

Saul Bellow, an exemplary writer of this generation, expresses most clearly the philosophical and religious quest necessarily contained within an abiding sense for passing things. All his work seems to ask the question, "Why am I here?" And answers in his comic mood: "Because I'm here — that's enough!" And in his mood of despair: "Because I'm here — that's not enough!" But his intensely lyrical and dramatic, onflowing participation in the life of his Chicago, his Africa, his universe, makes the underlying metaphysical question possible; and so his deepest answer seems to be: "Why? Because we are all here together on earth. It is both enough and not enough."

That is probably the only permanent answer to a question which never remains the same.

II. The Novel and the Story — The Long and Short of It

What the novelist seems to be doing at his philosophical best is to explore possibility. He cuts loose from the expected and sees another possibility for an entire life — his own, his characters', everybody's. The mystery of personality, that unheard sound, always the most heavy presence in a place, works its way to some concrete clap of existence through the tangle of growth which is a successful novel. The great novelists, hearing new sounds, building new worlds in the jungle of the real world, are also great moralists by implication — committed, before all else, to an intense valuation of human experience in the here and now. They are also dangerous and destructive moralists. With angry shouts and kicks they clear away their place in the jungle before they build. They tear down our customary ways of looking at things. They stare into the sun of alternatives. They tell us: You can choose this, you can decide that. You are free! Or if not, you must seek to be free.

In the short story, a writer does something rather different in degree and therefore different in quality. Of course, some novels are merely long stories, and some stories are merely foreshortened novels, but in general the short story is work conceived with greater rigor than the novel. The short-story writer pretty much knows what he is about when he begins; he puts on the smoked glasses of a limited form before watching the eclipse of the sun. The novelist, bound to freedom, may end up blind, roasted, stupefied, and lonely. He sets out with only a hint of the end of the voyage on which he has embarked with no maps but the sealed secret orders of instinct and intelligence. He is as blind as a Secretary of State on the brink of — he knows not what. He is chronically in a bad way, dazzled and sunburned, and heading full steam up shiftless creek.

Because of this necessity of psychic confusion crystallizing out toward inexplicable and miraculous clarity in the important novel — "novel" means new, and the novel brings us unwanted news of the world — the short story is usually more reassuring both to read and to write. The agony of doubt is relieved. The destructive power of a total re-evaluation of experience is not risked. The writer can put down some of his moral baggage. In the story he *knows* — and only doubt, hope, dread, expectation infect him with that inner debate of chronic invention. Knowledge is knowledge — certain-sure. It is as present and comforting as a baked potato. It is what it is. Add butter and salt and have no fear.

Yet, a story is not quite as sure as a baked potato. (*Nota bene:* Even the potato may have a worm baked into it.) The parables of the great prophets and saints are truer than their moral conclusions because tongue-tied and tail-tied to life, which means to unending reinterpretation and reunderstanding. (The word "truth" here is defined as the product of a viable manner of looking — with energy and love — rather than as a formulated conclusion.) Like the great parables, like a novel, a story opens out into a new world, too. At its best, as someone said of something else, it "goes on going on." Sometimes it won't stop going on. The most ruthless writer has trouble putting his stories away from him. Many a novel has been pried out of a writer by a dissatisfaction with what started out to be a story. He reads and thinks: No, no, that can't be all. Those people can't stop here. Now they should . . .

And all at once he finds himself committed to a year or two of griping, sweating, typing and retyping, scratching, poking, jumping out of bed at odd hours, like a parent with a cranky child, because a scene or a character or a situation does not let him sleep. He wants to shake his finger at each new story: "Promise you'll stay put if I give you your say?"

Part of the difference between the short story and the novel is the difference between a love affair and marriage. The first is piquant, exciting, less risky, but may cause beautiul troubles, such as wedlock. The second is long, complicated, noisy, unpredictable, very often unhappy, and absolutely prime to living on earth. The total commitment of marriage is very different from the lyrical joys of love. The novel is different from the story, and not merely because it is longer and heavier. The responsibility is total. "In dreams begin responsibilities" — in stories. "In the day responsibilities end, they end in responsibilities" —so the blessed total envelopment of a novel tells us. Those who read and write both forms treasure these two modes of experiencing fiction. And of course we love either a novel or a story as we love a girl — not for intelligence or virtue — but for the way it meets our gaze.

The short story, as it has developed since James Joyce, seems to be concerned with scene and incident, striking hot, like the lyrical poem. The novel since Dostoyevsky and Tolstoy has increasingly charged itself to make the whole man face the whole world — really the metaphysical enterprise, the bedrock sense of religious thought. Therefore a wholly questing writer like Ralph Ellison, forging or attempting to forge a total view of his world in which a man can stand, is poorly served by the short-story form and unrepresented here although his *Invisible Man* is one of the fine books of the decade and a representative one in its basic philosophical purpose. When the center does not hold, we try to make new centers. Or, in stories, the man whose center does not hold relies on the celebrational hope of poetry — this deed, this moment, this passing love or hate. A man may face the world alone in a story as in a novel, but he does not try to give himself his final name. He is less likely to be Melville's Ishmael than John Cheever's country husband, troubled in love, trying to make out.

The difference between the short story and the novel can be expressed also through another partly parallel, overlapping set of categories. The short story tends to control and formalize experience (though the expressionistic story does not); the novel tends to set forward experience in documentary detail (though the Jamesian novel does not). Fiction can be divided this way into two types: First, that which seeks the ordered ranging and mastery of ideas; second, that which seeks the mastery of experience by passionate avowal. The first writer says: "This is what I can do with it!" The second says: "This is how it is — all of it!" The writers who Avow have the virtues of weight of feeling, purgation by life, passion with its submissions and excesses. They run the risks of looseness, maudlin howling, self-indulgence. The writers who Control give the satisfactions of answering formal demands for order, of coming to an understanding of ends and causes and thus purging us of menace. They run the risks of a false, faked formalism, of giving us resolutions which do not resolve. As the Avowers may howl unnaturally, so the Controllers may build atrocious humps on their backs. One tries to go from the particular to the sublime, the other from the reticulated to the sublime.

No writer of any lasting interest is purely one thing or the other. The best writers of the Fifties have both expressed the disasters of the times and given us some tentative notions of order. And the great writer, who has the chance of producing a masterpiece, certainly combines both of these irreconcilables, the Avowed and the Controlled — just as estranged metals can finally be fused under great heat. With fire, pressure, and continued intensity, the great artist rises to the peak of emotion and the pitch of resolution in the same work — and so, as Aristotle says, we are at last purged of pity and terror. In some way, the moving image of desire has been expressed through the life of one person, that monster individual, the hero who at last represents us all.

III. The Writer as Cricken, Floozie, Elder Revolutionist, Young Fogie, Beautician, Mortician, etc., Including Far-Flung Flinger into Fans (Watch Out)

Harassed, often mistaken and mistook, blessed at his best by good hope and fruitful despair, the writer of the Fifties played hide-and-go-seek amid the disasters of the time.

He made a characteristic kind of fiction — anxious, humorous, demanding — in the image of man's hope during years when every thinking person had to be his own Don Quixote. The windmills surround us for the charging. Sheep may not safely graze, sheep in these days may not even safely gaze; but some writers munched and nosed and threw off their sheep's clothing. They ran against the furious windmills.

Who is the writer who gives us the strongest view of the time?

First, who is he NOT?

Not the fabricated fakes of television, Hollywood, and the mass magazines (not Harry Belafonte improving race relations by playing a Chinese version of *Green Pastures* in yellowface);

Not the Truth Trumpeters with a capital P (for Penultimate Reality), who are made of the nerves left over when Dr. Jekyll turned himself into Mr. Hyde;

Nor the Crickens (Critical Chicken-Hearts saying, "Complex it up, fellas, Russian it up a little!");

Nor the Floozies (Philosophical Oozers of Timeless Indifference);

Nor Sloan Wilson and Herman Wouk with their new upper-middle soap opera (an easier detergent for the togethered souls of suburban lads and lassies of whatever moribund condition);

Nor the Young Fogies queerly proclaiming a brotherhood of gang-bang and gangwhimper — real toadies in imaginary gardens ("I'm one Hell of a Guy, Damn! A-tearin' down society and grammar! A-preachin' of the gospel to all us delinquent kids! Man! Zip! Zen! Wow!");

Nor the Elder Tired Revolutionists ("I have found fair logos under the skirt of Henry James and in the handkerchief which Tom Eliot keeps up his sleeve");

Nor the Beauticians and Uglifiers like Tennessee W., Truman C., Speed L. ("It's so dreadful out here in the *world*. Lemme back, Ma!");

Nor the Morticians, those guilty refugees afflicted with severe cases of penance-envy ("I've read Kierkegaard, Simone Weil, Toynbee, Russell Kirk, Peter Viereck, and my own heart, which shrivels up inside me like the stretchsox off my foot, and I tell you, brethren, it was all a mistake. God meant us to go elsewhere, down below.");

Nor the various other crossbred jackals, bats, wood lice, small-eared asses, woolly barn owls, ferrets, and viewers with abstract alarm.

Then *who?*

Don Quixote, Jungle Jim, scapegoat, juggler, spinach-toothed President of Himself, the great writer of our times will be a person who loots the world for good reason, relishing his prize. He will not have a mediocre subject — himself. He will have a subject with grandiose boundary and tangled interior — *himself.* As a man of our time, he will sing about love, ambition, and mortality expressed through the events of days and nights, and buried within the miraculous willed accidents which move his people will be questions about the relation between freedom and isolation, independence and loneliness, love and weakness, that brutal egotism which is false personality, and the fearful abandonment of the risks of personality which is false socialization. The writer as bandit in the wide world does not know exactly what he will find, frozen shrimp or cash or a good swift kick in the assumptions, but he is bound to his life of sunny crime; he is committed to love, hate, death, and rebirth, as indeed we all are. The ophthalmologists tell us that exercise will not improve nearsightedness; the eye is not a muscle. However, it may be that the soul is a muscle and that myopia of the soul can be ameliorated by stretching the imagination.

If there is a will by the reader.

If the artist has both the will and a strong inner chart.

✻ EDMUND FULLER

The New Compassion in the American Novel

NEVER a glycerin tear shed to the tune of "Hearts and Flowers" in a Victorian tear-jerker was so sloppy and false as is the weird sentimentality in some of the roughest and supposedly most "realistic" of modern novels. An inverted pathos has sprung up among what Maxwell Geismar has called "the brutes." For some years, authors, publishers and reviewers have kicked around the word *compassion* so loosely that its meaning may become corrupted and lost.

The present decline of compassion (which also is the decline of tragedy) began in an odd and relatively innocuous way. It started with the vogue of the lovable bums, and at first it was no worse than a foolish romanticizing of the scalawag: a beery, brass-rail sentimentality. This pattern was not completely new — we see a bit of it in all the classical picaros — but never had it been so elaborated as it began to be in the thirties. It had charm and appeal, at times, dealing good-naturedly with human foibles. It is possible to look affectionately upon such people, as with Wilkins Micawber, if you keep your head and don't elevate a mood into a philosophy.

Some writers, especially those talented men William Saroyan, in *The Time of Your Life,* and John Steinbeck, in several books from his early *Tortilla Flat* to his recent *Sweet Thursday,* developed the lovable bums into the fallacy of "the beautiful little people" — which almost always meant the shiftless, the drunk, the amoral and the wards of society. A corollary was implied: if you didn't love these characters, you were a self-righteous bigot, hard of heart by contrast to the author's compassion and love for the common clay of humanity. Conversely, these books imply another world of respectable and economically stable people who vaguely are not nice, not right, compared to the ineffable and intransigent "little people."

Yet some, though not all, of this stuff called itself "realistic." Its absurdities reached a point in Steinbeck's *The Wayward Bus,* which inspired John Mason Brown to one of the most searching remarks

Reprinted from *Man in Modern Fiction* by Edmund Fuller, by permission of Random House, Inc. Copyright © 1957 by Edmund Fuller.

since the little boy said the emperor wasn't wearing any clothes: "If realism isn't real, then isn't it trash?"

A sinister twist came in the path some years ago, and abruptly this new soft streak lost its innocence. The lovable bum began to slip away, and in his place emerged the genial rapist, the jolly slasher, the fun-loving dope pusher. Now we see increasingly a technique of simple identification with the degraded which is miscalled compassion. It lacks the requisites for compassion as much as its subjects lack the requisites for tragedy.

What is compassion, anyhow? It means the sharing of a sorrow, a pity and sympathy, a desire to help — feeling another's pain or plight as if it were one's own, seeing "those in chains as bound with them." It applies to a man's moral as well as material or physical breakdown. In the moral realm it recognizes the sharing of all human guilt, the potentiality of evil in the most blameless, the element which the Christian calls original sin and the analyst calls the id. In the traditions of both tragic and pathetic literature there is an abundance of authentic compassion.

A large and generous view of life and a distinct standard of values are necessary to establish compassion. These need not, of course, be formulated, but at least you must be able to discriminate between a happy state and an unhappy one; you must be able to discern the difference between a man destroyed through his own fault and one destroyed through no fault of his own, with all the delicate gradations possible between. You must set a moral value on man's actions and circumstances. Compassion is not a suspension of judgment, it is a judgment tempered and chastened according to the facts under some definable theory of the human condition. Compassion is discernment of the gap between the man that is and the potential man that was.

Two old saws contain much of the truth about the compassionate view of life and, incidentally, remove its unavoidable judgments from any taint of smugness: "There but for the grace of God go I," and "To understand all is to forgive all." How these apply to the phony compassion in many current novels we shall see.

In the enthusiastic critical reception of *From Here to Eternity,* culminating in the National Book Award, the word *compassion* was sprayed all over the scene by the critical fraternity. The writing of James Jones may well have many admirable attributes, but I do not see wherein compassion is one of them.

Like all the other pseudo-tough young writers engaged in this peculiar transposition of values, Mr. Jones is shamelessly and laughably sentimental. This is missed by some simply because he isn't sentimental about Mother or Dad or the Pure Girl or Jesus or Darling Babies. Instead, he is sentimental about incorrigible antisocial and criminal types and whores. He is said to be compassionate toward these — which is as you choose to think. Certainly, though, if you are *not* one of these you may expect short shrift from Mr. Jones, for he has precious little compassion for anyone else.

If you can wipe Mr. Jones's tears out of your eyes, you will see that the famous Private Robert E. Lee Prewitt is not a social being, nor are his buddies. Prewitt is not the most extreme of them, but he is the "hero." His type is a social hazard. Since many men have endured as much in the way of background experience as Prewitt did, he is no more the helpless creation of something outside him than anyone else. His character is partly, even largely, self-created, as is true, for practical purposes, of most of us.

But, says Compassionate Jones: Prewitt, Maggio, Stark and the others, drinking and whoring, knifing and slugging, rolling homosexuals, defying authority indiscriminately and eternally, are good, good people. All authority, all sobriety, all the rest of the world, are bad. He is vindictive against the socially adjusted or constructive. If you listen to him long you'll be ashamed to be sober and out of jail. This is not compassion; it is paranoia.

And this is why some of us regard *From Here to Eternity* not as a controlled work of art, but as a clinically interesting projection of personalities by a man endowed with genuine gifts for narrative and pictorial characterization. Whether we are right or wrong, the minority holding this opinion must state it, in the face of reviews, sales and awards.

The most interesting case I've seen since Jones is a first novel of some seasons ago by George Mandel, *Flee the Angry Strangers*. It made no special mark in hard covers, though circulated widely in paper reprint. I choose it as a peculiarly apt illustration of a tendency which can be demonstrated in variations in many novels. In it the false compassion takes the ever more common form of complete negation of values and denial of responsibility. The author's interpreter, in the book, looks on the world of dope addiction and shrugs away any helpful intervention on these grounds: "Who the hell am I to stop it? Who am I to decide about people? There's no harm in anything. You can't stop any of that. You have no right. Nobody has."

With this view, he concludes that all the fallen are the result of repressive nay-saying by the unfallen. (Why the unfallen didn't fall is never explained.) And again emerges the teary slobbering over the criminal and degraded, the refusal to assign any share of responsibility to them, and a vindictive lashing out against the rest of the world.

This particular "compassion" is the sentimental pretense that things are not what they are. Mr. Mandel's eighteen-year-old heroine, addicted to drugs, sexually delinquent, mother of an illegitimate child, finally has been put in an institution. Mr. Mandel supports her in the outraged lament, "My own mother put me there."

As this girl escapes, steps up the dope, takes on more men indiscriminately, and tries a little prostitution, she can still say, reproachfully, "You think I'm a tramp."

"Shucks, kid," is the general attitude of the new-compassion boys, "just going around and doing everything a tramp does, doesn't make a good, sweet, clean little kid like you a tramp."

In short, the new compassion is the denial that men and women are what their consistent, voluntary (and involuntary) patterns of action make them. The elements of true tragedy and compassion — the fall from a standard, responsibility however extenuated, repentance, and the struggle for rehabilitation — are not in this philosophy.

What is wrong with Mandel's approach to his delinquent heroine? He feels sorry for her — don't we all? Can he deny that she has become a tramp? Compassion is to see precisely what she is (which he evades), analyze how she got that way (which he distorts or oversimplifies), and seek for what can be done to rehabilitate her (which he refuses). This is the weakness of many such novels.

It is no casual matter that authors, publishers and reviewers should blandly accept such attitudes as compassion. It may be the most unwholesome and dangerous single symptom in modern literature, for as there is nothing more appealing than the cloak of compassion, there is nothing more treacherous when it is false. In literary art, this is the absolute end product of ethical relativism. No valid compassion can exist without a moral framework. The Greeks had such a framework. The Judaeo-Christian tradition has one. Only in recent years, and so far only in a handful of writers, especially in the French existialist movement, has the moral framework quietly and completely dropped away. This new compassion is a danger to the art of writing, and a deadly one when it is accepted on its claims.

These writers are trapped in a terrible contradiction. Their form of compassion is not to blame, and they find that they cannot portray life at all without assigning blame. Therefore, since their concept of compassion will not permit them to blame anything upon the criminal, the degraded and the destroyed, they blame everything upon the noncriminal, the nondegraded and the undestroyed. It is a kind of counter-puritanism.

The irony is that these writers have no immediate ground. Many so-called good people are responsible for the destruction of others. All of us are involved in the guilt of mankind. Throughout literature and life we see it. But you have to have a standard of values in order to see how corrupt, warped, misdirected values destroy themselves and others. That's the realm of tragedy, of individuality and subtlety. If you have no values, and see no values, you cannot distinguish the hypocrite from the virtuous man, the self-righteous man from the genuinely good, the Uriah Heep from the man of honest humility. The world contains them all, and more. Beginning by seeing only bad, the new compassion ends by inverting it to be a cautious "good" to which normal life stands as a kind of "bad." "Evil, be thou my good"; this is the key to our paranoid novelists.

The existentialists and those influenced by them, and many who unconsciously have been practicing existentialists without the fancy jargon, portray human depravity and degradation without comment, presumably as they see it. This is a kind of moral neutralism. It makes no judgment, on the grounds that there is no judgment. But these writers show phenomena without meaning. If we give depravity no significance we imply that it has no significance. Far from being neutral or unmoralistic or undogmatic, this is a highly partisan, positive philosophical position indeed.

The conflict between good and evil is a common thread running through all the great literature and drama of the world, from the Greeks to ourselves. The principle that conflict is at the heart of all dramatic action, when illustrated by concrete example, almost always turns up some aspect of the struggle between good and evil.

The idea that there is neither good nor evil — in any absolute moral or religious sense — is widespread in our times. There are various relativistic, behavioristic standards of ethics. If they even admit the distinction between good and evil they see it as a relative matter and not as the whirlwind of choices at the center of living. In any such state of mind, conflict can be only a petty matter at best, lacking true universality. The acts of the evildoer and of the virtuous man alike become dramatically neutralized. Imagine *Crime and Punishment* or *The Brothers Karamazov* if Dostoevsky had thought that the good and the evil in those books were wholly a relative matter and had had no conviction about them.

You can't have a vital literature if you ignore or shun evil. What you get then is the goody-goody in place of the good, the world of Pollyanna. *Cry, the Beloved Country* is a great and dramatic novel because Alan Paton, in addition to his skill of workmanship, sees with clear eyes both good and evil, differentiates them, pitches them into conflict with each other, *and takes sides.* He sees that the native boy, Absalom Kumalo, who has murdered, cannot be judged justly without taking into account the environment that has partly shaped him. But he sees, too, that Absalom, the individual, not society the abstraction, did the act and has responsibility. Mr. Paton understands mercy. He knows that this precious thing is not shown on sentimental impulse, but after searching examination of the realities of human action. Mercy follows a judgment; it does not precede it.

One of the novels of the talented Paul Bowles, *Let It Come Down,* is full of motion, full of sensational depravities, and is a crashing bore. For the book recognizes no good, admits no evil, and is coldly indifferent to the moral behavior of its characters. It is a long shrug. Such a view of life is nondramatic, negating the vital essence of drama.

Charles Jackson is a novelist unmistakably sensitive and gifted. His novels are terrifyingly preoccupied with modes of demoralization and collapse. They depict these faithfully, but take in no other aspects of life at all. He admires and partly emulates Dostoevsky, but he does not appear to realize that the difference between the dark tones of his own work and those in Dostoevsky's novels is precisely that Dostoevsky took sides. He was not neutral in the conflict between good and evil. The gulf fixed between Jackson and Dostoevsky is not one of literary craftsmanship but of moral sense.

Dostoevsky views Raskolnikov with compassion, for he sees and interprets for us the moral fallacy that entrapped Raskolnikov. If there were no such fallacy, if Dostoevsky had perceived no moral standard to be warped, Raskolnikov (whose name means "the dissenter") would have been a mere Russian Robert E. Lee Prewitt, and there would have been no tragedy. The great depth of *Crime and Punishment* (the very title states it) is that both Dostoevsky the author and Raskolnikov the created character are conscious of the moral dilemma.

Dreiser, in *An American Tragedy,* sees Clyde Griffiths with compassion because he shows us how the boy has been undermined by a shoddy set of material values and is poorly equipped to appraise them. Dreiser sees the good and evil in the American era he portrays; the social tragedy is that there are those like Clyde who can see them only dimly, if at all.

The original muckrakers portrayed horrors with a fierce indignation against the social injustice they saw as causative; if sometimes too simply. So it is in Upton Sinclair's *The Jungle.* But these men were reformers. Their eyes were fixed upon a good of which they saw men deprived, and which they were determined passionately to restore. In the writers we are discussing, the vision of the good is lost. They stare hypnotized upon the mess as if they conceived it to be the sole, or total, reality of life.

Many novelists of talent other than those named are more or less involved in the confusion of identification with compassion, in the process of representing a facet of life as if it were the whole, and of presenting phenomena without the evaluation which the greatest of writers, and even the mere reformers, never have shrunk from offering. They feel that by detailing innumerable horrors without visible revulsion they are somehow demonstrating sympathy. They conceive their virtue as not casting stones at the sinner, but many cast stones in other directions, and some reverse the words of Jesus to say, in effect, "Neither do I condemn you — go and sin some more."

National Book Award juries have shown an affinity for new-compassion novels. In addition to *From Here to Eternity,* they have given the palm to Nelson Algren's *The Man With the Golden Arm* and Saul Bellow's *The Adventures of Augie March.* In Algren's skillful work, including the recent *A Walk on the Wild Side,* there may be sympathy, but it remains the one-sided sympathy of the new compassion. The promising talent of Norman Mailer has collapsed utterly into this genre in *Barbary Shore* and *The Deer Park.* Leonard Bishop's novels belong there, and Irving Shulman's at least lean that way. The total catalogue of writers and books within this category would be burdensome to compile.

Some borderline books of the kind we are discussing are no more than crying novels or — to be more blunt about a few — sniveling novels. A vast and blurred self-pity is appliquéd upon the fictional characters — as if to do this represented compassion in the author. In some cases it is simple transference of the author's own self-pity, as shown by the inability to see or move beyond it in portraying life. In some, the assiduous stockpiling of depravities has an unmistakable element of reveling, of wallowing, of bad-boy's glee. Many of these writers cry, "Look, Ma, I'm blaspheming."

There are merely fitful glimmerings of life and agitated motions in the books of such novelists. The vital questions which would bring them to profound life have been nullified. You cannot say of their attitude toward their characters, "To understand all is to forgive all." They see much but understand nothing. They do not understand all — they *devalue all.* They do not forgive all. They do not forgive anything. They say there is nothing to forgive. They take murder, rape, perversion and say, belligerently, "What's wrong with it?"

You cannot say of their characters, "There but for the grace of God go I," because you cannot find in their work any chain of moral cause and effect by which *you* could get from where *you* are to where their characters are (as you can in Dostoevsky and Paton). The placement of these characters in their situations is arbitrary and mechanical, as is the inversion of good and bad.

The irony of ironies is that these are not the most compassionate, but the most vindictive writers working today, not the most humble, but the most arrogant; not the binders of the wounds of their fallen brothers, but the destroyers of the social order. "Down! Down everybody!" they scream. "Down with us all!"

Dostoevsky anticipated this moral phenomenon as he did so many others. These paranoid novels are books that some of his brilliantly studied characters might have written. Ivan Karamazov said, "Everything is permitted," and Smerdyakov, acting accordingly, murdered. Raskolnikov saw moral law as inapplicable to some men, and acting accordingly, murdered. Ideas are more than abstractions, Dostoevsky shows us again and again. Ideas have consequences. God preserve us from the consequences of the ideas implicit in the novels of the new compassion.

JOSEPH J. WALDMEIR

Quest without Faith

COMMITMENT to an ideology, affiliation with a cause; a tendency to argue, moralistically, in terms of white and black; indignation, optimism, disillusionment; rebelliousness — these are the most essential components for a definition of the traditional social-critical novel. Little American writing today fits the definition. There are the potboilers concerned with teen-age gangs, beatniks, Hollywood, Washington, suburbia, and crime during the 1920s. And there is the pseudo-social criticism of Cameron Hawley, Sloan Wilson, Herman Wouk, James Gould Cozzens, Ayn Rand, and the Dos Passos of *Midcentury,* writers who are in reality apologists of expediency and affiliates of the *status quo.* But among the serious new American novelists — those who have done their best work since 1949 — only a handful are traditional social critics; and among these, most are those World War II novelists who identified fascism as a universal ideological immorality and saw themselves as crusaders against it.

The majority of the serious new novelists conceive of society and a man's place in it in quasi-naturalistic terms; hence they cannot be social critics in the traditional sense. The specific social villains — factory owner, orchard owner, inimical environment, "systems" such as capitalism or Nazi-fascism — against which the social critic has always fought are for them merely aspects or symptoms of a universal illness. And to attack, even to cure, a symptom is hardly to guarantee a cure of the illness, or even to prevent the rise of new symptoms. One may defeat Nazi-fascism, for instance, without disturbing in the least that middle-class morality which permitted Nazi-fascism to exist in the first place, and which permitted McCarthyism to replace it as symptom. As the new novelists see it, society — amorphous, all-pervasive, uncontrollable, capricious — is invulnerable. Optimism, disillusionment, angry indignation are irrelevant in this conception; ideologies and causes are teapot-tempest anomalies.

Resolution of the implicit dilemma would seem impossible; a man either compromises with, or conforms to, such a society, or he is

Reprinted from the *Nation,* November 18, 1961, pp. 390–396, by permission of the publisher.

destroyed by it. But the novelists resolve it neatly by the creation of a third choice: disaffiliation, both from society and from crusades against social evils. In so doing, they have forsaken pure naturalism, and have thereby softened the dilemma into a paradox: society is deterministic, but the individual, though a part of society, is remarkably free — indeed, sufficiently free that he is able to ignore society utterly, if not actively to subtract himself from it.

Whether by force or by choice (since a too great concern with the problems of existence in an age of conformity can push one willy-nilly outside the pale) the heroes of the new American novel are disaffiliates. Saul Bellow's Augie March and Henderson are both irrevocably separated from society. So too are Norman Mailer's Sergius O'Shaugnessy and Mikey Lovett, Nelson Algren's Frankie Machine and Dove Linkhorn, Bernard Malamud's Frank Alpine, J. D. Salinger's Holden Caulfield, William Styron's Cass Kinsolving and Peyton and Milton Loftis, Herbert Gold's Bud Williams, Paul Bowles's Port and Kit Moresby, Vance Bourjaily's U. S. D. Quincy and violated violators, and Jack Kerouac's Jack Kerouac. Even Ralph Ellison's invisible man, and the menagerie of factory workers in Harvey Swados' *On the Line* — though Swados and Ellison come very close to being social critics in the traditional sense — are outsiders.

None of these characters is capable of conformity, nor can any of them actively engage in social protest. In fact, Holden Caulfield, Bud Williams, Frank Alpine and the Moresbys are never even faced with a situation which might challenge their social consciousness. But many of the others are, and their reactions are revealing. Augie March, for example, is caught up in both labor and Communist activities, but is completely apathetic toward both except as they affect him directly. Peter Leverett in Styron's *Set This House on Fire* is dutifully respectful of his father's devotion to the New Deal, but his feelings go no further than a sort of wistful nostalgia for a commitment not his. Bourjaily's Quincy sees his youthful devotion to communism as naive enthusiasm, unworthy of the mature man of the world. Ellison's nameless hero becomes entangled with both the Left and the Right ideological wings, but ends as an absolute loner. And Mailer's Mikey Lovett, surrounded by an ex-Stalinist, an ex-deviationist and a corrupt representative of the extreme Right, finds all ideology floating away on the waves of meaningless political chatter, leaving him clutching nothing and swearing to defend it to the death.

Accompanying this social disaffiliation in the novels, which follows from the assumption that society is naturalistic, is a sort of moral disaffiliation, based on the further assumption that morals are social, hence, are at best relative, and at worst illogical. Most of the novelists deal with the common conceptions of immorality quite graphically, but seldom judgmentally. They do not condone, neither do they condemn; rather, they portray and explain and, as it were, attempt to understand. Augie March is a cheat and a thief from the beginning of his story to the end; Bud Williams is a con artist and pickpocket, as part of his with-it-ness; Nelson Algren's wild-siders are thieves, whores, drunks and perverts; William Styron's Cass Kinsolving is a drunken murderer, and his Milton and Peyton Loftis in *Lie Down in Darkness* are, respectively, a sot and a nymphomaniac; the characters in Vance Bourjaily's *The Violated* are so morally slippery that it is impossible to know who is violating whom — and very much the same thing must be said about the people in Chandler Brossard's *The Double View* and those in George P. Elliott's *Parktilden Village*.

But the two works which most clearly illustrate this amoral aspect of the new novels are Mailer's *The Deer Park* and Paul Bowles's *The Sheltering Sky*. The former is the story of the return to sexual potency (the redemption?) of Sergius O'Shaugnessy through the medium of Hollywood-nik sexual experiences. It has a little politics mixed in, and a touch of the-motion-picture-as-art discussion; but by and large, it is a book of, about and for illicit sex. *The Sheltering Sky* is also focused on sex, though not of the orgiastic variety. Kit Moresby punishes herself for her husband's death (over which she has no control — Bowles is clearly the most naturalistic of the new novelists) and for her failure to be present at his dying (over which she does have control — she is pursuing an affair with her husband's friend, Tunner, at the time of his death) by indulging her latent nymphomania as an ex officio member of a sheik's harem. Kit ends in madness, fleeing to avoid facing her guilt; but the reader is not led to believe that this is her punishment for evil — merely that this is the way such people often end up. One comes away from both books with the impression of remarkable talent, and, at the same time, with a distinctly crawly feeling. But be it noted: this must be precisely the feeling that Mailer and Bowles want the reader to be left with, else they'd have offered at least a moral judgment, if not justice, to help us wash it away.

Mailer, Bowles, the majority of the new novelists, are unable, or flatly refuse, to distinguish, except relativistically, between the accepted conceptions of good and evil; and so they see judging or choosing sides to be useless, as attempting to reform the world is useless. They drag us into depths of degradation, enervation and defeat. But most of them do not drag us into the depths simply for the sake of the dragging or the depths; nor do they leave us there. Their subject matter may be negative, but their "message," if they will pardon the expression, is positive.

The message is far from resoundingly optimistic. It is little more than a cautious hope, without promises or guarantees. Simply stated, it is the belief that somewhere, somehow, there exists a transcendent set of values which the individual can discover and achieve, if he suffers long and hard enough, and is very lucky in his search for them. The message is almost medieval, though of course defrocked, for there is no fixed religious system to impose order and control on the novelists' world, and no God to whom the individual can appeal for guidance or aid in identifying true values from false. The individual seeks the values either by pursuing them away from society, into the monastery with Frank Alpine, or into the wilderness with Henderson or the Moresbys; or by pursuing them into society with the majority of the characters we are discussing, armed and armored against society's pitfalls.

Thus, one achieves order and value, if at all, as a result of a quest, much as the medieval holy man and the knight achieve them. The difference rests in the certainty of the holy man and the knight that they knew what they sought; the heroes of the new novels cannot know, for who or what in a naturalistic universe can tell them? The values are at once personal and internal, universal and transcendent. The search begins and ends with the individual; it is he alone who must beat his way toward order, hoping only that he will know it when he finds it. Logically, then, the quest itself is at least as important and interesting as the finding, just as the temptation of the holy man is of as much moment as the vision, or as the perilous journey across the wasteland is as interesting as the Grail.

And just as logically, the fact that the quest sometimes fails does not negate the novel's message — any more than Lancelot's failure dimmed the significance of the Grail — unless the novelist conceives of the quest as a circular detour, as does Bourjaily in *The Violated,* Elliott in *Parktilden Village,* Styron in *Lie Down in Darkness,* and John Updike in *Rabbit, Run.* The quest does not simply fail in these novels; in reality, it hardly seems to be pursued at all. They are quest novels without a quest; hence, they lack a message as well. Bourjaily's people go nowhere, largely because their creator has nowhere to take them. Guy Cinturon is the only one who seems to have an aim in life: "the documented seduction of 350 women"; the rest are simply along for the ride. Bourjaily's interest in them extends no further than their private sensibilities, which he chronicles expertly. The inhabitants of *Parktilden Village,* though they too are carefully drawn and reasonably well motivated, stumble along in a vacuum, seeming to be headed somewhere but never arriving, until Elliott steps forward, drops his heroine melodramatically from the stage, summarily dismisses his hero, and ends on a bit of moralizing through the medium of his fourth most important character. Styron's magnificently articulate oddballs — a lush married to a paranoid and father to a moron and a congenital bitch — appear to be reaching toward some Truth through 400 pages of agonizing self-appraisals until, at the end, the reaching has become groping, and we end exactly where we started, having been nowhere. *Rabbit, Run* is the clearest example of this non-quest quest novel. Harry Angstrom is a man dedicated to finding value in a valueless world, and Updike encourages him, endows him with a merciless conceit and, paradoxically, with a tremendous desire to love. But Harry's search is no search at all; for all his moving, he stands stock-still; the more he wriggles, the deeper grows the hole which he digs for himself. Rabbit's quest is really flight; his values are vain dreams; the only order for him is the order which entraps him.

The only message it is possible to draw from these books is that there is no message to be drawn from them. These four writers are saying that this is the way life is, that when you have passed through it you find that you are exactly where you started.

Perhaps they are right, but it is a very difficult position to maintain and still write novels. There is a finality to it that would make saying it twice rather pointless. Bourjaily may have come to the same conclusion (Styron certainly has, for *Set This House on Fire* is the story of a successful quest, and will be discussed as such later). *Confessions of a Spent Youth* is decidedly a quest novel in which U. S. D. Quincy searches through his past for a permanent order by which his present can be justified and on which his future can be built. But he learns that a man is not made by his past, only by his present and future; that values are transitory; that commitment to love, ideology, religion or blood is impossible for him. The quest fails, but not because Bourjaily failed to send Quincy on it. The reflection of life here is as devastating as that in *The Violated,* but it no longer seems to be devastation for devastation's sake. Paul Bowles's work is even more destructive and depressing than Bourjaily's; as I said above, *The Sheltering Sky* leaves the reader with a distinctly crawly feeling. But here again we have a quest novel; Port and Kit Moresby enter the desert in a search for order and value outside or above time and space. That the search is fruitless, that they find instead disorder and physical and moral decay, does not nullify Bowles's point that life is a quest for order and value. The very fruitlessness fixes the point.

Perhaps the key book among those in which the quest fails is Norman Mailer's *Barbary Shore*. In fact, Mailer is in many ways the key figure in this discussion. *The Naked and the Dead* was a powerful novel of social criticism. Mailer's liberal anti-fascism is evident in the moral-ideological struggle between Cummings and Hearn as well as in the physical struggle between Croft and Hearn. And the death of Hearn is the liberally committed Mailer's warning to society that, unless it be alert, the Cummingses and the Crofts will prevail. Some of the war novelists continued their anti-Fascist crusade after the war (Irwin Shaw, for example, in *The Troubled Air*); but for Mailer, the end of the war brought the end of ideological certainty.

He lost conviction, and his writing shifted away from certainty toward the search for something to be certain of, away from crusade toward quest. Thus, Mikey Lovett, the hero of *Barbary Shore,* is a returned veteran without a past, for his memory is gone, trying to find himself and some justification for his existence in an enigmatic universe. His search takes him, as Mailer puts it in *Advertisements for Myself,* "into the psychic mysteries of Stalinists, secret policemen, anarchists, children, Lesbians, hysterics, revolutionaries." He searches for order and value in this, "the air of our time, authority and nihilism stalking one another in the orgiastic hollow of this century." But the search fails; political gibberish is all that Lovett has at the end — that, and the right to defend an ideology which he does not understand even sufficiently to identify. These, and the memory of the taste of Guinevere.

Barbary Shore is not a negative book, despite the failure of the quest. Mailer would have a difficult time becoming a negative writer, since he needs so badly to believe, and belief is a positive motivation for the quest. But the process of arriving (or, in Mailer's case, of re-arriving) at convictions is slow and painful for the honest, serious novelist. There are no short cuts, and substitutions are unsatisfactory, as Mailer has inadvertently proved in *The Deer Park* and may be proving again in *The Time of Her Time.* Sex, the memory of the taste of Guinevere, is the substitution he has made for order and value. Yet, even here, Mailer is not negative; he is simply at (it is to be hoped) a temporary dead end.

But the lovelessness, not the sex, is the dead end. All human desires and experiences, sex prominently among them, play important parts in the quest novels. They are life, and life is all that the modern quester has to guide him. He is separated socially and morally from the systems of value and order surrounding him; he is separated from religious certainty. He cannot regard desires and experiences as temptations and trials, as could the medieval holy man and knight, and eschew them as the means of success in his quest. He seeks for, rather than seeks in the name of, a higher moral order; and only through living can he hope to achieve it. But the quest novelist, whether the quest succeeds or fails for him, does not confuse desire and experience with achievement. Love is a value, not sex. Love, finally, is what Mikey Lovett and U. S. D. Quincy and Kit Moresby are denied, and so their quests fail, though they have about all the sex they can use.

Love, with and without sexual involvement, is the ultimate permanent and true value in the novel of the successful quest. It is love that sets Cass Kinsolving's house on fire and restores his manhood to him. It is love that matures Bud Williams away from with-it-ness, and forces Holden Caulfield finally to sort the real world from the unreal. It is love that chases Ralph Ellison's invisible hero into his dungeon, and at the end, causes him to resolve to leave it. It is love that places Frank Alpine hopelessly and helplessly behind the grocery counter. Love makes it possible for Augie March to rise above all that he learns about life, and to go on living, and laughing, despite the hopelessness of life. And it is love that sends Henderson running round and round that airplane clutching the child to his breast.

Sometimes the love is directed toward specific persons, as in the case of Cass Kinsolving and the peasant girl, Francesca; Bud Williams and his wife, Joy, and his friend, Grack; Holden Caulfield and his sister; Frank Alpine and the grocer and the grocer's daughter; and Henderson and the African lion king. Often it is far more general. Augie March comes to love nearly all the people he meets, and Ellison's nameless hero finds eventually that he must love the people he is trying to help more than he loves himself. And often, too, the love is universal, as it is in the novels of Nelson Algren and Jack Kerouac. Perhaps indiscriminate compassion is a better description than universal love here, for these two novelists seem intent on proving that all humanity is worthy of love by portraying the most unlovable in the sweetest terms. The success of the quest is mitigated, in the novels of Algren and Kerouac, by this Steinbeckian compassionate sentimentality which is at bottom irresponsible and lacking in conviction. Such sentimentality is not love at all, as the other novelists of the successful quest would define the term. For them, love must be conviction if it is to be value, and conviction means commitment, means individual responsibility for individual human actions — the only kind of responsibility possible, given a naturalistic view of the universe and of society, and given as well the ability to disaffiliate.

Again the parallel between the modern and the medieval quest is apparent. For the moderns, love of man rather than love of God is the key, and responsibility to the self rather than to a prescribed code; but this is merely a difference of emphasis or direction. The holy man and the knight were human, capable of sin and a powerful sense of guilt and an awareness of the necessity of expiation; so too are the modern questers. The sin in both cases is not loving strongly enough to live up to your responsibilities, and the resulting guilt is overpowering, as is the desire to be shriven.

Gold's Bud Williams is torn by guilt for deserting his friend when he needed Bud most, and for deserting his own past. He tries to atone by shifting responsibility — by retreating to a further past in the form of a touch football game and his high school sweetheart; by wishing his father dead, thus destroying the further past; and by marrying his immediate past, thus making it part of the present. But the guilt remains until he fulfills his obligation, until he does all that it is in his power to do for Grack. Ellison's hero, neither white nor Negro, "hurt to the point of invisibility," finds through his hibernation the necessity of love, which leads him to the guilty conclusion that the hibernation is perhaps "my greatest crime . . . since there's a possibility that even an invisible man has a socially responsible role to play."

Styron's Cass Kinsolving is a derelict, driven by a nameless guilt upon his quest, and escaping from failure after failure into drunkenness and clownishness. Francesca's murder is the catalyst which activates his sense of responsibility and sends him to execute Mason Flagg as a means of dispensing justice and expiating his own culpability. That Flagg is not guilty of the murder makes little difference. He personifies the corruption and guilt of Cass, the sore which Cass is obliged to burn out before he can live again. But succeeding in the quest by means of such violence — even though from Cass's point of view, and Styron's, the violence is not evil — is terrible, and Cass wants to surrender himself. But his friend Luigi frees him instead (" 'Consider the good in yourself! Consider hope! Consider joy!' "); and the book ends with Cass denying that he has found grace or belief at the end of his quest, but asserting that he has found the ability to live, to be "what I could be for a time. . . . And that for a while would do, that would suffice."

Bellow's Henderson is much the same sort of derelict as Cass, with the same tendency toward excess and violence. His quest carries him by gradual stages back to the utterly primitive, the cry, "I want!" constantly in his heart and on his lips. In Africa, through long philosophic discussions with the doomed lion king, he comes to understand both love and responsibility, and their interrelationship, and he resolves to return to his Lily and to her theory that one should live not for evil but for good, not for death but for life. And it is this understanding spilling over which causes him to clutch the little Persian orphan boy to him as he circles the plane in the frozen Arctic air. Again, there is no tremendous brilliant light at the end of the quest, no heart filled with Grace nor mind with Belief. But there is life and love and hope and the feeling that the individual can do something besides simply disaffiliate. And, Bellow and Styron appear to agree, this would indeed suffice.

Malamud and Salinger both lead their heroes upon successful quests, too. Frank Alpine becomes the grocer's assistant out of guilt for his part in the robbery and assault, and he continues with his hopeless task as love and responsibility grow in him, fed by successive waves of guilt for his thievery and for his rape of Helen. With the death of Morris, his willing entrapment is complete, the sacrifice is consummated, he becomes his lover's father, and thus he gains his reason for living. Holden Caulfield wanders across the face of his world from end to end, his heart and mind split apart by his precocious adolescence. His is the eternal quest of the adolescent for maturity, a quest always accompanied by disaffiliation and iconoclasm. It succeeds for Holden through the love he bears for his sister, and his awareness at the end that he is somewhat responsible for her now and for what she will become.

But love for his sister is more an end than a means for Holden Caulfield, just as conversion to Judaism is more an end than a means for Frank Alpine, and returning to his father's trucking business in Pittsburgh is for Bud Williams. Admirable though they may be, these are pat, somewhat sentimental, solutions to the terrible problems facing these characters. Admittedly, they are convenient endings to the novels, as Herbert Gold points out in the cute last line of *The Man Who Was Not With It*: "There's a good and with it way to be not with it too"; but they are not what most of the other quest novelists, whether their quests succeed or fail, mean by acceptance of responsibility. It is the difference between means and end, broadness and narrowness or, perhaps, sign and symbol. For strangely enough, running around an airplane with a Persian orphan in your arms *is* what the other novelists mean.

Edward Loomis's brief and brilliant existentialist novel, *The Charcoal Horse*, illustrates this distinction with utmost clarity. Gillespie, the hero, is a soldier who has accidentally committed a minor offense. He fears that confession, that is, acceptance of his responsibility, will cast suspicion upon him for another more serious, though still minor, crime. He chooses to do nothing, and as a consequence, a murder is committed and the murderer is sentenced to hang. Driven by guilt — which, rather than love, is the permanent value in existentialism — Gillespie pursues a quest for expiation. He tries to assume sufficient responsibility to keep the murderer from being hanged, but he is not permitted to do so, for the murderer too is responsible. In fact, Gillespie is not allowed even the solace of public expiation. There will be no punishment, no consequences, he is told. The responsibility is his entirely; the consequences are private and personal, and so is the guilt.

This is the order which the modern quester seeks, the order of pure individual responsibility. Gillespie is utterly free at the end, as far as the world outside himself is concerned. The only crutch the army permits him is the command to stand at attention. There is no pat answer for Gillespie. No simple way out — no way out at all. He must do and be exactly what he must do and be, just as Henderson must, and Cass Kinsolving.

But Styron, Bellow and the other quest novelists are not existentialists (despite Styron's clever manipulation of being and nothingness at the conclusion of *Set This House on Fire*). Their circles of love and responsibility expand outward rather than retreat inward. Their sense of guilt is instrumental; expiation is possible if the quest succeeds. Still, they and Loomis are in close agreement; Loomis simply has pushed the concept of individual responsibility to its logical extreme.

The problem in either case is to find a way to exist with dignity and self-respect within an enigmatic universe. The serious new American writers whom I have discussed here — and many others who could have and perhaps should have been discussed: James Baldwin, Flannery O'Connor, John Hawkes, William Goldman, Gore Vidal, Anton Myrer — are primarily novelists upon a quest to find that way. They are not, as I said at the outset, social critics in the traditional sense — the value and order they seek exist beyond causes and ideologies; but they are certainly social critics in the broader sense that the quest itself is implicitly a rejection of society's values. To seek a new approach and a new answer to the problems of the human condition is to criticize the old. And to find or reaffirm the most ancient of answers, love and individual responsibility, is to make that criticism explicit — to make it at once an accusation, a challenge, and a demand for reform.

✴ RICHARD LEHAN

Existentialism in Recent American
Fiction: The Demonic Quest

JEAN-PAUL SARTRE has commented on the literary debt that he and Albert Camus owe the American novel. Sartre has outlined the influence Hemingway had on Camus' *L'Etranger* and the effect of Dos Passos' *U.S.A.* on Sartre's own *Les Chemins de la Liberté (The Roads to Freedom)*.[1] Thelma Smith and Ward Miner[2] as well as Claude Magny[3] have called detailed attention to the popularity of American fiction in France after the Second World War. No one, however, has yet attempted to demonstrate the influence the postwar French novel has had on new American novelists. Paul Bowles, for example, has translated Sartre's *Huis Clos (No Exit)* for the Broadway stage. Bowles has attached the same emotional and intellectual significance to North Africa as has Camus, and uses this scene in a way remarkably similar to the way Camus uses it in his fiction. Moving to Paris in 1946, Richard Wright has come under the direct influence of Sartre, who published part of Wright's *Black Boy* in *Les Temps Modernes*, a literary and philosophical journal edited by Sartre. Cross Damon, the hero of Wright's *The Outsider*, uses an existential jargon and acts out of obvious existential motives. Recent novels by Ralph Ellison and Saul Bellow also seem to employ an existential hero in search of existential values.

Yet the problem is not entirely one of influence. The influence of Continental fiction on Bellow and Ellison is most remote, and it would be indeed difficult to prove that they have written conscious existential fiction. The problem is more one of an affinity of mind or spirit. The Americans are preoccupied with the same problems and themes that

Reprinted from *Texas Studies in Literature and Language*, I (Summer, 1959), 181–202, by permission of the author and the editors.

[1] Jean-Paul Sartre, *Situations* (Paris, 1947–49), trans. Annette Michelson (London, 1955). See also Sartre's essay "American Novelists in French Eyes," *The Atlantic Monthly*, CLXXVIII (August, 1946), 114–118.

[2] Thelma Smith and Ward Miner, *Transatlantic Migration, The contemporary American Novel in France* (Durham, N.C., 1955).

[3] Claude Magny, *L'Age du roman américain* (Paris, 1948).

fascinate and puzzle the French writers. Sartre, Camus, Bowles, Bellow, Wright, Ellison — all are concerned with the meaning of identity in the modern world, the nature of good and evil, the possibility of fulfilment in the contemporary society, the source of values in a world without God, and the possibility and meaning of action in an ethical vacuum. The new American hero is similar to the French existential hero because he shares a common world and a similar world view.

In a recent edition of the *Kenyon Review,* Mr. Murray Krieger makes some observations applicable to both the Continental and the American variation of the existential hero. Krieger's express purpose is to define what he calls the modern "tragic vision." Such a vision stems from the interactions between a protagonist and a disordered and chaotic world. Aristotle's definitions of tragedy are really inapplicable to modern drama because the Greeks took for granted an ordered world. As a result, "the fearsome chaotic necessities of the tragic vision [were surrendered] . . . to the higher unity which contained them."[4] Hegel also was unable to perceive the essence of the modern vision because he subsumed the tragic hero within an "ethical substance," a metaphysical equivalent to the unity of the Greek world. Kierkegaard, Krieger rightly points out, altered the focus from the universal and generic to the particular and individual. Faith, said Kierkegaard, "is precisely this paradox, that the individual and the particular is higher than the universal."[5] Nietzsche pushed Kierkegaardian principles to their limit. Once the all-embracing moral order was lost, Nietzsche's hero stood outside the universal — outside justice, society, and political institutions. Nietzsche's vision served to pre-empt the Dionysian forces (chaotic, primordial, orgiastic) to the exclusion of the Apollonian principles (civilizing, measured, sublime). Our modern tragic visions, says Krieger, are the Dionysian vision, "except that the visionary is now utterly lost, since there is no cosmic order to allow a return to the world for him who has dared stray beyond."[6]

I believe that the pattern of Camus' and Sartre's heroes follows exactly Krieger's preclassical definitions of tragedy. The existential hero does not reaffirm his identity through a tragic fall. Rather his tragic quest usually allows no noble form of self-fulfilment or higher return to the community, and often leads to a form of self-destruction. The fate of the hero is really consistent with existential theories of absurdity and society. Dostoyevski's Kirillov is probably the first modern hero to destroy himself out of the demonic desire to prove

---

[4] Murray Krieger, "Tragedy and the Tragic Vision," *The Kenyon Review,* xx (Spring 1958), 284.

[5] *Ibid.,* p. 287.

[6] *Ibid.,* p. 290.

that he is beyond any form of divine mandate — that he is his own God. In the absurd world one act has no more meaning than any other, except the act of dying, a form of fulfilment as well as destruction. The first existential martyr, Kirillov affirms his identity by destroying it. Such is the logic of absurdity.

Camus' Meursault is not unfamiliar with this logic of absurdity. He undergoes a shock of recognition when he murders the Arab on the Algerian beach and, possessed by a demonic urge to be the source of his own fate, fires four additional shots into the prostrate body, knowing that this will cost him his life. Meursault's act obliquely parallels Kirillov's suicide. Camus' hero realizes his own identity by putting it in jeopardy of death. Meursault and Kirillov are inverted Christ-figures, demonic heroes who die so that others may understand the nature of absurdity. Camus' metaphysical rebel, a satanic hero, rejects a God who allows a world of pain and suffering. "When the throne of God is overturned," says Camus, "the rebel realizes that it is now his responsibility to create the justice, order, and unity that he sought in vain within his own condition, and, in this way, to justify the fall of God."[7] The transition from Meursault to Jean-Baptiste is in many ways a logical one. Jean-Baptiste tries to usurp the power of God and ends up winding his way through the nine concentric circles of Amsterdam. Satan has once again become the modern hero, Hell the modern scene.

The philosophy of Jean-Paul Sartre contains a destructive principle at its very center. Sartre sees life as a struggle between mutually exclusive states of being — matter and consciousness. He believes the most perfect form of human attainment is that state which simultaneously contains pure matter and pure consciousness. Sartre recognizes that such a state is a form of self-destruction: to be pure fixity and pure consciousness at one and the same time is to be both God and dead, mutually inclusive terms. Since it is in the very nature of Sartrean freedom to overreach oneself, to strive for total completion, the Sartrean hero continually destroys himself at the very moment he achieves a kind of self-completion. It is no accident that characters such as Mathieu and Hugo die at the moment they most fully realize their freedom. Sartre often compounds his hero's trouble, often frustrates the will of his hero, by insisting that he recognize the need for social commitment as well as the need to be a *causa sui,* obviously exclusive pursuits. The irresolute Mathieu, torn between a desire to engage himself in the Spanish Civil War and a desire to pursue his own individual preoccupations, lacks the capacity for unimpeded ac-

[7] Albert Camus, *The Rebel,* trans. Anthony Bower (New York, 1956), p. 25.

tion and almost destroys himself by an inability to direct his restless energy toward a definite end. Sartre has been unable to finish *The Roads to Freedom* tetralogy because he has been unable to decide whether Brunet should pursue his ideals within or outside the Communist party, within or outside society. Sartre himself seems to be torn by the same irreconcilable choices, and seems to suffer the same paralysis of will that characterizes his hero.

No one has illustrated the tenets of existential philosophy better than Paul Bowles. The principal characters in *The Sheltering Sky,* Bowles' first novel, are Port and Kit Moresby, both ineffectual and overcivilized Americans who discover new depths of being after several months of primitive life in the desert. The novel functions in terms of Camus' vital universe and Sartre's theories of consciousness. It reveals Camus' belief in the destructive power of creation and Sartre's belief in the destructive nature of self-fulfilment. The novel takes place in Camus' North Africa, in and around the borders of the Sahara. The land is completely antihuman: the sun burns without mercy; the sky cracks with heat; the wind singes the skin like a gust from a blast furnace; and the red earth burns like an ember of molten lead. These elements are manifest extensions of the destructive powers lying behind the protective shield of the sky. The sky is a thin veil protecting man from the cosmic violence beyond; it "shelters the person beneath from the horror that lies above."[8] Port and Kit find new depths of being in an elemental contact with the desert before they are eventually consumed by the vital but destructive forces that sustain life.

Port's death functions in a dual capacity — symbolic and structural. Attempting to transcend the human condition, he refused to recognize the reality of death; he also founded his existence upon a cold antihumanism, "was unable to break out of the cage into which he shut himself, the cage he had built long ago to save him from love." (68) It is dramatically appropriate that Port dies of meningitis, shaken with chills. The chills are the objective equivalent of his cold antihumanism, his impersonal being. In *The Plague* Father Paneloux died a "metaphysical death." Port also dies of the plague to demonstrate an existential truth — that one cannot be so completely self-contained that he can transcend physical reality or be protected from the malevolent element that lies beyond the sheltering sky. Port's death also has a structural significance. Since Kit relied completely on Port, she is suddenly thrown totally upon herself. When this happens, she becomes aware of the absurd, the gratuity of her existence, the "sudden surfeit

---

[8] *The Sheltering Sky* (New York, 1951), p. 217. After the initial footnote, all references to primary texts will be shown in parentheses following the quoted material.

of time, the momentary sensation of drowning in an element become too rich and too plentiful to be consumed, and thereby made meaningless." (165) Kit desires to exist within Sartrean states of mutually destructive being — to maintain a free yet rocklike consciousness, to live within the world but outside of death, to possess the joys of sensual being in a state of godlike eternality. Her quest functions within the existential vocabulary, its dramatic pattern, and its tragic finale. As Sartre would explain it, she tries to push her freedom to a form of perfect completion; she desires to be one with pure consciousness and yet still be one with a sensual world, to be pure thought and pure sensation at the same time, to be both in and out of the world. As a result she becomes so self-involved that the delicate balance between consciousness and reality gives way to an extreme form of dementia. As Camus would put it, Kit finds new regions of sensual being only by becoming one with the universe and establishing a contact with the element that ultimately destroys her sanity.

Let It Come Down, Bowles' second novel, repeats almost exactly the general pattern of action in *The Sheltering Sky* and also functions within terms of a destructive and demonic element. Nelson Dyar (the surname hints at an element of the demonic suggesting "dare" and "desire")[9] comes to Tangier to escape the limitations of life in America. He also finds a new life in a physical and elemental relationship with the natural life. Although Dyar wants to be the sole source of his being, he lives in anguish, knowing that existence is completely fluid and unfixed. He attempts to secure a rigidity of being — first by stealing Jack Wilcox's money and then by murdering the Arab Thami — through acts of commitment so extreme that they transfix his being in relation to himself and the world. The scene that leads Dyar to this extreme action has most remarkable parallels to the beach scene in *The Stranger.* One morning as Dyar walks down a sun-drenched beach, he feels an explicit kinship with the world. He is suddenly at one with the universe. His very breath becomes part of the wind; the natural life "cleanses" him and washes away his bitter futility; (128) his strength "came out of the earth, nothing which would not go back into it. He was an animated extension of the sunbaked earth itself." (269)

As we have seen, Meursault also incarnates the universe and becomes a very extension of a destructive element when he murders the Arab. Since Dyar and Meursault are both sensual neopagans, both are primitivists who refuse to go beyond the world of matter; both maintain a completely unilateral view of life; one act, one situation, has no more meaning or importance than the next. "The whole of life does not equal the sum of the parts," Dyar maintains. "It equals one of the

[9] *Let It Come Down* (New York, 1952), cf. p. 169.

parts; there is no sum." (186) Life is purposeless; existence has no
meaning outside of itself. There is no grand design, no transcendent
justification. Dyar and Meursault make no attempt to restrain their
actions in this ethical void. By refusing to limit their extreme action,
they become complicit with the destructive element, immersed in an
evil which eventually consumes them.

Let It Come Down takes its title from the rain that continues to fall
throughout the story. The rain — along with the wind, the sun, the
violent sea — is the dramatic incarnation of the unseen forces which
constitute the conditions hostile to man. The desire of the beetle to
destroy the ant is only "infinity in a grain of sand." (269) Dyar wants
to be so self-involved that nothing from this hostile world can harm
him. To use Sartre's vocabulary, he desires to be his own *causa sui* —
pure being and pure consciousness at one and the same time. After
he has stolen Wilcox's money, Dyar flees with Thami to a small Arab
town, high in the Spanish mountains, where they find sanctuary in
Thami's small cabin. As Dyar tries to sleep at night, the wind bangs
the door back and forth. The rattling door reminds him of outside
reality: "the loose door was equivalent to an open door. A little piece
of wood, a hammer and one nail could arrange everything: the barrier
between himself and the world outside would be much more real."
(262–63) The next night — thoroughly fortified with *kif,* exhilarated
by vicarious participation in a frenetic native dance — Dyar is again
awakened by the banging door. He gets up to drive a nail into the
door — instead he drives the nail into Thami's head. With this drastic
act, Dyar bolts the door between him and humanity and seals himself
within his own consciousness: "his existence, along with everything in
it was real, solid, undeniable . . . he was conscious of the instantaneous
raising of a great barrier that had not been there a moment before,
and now suddenly was there, impenetrable and merciless." (310–11)
At this moment Dyar incarnates the absurd and becomes the source of
his own being — a modern satanic hero, an avatar of malevolence
driven by essentially demonic motives to be his own *causa sui.* Now
outside the realm of humanity, his being has all the fixity of death.
Like other existential heroes Dyar destroys himself at the moment he
fulfils himself.

The Spider's House, Bowles' latest novel, has oblique parallels to
Camus' *The Plague.* The novel takes place in Fez, at the time in a
virtual state of siege. Morocco is being torn in half by two factions,
the relentless French colonialists and the greedy Istiqlal nationalists.
Like Camus' Oran, the stock way of life has been violently interrupted,
the old order has suddenly given way, and the individual is forced to
construct a new way of life in an extreme and absurd world that has
no moral base or center. As in Camus' fiction, the suffering and vio-

lence in Fez has no meaning outside of itself and is meant to be taken as an indivisible part of the total human condition.[10] Again, as in Camus' fiction, the world of Bowles is without causal links. Existence is completely gratuitous. An object has no meaning except in and for itself. As the protagonist, John Stenham, puts it, this is a world of "and then" rather than of "because"; "one thing doesn't come from another thing. Nothing is the result of anything." (187) A world without links defies coherence. Since the world of Fez is both irrational and malevolent, it is by necessity absurd. In this cause *The Spider's House* is an oblique commentary on the psychological state of mind that motivated action in Bowles' earlier fiction. Port and Kit Moresby and Nelson Dyar sought protection from the absurd forces around them within the well of consciousness. John Stenham tells Lee Veyron that the populace of Morocco also wants to dissociate itself from "the whole world outside [which] is hostile and dangerous." (186) Camus and Sartre never carried their concept of the absurd to the extreme conclusions of Bowles, but it certainly seems evident that the existentialists and Bowles start out with the same general premise and that there is an explicit relationship between their two orders of fiction.

The relationship between Saul Bellow and French existentialism is more difficult to determine precisely. Yet *Dangling Man*, Bellow's first novel, is very similar to Sartre's *Nausea* and Camus' *The Stranger*.[11] Joseph, Bellow's hero, is suddenly tumbled out of a comfortable way of life when he receives an induction notice from his draft board. While Joseph knows he will eventually be called into the army, his immediate induction is postponed and he is left dangling. Joseph resembles Meursault and Roquentin in many ways: he is a minor clerk (like Meursault); initially he is caught up in the stifling ritual of daily activity; he is most susceptible to physical stimuli; he is an empiricist; he lives in a world divested of ends; he grows from philosophical innocence to a state where he questions the nature of creation and human existence; he records this progress in a journal (like Roquentin). In sum, *Dangling Man* follows the dramatic pattern of *The Stranger* and *Nausea* — reveals an innocent mind coming in contact with the absurd and portrays the effect this has on the hero and his relationship with others.

In *The Myth of Sisyphus* Camus outlined the psychological process that precedes and follows awareness of absurdity. Joseph develops in relation to this pattern. He is caught up initially in the mechanical pattern of daily activity; his induction notice suddenly interrupts this

[10] *The Spider's House* (New York, 1955), cf. pp. 211, 231, 335.

[11] *Dangling Man* (London, 1946) was originally published in 1944, six years after Sartre's *Nausea* (Paris, 1938) and two years after Camus' *The Stranger* (Paris, 1942).

routine; life thereupon is robbed of all meaning. Joseph begins to live at a distance from the world, outside the realms of ordinary men, carrying the full weight of his undirected existence. " 'I am forced,' he says, 'to pass judgments on myself and to ask questions I would far rather not ask: "What is this for?" and "What am I for?" and "Am I for this?" My beliefs are inadequate, they do not guard me.' " (123) Like Meursault and Roquentin, Joseph journeys a path of continued anxiety. His quest for identity takes him outside the order of men to a point of self-autonomy so complete that he almost is unable ever again to accept his original world view, to return to society, or to reaffirm his initial identity.

Meursault and Roquentin are unable to find any meaning in the communal life. Joseph also rejects the order of men when, at Mitta's party, he suddenly realizes that his friends band together for mutual protection, behave the way the group expects them to behave, assert the group values, scorn all that is outside the clique, and ridicule all that threatens the general definition. He also rejects his materially minded brother, Amos, and Amos' daughter, Etta. Joseph even begins to reject Iva, his wife, who is sympathetic but not really understanding of his sudden deracination.

Joseph's disillusionment in people prefaces his disillusionment with the whole nature of creation; the world suddenly becomes a very indifferent thing, and he is no longer willing to live in a passive relationship with it. "The world comes after you," he says, (137) and there is a "feeling of strangeness, of not quite belonging to the world at large." (30) An indifferent world precludes a beneficent and personal God, and Joseph asserts that "there are no values outside of life. There is nothing outside of life." (165) Joseph rejects God for the same reasons as do Meursault and Roquentin; he insists that God is born out of "a miserable surrender . . . out of fear, bodily and imperious . . . I could not [he says] accept the existence of something greater than myself." (68)

Once he has rejected society, the world, and God, Joseph, like all existential heroes, longs for the purity of the completely self-contained existence, the very internal necessity of an art object. "We need," he says, "to give ourselves some exclusive focus, passionate and engulfing." (141) In *Nausea* Roquentin is fascinated by a jazz tune, *Some One of These Days,* he hears on a phonograph in the café, Railwaymen's Rendezvous. He longs for the constituted fixity of an art form. "When the voice was heard in the silence," he says, "I felt my body harden and the Nausea vanish. Suddenly: it was almost unbearable to become so hard, so brilliant . . . the music . . . filled the room with its metallic transparency, crushing out miserable time against the walls."[12] Without transcending the human condition, the music unifies a shapeless reality, orders a discordant flux of time, and lends intensity and meaning to human suffering:

> A glorious little suffering has just been born, an exemplary suffering [says Roquentin]. Four notes on the saxophone. They come and go, they seem to say: "You must be like us, suffer in rhythm." (233).

Joseph listens to a Haydn *divertimento* with the same intensity as Roquentin listened to his jazz tune. Joseph also wants to give his life the integrity of an art object, his suffering the brilliance of formal arrangement, and his existence the inner necessity and proportion of a harmonious order of creation. It is difficult to believe that Bellow wrote this scene without conscious recall of Sartre's *Nausea*. Joseph echoes the exact sentiments and ideas of Roquentin:

> It was the first movement, the adagio, that I cared most about. Its sober opening notes, preliminaries to a thoughtful confession, showed me that I was still an apprentice in suffering and humiliation. I had not even begun. I had, furthermore, no right to expect to avoid them. So much was immediately clear. Surely no one could plead for exception; that was not a human privilege. What I should do with them, how to meet them, was answered in the second declaration: with grace, without meanness. And though I could not as yet apply that answer to myself, I recognized its rightness and was vehemently moved by it. Not until I was a whole man could it be my answer, too. And was I to become this whole man alone, without aid? (67–68)

Like the existentialists, Bellow is not only trying to depict the emotion of abandonment that accompanies the loss of fixed traditional values; he is also trying to depict the motives that lead to the self-enclosed hero. In a prolapsed world, in a state of continued suspension, the hero carries his personal existence in its total weight. He can live in terms of no future reality — except death. He can act in terms of no emblem — except self-definition. All of his actions have no meaning outside of themselves; his existence is completely autonomous and self-enclosed.

The dichotomy of self-affirmation and self-negation — of total rejection of a fixed social order and total acceptance of unfounded existence — almost destroys Joseph, as it destroys Kit Moresby and Nelson Dyar. Like other existential heroes, Joseph desires an ideal existence almost at the expense of his real existence. The Spirit of Alternatives, Joseph's alter ego, is the voice of "Unreason" which

[12] *Nausea*, trans. Lloyd Alexander (Norfolk, Conn., n.d.), p. 34.

keeps him dangling between irreconcilable orders — hope and actuality, the ideal and the real, life and death:

> "The vastest experience of your time doesn't have much to do with living. Have you thought of preparing yourself for that?" [says the Spirit of Alternatives]
> "Dying? . . ."
> "I mean it."
> "What is there to prepare for? You can't prepare for anything but living. You don't have to know anything to be dead. You have merely to learn that you will one day be dead. I learned that long ago. No, we're both joking. I know you didn't mean that."
> "Whatever I mean, you get it twisted up."
> "No. But I'm half-serious. You want me to worship the anti-life. I'm saying that there are no values outside of life. There is nothing outside life." (165)

> "Apparently we need to give ourselves some exclusive focus, passionate and engulfing."
> "One might say that."
> "But what of the gap between the ideal construction and the real world, the truth?"
> "Yes . . ."
> "How are they related?"
> "An interesting problem."
> "Then there's this: the obsession exhausts the man. It can become his enemy. It often does."
> "H'm."
> "What do you say to all this?"
> "What do I say?"
> "Yes, what do you think? You just sit there, looking at the ceiling and giving equivocal answers."
> "I haven't answered. I'm not supposed to give answers." (141)

The Spirit of Alternatives brings out rather clearly the difficulty of being a law unto oneself when every possible course of action suggests an alternative. Bellow, of course, is here expressing an existential idea — the ambiguity of ethics, the difficulty of choice between two courses of action that are not morally exclusive of each other.

Joseph's discussion with the Spirit of Alternatives calls to mind Ivan's talk with the Devil. It is a rather curious coincidence that Joseph's journey leads to a form of demonic union. Mrs. Harscha calls him Mephistopheles, and Joseph says, "She had seen through me — by some instinct, I thought then — and, where others saw nothing wrong, she had discovered evil. For a long time I believed there was a diabolic part to me." (77) I believe that Bellow is merely playing with ideas here. Joseph is not a thoroughgoing satanic hero, and he himself rejects the label. The interesting thing is that Bellow and Camus are both concerned with the possibility of life outside the social order, and both are willing to recognize that such a life borders upon a satanic existence — the rebel in the underground.

Bellow's hero dangles between accepting and rejecting his freedom, is torn by the nature of alternatives (as his alter-ego signifies). Like other existential heroes, once Joseph has divested the world of meaning he finds it impossible to act in terms of commitment. Joseph's state of suspended activity is a form of death in life; his new identity brings him to the edge of a peculiar kind of self-destruction. As Sartre has pointed out, matter has to be infused with consciousness before it assumes a momentary meaning; freedom too must be directed outside itself in a form of (say) political commitment before it takes on meaning. Joseph is the completely autonomous hero who is unable to direct his energy outside of himself and almost burns himself out in fits of insignificant restlessness. He is like the character in *The Plague* who spends all his time counting a bushel of peas from one basket into another, or the one who spends all his time rewriting the first sentence of his novel, or the character who appears each noon, calls the neighborhood cats to his balcony, and then spits upon them with great accuracy.

The *Dangling Man* is similar to *The Plague* in another rather significant way. The plague brings Camus' characters to a moment of self-awareness. The majority of Camus' characters invest their freedom with a kind of meaning by fighting the plague (even though they know that their efforts will have no permanent avail). Joseph, however, does not invest his freedom with any outside meaning and, as a result, dangles between a kind of existential integrity and bad faith. The close of the plague marks the end of a forced awareness; the end of Joseph's waiting marks the end of an imposed consciousness. It is interesting to note that both Joseph and the plague-stricken are able to reaffirm their initial identity and to return to the original community. The quest stops short of self-destruction because it stops short of any kind of cosmic identification or total autonomy. Joseph welcomes release from his unfixed state of being, and his surrender is marked by a refreshing breath of air — almost the seablown air that greets Diego after the termination of the plague in Camus' play, *State of Siege*. Joseph was on the threshold of freedom, but recognized that its consequences were too great:

> We are afraid to govern ourselves [he declares]. Of course. It is too hard. We soon want to give up our freedom. It is not even real freedom, because it is not accompanied by comprehension. It is only a preliminary condition of freedom. But we hate it. And soon we run out, we choose a master, roll over on our backs and ask for the leash . . . That's what happens. It isn't love that give us weariness of life. It's our inability to be free. (167–68)

Freedom imposes too great a burden; it can lead to extremes, and extremes can lead to self-destruction. "I am no longer to be held accountable for myself," Joseph concludes upon entering the army. "I am grateful for that. I am in other hands, relieved of self-determination, freedom cancelled. Hurray for regular hours! and for the supervision of the spirit! Long live regimentation!" (191) It is noteworthy that Joseph's journey stops short of social alienation, and that Bellow possibly saves Joseph from the fate of Nelson Dyar.

Cross Damon, the hero of Richard Wright's *The Outsider,* is another modern hero whose existential motives lead to overreaching and personal disaster. *The Outsider* is the most express treatment of the existential theme in American fiction. The novel, however, does not reveal a major talent and has most serious limitations: it is a philosophical *tour de force,* exploits the sensational, relies upon existential ideology to fill out character motivation, and editorializes far more than the most tendentious Continental existential novels. Wright, however, does understand the basic philosophies of both Sartre and Camus, and his portrait of the modern satanic hero is documented in existential terms.

Cross Damon is also in search of a new identity. When he is listed by mistake among the dead of a horrible train wreck, he repudiates an identity in which he can no longer believe. His problems are supposed to be the problems of modern man: he is "the twentieth-century writ large."[13] He rejects the common values because he can find no meaning in society, and because he is unable "to relate himself to others." (127)

Damon's dilemma is in a way also Meursault's — "the dilemma of the ethical criminal, the millions of men who lived in the tiny crevices of industrial society completely cut off from humanity, the multitudes of little gods who ruled their own private worlds and acknowledged no outside authority." (302) Like Meursault, once Damon is outside the social order he enters into a diabolical cosmic relationship, becomes a law unto his own undefined nature, and becomes the source of all good and all evil:

> Damned is the man who must invent his own god! [says Damon, anticipating his own ultimate damnation] Shun that man, for he is part of the vast cosmos; he is akin to it and he can no more know himself than he can know the world of which he is in some mysterious way a part . . . what does this mean — that I don't believe in God? It means that I, and you too, can do what we please on this earth. (314)

Damon's cosmic identity becomes licence for murder. Although both Meursault and Damon are metaphysical murderers, they are also "inno-

[13] *The Outsider* (New York, 1954), p. 284.

cents" — innocent because society is guilty. Meursault kills the Arab because he is an automaton and merely reacts to an unpleasant series of sensations. The point is that Meursault is an automaton because of the meaningless workaday world: the rising at seven, breakfast, tram, work, lunch, work, tram, dinner, the rising at seven again. The robot woman in Céleste's restaurant, who mechanically wolfs her way through dinner so that she can get home to the evening radio programs, is meant to be read as society writ small. Damon is also innocent because society has given him no values in which he can believe and by which he can live. Damon murders with impunity because, as Wright puts it, "there was a kind of innocence that made him want to shape for himself the kind of life he felt he wanted." (78) Damon protests his innocence at the end of the novel, after he has been shot and is about to die. "In my heart," he says, "I felt . . . I'm innocent . . . That's what made the horror." (384)

The Stranger is constructed on a strict ironic framework since society is both at the source of Meursault's murder and of his death sentence. Meursault is a victim; he thinks of himself as a martyr, the new Christ. Cross Damon continually refers to himself as a victim also (cf., for example, 350). Like Meursault, Damon is also an inverted Christ-figure. His very name suggests that he is both satan and saviour — that "a genuine atheist is a real Christian turned upside down." (369) Named by his mother after the cross of Christ, Damon is indifferent to his mother (Meursault is similarly indifferent to his mother) and follows the wayward footsteps of his father (Camus also sees the destructive principle in terms of the father or the judge). The name "Cross" is significant because it suggests the hero's godlike desire to be the autonomous and self-enclosed martyr. Damon wants to be either pure consciousness or pure matter, *pour-soi* or *en-soi,* to use Sartre's terms for the Godhead. He wishes "to swap the burden of this sorry consciousness for something else! To be a God who could master feelings! If not that, then a towering rock that could feel nothing at all." (123) The name "Damon" is significant because it represents "the quality of the demonical in him." (120) Near the end of the novel, Damon tells Sarah, "Remember, He said: 'Come unto me, all ye that labor and are heavy laden, and I will give you rest'?"

"But you don't believe that," [Sarah] protested, baffled, half-scared. "I know you don't. Do you?"

"No." He could not resist telling her the truth.

"Then why do you tell *me* that?"

"Perhaps God uses the Devil to guide people home," he told her. . . .

"You are the *devil*!" she burst out bitterly. (362–63)

Like Roquentin, Damon listens to jazz music in an attempt to realize a new identity. Roquentin envies the internal necessity of the art form. Cross Damon believes that by listening to jazz he can systematize his sensual impulses and become a kind of God. He refers to its "demonic contagions" and, as Wright tells us, the "blue-jazz became his only emotional home . . . He came to feel that this music was the rhythmic flauntings of guilty feelings, the syncopated outpourings of frightened joy existing in guises forbidden and despised by others." (125)

As we have seen, the dichotomy between rejection of a fixed social order and acceptance of an unfixed existence almost destroys Joseph. Once Damon becomes self-enclosed, he finds that there is no return to the community, and his plight becomes that of the Moresbys and Nelson Dyar. Damon, a variation of Camus' Jean-Baptiste, finds no redemption from modern hell. (cf. 165) He is exposed by Bob Houston, the District Attorney, a hunchback who has the psychological makeup to understand the motives of a satanic hero:

> Houston, a hunchback, an outsider, a man whose physical deformity had forced him to live in but not of the normal rounds of ritualized life, knew the demonic feelings of men who played god because he himself was of the demon clan, having hidden his kinship with the rebellious by publicly upholding the laws and promises that men live by. (224)

One demonic consciousness upends another; and when Damon recants at the end of the novel, he is in essence expressing the tragic consequence of existentialism — the cosmic hero becomes self-enclosed only by traveling the path of self-destruction. Like Kit Moresby and Nelson Dyar, Damon's end was in his beginning. Nietzsche's man of power assumes a satanic mask, and the flight toward identity leads up a road that never turns back to man.

The hero of Ralph Ellison's novel, *Invisible Man,* also destroys his original identity and quests unsuccessfully to reaffirm another one. He is still another contemporary hero who is unable to redeem himself from a fallen world, a modern hell. While relationship between Ellison and the existentialists is most remote, they are bound together by definite preoccupations with the nature of identity in the absurd world. Ellison's hero ultimately comes to very existential attitudes toward life: "I knew it was better," he says at the end of his journey, "to live out one's own absurdity than to die for that of others."[14] "Our task is making ourselves individuals," he says elsewhere. "We create the race by creating ourselves." (268) "Life is to be lived, not controlled, and humanity is won by continuing to play in face of certain defeat." (435)

---

[14] *Invisible Man* (New York, 1947), p. 422.

Sisyphus could not have expressed himself more clearly, or in more distinct existential terms. If he is speaking for himself, Ellison certainly does not overstate the case when he says that Sartre, Kierkegaard, and Unamuno are the chief literary heroes of the modern world.[15]

Ellison's unnamed hero loses his identity when he is expelled from a small Southern Negro college. His only offense is to expose a wealthy northern philanthropist to the realities of Negro life in the South. Mr. Norton thinks of the Negro as an abstract extension of his personal destiny. Dr. Bledsoe, the president of the college, endeavors to preserve this God-subject relationship between Norton and the Negro. By keeping Norton in contact with only the most idealistic aspects of Negro existence, Bledsoe is able to keep him in contact with a nonentity, an abstraction, an invisible generic animal.

Norton is a symbolic Godhead; the college is a symbolic Garden of Paradise. Nameless and without precise location, the college has an air of otherworldliness. Norton visits the school each spring; his presence accompanies the cycles of life, and the campus is beautifully in bloom; yet beneath the appearance of life and fecundity is the stark reality of arid death. "Why is it," the hero asks, "that I can recall in all that greenness no fountain but one that was broken, corroded and dry?" (29) A forbidden road runs through this paradise on "past the buildings, with the southern verandas half-a-city block long, to the sudden forking, barren of buildings, birds, or grass, where the road turned off to the insane asylum." (27) Here again is the familiar road, the possibility of the journey outside society, the insane asylum at journey's end.

Ellison's hero journeys down the forbidden road — bringing Mr. Norton with him. Once Norton sees Jim Trueblood and the veterans at the Golden Day, he can no longer think of the Negro as an extension of his beneficent nature, and Ellison's protagonist can no longer think of Norton as God. As the protagonist leaves the college, never more to return, he notices a snake crossing the highway. The loss of the old identity is worked out in terms of the Fall. The quest for the new identity is both frenetic and unsuccessful, and the hero eventually ends up alone, abandoned, on an underground coal pile. There is a humor here — but rather a demonic humor, a kind of satanic glee, the shrill laugh of Dostoyevski's possessed or underground hero with whom Ellison's protagonist is indeed blood brother.[16] After he killed the Arab, Meursault tells us that he feels doomed. Ellison's hero also

[15] Ralph Ellison, "Society, Morality, and the Novel," *The Living Novel: A Symposium,* ed. Granville Hicks (New York, 1957), p. 79.

[16] Wylie Sypher, "The Meaning of Comedy," *Comedy* (New York, 1956), has seen this relationship between the comic and the absurd, especially in Dostoyevski and the existentialists; cf. pp. 193–197.

recognizes a kind of inevitability in his flight outside of man. "My end," he tells us, "was in the beginning." (431)

The coal pile becomes a retreat from both society and self. Like Kit Moresby and Nelson Dyar, Ellison's hero ends in a state between being and non-being. "All dreamers and sleepwalkers must pay the price," he says, "and even the invisible victim is responsible for the fate of all. But I shirked that responsibility; I became too snarled in the incompatible notions that buzzed within my brain. I was a coward." (12) No writer, on either side of the Atlantic, has found a more powerful image to convey Sartre's concept of bad faith. Yet it is a bad faith which follows from the tenets of existentialism itself. Existential choice and freedom are constructed along asocial lines; existential commitment, on the other hand, is a principle of social involvement. The hero is thus torn between the instinct to live outside society and the guilt which follows such a choice. These two positions are mutually exclusive — and yet to see them both in existential philosophy is only to place Sartre's *No Exit* next to his *What Is Literature?* Like Mathieu, Brunet, Jean-Baptiste, Invisible Man — aware of both necessities, unable to act in terms of either — frustrates his will and is consumed by his very logic.

Destruction — either death or a kind of insanity — is at the end of the existential quest. And yet the quest, the dramatic means of revealing a free will in search of identity, is absolutely necessary to existential literature. The existential hero believes at times that hell is other people. He also believes that there is no longer a dichotomy between good and evil and that evil is a gratuity, a latent part of existence. The existential hero desires to master the malevolent element rather than let it master him. These motives — the desire to be a moral or social law unto himself, the desire to be so self-involved that the outside world is no longer a threat — lead to the flight, the quest, towards a new identity in which the hero is completely autonomous and creation is a mere extension of his will. This explains why the existential hero often assumes the guise of the sensualist, the man who is able to say *no* to death by making an eternity of the moment, the atheist who is able to fill the moral void by making the all-consuming experience the end of existence. "To feel" is often the first step in the desire "to power." The sensualist is the satanic hero who has incarnated the Nietzschean will.

Ivan collaborated with the Devil, and Camus (perhaps unjustly) maintains that Ivan is the character who most captivated Dostoyevski's imagination. Certainly Ivan, the rôle Camus played in his dramatic adaptation of *The Brothers Karamazov*, is the character who most captivates Camus' imagination. American novelists have also been fascinated with the figure of Satan. Young Goodman Brown and

Ethan Brand meet him. It is not, however, until Faulkner's Joe Christmas that the American hero actually *becomes* the Devil. Christmas is
explicitly referred to as the Devil ten times, and the label is certainly
consistent with his nature.[17] The Moresbys, Nelson Dyar, Joseph,
Cross Damon, Invisible Man — all, in various ways, continue the tradition of the demonic hero. Without family, outsiders, physically dislocated, they are the sensualists who desire the all-consuming experience. Save Joseph, they are plagued by the emotions of loneliness
which haunt their journey. Like Satan, they are their own destroyers;
they reject society, plot against it, seek a new reality, a supreme
identity, and thereby destroy themselves.

The modern hero stands at a crossroads — one path leads to the
society, the other away from the community. Joseph, torn by the
struggle of choice, almost burns himself out trying to reconcile the
alternatives. The Moresbys, Nelson Dyar, Invisible Man — all take
the path outside the community and pursue it to a form of ultimate
doom. Along with Meursault and Joe Christmas, they are the first
of the existential martyrs. The irony of their deaths is part of the
absurdity of their lives. Society makes them and then destroys them
for what they are.

It is interesting to note that the existential hero of late is taking the
path to the community. Camus' Rieux, Tarrou, D'Arrest, Sartre's
Brunet, Bellow's Leventhal and Wilhelm — all possess a new compassion, and the existential struggle is not quite so antiheroic, so satanic
in character. Perhaps this is only the natural difference between the
underground existence of Sartre and Camus during the Resistance and
their rather prominent social positions after the war.

Perhaps the death of the satanic hero anticipated this return to society all along. In *The Rebel* Camus says "the individualist cannot
accept history as it is: he must destroy reality not collaborate with it,
in order to affirm his own existence."[18] The modern writer destroys
reality by destroying the modern hero who incarnates it in its most
malevolent form. The modern novel exorcises the devil in a very real
way and thereby establishes a sense of what *should be* rather than
what *is*. The death of the antihero is a form of protest as well as a
form of hope — a way of saying that the world *should* and perhaps
could be a better place in which to live, that the world cannot be
changed but that man can as long as he is free to choose and act. This
is only saying, in sum, that existence precedes essence. The death of
the modern hero is an instance in which art subsumes reality and
perfects it. Malraux, Camus, Sartre, Hemingway, Bellow, Wright —

[17] William Faulkner, *Light in August* (New York, 1950); cf., for example, pp. 111, 173, 326–327, 333, 335, 337, and 379.

[18] Cf. *The Rebel,* pp. 288–289.

all give deference to the artist in his many manifestations. Is it any wonder the artist has become a supreme figure, the very hope of the modern world?

It would be misleading to leave the impression that the treatment of the existential theme in America is of a piece. The handling of the theme varies radically. Bowles' novels are constructed around a symbolic scene. There is an objective correlative between the violence of the scene and the violence of the action. Bellow's four novels are so different that it is difficult to generalize about his methods. *Dangling Man* —similar in character presentation, dramatic pattern, tone and point of view to *The Stranger* and *Nausea* — is a masterpiece of compression, probably the closest American adaptation of existential techniques. Wright has never recovered from the influence of Dreiser. In *Black Boy* he tells us

> I read Dreiser's *Jennie Gerhardt* and *Sister Carrie* and they revived in me a vivid sense of my mother's suffering; I was overwhelmed . . . It would have been impossible for me to have told anyone what I derived from these novels, for it was nothing else than a sense of life itself. All of my life had shaped me for realism, the naturalism of the modern novel, and I could not read enough of them. Steeped in new moods and ideas, I bought a ream of paper and tried to write.[19]

In *How Bigger Was Born,* Wright tells us that he worked on *Native Son* like a "scientist in a laboratory," inventing "test-tube situations [and placing] Bigger in them."[20] *Native Son*[21] is indeed a naturalistic novel. Wright assumes his theme as a scientific fact (that man is determined by his society), invents a situation to control this theme (Bigger's murder), and then documents excessively (cf. the long speech of the lawyer at the end, pp. 324–46). *The Outsider* uses the same methods. Wright assumes his theme as a scientific fact (that modern men, especially Negroes, are unable to accept social values), invents a situation to control this theme (Cross' murder), and then documents at length (cf. Cross' long speech at the end, pp. 307–22). Wright, in other words, has used exactly the same structure in an avowed existential novel that he used in an avowed naturalistic work. The technique of *The Outsider* contradicts the philosophical position of the work itself. Wright insists that one's existence is limited to one's situation; yet *The Outsider* is written from an omniscient point of view. The novel employs the familiar "block method." The narrator, outside the action, accumulates a great mass of material and arranges it into blocks or units. There is little relationship between these units, and the

---

[19] *Black Boy* (New York, 1945), p. 219.
[20] *How Bigger Was Born* (New York, 1940), p. 21.
[21] *Native Son* (New York, 1940).

progression of the novel stems from a necessity no greater than that of chronology. Each unit is related to another only because it is related to the main theme, and each block repeats or enlarges the central theme. *The Outsider* employs the repetitive form of the naturalistic novel.

Invisible Man employs a diametrically different technique. Ellison constructs his novel in terms of a number of key symbols, images or metaphors. The metaphor of invisibility correlates the position of the Negro with the properties of glass: one can look through the Negro as one can look through a pane of glass without being aware of a substance, a property of existence. The metaphor of blindness reinforces the major metaphor: Homer A. Barbee, who extols the work of Bledsoe, is blind. Jack, the Communist who sees the Negro in terms of a group caught in a dialectical process, has a glass eye. The hero himself is initially blinded by his ambitions; at the town meeting he is appropriately blindfolded, sent out to box a number of his companions; he does not begin to see until Mr. Emerson shows him Bledsoe's letter.[22] Appearance hides reality in this myopic world, and the impostor reigns supreme. The images of darkness and light complement the metaphor of blindness. On the coal pile, the hero cannot see; yet he no longer lives in the world of blindness. He secures light, first by burning his high-school diploma (thereby rejects white man's institutions), then by burning a Negro doll (rejects stereotype Negro), and finally by burning his party correspondence and name tag (rejects political abstractions). He manages to tap an electric line and wires his underground home with lights. Light itself is an objective manifestation of his new-found intellectual repository for various objects the narrator picks up on his journey — a toy bank in the image of a Negro, a Negro puppet manipulated by an invisible black string, a link in a leg chain. The objects symbolically depict the Negro as an economic pawn.

As the variety in technique would indicate, the American writers did not go to the French novelists in any systematic or inclusive way. The Americans, in fact, often use elements from the writings of both Sartre and Camus, seemingly unaware that Sartre and Camus split in 1952 in an argument over Communism. Despite the variety of technique, despite the electric nature of American existentialism, there is a distinct similarity of theme in Continental and American fiction which, it seems to me, goes beyond mere accident. Both orders of fiction reveal the hero functioning in a moral vacuum, a law unto him-

---

[22] The name is obviously meant to suggest Ralph Waldo Emerson, whom the Negroes regard more as an abolitionist than a transcendentalist. For a brief account of Emerson the abolitionist see Philip Butchere, "Emerson and the South," *Phylon*, XVII (1956), 279–285.

self, the society a prison restraining his free and natural impulses; both orders of fiction depict the reality of death, a centripetal universe folding in upon the hero,[23] and the feeling of ethical abandonment which accompanies the realization that all activity is directed toward no ethical purpose; both depict the shock of moral recognition which accompanies the realization that the world is absurd and that one has been complicit in its malfunctioning; both extol the sensualist who tries to order his sensations in such a way that the moment says no to death; both express the feelings of loneliness and abandonment which come with the loss of the family and traditional beliefs and values; both employ forms of the demonic and dislocated hero, the Antichrist and conqueror of God, the outsider in search of identity.

These preoccupations, of course, exist in a historical framework more inclusive than existentialism:

> The man of the future [writes Nietzsche], who in this wise will re- deem us from the old ideal, as he will form that ideal's necessary corollary of great nausea, will to nothingness, and Nihilism; this tocsin of noon and of the great verdict, which renders the will again free, who gives back to the world its goal and to man his hope, this Antichrist and Antinihilist, this conqueror of God and of Nothing- ness — *he must one day come.*[24]

The preoccupations of existentialism are the preoccupations of an age. Sartre and Camus have major talents and their contributions are sig- nificant. They have continued the tradition of the nineteenth-century thinkers and turned modern man back to the truths of Nietzsche, Dostoyevski, and Kirkegaard. Existentialism as a modern philosophi- cal theme has now gone beyond the limits of a specific country or even continent. Sartre and Camus will undoubtedly continue to go their separate ways. Sartre no longer has the popular appeal he had fifteen years ago. Camus, however, has captured the imagination of today's young intellectuals and writers in an almost unprecedented way. Amer- ican criticism of Camus' fiction is continually growing.[25] *The Stranger*

---

[23] As Camus' hero gets nearer to death, his universe gets smaller until his whole absurd condition almost crushes him: cf. Meursault going from a smaller to smaller cell, Jean-Baptiste descending from "mountain tops" to a bedroom the size of a coffin. As Bowles's Port Moresby lies on his deathbed, his world folds inward and its walls enclose him within a dimin- ishing center; cf. *The Sheltering Sky,* p. 157. A prison cosmos also contains Bellow's Joseph; cf. *Dangling Man,* p. 92.

[24] Friedrich Nietzsche, "The Genealogy of Morals," *The Philosophy of Nietzsche* (New York City, 1927), p. 716.

[25] Henry Regnery Company has recently published Thomas Hanna's *The Thought and Art of Albert Camus* (New York, 1958); George Braziller, Inc. has issued Herm Briffault's translation of Albert Maquet's *The Invin-*

has been adapted for translation in American French courses,[26] and is bound to have a certain effect on many promising writers now in the college classroom. Camus died without fully realizing his talent. His later works, especially *Exile and the Kingdom,* reveal a falling off. Yet Camus made his mark, and his presence is still felt. One can hear the language of the rebel in William Styron's *Set This House on Fire.* One can detect the influence of *L'Etranger* on Walker Percy's *The Moviegoer.* Undoubtedly Camus will continue to influence many new novelists — both on the continent and in America.

---

cible Summer (New York, 1958). Rutgers University Press has published Germaine Brée's *Albert Camus* (New Brunswick, N.J., 1959). Also available to American readers is Philip Thody's *Albert Camus: A Study of His Work* (London, 1957). Camus is also treated in R. W. B. Lewis' study of the modern hero, *The Picaresque Saint* (New York, 1959). The more popular American journals have recently taken an interest in Camus. *Esquire Magazine* has published "The Growing Stone" (from *Exile and the Kingdom*) and *The Atlantic Monthly* (May, 1958) has printed a laudatory article on Camus by Charles Rolo along with Camus' Nobel Prize speech.

[26] Eds. Germaine Brée and Charles Lynes, Jr. (New York, 1955).

✣ LESLIE A. FIEDLER

The Breakthrough: The American Jewish Novelist and the Fictional Image of the Jew

THOUGH there were American Jewish novelists of real distinction in the first three decades of the twentieth century, it is not until the 'thirties that such writers play a critical role in the total development of American literature. From that point on, they have felt themselves and have been felt by the general public as more than pioneers and interlopers, more than exotics and eccentrics. Indeed, the patterns of Jewish speech, the experiences of Jewish childhood and adolescence, the smells and tastes of the Jewish kitchen, the sounds of the Jewish synagogue have become, since 1930, staples of the American novel.

It is, of course, Jewish urban life in particular which has provided a standard décor for the novel: the life of New York, and especially of the ghettos of the East Side, Williamsburg, etc. In a certain sense, indeed, the movement of Jewish material from the periphery to the center is merely one phase of a much larger shift within the world of the American novel: that urbanization of our fiction which accompanies the urbanization of our general culture.

Our literary 'twenties were dominated by provincial writers like Theodore Dreiser, Sherwood Anderson and Sinclair Lewis, even Faulkner and Hemingway, who close that period and provide a bridge into the age that succeeds it. Whatever their talents, they remained essentially country boys who had come to the big city, who had wandered under their own power into New Orleans or New York, who had been transported by the A.E.F. to Paris. Whether they stayed or returned home again did not finally matter; even when they wrote about the city, they wrote about it as seen through the eyes of one who had come late into it and had remained a stranger.

Despite an occasional sport like Myron Brinig, who writes about Montana, or MacKinlay Kantor, whose subject matter includes hound-dogs, Jewish writers do not fit into such a provincial pattern, which does not, in any case, reflect the typical, the *mythical* Jewish experience in America. Their major entry into the American novel had to

Reprinted from *Midstream,* IV (Winter, 1958), 15–35, by permission of the author and the editors.

wait its urbanization, though that entry is not, to be sure, only a function of such urbanization. It is an extension, too, of the break-up of the long-term Anglo-Saxon domination of our literature which began in the generation just before the First World War. The signal that this double process had started was the emergence of Dreiser as the first novelist of immigrant stock to take a major position in American fiction. There is something ironic in the fact that the breach through which succeeding Jewish writers poured was opened by one not innocent of anti-Semitism; but once the way was opened for immigrants in general, it was possible for Jews to follow.

At any rate, by the end of the 'thirties (a recent historian of Jewish literature points out) there were some sixty American Jewish writers of fiction who could be called without shameless exaggeration "prominent." A close examination of that historian's list proves rather disheartening; for of the sixty-odd names he mentions, fewer than ten seem to me worthy of remembering; and three of these (Abe Cahan, Ludwig Lewisohn and Ben Hecht) belong, in theme and significance, to the 'twenties in which their major work was accomplished. The writers who remain of the original sixty are Edward Dahlberg, Leonard Ehrlich, Daniel Fuchs, Meyer Levin (recently come to life by reaching back into the Jewish Society of the 'twenties for an image of violence and disgust stark enough to move us) and Henry Roth. Even if one were to add to these certain others not included in the original group, say, Waldo Frank, Maurice Samuel, Isidor Schneider and Michael Gold, who are at least symptomatically important, it would make a constellation by no means inspiring; for no one of them is a figure of first importance even in the period itself.

Fuchs and Roth are writers of considerable talent, even of major talent, perhaps; but for various reasons, their achievement is limited. Roth is the author of a single novel, *Call it Sleep;* and Fuchs, though he wrote three before his retreat to Hollywood and silence (and despite a recent come-back in short fiction), wrote only one book of considerable scope: *Homage to Blenheim.* There remains, of course, Nathan Wallenstein Weinstein, who preferred to call himself Nathanael West — and whose long neglect by official writers on the period is now being overbalanced by his enthusiastic rediscoverers. For a long time, scarcely anyone but Henry Popkin[1] considered him worth touting; but now the republication of his whole works and his translation into a Broadway play have given West back a full-scale existence. There is no use being carried away, however; no use in concealing from ourselves the fact that what has been restored to us is only another tragi-

[1] I have in conversation, as well as through reading his articles, so long exchanged ideas with Henry Popkin on the American Jewish novelist that I am indebted to him everywhere.

cally incomplete figure, whose slow approach to maturity ends in death. And there remains further the troublesome question: is West in any effective sense a Jew?

Though the 'thirties mark the mass entry of the Jewish writer into American fiction, they do not last long enough to see any major triumphs. There is no Jewish writer among the recognized reigning figures of the period: no Dos Passos, no Farrell, no Steinbeck; there is no Jewish writer who played a comparable role to the continuing major novelists of the 'twenties: no Fitzgerald, no Hemingway, no Faulkner. There is no Jewish author (with the possible exception of West) who can rank even with middle-generation fictionists like Robert Penn Warren, who seemed at the end of the 'thirties promising young men.

Even in the creation of images of the Jew, a job the Jewish writer in the United States has long been struggling to take out of the hands of the Gentiles, there is no Jewish writer who can compare in effectiveness to Thomas Wolfe. Just as Sherwood Anderson and Hemingway and Fitzgerald succeeded in making their hostile images of Jews imaginative currencies in the 'twenties, Wolfe succeeded in imposing on his period a series of portraits derived from his experiences at New York University: enamelled Jewesses with melon breasts; crude young male students pushing him off the sidewalk; hawk-beaked Jewish elders, presumably manipulating the world of wealth and power from behind the scenes.

What, then, was the modest contribution of the Jewish writer to the fiction of the 'thirties, and how did this prepare for later successes going beyond anything he himself achieved? Predictably enough, a large number of American Jewish writers of the period were engaged in the production of the best-advertised (though, alas, quite infertile) art-product of the period: the Proletarian Novel. Perhaps the best way to define that sub-form of the novel is to remind ourselves that it is the major result of applying to the creation of literature the theory that "art is a weapon"; and that therefore it was in intent anti-art, or at least, opposed to everything which "petty-bourgeois formalism" considered art to be. Perhaps because of the contradictions inherent in such a view, it had one of the shortest lives ever lived by a literary genre. One speaks of the Proletarian Novel as a form of the 'thirties, but in fact it was finished by 1935 or 1936, becoming at that point merely formula writing, completely at the mercy of political shifts inside the Communist movement.

In any case, the Proletarian Novel is not, as its name suggests, merely a book about proletarians; it is alternatively about poor farmers, members of the lower-middle class; and most often, in *fact* if not in theory, about intellectuals: especially about the intellectual's attempt to identify himself with the oppressed and with the Movement which claimed to represent them. The Proletarian Novel was, then, ideological fiction dedicated to glorifying the Soviet Union and the Communist Party, and to proving that that Party was the consciousness of the working class in America as well as in the rest of the world. Yet the most characteristic aspect of such novels escapes ideological definition completely, for it is a product of the age as it worked on writers beneath the level of consciousness of class or anything else. This is the *tone* of the Proletarian Novel: a note of sustained and self-satisfied hysteria bred on the one hand of Depression-years despair and on the other of the sense of being selected as brands to be snatched from the fire.

The Stalinist movement in the United States has always attracted chiefly marginal and urban groups; and if one thinks of the marginal and urban in the United States, he thinks, of course, largely of Jews. Especially in its cultural activities, in the John Reed Clubs, on the *New Masses* (and those cultural activities were of major importance in the 'thirties, when the Communists captured few factories but many publishing houses), Jews participated in a proportion completely out of accord with their role in the total population. Indeed, the Movement was by way of being the typical strategy of the ambitious young Jew in a time of Depression for entering fully into American life. Jews who would have been dismayed by older kinds of bourgeois assimilation, embraced this new method which allowed them at once to identify themselves with America and protest against certain aspects of its life.

Similarly, the intellectual, whether Jewish or not, found in the Movement an escape from the sense of alienation from American society which the 'twenties had brought to acute consciousness. One must realize the attractiveness of the orthodox Communist "culture" sponsored by the *New Masses* for the young man who was both an intellectual and a Jew. It is scarcely surprising that so many of them turned to the Proletarian Novel as their chosen form; even those who for aesthetic reasons found the genre unpalatable apologized for their apostasy, or tried to make up for it: like Nathanael West feeding his more orthodox contemporaries at the family hotel and boasting of having walked the picket line with James T. Farrell and Leane Zugsmith.

Still, no matter how alluring the Proletarian Novel might have been to the un-proletarian Jewish writer, he could not, of course, write such a novel *as a Jew*. It was during the 'thirties, one remembers, that the Stalinists were officially condemning Jewish chauvinism in Palestine, and attacking Ludwig Lewisohn (who had entered his Zionist phase) as the blackest of reactionaries; and in those days, "race consciousness" was thought to be inimical to class consciousness. It is not surprising, after all, that a recent survey of the literature of the period, in a book called *The Radical Novel in America,* can point out only *one* Proletarian Novel which dealt specifically with anti-Semitism. This is a problem which must wait for the Popular Front novel and the Middlebrow Liberal Novel, which is to say, for the 'forties.

All of which does not mean, of course, that a Jewish writer could not *begin* with his Jewishness; and, as a matter of fact, Michael Gold's *Jews Without Money,* which appeared in 1930, was the prototype of the Proletarian Novel, going through eleven printings in its first year and setting a pattern for succeeding writers. Not quite a novel really, or quite an autobiography, it seems more than anything a collection of vignettes of Jewish life making a moral point — a conversation tract illustrating the passage of a thinking man from Judaism to Communism. The pattern is simple enough (it is picked up and reinforced later in Isidor Schneider's *From the Kingdom of Necessity*): to make of "Jewish nationalism" and the Jewish religion the chief symbols of reaction; the pious man, the pillar of the synagogue, appears as a landlord and an owner of whorehouses; the rabbi becomes an old lecher; and the rituals of the Jews instances of hypocrisy and backwardness. The *Seder* (one thinks of what Herman Wouk will be doing fifteen years later to redeem all this!) an especial horror: "Ironical, isn't it? No people has suffered as the Jews have from the effects of nationalism and no people has held to it with such terrible intensity. . . ."

Can there be, then, in the American Jewish proletarian writer any Jewishness beyond a peculiarly Jewish self-hatred, a Jewish anti-Jewishness? To be sure, there is always available to him Jewish local color: the stumbling speech, the squalor, the joy peculiar to the Lower East Side or Brownsville; but these are by the 'thirties already sentimentalized clichés also available to the makers of Cohen and Kelly type movies. There is, beyond this, the constant awareness of alienation which belongs to the Jew: the sense of loneliness not as an accident but as a kind of chosenness; and in a writer like Gold the ancestral cry of *"Eli, Eli . . ."* persists. "In my ears still ring the lamentations of the lonely old Jews without money: 'I cash clothes, I cash clothes, my God, why hast thou forsaken me!' "

Not only has the concept of the choosing of all Israel in an election which seems an abandonment been transferred from the whole people to a part — to the poor alone; but in the process, what began as a mystery has become hopelessly sentimentalized. It is not for nothing that Mike Gold has been called the Al Jolson of the Communist Movement; indeed, in and through him, a cloying tradition of self-pity, which is also, alas, Jewish, and which had already possessed the American stage, moves on into literature. If the Communist Jewish writer can sing *"Eli, Eli . . ."* to his own tune, he can also sing *"A*

Yiddishe Mamme" in a proletarian version. Here is Mike Gold once more: "My humble funny little East Side mother. . . . She would have stolen or killed for us. . . . Mother! Momma! I am still bound to you by the cords of birth. . . . I must remain faithful to the poor because I cannot be faithless to you."

All of this is secondary, however; the special meaning of Judaism for the radical writer of the 'thirties is, expectedly enough, its Messianism. "I believed," Gold writes, "the Messiah was coming, too. It was the one point in the Jewish religion I could understand clearly. We had no Santa Claus, but we had a Messiah." It is understandable, after all, that Marxism should feel at home with the Messianic ideal, since Marx seems to have envisaged himself, more often than not, as a prophetic figure: the last of the prophets promising a new heaven and a new earth. With the Russian Revolution, however, and the differentiation of Bolshevism, a new tone is apparent in Socialist messianism: a note at once apocalyptic and violent.

The old-fashioned sanity that characterizes Abraham Cahan is abandoned; and especially anything that smacks of the pacifism of the 'twenties is rejected in favor of an ideal of "hard Bolshevism" and class war. Two quite different sorts of feelings are involved, often confused with each other but logically quite separable: on the one hand, the desire, compounded of the self-hatred of the Jew and the self-distrust of the intellectual, that the good, clean, healthy workers of the future take over and destroy all that has come before them; on the other, an impulse to identify oneself with the future, to feel oneself for once strong and brutal and capable of crushing all that has baffled and frustrated one's dreams. "Oh workers' Revolution," Gold's protagonist cries out at the book's climax, "You brought hope to me, a lonely suicidal boy. You are the true Messiah. . . ."

Jewish American fiction in the 'thirties, whether specifically "proletarian" or not, is characterized by this frantic religiosity without God, this sense of the holiness of violence. Wherever one turns, there is the sense of a revelation, mystic and secular and terrible as the only possible climax: the challenge to an unbelieved-in God to redeem Williamsburg at the end of Fuchs' first novel; the prayer to Pure Mathematics as a savior in Maurice Samuel's *Beyond Woman;* the invocation of the holy rage of John Brown in Leonard Ehrlich's *John Brown's Body;* the baffled and self-destructive attempt of Nathanael West's Miss Lonelyhearts to become Christ in a Christless world. . . .

The Jewish novel of the 'twenties has as its typical theme assimilation and as its typical imagery the erotic; but the novel of the 'thirties is in theme and imagery, as well as politics, apocalyptic. Sex does not disappear from it completely, for the conquest of erotic taboos is a continuing concern of the contemporary novel; but its meaning and importance alike have been altered as compared with, say, *The Rise of David Levinsky* or Ben Hecht's *A Jew in Love*. From the Jew in love to the Jews without money of the 'thirties is a long way whose direction is indicated by Maurice Samuel's title *Beyond Woman*. Where erotic material does appear, it is likely to have the function which it assumes in Gold's book, to have become one more exhibit in the Chamber of Horrors: evidence of the evils of prostitution or the prevalence of homosexual rape of small boys under Capitalism. More generally speaking, after Mike Gold, sex tends to be treated as just another sort of volence in a violent America.

In the 1930's, the Jewish American novelists, like most of their Gentile fellows, become subscribers to the cult of violence; though for the Jewish writer such an allegiance has a special pathos because of the long opposition to violence in the Jewish inheritance. It is one more way of denying his fathers. And what could he do in any case? In those shabby, grey years the dream of violence possesses the American imagination like a promise of deliverance. Politics is violent and a-politics equally so; whatever else a man accepts or denies, he does not deny terror.

Obviously, the 'thirties did not invent terror and violence in our fiction; as far back as our books go, there are images of horror: the torn corpse stuffed up the chimney; the skull split by a tomahawk; the whale spouting blood. Even a "funny book" like *Huckleberry Finn* has more corpses than anybody can ever remember. There are, however, two transformations in the 'thirties of the role and handling of violence.

The first is the *urbanization of violence;* that is to say, violence is transferred from the world of nature to the world of society, from what man must endure to what man has made. There is, of course, a special horror in considering the law of fang and claw walled in but unmitigated by the brick and glass of the city-planners. Even a provincial writer like Faulkner is driven in those years to move into the city streets for images of terror adequate to the times; and *Sanctuary* remains of all his books the most appalling, and Popeye, his sole urban protagonist, his most monstrous creation.

But the 'thirties mark the climax of an even more critical change: the ennobling of violence as "the midwife of history." Under the name of the Revolution, violence becomes not something to be fled, not the failing of otherwise admirable men, not a punishment for collective guilt — but the crown of social life. What had begun just after 1789 with the Terror and had been hailed in America by the theoretically bloody Jefferson, received in an age of mechanized warfare and mass production its final form. The lust for pain of Nietzsche and the hypostasizing of History by Hegel culminated in the twin horrors of

Nazi and Soviet brutality; but a worse indignity had already been worked on the minds of intellectuals, conditioned in advance to accept one or the other.

In light of this, it is easy to understand that questions of ideology are secondary, that it is the pure love-fear of violence which distinguishes the novel of the 'thirties: a kind of passion not unlike that which moved the Germans before their final defeat, a desire for some utter cataclysm to end the dull dragging-out of impotent suffering. Not only Communist-oriented writers produced such horror literature, but southerners like John Peale Bishop (in *Act of Darkness*) or Robert Penn Warren (in *At Heaven's Gate*); Hemingway made his obeisance to the mode in *To Have and Have Not;* and even so mild an upper-middlebrow traditionalist as James Gould Cozzens produced in *Castaway* a novella of the required shrillness.

In the official Communist version, the vision of the apocalypse is translated into that of the "Final Conflict" between worker and boss, Good and Evil; but this pat formula the better Jewish American novelists could not quite stomach. Rather typically they temper the violence they cannot reject with humor, an ironic refusal to enter the trap completely. At the close of Daniel Fuchs' *Homage to Blenheim,* the three *shlemiels* who are his protagonists have reached the end of their illusions and are looking at each other in despair. One has come to realize that he will run a delicatessen for the rest of his life; another has come to see that the greatest event in his career will be winning three hundred dollars on a long-shot.

> "Well," said Coblenz, "don't take it so hard. Cheer up. Why don't you turn to Communism?"
> "Communism?" cried Mrs. Balkin. "Listen to Mr. Bungalow. Communism!"
> "What has Communism got to do with it?" Munves sincerely wanted to know.
> "It's the new happy ending. You feel lousy? Fine! Have a revelation and onward to the Revolution!"

Fuchs' protagonists remain to the end victims and anti-heroes, incapable of any catastrophe more tragic than the pratfall; but this is the traditional strategy of the comic writer. In a more complex way, Nathanael West and Henry Roth manage to achieve at once the anti-heroic and the almost-tragic. In West, the comic butt is raised to the level of Everybody's victim, the skeptical and unbelieved-in Christ of a faithless world; in Roth, the *shlemiel* is moved back to childhood, portrayed as the victim of circumstances he can never understand, only transcend.

West, of course, remains a humorist still; though in him humor is expressed almost entirely in terms of the grotesque, that is to say, on the borderline between jest and horror. In his novels, violence is not only subject matter; it is also technique, a way of apprehending as well as a tone and theme. Especially in the *Dream Life of Balso Snell,* one can see what West learned from the Surrealists during his stay in France: the violent conjunctions, the discords at the sensitive places where squeamishness demands harmony; the belly-laugh that shades off into hysteria.

Yet he is a peculiarly American case, too. In one of his few published critical notes he announces: "In America violence is idiomatic, in America violence is daily." And it is possible to see him as just another of our professional tough guys, one of the "boys in the back room" (the phrase is Edmund Wilson's — the title of a little book in which he treated West along with John O'Hara). But West is, despite his own disclaimers, in a real sense, a Jew. He is racked, that is to say, by guilt in the face of violence, shocked and tormented every day in a world where violence *is* daily. In *Miss Lonelyhearts,* he creates a kind of portrait of himself as one all nerves and no skin, the fool of pity whom the quite ordinary horror of ordinary life lacerates to the point of madness. His protagonist is given the job of answering "letters from the lovelorn" on a daily newspaper; and finds in this job, a "joke" to others, a revelation of human misery too acute to bear.

But this is West's analogue for the function of the writer, whom he considers obliged unremittingly to regard a suffering he is too sensitive to abide; and in no writer is there so absolute a sense of the misery of being human. He is child enough of his age to envision an apocalypse; but his apocalypse is a defeat for everyone. The protagonist of *Miss Lonelyhearts* is shot reaching out in love toward a man he has (against his will) offended; the hero-*shlemiel* of *A Cool Million: or The Dismantling of Lemuel Pitkin* goes from one absurd anti-Horatio Alger disaster to another, and after his death becomes the hero of an American Fascist movement. But the real horror-climax of his life and the book comes when, utterly maimed, he stands on a stage between two corny comedians, who wallop him with rolled up newspapers in time to their jokes until his wig comes off (he has been at one point scalped), his glass eye falls out, and his wooden leg falls away; after which they provide him with new artificial aids and begin again.

It is in *The Day of the Locust,* however, West's last book and the only novel on Hollywood not somehow trivialized by its subject, that one gets the final version of The Apocalypse according to Nathanael West. At the end of this novel, a painter, caught in a rioting mob of fans at a Hollywood premier, dreams, as he is crushed by the rioters, his masterpiece, "The Burning of Los Angeles":

Across the top he had drawn the burning city, a great bonfire of architectural styles . . . Through the center . . . spilling into the middle foreground, came the mob carrying baseball bats and torches — all those poor devils who can only be stirred by the promise of miracles and then only to violence, a great United Front of screwballs and screwboxes to purify the land. No longer bored, they sang and danced joyously in the red light of the flames.

West does not seem to me finally a really achieved writer; his greatness lies like a promise just beyond his last novel and is frustrated by his early death; but he is the inventor for America of a peculiarly modern kind of book whose claims to credence are perfectly ambiguous. Ones does not know whether he is being presented with the outlines of a nightmare endowed with a sense of reality or the picture of a reality become indistinguishable from nightmare. For the record, it must be said that the exploiters of such ambiguity are typically Jews: Kafka for the continent, West for us.

But in what sense is West a Jew at all? There is a violent flight from Jewish self-consciousness in his work; indeed, in *Balso Snell,* there is a bitter portrait of the kind of Jewish artist who feels obliged to insist on his origins:

"Sirrah!" the guide cried in an enormous voice, "I am a Jew! and whenever anything Jewish is mentioned, I find it necessary to say that I am a Jew. I'm a Jew! A Jew!"

Indeed, whenever a Jew is directly identified in West, he is portrayed viciously enough to satisfy the most rabid anti-Semite; although one must hasten to add that this is balanced by portraits of anti-Semites which would gratify any Jew. Finally, however, anti-Semitism and anti-anti-Semitism do not really add up to Jewishness, much less cancel each other out. West's changed name is surely a clue; he is the first American Jewish writer to wear a name which is a disguise; the exact opposite of Henry Harland, first author of an American book with a Jewish milieu, who called himself Sidney Luska and tried to pass as a compatriot of his protagonists.

West, we are told, made a point of dressing in a Brooks Brothers suit, carrying a tightly rolled umbrella and going, conspicuously, on hunting trips — which is to say, he insisted in all ways on making himself the antitype of the conventional Jewish intellectual. Yet it seems to me inconceivable that anyone but an urban, second-generation Jew in revolt against his background could have produced the novels from *Balso Snell* to *The Day of the Locust.* Certainly, the epigram of C. M. Doughty, which he himself quotes, seems applicable to Nathanael West:

"The Semites are like a man sitting in a cloaca to the eyes, and whose brows touch heaven."

Henry Roth is quite another matter. *Call it Sleep,* which appeared in 1935, and which no one will reprint despite continuing critical acclaim, is a *specifically* Jewish book, the best single book by a Jew about Jewishness written by an American, certainly through the 'thirties and perhaps ever. Technically, Roth owes a great deal to James Joyce; and, indeed, it is the strategy of intense concentration on fragmented detail and the device of stream-of-consciousness (both learned from *Ulysses*), which protect his novel from the usual pitfalls of the ghetto book. He reverses the fatal trend toward long-winded chronicle, which had at once inflated and dimmed the portrayal of Jewish immigrant society from Abe Cahan's life-long study of David Levinsky to Ludwig Lewisohn's "saga" of four generations. The events of *Call it Sleep* cover two years of ghetto life, from 1911 to 1913, and are funnelled through the mind of a boy who is six at the start of the book. It is through the sensibility of this sensitive, poetic, mama-haunted, papa-hating Jewish child, full of fears and half-perceptions and misunderstandings, that the clichés of the form are redeemed to poetry.

But he serves another purpose, too; that of helping the author, apparently committed to the ends of the Movement, evade ideology completely. In the place of the Marxian class struggle, Roth sets an almost Dickensian vision of the struggle between the child and society, of the child as Pure Victim. The lonely boy and the hostile city make only the first in a series of counterpoints on which the book is based: the greenhorn and the American; a subtle and lovely Yiddish and a brutal, grey English; grossness and poetry; innocence and experience, finally Gentile and Jew. In a way, quite unexpected in the 'thirties, Roth plays off the values of the *Cheder* against the values of an outside world dedicated to a pagan hunger for sex and success.

The climax of the book comes when David, the younger protagonist, thrusts the handle of a milk-ladle down into a crack between streetcar rails and is shocked into insensibility. He has learned earlier of the power of the rails, when captured and tortured by a gang of Gentile hoods on the previous Passover; and has come somehow to identify that power with the coal of fire by which the mouth of Isaiah was cleansed. He feels the need of a similar cleansing, for young as he is, he has the sense of having played pander to his cousin Esther and a Gentile boy in order to be accepted in that boy's world. Just before he passes into complete unconsciousness, David is granted a vision — once more the apocalypse — in which all that troubles him is healed: his father's paranoic rage and fear of cuckoldry; his mother's mute suffering and erotic fantasies; his own terrors and apostasies. Blended into his vision are the harsh cries of the street and the voice of a Socialist speaker prophesying the day on which the Red Cock will crow. For the vision neither the eight-year-old David nor the author have a name; and as the boy falls from consciousness, he thinks: "One might as well call it sleep."

After this spectacular achievement, Roth wrote no more novels; he works now, one hears, in an insane asylum in upstate New York — and an occasional story reveals him still haunting his old material without conviction or power. It is not an untypical case in the history of American Jewish writers in the 'thirties. Gold and Schneider lapsed into mere pamphleteering; West and Fuchs moved off to Hollywood, where the former died; no promises were fulfilled. Looking back, one sees a series of apparent accidents and ideological cripplings, acts of cowardice and despair; and yet there is a sense that this universal failure is not merely the function of personal weakness but of a more general situation. Although all outward circumstances in the time of the Great Depression conspired to welcome the Jewish writer, the inward life of the Jewish community was not yet defined enough to sustain a major writer, or even to provide him with something substantial against which to define himself in protest.

II

It is only during the past fifteen or twenty years that such a definition has been achieved. In this period, Jewish self-consciousness in America has endured certain critical readjustments under pressure from world events: the rise and fall of Hitler; the consequent dissolution of virtually the whole European Jewish Community; the establishment of the State of Israel, and the need to redefine the allegiance of American Jews as Jews and as Americans. Other less spectacular developments have exercised an influence, too: the closing off of mass immigration and the slow disappearance of Yiddish as a spoken language; the elimination of the "greenhorn" as a typical Jewish figure — all this accompanied by an increasing general prosperity for the majority of American Jews. No longer is our story that of the rise of an occasional David Levinsky, but that of almost the whole Jewish people on the march toward the suburbs; of the transformation of essential Jewish life into bourgeois life.

At the same moment, there has been a complementary entry of the Jews into the academic world. One reads with surprise and incredulity that when Ludwig Lewisohn was graduated from Columbia, he was advised not to hope for a job teaching English anywhere in America. More and more these days, even in this sensitive Anglo-Saxon area, Jews have come to write and teach; and only the most unreconstructed backwoods anti-Semite is heard to murmur bitterly about men named Greenspan or Schwartzstein lecturing on Emerson or Thoreau. Jews, indeed, have come to control many of the positions of prestige in the intellectual world of America, as editors and journalists and lay critics as well as teachers and writers.

We live at a time when there exists what can be called either a temptation or an opportunity, at any rate, the possibility of Jews entering fully into the suburban-exurban pattern of success, conformity and acceptance in an America where right-minded citizens protest teaching *The Merchant of Venice,* and blatant anti-Semitism exists chiefly in the most backward elements of the working class and in the backwoods of the South. For better or for worse, the task of the Jewish-American novelist now is to give some sense of the settling down of Jews in our steam-heated, well-furnished *Galut;* or to struggle against it, if such a struggle is still possible.

For this reason, we are through with the traditional "up from the ghetto" kind of Jewish fiction as a living form. In such books as Alfred Kazin's *A Walker in the City,* Isaac Rosenfeld's *Passage from Home,* or *An End to Dying* by the very young writer Sam Astrachan, one sees attempts to redeem the old pattern; but such attempts seem finally nostalgic and vestigial — echoes of yesterday's concerns. What, then, is central and vital in the recent novel as written by American Jews? Perhaps the best way to begin to answer this is to consider the situation left by the collapse of the Proletarian Novel and the exhaustion of the messianic spirit.

Even before the end of the 'thirties, when the most aware began to feel that the post-World War I era was over and the pre-World War II era had already begun, proletarian fiction was officially liquidated. The Communist Party through its cultural organs began to prepare for the Popular Front Novel, for a kind of fiction *pious* rather than *apocalyptic* in its approach. No longer was intransigeance the keynote, but cooperation; no longer were the "workers" the subject, but "the little people"; no longer was the *International* required mood-music, but *America the Beautiful.* Sentimentality had replaced terror; and those who looked back longingly toward bloodier days were condemned as "infantile leftists."

Most crucial of all, the American Left, which had traditionally associated itself with the avant-garde in literature, turned away toward Hollywood and Broadway and nightclub folksingers from the Village. The concept of Art as a Weapon no longer led to old-fashioned Agitprop productions, but to slick creations provided by movie writers or Madison Avenue ad-men with bad consciences. The distinguished names, available in the 'thirties at least for petitions and pamphlets, Dreiser or Farrell or Dos Passos, began to be replaced by

Rex Stout and Donald Ogden Stewart, Dashiell Hammett and Howard Fast.

Fast is particularly interesting as the last full-time bard of the Movement, its most faithful middlebrow servant in the arts. He has in recent months reached a final crisis of conscience and has made at last a public break with the Communist Party; but for some fifteen years beginning in 1942 he managed almost alone to create a kind of sub-literature in tune with its changing political line. In *The Un-vanquished* and *Citizen Tom Paine,* he found a way of adapting the historical novel to Stalinist uses, of making its sentimentality under-write the pieties of "progressive politics"; and thus broke out of the long silence which had followed the collapse of proletarian fiction. If he turned at last into the most dogged sort of formula writer, it was due only in part to his natural limitations. No one could have stood up long under the demand to redeem George Washington when "Americanism" becomes respectable; to refurbish Judah Maccabee when Judaism comes back into fashion; or to get Sacco and Vanzetti out of the mothballs when all else fails. That the official Popular Front hack be a Jew is in some ways ironical but not unexpected; for among the last faithful left to the Communists in America were certain Jews clinging to the ragged cliché that in the Soviet Union, at whatever price, anti-Semitism had been eliminated.

The accommodation of the Stalinist left to middlebrow pressures (and the more complicated adjustment of the anti-Stalinist left in the pages of *Partisan Review*) has left no place for the instinctively radical writer to turn. There is no more dismaying prospect than the loneliness and bewilderment of the belated apocalyptic writer, especially when he is too young for the experience of the 'thirties, and has to make a second-hand, home-made version of class struggle fiction — out of G.I. platitudes and memories of Marxism. James Jones is, perhaps, the outstanding representative of the group; and Norman Mailer its chief Jewish proponent. In the latter's *The Naked and the Dead,* for instance, the Fascist villain out of a hundred weary Agitprop entertainments appears as General Cummings, surely one of the most improbable characters in all fiction.

Such writers, having no center, are provincials in the deepest sense of the word: that is to say, they repeat what they have never heard and invent all over again what is already worn out. Mailer is a case in point, recapitulating the whole recent history of literature before him: he rewrites the anti-war novel in *The Naked and the Dead,* the anti-Hollywood novel in *The Deer Park,* the novel of political disillusion-ment in *Barbary Shore.* Only the hectic sexuality which threatens, despite his conscious intent, to replace politics completely, seems his own; the rest is unacknowledged (I suspect, unaware) quotation.

As in the writers of the 'thirties, in Mailer what remains of Jewishness is translated into social protest; though the chief rebels of his
books are (like West's) almost pointedly *not* Jews. And yet in one
sense, he is more the child of his sentimental times than he would be
pleased to admit; certainly there appears for the first time in *The
Naked and the Dead,* what is to become a standard character in the
liberal-middlebrow war book: the Jewish Sad Sack. In Mailer's Gold-
stein, who finds the chief horror of war anti-Semitism in his own
ranks, there is present in embryo Irwin Shaw's Noah Ackerman —
and the protagonist of a score of movies to come.

Such lapses into the banal vocabulary of the middlebrows are, however, rare in Mailer. He may be clumsy and provincial, but he is
above all things honest; and he refuses to endorse the clichés of enlightened liberalism. There is something healthy, I think, in preferring yesterday's platitudes to today's; for they are at least unfashion-
able, assurances that the writer is not merely on the make. Mailer is
not, in any case, a typical figure, standing apart as he does from the
two major developments which have followed the collapse of the
Proletarian Novel.

Both these developments are of considerable importance for an
understanding of Jewish writers in America, since both are in large
part products of Jewish writers, and both help to establish the background against which the later Jewish writer defines himself. The first
development is a kind of literary Jacobinism: a resistance to the separation of radical politics and avant-garde art. Its adherents would
reconstitute the alliance of anti-bourgeois social criticism and anti-
bourgeois literary experiment; but this they would do outside of any
party orthodoxy. The second is a species of literary liberalism which
aims at rescuing Popular Front art, that is, self-righteous, middlebrow
art, from the Communists in favor of an enlightened segment of the
bourgeoisie. Let us consider them in reverse order.

The middlebrow liberal or liberal-colored fictionist responds to the
demands of a certain novel-reading section of the middle class which
would like to be Philistine in a really arty kind of way. Such readers
are more concerned with social problems than with art, and turn to
novels merely as occasions for thinking about such "important problems." The kind of middlebrow fiction produced for their benefit has
established itself everywhere from *Good Housekeeping* and the *Saturday Evening Post,* on the one hand, to the *New Yorker,* on the
other. One of its newer sub-varieties, science fiction, has opened up
a whole series of periodical and book-length markets; and in its more
traditional forms it has even won real triumphs in the major book
clubs.

This kind of novel in form combines a clear narrative line (no confusing flashbacks or troublesome experiments in style) with a pious celebration of social protest in favor of Negroes, Jews, children of adulterous mothers, paraplegics, Hungarians — whatever is thoroughly unexceptionable and, of course, *up to date;* for such books must compete with the daily newspaper. In these works, a new, urban, professional, liberalized, and, I think, largely Jewish elite comes to terms with its own vague feelings of guilt at being so prosperous in a troubled world. The kind of people who learn all about their children from reading Gesell, who go to the Museum of Modern Art, who subscribe to *The Reporter,* who vote for Adlai Stevenson, also buy the novels of Budd Schulberg and Irwin Shaw to get the latest word on the "little people," with whom they sentimentally identify themselves.

Naturally enough, considering the strength of Jewishness in this group and the impact of Hitler on the whole newspaper-reading world, the first "little people" to be celebrated in the liberal novel were the "little Jews." Not only Jewish writers, but Jews and Gentiles alike, discovered at once this new form of the novel and the new subject (so ignored in the 'thirties) of anti-Semitism. Arthur Miller's first novel *Focus,* Laura Z. Hobson's *Gentlemen's Agreement,* Mary Jane Ward's *The Professor's Umbrella* — there is a whole stream of such books mounting to a kind of flood-peak with John Hersey's *The Wall.* They are profoundly sentimental in theme and tone and are written in the slickly finished style proper to a literary no-man's land existing somewhere between Hollywood and Madison Avenue and blanketed with old copies of the *Saturday Review of Literature,* the *New Yorker* and the *Princeton Alumni Weekly.*

What is oddest about such fiction, however, is the way in which it is typically hoked-up; the books are never simply studies of anti-Semitism in action, they are studies of anti-Semitism with a gimmick. Miller, for instance, deals with a man who, though a Gentile, *looks* like a Jew when he puts on glasses, and is persecuted when his eyes fail. Mrs. Hobson's book is about a reporter who *pretends* he is a Jew and brings down upon himself the discrimination of anti-Semites. It is not only a certain middlebrow ideal of form which demands the gimmick, but a basic uncertainty which is aptly symbolized by such a tricky device. What, after all, *is* a Jew in this world where men are identified as Jews only by mistake, where the very word becomes merely an epithet arbitrarily applied? It is difficult to make a novel about anti-Semitism when one is not sure exactly what, beside being the butt of anti-Semites, makes a man a Jew.

There are, to be sure, occasional portraits of real Jews beside the imaginary ones; but the former are such monsters of humility and gentleness and endurance and piety that it is impossible to believe in them. Such protagonists are no more real than the happy endings which await them: reconciliations in an atmosphere of goodwill even less credible than the atmosphere of exaggerated hostility with which such fables typically begin. The pattern is set once and for all in a story of Irwin Shaw called "Act of Faith," in which a young man, scared by his father's accounts of anti-Semitism at home, decides to keep as insurance a *Luger* he has picked up on the battlefield. He thinks, however, of his war-time buddies, "of all the drinks they had had together, and the long marches together, and all the girls they had gone out with together" and decides to sell the pistol after all. "Forget it," he says finally, "what could I use it for in America?" What begins as a political problem (touched with hysteria) is solved as a sentimental one (touched with politics).

From a story of anti-Semitism to one of war is an easy jump; indeed, the liberal war novel is only one more species of the high-minded literature of social reform: a sub-variety, in the hands of Jewish writers in particular, of the novel of anti-Semitism. Shaw's *The Young Lions* is the prime example of the genre, anticipations of which we have already noticed in Mailer's *The Naked and the Dead*. In a fundamental sense, there is nothing *new* in such novels; they do not change the protest form of the war-book invented just after World War I; but the method has been perfected: the tone of superficial realism set by unflinching descriptions of death, rape and the other usual calamities of combat; the rejection of certain more obvious stereotypes of the enemy, and the exploitation of others: the reactionary American General, for instance, but especially the "representative platoon," with the Jewish Sad Sack to help make up its roster.

One raised entirely on such literature and the movies based on their clichés would believe the United States Army to be carefully organized so that each platoon contains a pure, sentimental sample of the "little people" at war: a cocky, slight Italian, a Brooklyn Jew, a raw-boned, blonde farmboy etc. Certainly, no such group would dare set off without its Jew, the kind of understanding victim, who, in the recent liberaloid film *Attack,* is portrayed as reciting *Kaddish* for a Catholic thug who dies while trying to reach a gun and kill (naturally!) an evil officer.

Shaw's Jew is Noah Ackerman, a self-educated intellectual, hated at first by his buddies in part because a copy of James Joyce is found in his foot-locker, but later much admired after offering to fight the six or eight toughest men in his platoon. In him, we meet the stereotyped anti-stereotype of the Jew: since the old stereotype makes the Jew a coward, he is brave; since it makes the Jew a war-resister, he is a combat hero; since it makes the Jew an enemy of personal violence, he is (for quite high-minded reasons) dedicated to it. What Hemingway had satirized as over-compensation in Robert Cohn is here glorified.

There are, however, two other major characters in *The Young Lions* beside the Jew as Fighting Sad Sack: the anti-stereotype stereotyped Nazi, and an enlightened, sensitive American who has passed from Broadway to the front and is the eye of the book. The Nazi is permitted to kill the Jew, but Michael Whiteacre, the emissary from the world of Popular Culture, kills the Nazi. This is all quite satisfactory to the readers; for Michael is clearly intended to be their representative in the action: a projection of the mind for which Shaw is writing, the social group for which he speaks.

His work fulfills the ideal proposed to himself by the bureaucratized intellectual dreaming of what he would do if released by Hollywood or the T.V. network. *The Young Lions* is, one remembers, the book which the gigolo-scriptwriter in *Sunset Boulevard* (and presumably the scriptwriter behind him) reads in his spare time. Budd Schulberg is, of course, another novelist who speaks for the same audience; and his *What Makes Sammy Run?* is as appropriate a representation of the Hollywood novel on the middlebrow level as *The Young Lions* is of the war novel (or, indeed, as Schulberg's own *On the Waterfront* of the liberaloid labor story).

When Schulberg's earlier book appeared, there was much pointless and confusing comment on the presumably anti-Semitic implications of his portrayal of Sammy Glick; as if this were the first portrait of an evil Jew to have appeared in American literature. In the midst of such properly middlebrow polemics, most readers failed to notice the more unforgivable travesties of Jews in Schulberg's noble scriptwriters, who read Silone's *Fontamara* in *their* spare moments, and fought the good fight for the Screen-writers' Guild despite blacklisting and redbaiting.

Schulberg's novel, like all sentimental melodramas, splits into opposing symbolic characters what in fact exists in one contradictory soul. Once understood in this light, the book may be read as a portrait of the artist as a Hollywood employee: that is, a writer like Schulberg (and Shaw) is in part the noble Jewish supporter of the Loyalists and trade-unionism, but in part, too, Sammy Glick, the poor boy on the make. They, too, are sons of a first generation of immigrants which had destroyed itself for their sake in a strange world; they, too, are eager to be heard, to be effective, to be successful — and to break out of the trap of a stereotyped Jewishness without money. They are more complicated men, to be sure, than Sammy Glick; but then everyone is: even Herman Wouk.

Wouk's work does, however, possess a certain importance for revealing on a less sophisticated level ambitions analogous to those which inform *What Makes Sammy Run?* and *The Young Lions*. If

Shaw and Schulberg can be said to speak for the mass entertainers with yearnings to transcend their world, Wouk can be understood as representing the ad writers and gag writers who are convinced that the same slick techniques by which they earn their livings can do justice to certain modest liberal values, and that those values are compatible with the suburban lives they lead. Turning from Shaw and Schulberg to Wouk, one notices certain differences: less shock, fewer dirty words, less stylistic pretension. His is a world that cries "Keep it clean!" and the one thing that that world finds dirtier than four-letter words is high-brow art.

A common sentimentality, however, binds them together and a common store of stock "little people." Greenwald, the Jew of Wouk's war novel, *The Caine Mutiny,* is blood-brother to the Ackerman of Shaw's *The Young Lions:* both are Jews who face up to Gentile versions of courage and honor which exclude them, not by challenging those codes but by aping them; both attempt to prove, despite the handicaps of a Jewish physique and a long tradition of non-violence, that they can outdrink and outfight any *goy.* But Greenwald has adapted to the world that surrounds him even more shamelessly than Ackerman, having neither a taste for James Joyce nor a principled distrust of the armed forces. The villainous intellectual who does is called Keefer, and is clearly (thank God!) not a Jew.

The reconciliation which Wouk demands goes far beyond the embracing of one's fellow yahoos in battle camaraderie as advocated by Shaw. It requires embracing the whole military, the whole social order in all its smug security, because, as Greenwald reminds especially his Jewish readers, it was Captain Queeg who kept mama out of the Nazis' soap-dish. "Captain Queeg, yes, even Queeg and a lot of sharper boys than any of us. Best men I've ever seen. You can't be good in the Army or Navy unless you're goddam good, though maybe not up on Proust and *Finnegans Wake* and all." *The Stars and Stripes Forever* blend with *A Yiddishe Mamme,* as Gold had once blended the latter with the *International* — and the way is clear for Marjorie Morningstar.

Marjorie is, indeed, our new middlebrow muse, translated from Wouk's book to the cover of *Time* to the movies with scarcely a pause for breath: a portrait of accommodation as the young girl. That she is Jewish is the final touch: a tribute to the triumph of liberalism in the suburbs, the truce with anti-Semitism of the American middle-class, and the end of surly intransigence among the Jews. In the form of Noel Airman, Wouk has isolated all that is skeptical, anti-Philistine and indifferent to bourgeois values in the Jewish American tradition; and Airman he has made his villain. With him he identifies everything that stands between the Jew and social acceptance, the novelist and popularity; with Marjorie he identifies all that makes the Jew acceptable and the Jewish novelist a best-seller. It is one of the melodramatic fissions like the one we have noticed in Shaw and Schulberg; though this time the author isolates and casts out of himself symbolically not his greed for success but all that stands between him and that success.

What is truly strange is not that Marjorie should seem representative to the bourgeois Jewish community, but that she should also strike the American community at large as a satisfactory image. Yet it is comprehensible in the end that the enlightened American *allrightnick,* Gentile or Jew, should find in the suburban Jewish housewife the proper symbol of interfaith "tolerance," the vision of unity in diversity possible where no one any longer believes in anything but the hundred-percent Americanism of just believing.

This is not yet, however, a total picture of the middlebrow novel as written by the Jewish American writer. If Shaw defines the middle of the middle, and Wouk its lower limits, it is J. D. Salinger who indicates its upper reaches. Though Salinger has written always for the circle of middlebrow periodicals that includes *Good Housekeeping* and the *New Yorker,* he has maneuvered constantly (though at first almost secretly) to break through the limits of that circle. He has piously acknowledged in his stories the standard ritual topics of the enlightened bourgeoisie: the War and anti-Semitism; but he has been concerned underneath with only a single obsessive theme: the approach to madness and the deliverance from it, usually by the intervention of a child. His "little people" are often quite literally little, usually small girls; and his favorite protagonists are under twenty, their typical crisis the last pre-adult decision of deciding whether or not to remain in school.

The themes that find full expression in *Catcher in the Rye* are tried early in short magazine fiction. In "A Girl I Know," there first appears the familiar, six-foot two, blackhaired boy, cast out of school; though in this case he is eighteen, has been expelled from college, and finds his way to Austria where he becomes involved in a brief, utterly innocent love affair with a Jewish girl, who can speak no more English than he can German. The War separates them and he returns to Europe to find her dead, killed by the Nazis. In the much-reprinted "For Esme with Love and Squalor" the other half of the obsessive fable is sketched in: the story of a man redeemed from a combat breakdown by a gift from an orphaned, twelve-year-old, upper-class girl, with whom he has had a brief tea-table conversation in England.

In *Catcher in the Rye,* the blackhaired boy on the lam from school and the man threatened with insanity are joined together; the savior becomes the little sister — and the sentimental-political background is sloughed away in favor of a discreetly hinted-at world of religious implications. One has the sense that Salinger is making a real bid to break out of the trap of middlebrow "understanding" into the realm of the tragic; but the attempt fails. It is impossible to believe in Holden Caulfield finally, for he is too unreal, a creature of tricks of style, set against an utterly unconvincing family background. One knows that he is intended to represent a holy innocent against whom the rest of the world is measured: a kind of prep-school, upper-income-bracket Huckleberry Finn, who cannot quite light out for the Territory but is redeemed by a little girl in a climax essentially sentimental; yet he ends as the prep-school boy's dream of himself, a slickly amusing model imitated by a hundred seventeen-year-olds in a score of secondary-school magazines from coast to coast.

In "Zooey," a recent novella published in the *New Yorker,* Salinger seems to me to have recast his story, so often unsuccessfully attempted, in much more convincing form. If "Zooey" moves us where *Catcher in the Rye* merely amuses, it is because for once the madness of the theme is allowed to break up the slickness of the style; and the family tragedy which is Salinger's essential theme is uncontaminated by required subject matter, erotic or political, essentially alien to him. The only romance to which he really responds is the family romance: Orestes saved from the furies by Electra (though this time he has reversed the roles); and he has brought his myth in all purity *home,* to his own Manhattan and to the Jewishness with which he has had so much trouble coming to terms. His protagonists may find their final peace in a religious revelation compounded of Zen Buddhism and Christian mysticism; but they begin at least in a Jewish milieu (half-Jewish only, he insists) of quiz-kids and memories of the Pantages circuit. Salinger seems to me by all odds the most interesting of the middlebrow writers, torn between a professional knowledge of what is permitted the entertainer and a desire to surrender all striving to the attainment of a mystic's peace. The assertion at the end of "Zooey" that the Fat Lady of the middling audience is "Christ Himself. Christ Himself, buddy!" seems to me one of the wackiest and most winning attempts to compromise these contradictory impulses.

The second major direction of recent fiction, what I have called earlier the Jacobin protest, is a last attempt to maintain the snobbism of the highbrow in a world which undercuts his existence. It is associated, in its Jewish manifestations at least, with *Partisan Review* and the publications that flank it: *Commentary, Encounter* and the *New Leader,* on the one hand; *Kenyon Review, Sewanee Review* and certain other literary quarterlies, on the other. It is not especially relevant from our point of view that *Partisan* was originally political in nature, pledged to retaining the purity of Marxism at a time when the official Communist movement was in retreat toward Popular Front-ism; what *is* important is that it was pledged also to maintain against the bourgeoisie the alliance of high art and radical thinking.

By the 1950's as a matter of fact, Marxism had become a memory, a special condition of their youth, to most of *Partisan Review's* remaining collaboration; respectability crept inexorably in upon it. At various points, indeed, certain super-Jacobins left the magazine's pages in despair. Not the least interesting of these is Paul Goodman, who wanted to maintain an uncompromised allegiance to pure bohemianism and non-accommodation. He is at present a lay analyst, influenced in his practice by the teachings of Wilhelm Reich; and his concern with depth-psychology helps shape his fiction, which is also based in part on the techniques of Kafka and the devices of Yiddish folk humor.

Yet even those who remain and have most blatantly accommodated to the world around them still share something with further dissenters like Goodman, something which separates them clearly from the middlebrow writers we have been discussing. What is it that they share beneath all their differences? I have called it earlier the snobbism of the highbrow; and their enemies are likely to label it "negativism." Perhaps it is best thought of as a sort of vestigial, spiritual Trotskyism: an obligation to the attitudes of dissent which survives the ideological grounds for dissent. It arises in any case from their early conditioning in endless polemics on Marxian theory and their exposure from adolescence on to Freudian concepts; and makes them more closely kin in certain ways to European intellectuals than to more traditional American writers.

Perhaps most important of all is the fact that such writers possess in common a brand of experience which is rich and suggestive. They are urban; they are second-generation Americans; they are men and women whose adolescence and early youth came between the Great Wars, was influenced by the Civil War in Spain and haunted by the Depression; they remain strangers in the world of prosperity in which they now, quite comfortably, live. They are joined to each other and separated from the rest of their generation by the experience of having accepted and rejected Communism.

They are, finally, typically Jewish: secularized, uncertain Jews in most cases to be sure; but in all cases possessed by the ghosts of their Jewish past; and they continue to wrestle with the lay messianism which was the gift of that past to them. Their peculiar relationship to their Jewishness emphasizes their sense of alienation (it is a favorite word of theirs, very annoying but inescapable), and protects them against the Wouk-Shaw-Schulberg kind of simple-minded, liberal-middlebrow accommodation.

Yet the blessing which has fallen upon Wouk has also been bestowed (even more fantastically) upon *Partisan Review*. For better or for worse, the time has come when each cultural level in America looks to some Jewish-sponsored myth for a justification of its existence and its dreams; for some the Superman of the comics, for some the moralistic robots of Isaac Asimov, for some Marjorie Morningstar, for some images of urban alienation out of the pages of *Partisan Review*. Certainly, that magazine despite the tininess of its actual subscription list exercises at home and abroad a fantastic influence. If the concept of the highbrow has become for most Americans associated with the notion of the urban, Jewish, former Communist, this is in part the work of *Partisan Review*.

Certainly, as far as literature is concerned, it has introduced over the past fifteen years a group of writers rivalled in their variety and the richness of their common themes only by the southern group which includes Eudora Welty, Carson McCullers etc. Among them are writers like Delmore Schwartz, who has not yet produced a novel, but who has, in the short stories collected in *The World Is a Wedding,* managed to evoke the tone and texture of second generation life in America better than anyone I know. To render an undramatized sense of grey people in grey cities, speaking to each other in grey voices and grey words, he has evolved a desperately flat style, which, when it does not succeed, can be boring beyond belief; but which, when it works, carries an unparalleled conviction. There are further the *Partisan Review* adaptors of Kafka, in particular Isaac Rosenfeld, who made in his short stories something new and disturbing of Kafkaesque ambiguity and grotesque humor; and who pushed forward the possibilities of Kafkaesque form, the symbolic statement neither quite essay nor quite story. There is, finally, Bernard Malamud, currently the *Partisan* Fellow in fiction, more metaphysical than most of his colleagues and richly inventive as they seldom are, but produced by the same milieu, the same vestiges of urban Jewishness. In his second novel, *The Assistant,* he has dared a full-scale Jewish theme, opening up dazzling new possibilities by setting back on its feet again the conversion story turned upside-down by the Marxists after Mike Gold.

Malamud's meaning seems to me to be just now defining itself and to belong to what lies ahead, unlike that of the two major figures of the last decade to whom I now come. The first is Lionel Trilling, who is to me an endlessly fascinating case, though finally, I fear, a disappointing one. Indeed, the clue to his fascination lies in the last-minute failure of what is a complex and subtle sensibility; in the fact that as a fictionist, he doesn't quite work. Yet he was willing to attempt in *The Middle of the Journey* the novel which some writer of his kind must someday achieve: the story of the allure of Communism and of the disillusion with it. Norman Mailer has tried his hand at it, to be sure, but without having quite lived through the experience, and Isaac Rosenfeld has explored it a little obliquely in one short story; while Leslie Fiedler has endlessly circled around it in his shorter fiction. Only Trilling has made the full-scale attempt; and it is perhaps a certain air of schematism in his approach, a sense of his having reached this item on a list of Important Things to be Done, which mars the book.

The events of the novel, at any rate, finally remain unconvincing, both on the symbolic level (despite their relationship to the central experience of a generation) and on the literal one (despite their resemblance to the newspaper story of Hiss and Chambers); because they come to us refracted through the mind of a singularly unconvincing protagonist, a kind of cross between Matthew Arnold and E. M. Forster, caught at the moment of his entry into middle age and at the point of recovery from a wasting disease. He is both genteel and Gentile, this Laskell, through whom the working class characters of the book become caricatures and its passion merely literary — not Trilling, of course, but a mask Trilling prefers to assume, a mask of the bourgeois academic who is beyond Judaism as he is beyond the clichés of middlebrow liberalism. I do not know whether Trilling lacks vitality because of his failure to tap his own Jewish sources, or whether he fails to tap those sources because of an initial lack of vitality; but somewhere here there is a clue to his failure, a failure whose outward symbol is the lack of Jewish major protagonists in a novel by a Jew about an experience deeply rooted in Jewish life.

He is much more successful in certain short stories, in "Of This Time, of That Place" and "The Other Margaret," where he can concentrate on a narrower world of university-oriented, genteel, New York, middle-class culture, in which Jewishness survives chiefly as what used to be called "ethical culture," a kind of diffuse moral concern. When he enters the larger world of the novel and confronts in particular the absurdity essential to the Communist experience in America, he is defeated by the very talents which make him so much at home in the world of late nineteenth century British fiction.

Saul Bellow is quite another matter. The author of *The Dangling Man, The Victim, The Adventures of Augie March* and a recent collection of shorter fiction called *Seize the Day,* he is already an established writer; although in the annoying fashion of American journalism (he is after all younger than Faulkner or Hemingway) he is still referred to as a "young novelist." Looking at the whole body of his work, one has the sense of a creative restlessness, an adventurousness, which distinguish him quite sharply from such other established fictionists as Trilling, on the one hand, or Irwin Shaw, on the other. Even such younger, dissident middlebrows as Herbert Gold seem beside him to lack technical courage and real commitment.

Bellow can, on occasion, mute his style as he has done in *The Victim* and in the novella which gives his most recent collection its name; but even under wraps, his language has a kind of nervous life, a tough resilience unequalled by any other American Jewish writer of the moment. Perhaps the fact that Yiddish was his first language has something to do with the matter, but when he unleashes his fancy and permits himself a kind of rich, crazy poetry based on the juxtaposition of high language and low, elegance and slang, I am reminded of *Moby Dick*. The dialogue of his books possesses a special vitality; he can report a passage of conversation about ideas which leaves one feeling that his characters have exchanged more than words, have really touched each other as with a blow or a kiss.

In the body of his work, the ideas of the *Partisan Review* group (it does not matter how far he thinks he has left them behind) come fully alive in literature for the first time; they exist, that is to say, as they existed at their best in the minds of the men who held them; for those men at their best *lived* such ideas and did not merely believe them. Not only does Bellow have a style more vigorous than that of Trilling; but he moves in a world which is larger and richer and more disorderly and delightful — a world which he calls most often Chicago, though it is the externalization of fancy as well as memory. Implicit from his beginnings is the impulse toward the picaresque, which broke free finally in the sprawling, episodic shapelessness of *Augie March* — whose very formless form protests the attempt to impose tight, aesthetic patterns upon a world whose essence is chaos.

Bellow is, not unexpectedly in an age when writers in general have entered the university and Jews in particular have found a home there, a teacher like Trilling. The Jim Tully ideal of the author-bum, still played at by novelists like Nelson Algren, has never had much appeal for the Jewish writer in America; but though Bellow rejects the mask of the hobo bard, he does not assume that of the cultured humanist. His myth of himself is not that of the morally discriminating bourgeois at home over cocktails; but of the lonely city dweller moving among boarding houses and cheap hotels, shabby restaurants and grey city streets in the heat of midsummer. The typical Bellow protagonist is the man whose wife has left him or has gone off to her mother's, the man returning to a house in disorder.

He is the person who, all amenities stripped away, feels himself stripped to his human essence. And the human essence, the naked fact of a man in a Bellow book is never an answer but always the question: what am I, after all? What, after all, is man? To which the unpromising answer is returned: you are what asks; go on asking. Here is Bellow's true center as well as what makes him central for all of us; he has realized not more clearly, perhaps, but more passionately than anyone what the collapse of the Proletarian Novel really meant: not the disappearance only of a way of writing, never very fruitful in any case, but also the dissolution of the last widely shared definition of man — as victim or beneficiary of the social order.

Because Bellow does not subscribe to the liberal's illusion that the definition of the human in social terms is still viable; because he knows that Man, in the old sense, is dead — he is able to redeem all the typical books of the middlebrow-liberal canon. *The Dangling Man* is his book about the war; *The Victim,* his novel of anti-Semitism; *Augie March,* his examination of the perils of success; *Seize the Day,* his fable of failure in a world of prosperity — his own *Death of a Salesman.* But in each, ambiguity has replaced sentimentality, the tragic or the joyous displaced self-congratulation and self-conscious piety. The Jew and the anti-Semite, the machiavellian and the *shlemiel* come alike to the same revelation.

It is because he manages to exact from the most unpromising material the stubborn vision of lonely man in a world which no longer provides his definition, that Saul Bellow is able at last to create the most satisfactory character ever projected by a Jewish writer in America: Augie March. With the book itself, shrill, repetitious, in spots hysterically euphoric, I have certain quarrels; with Augie, none. He is an image of man at once totally Jewish, the descendant of the *shlemiels* of Fuchs and Nathanael West, and absolutely American — the latest avatar of Huckleberry Finn. In him, there is blended in perfect irony those twin, incompatible American beliefs: that the answer is just over the next horizon, and that there is no answer at all.

It is, I think, the final commentary on our age and on the place the Jew occupies in its imagination, that Huck Finn, when he returns to our literature not as an item of nostalgia but as an immortal archetype, returns without his overalls, his fishing pole and his freckles, as a Chicago kid making his way among small-time Jewish machiavellians. More was needed, however, than the age; the moment demanded a Jewish hero, perhaps, but hesitated indifferently between Augie March and Marjorie Morningstar. What was demanded was the talent and devotion and conviction which belong particularly to Bellow, and the rich, complicated milieu out of which he has emerged.

❧ WOLFGANG B. FLEISCHMANN

A Look at the "Beat Generation" Writers

WE are all familiar with the term "beat generation." It has come, within the last three years, to connote a variety of American artistic and social phenomena. In its widest sense, "beat generation" describes a group of people involved in a way of life, the positive features of which are general resistance against the values and mores of the American middle class, a total acceptance of all types of sexual behavior, general predilection for "cool jazz," and the adoption of Oriental mysticism in the form of Zen Buddhism as a unifying metaphysics and philosophy of life. The negative features of the way of life described by the adjective "beat" are withdrawal from politics and from the responsibilities of citizenship, withdrawal from the universities and academies, and withdrawal of recognition from all institutions the State provides.

Less widely defined, the "beat generation" is thought of as a group of bohemians, made up of jazz-musicians, writers, artists, college students, and generally dislocated personalities who lead *la vie* "beat" in San Francisco, New York, or Boston — also, in a more isolated manner, in Mexican villages, on the beaches of Southern California, and at various spots in the Rocky and Smoky Mountains. The names of individuals play a larger role in this second visualization of a "beat generation" than in the first. We find grouped here jazz-musicians like Lennie Tristano, Dave Brubeck, and Lester Young, photographers like Harry Redly and Harold Feinstein, writers like the popular novelist Norman Mailer, as well as the poets and authors engaged in the more specifically literary contexts of the movement. These personalities often, though not always, gather in cafes of Bohemian character, surrounded by a coterie made up of the curious and interested. In some of the bars thus frequented, the central attraction is the reading, to the accompaniment of jazz, of the works of the "beat generation's" writers and poets.

It is the fairly unorganized group made up of these authors which comprises the most narrow concept subsumed under the term "beat

Reprinted from the *Carolina Quarterly*, XI (Spring, 1959), 13–20, by permission of the author.

generation": the literary movement of that name which, so baptized by its main prose author Jack Kerouac, has attracted wide attention ever since some of its members gathered in a San Francisco art gallery in the fall of 1955 to rebel consciously against the academic tradition in American poetry.

Who are the "beat generation" authors? Even a cursory glance at their biographies shows that they are not a generation in terms of age, ranging, as they do, between the ages of twenty-odd and fifty-odd. Nor are their intellectual, social, and religious backgrounds of sufficient homogeneity to attribute to them a common denominator as to provenance. Are they, then, a "generation" in the sense of literary history — a unified movement of poetic innovation in style with a common philosophical set of beliefs? The answer to this question is not clear at first glance for, among certain ones of the group, a solidarity of style and ideas is readily apparent, though some salient differences also rise readily to view. It is hence necessary to take a closer look at the authors of the "beat generation" and at certain features some of these have in common.

Let us begin with the best known ones — Jack Kerouac and Allan Ginsberg. John (Jack) Kerouac is the author of thirteen novels, of which four, among them *On the Road, The Subterraneans,* and *The Dharma Bums,* are published. He is thirty-six years old, a former Columbia University football player and merchant marine sailor. According to Malcolm Cowley, publisher of *On the Road,* Kerouac works on typewriter strip-rolls without revising. He has defined, in the fifth issue of the *Evergreen Review,* a method of writing fiction based on Wilhelm Reich's theory of the orgasm. This method advocates self-expression in the total degree: the author creates his style by leaving his words and associations as they come from him in the hot pitch of creative frenzy.

Allen Ginsberg, four years Kerouac's junior, is the author of the "beat generation's" manifesto, the poem *Howl.* Other major lyrics by Ginsberg include the poem *America,* the opening lines of which:

America I've given you all and now I'm nothing.
America two dollars and seventy-seven cents January 17, 1956,

have endeared its author to European left-wing intellectuals, a long poem entitled *A Supermarket in California,* and, more recently, a series of lyrics called *Siesta at Xbalba.* Unlike Kerouac, who claims total originality, Ginsberg openly declares himself in his poems to be an imitator of Walt Whitman, Maiakowsky, and Guillaume Apollinaire and a student both of Zen Buddhism and of Mayan mysticism. Like Kerouac, Ginsberg is a product of Columbia University.

In the second string of "beat generation" poets a great and diverse collection of individuals may be placed. To proceed here from the sublime to the ultra-terrestrial, we should start this list with William Everson, now Brother Antoninus, O.P., a forty-six-year-old lay brother. Brother Antoninus' verse speaks, in tones reminiscent of Gerard Manley Hopkins, of the relations between man and God in a troubled universe. A second Roman Catholic poet, John Logan, has recently had verse of less eminent, but similar, sort published in the *Evergreen Review*. Philip Whalen, an ex-Reed College student and World War II veteran, closes, though in a different vein, the list of "beat generation" metaphysicals. He is a Buddhist mystic who, after a period in a Japanese monastery, has settled down to write meditative verse in Berkeley, California.

The authors we may call the "beat generation ultra-terrestrials" seem to be, on the surface, in greatest contrast to the spiritually concerned group of poets just spoken of. But this contrast is superficial: while the poetry of Ginsberg and the prose of Kerouac dwell deliberately on the sordid, the unmentionable, and the socially controversial, they have a concern with values beyond the material ones which is rather clearly stated. Beyond Ginsberg's bloody toilets and Kerouac's bowls of unsanitary oatmeal served in truckers' cafes there lie visions of a peaceful world made strong by the love of comrades and the joys of mystic insight. Zen Buddhism and a kind of comradeship reminiscent of the *Wandervogel* movement in the German Weimar Republic's days, are its ideals.

The works of two other "beat generation" writers beside Ginsberg and Kerouac are in this "ultra-terrestrial" vein: the poetry of Lawrence Ferlinghetti and the prose of Michael Rumaker. Ferlinghetti, thirty-nine, is a San Francisco publisher and the owner of the City Lights Bookshop in that city. Like Ginsberg, he exalts emancipation and resistance to institutions; unlike *Howl,* however, Ferlinghetti's *Pictures of the Gone World* and *A Coney Island of the Mind* are series of lyrics consciously imitative of William Carlos Williams' lighter verse and akin in technique to the work of E. E. Cummings. Rumaker, a twenty-six-year-old graduate of Black Mountain College, writes a prose highly reminiscent of Kerouac's but endowed with a distinctive gift for precise description. His story, "The Desert," printed in the second *Evergreen Review,* shows, as well, that even "beat" prose may gain value from proper punctuation.

Between the "beat generation metaphysicals" and its "ultra-terrestrials," a group of writers should be mentioned which might be termed "beat generation experimentals." Here we have poets who share a predilection for jazz-rhythm and a certain mystic tone with Whalen, on the one hand, and Ginsberg, on the other, but whose verse is neither topical nor philosophical but concentrated on a communication of images. A typical young "experimental" in this sense is Michael (Mike) McClure, like Rumaker twenty-six and a product of Black Mountain College, whose verse shows definite echoes of the American imagist movement (Amy Lowell, the early Pound) coupled with an imitation of "cool" jazz-rhythm. Another is Philip Lamantia, a fifty-ish ex-anarchist and ex-surrealist. In Lamantia's poems, the strains of "way-out" jazz give motion to a world of Dali watches and William Carlos Williams guitars, melted together in a mystical — but undirected — way. Thirty-nine-year-old Robert Duncan boldly plays with the *Structure of Rime* in a long *Evergreen Review* poem of that name. Josephine Miles, a full professor of English at the University of California (Berkeley), endows her rather conventional imagist verse, the latest of some years' production, with startling touches evocative of jazz.

Robert Duncan, Josephine Miles — as well as several other less prominent poets published in the City Lights Press, the Jargon Press, and in the *Evergreen Review* — make up a segment of the literary "beat generation" which shares with its "metaphysical" and "ultra-terrestrial" segments only a tolerance of unconventional form and language in poetry. Even more clearly than McClure and Lamantia, the minor "beat generation experimentals" are purely literary affiliates of the movement. Their presence within it indicates the "beat generation's" diverse poetic strains and its lack of a cohesive literary doctrine. For, upon further analysis, even my division of these authors into "metaphysicals," "experimentals," and "super-terrestrials" can be shown to be synthetic and arbitrary. Basically, the "beat generation's" authors are too distinctly individualistic to allow their work to be classified. Nor is there, in the maze of Zen Buddhism, Roman Catholicism, cynicism, hedonism, and surrealism which informs their work, any unified philosophical position, save, perhaps, that vague utopian and pacifist goal of man at ease with himself which is shared by both the religious and earthy "beat generation" writers.

We do not, then, have in the "beat generation," a literary movement as such a phenomenon is understood by most historians of letters. What unifying factors which draw the "beat generation" authors together may be found? Is the "beat" way of life their only cohesive force? Surely not, for Brother Antoninus, Josephine Miles, and John Logan, to mention only three *Evergreen Review* poets, can scarcely (being, respectively, a Dominican lay brother, a nominee for the Executive Committee of the Modern Language Association, and a family-man teaching at Notre Dame) be associated with hot-rods, dope-peddling, or wandering *On the Road*. We must turn, for an answer to this question, to the critical prose of Kenneth Rexroth, the literary apologist for the "beat generation."

Rexroth, a fifty-three-year-old poet, ex-anarchist, ex-Marxist present-day radio announcer has, within the past two years, published several essays on the "beat generation" writers which treat of these in a sympathetic vein. Rexroth's essays are all fairly similar to one another and revolve about four central points:

1. The "beat generation" writers and poets are a unique and startlingly novel phenomenon in American literature.
2. The "beat generation" writers revive a valuable — indeed the only real tradition in American letters.
3. The "beat generation" writers are the heroes of a long-needed revolution against academic and upper middle-brow writing and criticism in America.
4. The writers of the "beat generation" represent the true spirit of American youth today.

The last point we must leave to the sociologists and social philosophers; the first point is manifestly absurd. For a poet-critic like Rexroth, who has been reading American literature for some thirty-five years, must surely know that experiments in verse and prose have characterized it during that period. We need only recall Ezra Pound's *Cantos*, T. S. Eliot's *Four Quartets*, William Carlos Williams' *Paterson*, Hemingway's *Death in the Afternoon*, John Dos Passos' *42nd Parallel*, and Gertrude Stein's *Brewsie and Willie* — all eminent works with that characteristic published in the period 1923–1958 by authors of very diverse sensibilities, to be aware of that fact. To Rexroth's "San Francisco Renaissance" of the 'fifties we can oppose the fugitive agrarian movement of the 'twenties and the Marxist literary movement of the 'thirties — both, on the surface, collective efforts to bring American letters to a novel, startling, and unique re-birth.

Rexroth's other two assertions, however, that the "beat generation" poets revive a lost tradition in American literature and that theirs is a legitimate revolt against academic poetry and criticism contain enough truth to be looked into carefully. Though Rexroth may never have read Walt Whitman's late critical summary "A Backward Glance O'er Travel'd Roads," its last sentences are implicit in Rexroth's discussion of the "beat generation's" revival of the true American tradition. Whitman says here:

> Concluding with two items for the imaginative genius of the West, when it worthily rises — First, what Herder taught to the young Goethe, that really great poetry is always (like the Homeric or Biblical canticles) the result of a national spirit, and not the privilege of a polish'd and select few; Second, that the strongest and sweetest songs yet remain to be sung.

It is the democratic, rather than the aristocratic, the native, rather than the foreign tradition which are here, in 1891, praised as the desirable background for future American literature. And it is precisely the language of the native common man illuminating democratic sentiments which is, according to Rexroth, being revived in the prose of Rumaker and Kerouac, the verse of Ginsberg and of Ferlinghetti. The tradition which is revived by these is, according to Rexroth, that of Whitman's spontaneous and revolutionary verse, of Mark Twain's dialectal prose in *Huckleberry Finn,* and of Hart Crane's more energetic lyrics — all as set against the prose of Henry James and the poetry of T. S. Eliot, which are condemned as foreign, formalistic, and artificial. There is, at first glance, much truth in Rexroth's assertions, especially as he is careful to allow those foreign authors in whom Ginsberg shows interest (Apollinaire, Beckett, and Maiakowsky) a place in the "beat generation's" tradition and freely admits that some *Evergreen Review* and *City Lights Press* poets draw on other experimental traditions in their work. Yet there is one factor which Rexroth eliminates from his assessment which, as we shall see, bears some striking resemblances to outstanding "beat generation" work — the Marxist literary effort of the 'thirties.

It is interesting, in this respect, to look at a volume entitled *Proletarian Literature in the United States* (1935). Here we find, for instance, a poem entitled "Thalassa, Thalassa" by James Neugass. It deals with a strike of Greek merchant seamen in the harbor of Buenos Aires and the last stanza of it reads:

> "Romance, travel, adventure." So what? — saleswords for slavery.
> In Buenos Aires, they went out on strike and they went out solid,
> They sat on deck and stared at their officers, sang the Comintern.
> Two went under a third mate's Colt. The sharks got another,
> They went out solid, they didn't scab, they stayed out and they won
> . . . .
> Struck once and won the first small part of what shall be theirs,
> The Red Internationale of Seamen and Harborworkers!

For comparison we turn to the madhouse scene in Ginsberg's *Howl,* Part III:

> where there are twentyfive-thousand mad comrades all
> together singing the final stanzas of the Internationale
> . . . .
> where we wake up electrified out of the coma by our own
> souls' airplanes roaring over the roof they've come to
> drop angelic bombs the hospital illuminates itself imaginary
> walls collapse O skinny legions run outside O starry-spangled
> shock of mercy the eternal war is here O victory forget your
> underwear we're free . . .

It is unlikely that Neugass influenced Ginsberg directly. And Ginsberg's ideas differ from Neugass's: the latter's revolt is newspaper fact; the former's is a madman's delusion. Yet the tone, the terms, and the form of the statements are remarkably alike.

The same volume which carries "Thalassa, Thalassa" also brings a short story by Albert Maltz called "Man on a Road." Here an anonymous man gives a poor worker a ride and treats him to a cup of coffee:

> We went inside. For the first time since I had come upon him in the tunnel he seemed human. He didn't talk, but he didn't slip inside himself either. He just sat down at the counter and waited for his coffee. When it came, he drank it slowly, holding the cup in both hands as though to warm them. When he had finished, I asked him if he wouldn't like a sandwich. He turned around to me and smiled. It was a very gentle, a very patient smile. His big, lumpy face seemed to light up with it and became understanding and sweet and gentle.
>
> The smile shook me all through. It didn't warm me — it made me feel sick inside. It was like watching a corpse begin to stir. I wanted to cry out "My God, you poor man!"

And we turn to Jack Kerouac's *On the Road:*

> all dead bums forever dead with nothing and all finished and out — there — and this was the clientele in the Public Hair restaurant where I ate many's the morn a 3-egg breakfast with almost dry toast and oatmeal a little saucer of . . . my 26-cent breakfast, my pride — and that incredible semiqueer counterman who dished out the food, threw it at you, slammed it, had a languid frank expression straight in your eyes like a 1930's lunchcart heroine in Steinbeck . . .

where, once more, the resemblance between the Marxist and the "beat generation" style is striking. Maltz and Kerouac present the same mixture of dramatic human expression in similarly sordid surroundings. Their contexts are, of course, different: Maltz's old man is dying of silicosis from working in a mining tunnel; Kerouac's protagonist is an intellectual earning a full professor's salary as a railway brakeman who eats his 26-cent breakfast to prove that it can still be eaten in the San Francisco of the 'fifties.

Proof that Marxist prose is of importance for understanding the "beat generation's" literary tradition does not invalidate the latter. Nor does the absence of a social purpose in the "beat generation's" writings force us to condemn these and brand them feeble, pointless imitators of Marxist literature. For theirs is a different story, told to a different age. But Rexroth's assertion that Whitman, Twain, and Hart Crane make up the "beat generation's" direct ancestry must here be modified to include Marxist elements from the 'thirties.

Rexroth's statement that the "beat generation" writers are the gad-flies for a needed revolt against conventional academic poetry is perhaps the truest of his claims. For, since the end of the American Marxist movement in literature, no unified group of writers in present-day America has dared to be scornful both of the popular media com-munication (the press, radio, and television) and of the conventional unconventionality of upper middle-brow magazines of the *Atlantic Monthly* variety, before the "beat generation" writers took this step. No frontal attack but the "beat generation's" has been delivered re-cently, from an outlook neither openly Marxist nor patently *bourgeois,* against the control which the New Criticism and the agrarian fugitive tradition exercise today over the emergence of younger literary talents. It is impossible, in America today, to study American or English literature on the university level without being indoctrinated, at one point or another, with the critical views of John Crowe Ransom, Allen Tate, Randall Jarrell, R. P. Blackmur, or Lionel Trilling — to mention only the most prominent names among the professor-poet-critics who control the *Kenyon Review,* the *Hudson Review,* and the *Partisan Review.* It is very hard, by the same token, to break into print as a young writer or critic without being, in some way, a recognizable imitator of the older New Critics or ex-fugitive agrarians. The "beat generation" writers attack this rather rigid tradition, not because they oppose the creative and critical efforts of the Kenyon school, but because they resent the control of vested academic and publishing in-terests over the expression of the critical and creative spirit. And in this they are, I feel, right. Unfortunately, the "beat generation" has no unified critical doctrine, no poetics to support its polemic — the extreme individualism which gave the "beat generation" writers strength to launch their protest paradoxically negates the development of a strong intellectual point of view.

We have attempted, here, to give the "beat generation" writers and poets a close look. What we found is a group of young to middle-aged creative talents of some merit who neither perform in a unified literary style nor defend a common intellectual or spiritual point of view, save, perhaps, a tendency toward mysticism and pacifism cultivated by the metaphysical and ultra-terrestrial extremes of the movement. We found that, in the light of the experimental tradition in contemporary American poetry and prose, the "beat-generation" writers' claims to uniqueness and originality within it are absurd. We saw, as well, that proletarian literature of the 'thirties plays a significant part in their literary ancestry and disqualifies Rexroth's claims that Ginsberg and Kerouac bring to a renaissance the dormant spirit of American folk-literature as exemplified by Whitman and Twain. Finally we saw that the "beat generation writers' " polemic against the strangleholds both of commercialism and of the cliquish spirit of New Critics and ex-fugitive agrarians is a healthy and positive feature of their approach to contemporary American letters. If they could only develop a unified point of view to spearhead their critical attack, the writers of the "beat generation" could bring great benefit to our literary scene.

PART II

ON SOME INDIVIDUAL NOVELISTS

✻ MARCUS KLEIN

A Discipline of Nobility: Saul Bellow's Fiction

IN the 1950s the sensible hero journeyed from a position of alienation to one of accommodation. Accommodation to the happy middling community of those years, to the suburbs, to the new wealth and the corporate conscience, to the fat gods. But the accommodation was aware of itself and, for the spirit's ease, it saved a tic of nonconformity. That was the substance of David Reisman's lessons in autonomy, and no social prescription of the decade was so well-liked as his. The journey was the *reisemotif,* so to speak, of serious American fiction in the decade, and of less serious American fiction, too. When the retrieved awareness was small, as often happened, when Marjorie Morningstar accepted Mamaroneck and Sloan Wilson his tailor, when, that is, the progress toward accommodation was most successful, accommodation looked most like retreat.

Saul Bellow's novels, altogether the most exciting fiction of those years, worked too — quite beyond any question of Bellow's intentions — within the motion from alienation to accommodation. Indeed, from a certain distance Bellow's novels find their definition as a systematic exploration of the concerns of all the Wilsons and the Wouks. Only — and of course it makes all the difference — they were more aware, more imaginative, and more severe. Bellow's characters, despite the variousness of mood and style of his work, remain much the same: a youth and a fat man, with a quirky philosopher loitering nearby. And they face problems which are reducible to a single problem: to meet with a strong sense of self the sacrifice of self demanded by social circumstance. Alienation, the sense of separate and unconciliating identity, must travel to accommodation. Bellow's inspiration is finally in other, deeper sources, but as the novels have worked themselves out they have dealt in the terms presented by the history in which they have found themselves. The dialogue between alienation and accommodation is what first of all they are about.

Dangling Man, published in the mid-1940s, took its terms from the '40s and pushed a dour hero over the arc from the impossibility of

Reprinted from the *Kenyon Review,* XXIV (Spring, 1962), 203–226, by permission of the author.

121

alienation to the death in accommodation. Joseph in his idiopathic freedom is functionless and unbearably isolated, but when, by hurrying his draft call, he seeks accommodation, he sacrifices the freedom of the self. The problem, whose formal construction Bellow perhaps borrowed from debates in *Partisan Review,* is insoluble, and in Bellow's next book, *The Victim,* it yields to a more tangible problem in responsibility. Asa Leventhal must balance what he owes a man who is at once his persecutor, his victim, and also his companion in this universe against what he owes himself. He discovers that he has a moral obligation in each direction — and that the issue is not only a moral one. Life is a battle in which each engagement suggests the necessity of disengagement, and *vice-versa.*

It may be a comic battle. This is a proposition which all of the dozens of high adventures of Augie March will want, serially, to prove, and which Augie finally will want to preserve intact. Except that it can't be preserved. There is too much running and brawling in the proposition, and no possibility of real freedom or community or love. For that reason *Augie March* never really ends.

In *Seize the Day* Bellow suddenly made the problem and his fiction severe by bringing to the last extremity a hero who can run and brawl no longer, who must find a principle of life in this world that has beaten him — or die. Tommy Wilhelm (together with Bellow) manages it, though he just manages it, in his last, desperate, resonating adventure. He finds himself weeping at the bier of a stranger, and in the same motion discovers that he is moving "toward the consummation of his heart's ultimate need." That need, the whole of the novel comes to reveal, is the need not to die. At the moment of death, his motion is toward existence, the vitality that defines and unites everyone, and his weeping is an acceptance of it and therefore an act of love toward life.

What has been caught, but just caught, is a progress of the soul through its freedom, from isolation to affirmation of ordinary life in the world. The affirmation is made again in the first movement of *Henderson the Rain King.* "Grun-to-molani," man-want-to-live, an ancient African queen whispers to Henderson, and his heart fills with joy. But Henderson is ridden by high energies and lofty ambitions, and equipped therefore for the discovery that the principle of reconciliation is not enough. He needs further adventures, as the principle needs extension. Man wants to live, but in what shape and form? The communal principle fails Henderson as soon as he learns it when, in an impetuous gesture of good will, attempting to rid a cistern of frogs, he blows up his host's water supply. The idea of community imposes the idea of service, and Henderson possesses that idea fiercely. He would make men better, and free them from the law of decay. But his passion for service must be chastened and trained, and his further adventures under the tutelage of Dahfu, an African king who is part Wilhelm Reich, part Zarathustra, and part King David, provide him with just that spiritual exercise. He is put to lessons in self-transcendence. He must learn to contain humiliations. He must overcome fear. Like Zarathustra, he must empty himself in order to become a man again. Having done so, he can return to his home in Connecticut, to his wife, and he can make plans to enter medical school.

It is to these Nietzschean terms that the dialogue of *Dangling Man*, between alienation and accommodation, has come. The terms now, well over a decade later, are in no close sense the same terms at all. Bellow has got beyond them. But they are clearly consonant with their originals. They refer to the same problem, and the five novels show a strict struggle with it. What is remarkable is that Bellow has played it all by ear. The orderliness of his progress, and the intellectual unity, have after all been the wonderful accident of his commitment. The novels, with perhaps the exception of *The Victim*, are not even well-made. They spill over on themselves; they work themselves out according to the demands of character and frequently, one feels, out of the demands of gimmicks. They exhibit novelistic failures: *Dangling Man* is enclosed and short of action; Augie's exuberance runs down in the middle and becomes repetitive; Henderson suffers turgidity among his other sufferings. But they are shaped, and that is the excitement one feels in them, by an energy of total commitment, by an imagination that will confront human needs and greeds as they spill all over themselves and yield to clarity only after heavy labor.

A large and suffering appreciation of maelstrom, of personality filled with its own chaos and set down in the chaotic circumstances and the obscure obligations of the ordinary world, has shaped the novels and made them into a coherent vision. Bellow's alienated hero before he is alienated is a terribly oppressed individual, and it is with the feeling of his oppression that the fiction no doubt begins. Human beings crowd upon Bellow's hero and attempt to subjugate him. Human beings become burdensome to him. And it is not only those others who directly assault him who threaten his freedom. He begins in a condition of individuality imperiled, and his career is a series of adventures through a metropolis of perils. Bellow's hero lives among clutter, boredom, distraction, things. "Things done by man overshadow us," says Augie. "And this is true also of meat on the table, heat in the pipes, print on the paper, sounds in the air, so that all matters are alike, of the same weight, of the same rank, the caldron of God's wrath on page one and Wieboldt's sale on page two." Augie's complaint is diagnosed as *moha*, opposition of the finite, a curious complaint which is the start in fact of all the Bellovian protagonists.

It is the sheer weight of chaotic existence that first of all defines them. "The novelist is distracted," Bellow says in one of his discursive pieces. ". . . there are more things that solicit the attention of the mind than there ever were before." The novelist is menaced with "death by distraction," and not only the novelist: everyone on every level is exposed to the danger. We are menaced by the sheer distraction of sheer wealth. "The world is too much with us, and there has never been so much world," Bellow has said elsewhere. There is so much money now and there are so many possessions. "Love, duty, principle, thought, significance, everything is being sucked into a fatty and nerveless state of 'well-being.'" The fat gods of the new materialism are all about us demanding our energies.

We are menaced, distracted, and overborne by the sheer clutter of things. And of course it is to the point that Bellow, unlike the past masters, Hemingway and Faulkner, is entirely a city writer. (*Henderson* takes place mostly in Africa, to be sure, but not in the green hills of Africa. It is an Africa teeming with people and political intrigue, and with furniture; an Africa urbanized.) In the city there is much more to contend with. Things and others both are close and thick in Bellow's novels, and though Bellow is not without affection for nature, there is no escape into rural simplicities. In urban circumstances the rites of love are enormously difficult. Bellow's cities — Chicago and New York — are dense with neighbors and noise, with streetcars, subways, families, friends, soot, and filth. Joseph, living in a six-sided box within a Chicago rooming house, is victimized by the old man next door who coughs all night, leaves the door to the toilet open, steals socks, and throws empty whiskey bottles into the alley. *The Victim* begins: "On some nights New York is as hot as Bangkok," and all the gagging heaviness of a New York summer, the light of the sun like "the yellow revealed in the slit of the eye of a wild animal," the subways, the sweat, the listless crowds in the parks, the invincible dirt, the struggle for air, is brought upon Asa Leventhal's moral burden. Augie's Chicago, while it spawns heroic vitalists, is what he calls it in his first sentence, a "somber city." Those vitalists are all Machiavellians, omnipresent, dangerous, reaching out with too many clever hands. The somber city provides neither a recollection of Edenic childhood nor expectation of heaven. Augie is set down into "deep city vexation" and "forced early into deep city aims," and "what," he wants to know, "can that lead to of the highest?" His initiation into love is of the kind the city affords, love paid for and second hand. "That's what city life is. And so it *didn't* have the luster it should have had, and there *wasn't* any epithalamium of gentle lovers . . ." The character and the fate which are Augie's study are located first in his response to the enormousness and complexity of Chicago. "Crusoe," he says, "alone with nature, under heaven, had a busy, complicated time of it with the unhuman itself, and I am in a crowd that yields results with much more difficulty and reluctance and am part of it myself."

The clutter of the city weighs upon and shapes Tommy Wilhelm and Eugene Henderson, too. His existence lies upon Tommy Wilhelm like a hump, he is "assigned to be the carrier of a load which was his own self," but it makes a difference that he must carry it along upper Broadway on a summer's day. On a day after a sleepless, noisy New York night. Through the dust of the street and the fumes of the buses, through "pushcarts, accordion and fiddle, shoeshine, begging, the dust going round like a woman on stilts," talking to himself because there is no one else to talk to among the millions of a city like New York. "The traffic seemed to come down Broadway out of the sky, where the hot spokes of the sun rolled from the south. Hot, stony odors rose from the subway grating in the street." And when Dr. Tamkin, the tutelary confidence man of the novel, a deity of this inferno, tells Tommy that the world is full of murderers, Tommy answers helplessly that "there are also kind, ordinary, helpful people. They're — out in the country."

Henderson goes out in the country, first as gentleman pig farmer, then as an African explorer, but the spirit, the heat, the humanity, and the junk of the city are always at his back. His farm, become a pig kingdom, swarms with grunting animals. The city's steaming pavement becomes the strange, obscurely threatening "calcareous" rocks of King Dahfu's country. The heat of the city becomes the boiling African sun, felt as the jungle fever which oppresses Henderson throughout his spiritual adventuring. Tamkin is recreated in King Dahfu, Henderson's guiding spirit, king of the warlike Wariri, another prince of darkness. The clotted Broadway crowd becomes the frenzied savages who batter Henderson to his knees in the ceremony in which he is made the Rain King.

Henderson abandons things and people to make the trip to Africa. It is the notion of junk that is the immediate motive of his going. Climbing through the rooms of an old lady just dead, he is overwhelmed by her collected rubbish: "Bottles, lamps, old butter dishes, and chandeliers were on the floor, shopping bags filled with strings and rags, and pronged openers that the dairies used to give away to lift the paper tops from milk bottles; and bushel baskets full of buttons and china door knobs." And he thinks, "Henderson, put forth effort. You, too, will die of this pestilence. Death will annihilate you and nothing will remain, and there will be nothing left but junk." He puts forth effort to escape, but the city stays with him nonetheless. In Africa he talks city talk: "Now listen, Your Highness, don't sell me

down the river. You know what I mean? I thought you liked me."
He thinks, in Africa, in city metaphors and of city events; the city
maintains its pressure, and alive within his other speculations is the
city idea of people, nameless, faceless, with whom no communication
is possible. Tommy Wilhelm was condemned to talk to himself in a
city where every other man spoke a language entirely his own, and
Henderson is brought to the vision of Babel raised to include the
universe: "This planet has billions of passengers on it, and those were
preceded by infinite billions and there are vaster billions to come, and
none of these, no, not one, can I hope ever to understand. Never!"
He goes on to reflect that this matter of quantity, come up in another
view, need not bury you alive, that it is marvelous and not depressing
— but the reflection comes of his struggle and not of his primary
condition.

Under the mass of such quantity and confronted by such chaos in
the external world, Bellow's hero in his first motion moves toward un-
burdening and sloughing off. Civil society is too much, and indeed in
extreme moments even the cultural accumulations, the very history
and wisdom of civilization, are too much and are rejected. Most em-
phatically by the aging wise man, another Zarathustrian prophet, of
Bellow's monologue called "Address by Gooley MacDowell to the
Hasbeens Club of Chicago":

> Around our heads we have a dome of thought as thick as atmos-
> phere to breathe. And what's about? One thought leads to another
> as breath leads to breath. By pulling [it] into universal conscious-
> ness, can [we] explain everything from Democritus to Bikini? But
> a person can no longer keep up, and plenty are dying of good ideas.
> We have them in the millions, in compilations, from the *Zend
> Avesta* to now, all on file with the best advice for [one] and all hu-
> man occasions. . . . Look at us, deafened, hampered, obstructed,
> impeded, impaired and bowel-gutted with wise counsel and good
> precept, and the more helpful our ideas the worse our headaches.
> So we ask, will some good creature pull out the plug and ease our
> disgusted hearts a little?

It is a prayer Augie, too, records: "Anyway, there's too much of
everything of this kind, *that's* come home to me, too much history and
culture to keep track of, too many details, too much news, too much
example, too much influence, too many guys who tell you to be as
they are, and all this hugeness, abundance, turbulence, Niagara Falls
torrent. Which who is supposed to interpret? Me?" And Tommy
Wilhelm is overcome by the sheer information in Tamkin's discourses,
and Henderson, an overwhelmed millionaire, under the spur of a
similar impulse fills beautiful pieces of architecture with pigs and
then, seeking Eden, makes a safari to the pre-civilized past, "the real

past," he says, "no history or junk like that." And if all history and culture are rejected in a style that borrows widely from the world's accumulation of literature, that fact is more than irony. Bellow's style, which beginning with *Augie March* has become a racy vehicle bearing great freights of knowledge, is a thing that simultaneously admits and dismisses clutter. All its process of literary echoing goes to lend the rejection authority.

The matter has become more and more apparent, but since the beginning all Bellow's heroes have started in a gesture of escape from burdens, an extreme romantic gesture. It is a gesture which in its extremity brings Bellow into touch with one of the defining impulses of American character, into touch with at least all the classic Redskins of American letters, from Leatherstocking to Whitman to Mark Twain to Hemingway, all those who light out for the woods, the open road, the Territory, and into touch perhaps with the Palefaces, too. (The extreme need to escape burdens, to be free of all the clutter, is certainly as well a distinction of Hawthorne and Henry James.) Bellow's hero is tempted frequently to epiphanies of love for mankind in general, though never for things, and his motion is brought to various thematic significances, but he is in the first instance activated by the need to rid himself of the weight of the chaos.

He can escape from under that weight into harmony with natural laws vaguely realized as beneficent, or he can escape into himself, locate all value and reality in his person, or he can in various ways attempt to reconcile himself with external existence in all its chaos. And it is out of those three possibilities, the first two stretching toward the last, that the action and the total thematic construct of Bellow's novels have come.

Neither as a metaphysical conception nor in the pleasantness of its phenomena is Nature ever dominant as a motif, though it has become more emphatic as the novels have succeeded each other. Bellow's city imagination is not comfortable with the Natural Laws. He has little nature to bring to them. But his hero entertains a yearning for them and a provisional trust that they are good, because the circumscription of the possibility of escape demands it. Joseph dismisses "nature" when it is presented to him by a friend who complains of the treelessness and too-human deadness of New York, dismisses it as nostalgic sentimentality. Nevertheless his whole struggle toward what he calls the "facts of simple existence" is involved in a turn of the seasons toward fruitful harmony. The chaotic winter submits to spring. Joseph begins his journal in the dark Chicago December and surrenders himself, relieves himself of his freedom, in April. Bellow accents the matter by having Joseph look forward throughout his winter to walking in the park in his spring coat on the 21st of March, and he shifts the mood of the novel toward resolution with the coming spring.

Asa Leventhal, locked in New York's inhuman heat, has moments of freshness and deep breathing at sea on the Staten Island ferry, and the plot of the novel moves him toward the relief that will come with Labor Day. The attempted suicide of his antagonist, Allbee, on the eve of that day makes possible Leventhal's birth into a possible world, and the day itself brings cooling breezes. Nature as transcendent reality brushes Levanthal lightly once — for a brief moment of half-sleep he feels the whole world present to him and about to offer him a mysterious, it would seem redeeming, discovery. But the discovery blows by him and at the end of his action, having abandoned ultimate questioning and now re-entering a darkened theatre with his wife, he is no closer to a notion of reality.

But Augie comes, if not conclusively, at least wholeheartedly to the natural laws, his "axial lines" called "Truth, love, peace, bounty, use-fulness, harmony!" which, he says, quiver right through him when striving stops. They excite him in the moment after his perception of them to pastoral ambitions. He wants to own and settle on a Mid-western farm, to marry, and to teach orphans. His adventures carry him, however, into complexities which won't permit cessation of striv-ing. The axial lines, he says, are "not imaginary stuff . . . because I bring my entire life to the test." There is no doubting his sincerity, but this is one of the moments when Augie's hopefulness becomes shrill. His whole life does not validate the perception. The novel does not earn that leap into faith. In fact the novel is honest beyond Augie's knowing and it does not permit him so easy an escape. Nor is it an escape that Tommy Wilhelm, so strictly confined by authentic troubles, can practically afford to take. Not, anyway, in its romantic simplicity. Tamkin does offer him nature. "Creation is nature," he says. "Rapid. Lavish. Inspirational. It shapes leaves. . . . You don't know what you've got within you." But it is no solace to a middle-aged slob rapidly and lavishly dying in the middle of New York Ctiy. Tommy is simply confused by the offer.

It is Henderson who most clearly moves toward harmony with the natural laws. He goes among noble savages and to live with the beasts in the field — and if his Africa has the feel of Chicago and the smell of New York, that is apparently despite Bellow's first intention. Moreover it is Henderson who most clearly demonstrates the naïveté of the escape into nature. He makes a journey into the heart of dark-ness to discover the horror of it. He goes to Africa to discover Reality. A voice within him says constantly, "I want," and that is what it ulti-mately wants. "Truth" and "Reality" are ambitions always at his lips. His soul's progress is marked by a succession of emblematic beasts.

First a porcine pig farmer in a sty of piggish phenomena, he comes in the first stage of his journey upon a motley tribe of pious cow-worshippers and then he tries to do what none of them will do, to deal at first hand with a plague of frogs. He fails, but in failing he has pursued nature to a certain depth. His next, and most important, stop, with a tribe of lion-worshippers, brings him face to face with the thing itself. Under the tutelage of Dahfu — himself a refugee from civilization come home to meet Reality — Henderson is put to the task (following disciplines derived from the somatic psychology of Wilhelm Reich) of assuming and absorbing Dahfu's pet lioness. She is all lion, Dahfu observes. "Does not take issue with the inherent. Is one hundred per cent within the given." She is the way to Being, the end of Becoming, the unchanging truth prior to the cycle of desire and fear. She will force Henderson to the present moment. "She will make consciousness to shine. She will burnish you." She *is* Being — or, as it turns out, penultimate Being — itself. (Being, of course, not seen as daffodils. Bellow is never so lacking in severity as that.) And Henderson has some small success in overcoming his fear of the lioness and then in absorbing lion-ness. He meets the inhuman thing. In the same way, it happens, and within the same image as previous Bellow heroes have met it — Asa saw the yellow of the sun like that in the slit of the eye of a wild animal, "say a lion, something inhuman that didn't care about anything human and yet was implanted in every human being, too," and Augie had adventures with the lion's American equivalent, an eagle with a "pressed-down head, the killing eye, the deep life of its feathers." But Henderson goes further. The lion is pure fire, he says, forcing him to close his eyes. So are the stars pure fire, he realizes, and not small gold objects. He develops his consciousness of the matter beyond ways that are permitted Asa and Augie. He discovers that the inhuman fire is at the center of his humanity, too.

With that discovery he should achieve harmony. Here is the very principle of Augie's axial lines. But Henderson is hurried to a further pitch of Reality. Dahfu's lion is a pet lioness after all. Henderson is now made to confront the authentic lion, male and wild:

> Then, at the very door of consciousness, there was a snarl and I looked down from this straw perch . . . into the big, angry, hair-framed face of the lion. It was all wrinkled, contracted; within those wrinkles was the darkness of murder. The lips were drawn away from the gums, and the breath of the animal came over me, hot as oblivion, raw as blood. I started to speak aloud. I said, "Oh, my God, whatever You think of me, let me not fall under this butcher shop. . . ." And to this, as a rider, the thought added itself that this was all mankind needed, to be conditioned into the image of a ferocious animal like the one below.

That lion castrates and kills King Dahfu. The voice of the lion is the voice of death itself. And this Real, far from being the escape from chaos, is chaos and old night itself. To submit to the harmony it offers, on the principle that the lion outside is inside, too, would be to accept the inhmanity of the inhuman Real. Henderson had in one of his discourses with Dahfu parried Eliot by saying that humankind could not stand too much *un*reality, but Eliot wins the point. Henderson now reflects on the great inescapable rhythms of life, Augie's axial lines once again, but he reflects that he can't afford to worry about them. The old queen's advice, "Grun-tu-molani," man-want-to-live, comes to mean going about the business of living despite the death-dealing, chaotic Real.

That is very much, if not explicitly, the ground upon which Augie finally mounts his optimism. If Augie is only incidentally concerned with the nature of the real Real, he is completely engaged with the natural laws as they impinge on his larky and boisterous freedom, and the *animal ridens* rises in him *despite* their influences. His adventures are escapes from all determinisms, human and suprahuman. And that is the ground upon which Tommy Wilhelm, finally made to confront death as ultimate reality, can choose to live. The escape from under the weight of external chaos into the natural laws does not work. It is no escape at all. At the center of the universe are violence and death. The vague yearning for the natural laws lucent in the earlier novels is quite extinguished when the fiction works it out to the test.

There is an alternative dodge for Bellow's oppressed hero in the assertion of his own character as the locus of reality and value. In the face of cluttering chaos and with a swagger, he can assert personality broadly. "A man's character is his fate, says Heraclitus," says Augie with relishing approval, and if at the end he learns that a man's fate is his character, why, that is a fate good enough for him. Tamkin advises Tommy:

> Seek ye then that which art not there
> In thine own glory let thyself rest.
> Witness. Thy power is not bare.
> Thou art King. Thou art at thy best.

It is advice under which Tommy staggers. The hero of one of Bellow's short stories, "The Trip to Galena," a young man engaged in a war against the overburdening boredom of things and people, proposes that "a man is bound to do everything in his lifetime." He will conduct war by the simple exertion of personality. And Henderson, whose person is explicitly reflected in his body, is great and joyous in his body. His very suffering delights him because it is an exercise of personality. At the center of the universe, then, in this action, is the

individual self. The self constantly threatened, however, and presenting an obligation. The Bellovian hero will protect his personality from
the outside or, because he can't live in a nutshell, insinuate it in and
out of chaotic experience; but he will maintain it, attempt to maintain
it, always unbroken.

At the end the assertion is merely a dodge, and the escape is blocked
precisely because the inhuman outside *is* within — that, finally, is why
"alienation" is impossible. Nor can personality remain untouched.
The attempt at self-preservation raises severe moral problems. And at
the end the person must indeed be broken in order to achieve life.
But the motion of the escape meanwhile irradiates Bellow's writing. It
is the inspiration of his comedy. Because the need is desperate, the
assertion of the person is extreme — with *Augie March* and thereafter,
though there are hints of the mood before, the assertion is raised in
various characters to burlesque. Bellow's personalist hero yelps, quite
the gamecock of a new, urban wilderness, quite like his backwoodsman
prototype impelled to brashness by dispossession and inadequacy and
the feeling of threatening powers everywhere. He sings himself with
quite the same nervy insolence with which Walt Whitman met the
world, and like that witty comedian he makes a great gesture of including the whole world in himself, but then he adopts shifts and
evasions and contrarieties to keep free of it. And like Whitman, he
celebrates himself by the exercise of a free-wheeling, inclusive, cata-
loguing rhetoric, gripping great bunches of facts in sentences that just
manage to balance, racing through various levels of diction, saying with
every turn, "Look at me, going everywhere!" It is a gaudy fireworks
of style, in itself a brilliant affirmation of the self. At the same time it
performs the ironic function, by its calculated indiscriminateness (in
Bellow and in Walt Whitman, too), of discarding everything it picks
up. It is therefore the perfect expression of the dynamic, disengaging,
mock hero.

Dahfu accuses Henderson of being a great avoider, and the same
accusation may be made against all of Bellow's personalists. Augie is
the clearest instance. His famous "availability" is the flamboyant self-
asserting part of him, but it is perfectly and in every engagement
countered by his "opposition." At the end he still has all his availability; his great appetite for life and engagement is intact precisely
because he has spent it in no experience. He is presented taking what
amounts to still another oath of unsusceptibility to all the "big personalities, destiny molders, and heavy-water brains, Machiavellis and
wizard evildoers, big-wheels and imposers-upon, absolutists." The oath
is redundant, for his unsusceptibility is continuous. Indeed it is a
moral failing, and one which Augie is made to realize. The one advice
by his many advisers which cuts deep is that he can't be hurt enough

by the fate of other people. That is a failing in love, and the most strenuous part of Augie's action is in the problem it poses. It is a failing he never rectifies, for to do so would stop him cold.

Augie is a kind of Huck Finn, with his something adoptional about him, his participation in a linear series of adventures, his resilience, his mounting good humor. The comparison has been noted. But he is like Huck, too, in his reluctance to be civilized. He eludes. He is not to be caught by the shaping influences. He won't be determined. Moreover, he is Huck confined to a city populated by endless duplications of the King, the Duke, and Colonel Sellers. No matter that his adventures take him over two continents, he is always in Chicago, without a territory to light out for — so he is put to more muscular shifts of duplicity. What the Mississippi and the Territory could do for Huck, Augie must do for himself. His only territory is his personality, which he must keep free. Life is dramatic for Augie, it is process, and the process is that kind of evasion that keeps all events and the person from settling.

A new discipline and another notion of the possibilities of freedom will be needed by the personalist hero who is to avoid evasion and be hurt enough by the fate of other people. Bellow comes to it, but after *Augie* as before the strong assertion of independent personality secures all his lyricism, and without restriction to the personalist protagonists. Radical self-assertion, assertion of the real, untypical self, is an act of courage in Bellow's squeezing world. There is glamor in it which just for itself for the moment transvalues all moral obligations. It commands Bellow's love even for the very Machiavellians he loathes — sometimes, it should be added, with the disastrous result of turning them quaint.

Almost in the very beginning, in 1942 with his second published story, "The Mexican General," there appeared the first in Bellow's line of resolutely vital knaves. The General is a provincial opportunist who has secured his opportunity with the assassination of Trotsky. He is an arrogant ghoul, well-mistressed, a vile entrepreneur at the funeral of the Revolution, and he is made to bear a moral of political corruption. But he is also equipped with Lawrentian innuendoes of personality — he has Indian vigor, he is alive, he has personal force, he is an *Übermensch* just not yet attained to moral transcendence, and the pale moral sophisticate of the story is reduced by him to a fascinated helplessness. There is no doubt that the Mexican General is intended as a villain, but, perhaps despite his intentions, Bellow celebrates him. There will be many like him, with variations in virtue: Kirby Allbee and (also in *The Victim*) incidental chieftains, the patriarch Schlossberg; the matriarch Mrs. Harkavy; then Augie's Grandma Lausch and his "first superior man," William Einhorn —

and indeed every one of the thirty-odd Machiavellians in his adventures; then Dr. Tamkin; then King Dahfu with his "strong gift of life" and his extra shadow-casting intensity, and Henderson himself. All of them are, if not reincarnations of the General, at least apparently related to him. The descendants inhabit Bellow's shorter pieces as well: plays, stories, monologues, and a curious and festive interview (published in *The Reporter*) with Joe "Yellow Kid" Weil, an aged oligarch among the Chicago confidence men and among the Chicago intellectuals of Bughouse Square, "an elegant and old-fashioned gentleman" of "round phrases and leisurely speech," a reader of Nietzsche and Herbert Spencer, a masterful man who has refused to be society's obedient slave.

The virtue in the exercise of personality for its own sake is clearly a virtue derived from necessity. It is derived as well, seemingly, from the lessons in necessity inherent in one tradition of Yiddish literature, the tradition of what has been called *dos kleine menschele,* the little man of the Eastern European ghetto, the *stetl,* who is forced by the presence of perils everywhere to ingenious ways of personal survival. One of those ways is in mock-heroism. Yiddish conversation itself, a vessel of the spirit that produced *dos kleine menschele,* is, Bellow himself has said,

> full of the grandest historical, mythological, and religious allusions. The Creation, the Fall, the Flood, Egypt, Alexander, Titus, Napoleon, the Rothschilds, the sages, and the Laws may get into the discussion of an egg, a clothesline, or a pair of pants.

The conversation of Augie and his major successors is full of the same, sprouting comparative references to heroes from Jacob to Caesar to John Dillinger to Sir Wilfred Grenfell, to epical events from the Diaspora to the campaigning events of World War II. This manner of living on terms of familiarity with greatness, Bellow goes on to say, contributed to the ghetto's sense of the ridiculous. It also performed a more delicate feat of irony, and one to which Bellow is sensitive. On the one hand, the mock-heroics of the little man render all conventional heroism absurd. Mock-heroism in Bellow's fiction serves that function. But the mock-heroics of Bellow's protagonists and antagonists (both) are far from those of tradition — the tradition of Chaucer and Rabelais and Swift. They are not practised with such broad and easy security. On the other hand, the acts themselves constitute real heroism, a mode of strong self-assertion in a community that disallows the self. Given the prison of restrictive circumstances of the *stetl,* and then those of Bellow's city, it is the only mode by which personal identity can be emphasized. Augie's mythical mouthfuls provide rough fun; they burlesque his own bravado and dilute all pretension. At the same time they call Julius Caesar and John Dillinger to witness. There is courage in the insolence of it. The bravado is a thin mask for the bravery, rather than vice versa. Augie's frisky speech is the power he puts forth to win from all oppressive circumstances a right to exist.

The exercise of personality is everywhere in Bellow's world an act of courage. The salvation of the self, whether by defiance or evasion, is an honored behavior. The self is where felt reality is, and where meaning may be. But the rocks upon which simple exulting personality would founder were discovered at the beginning. Joseph, whose whole struggle was for the means by which the self might be preserved in a time of death, comes upon the disappointing fact of his own baseness and then on the necessity of goodness in community. Alone and allowed to test his dreadful freedom, he becomes irritable, self-indulgent, oversensitive, quarrelsome. Perhaps he has not achieved the highest freedom. Freedom should be the condition of dignity. But, meanwhile, he does not know what to do with the freedom he has. His free self becomes burdensome to him, and he has a continuous lesson in the end of ordinary free self-hood in Vanaker, the lonely, disgusting old man next door, grunting, hacking, thieving, and smelling away his existence. It is when Joseph sees a rat scurrying through some garbage that he resolves to give up his freedom and his self. The self he has held so dear is an "imprisoning self," and the end of his speculation about "ideal constructions" is that the highest of them is that which *unlocks* the imprisoning self. Alienation is not to be made into a doctrine. The other side of freedom is isolation. Alienation is, moreover, morally reprehensible. "What we really want," Joseph discovers, "is to stop living so exclusively and vainly for our own sake, impure and unknowing, turning inward and self-fastened." Joseph's talent is "for being a citizen, or what is today called, most apologetically, a good man," and "goodness," he is forced to know, "is achieved not in a vacuum, but in the company of other men, attended by love."

The notions of inherent baseness, of human nature sharing the bestiality of nature itself, and of love as an imperative lurk everywhere for the personalist hero. At some point in his adventuring each of Bellow's heroes finds the beast within. Asa Leventhal must wrestle with his own inhumanity. Augie, rich in spirit and rowdy as he is, is unable to stay with his purest feelings. He is confronted by the last of his many advisers with a vision of the human soul as composed of secrets, lies, and diseases. Tommy Wilhelm is confronted by Tamkin's notion of a corrupting "pretender soul" turning all human beings into murderers. ("Yes, I think so too," says Tommy. "But personally . . . I don't feel like a murderer. I always try to lay off. It's the others who get me.") Henderson sees himself as a bargain basement of deform-ities, his whole existence proposed in metaphors of beasts. And in one short lyrical instance, in an Easter sermon by one of Bellow's quacky truth-telling rejuvenators, cannibalism is imploded as the law of life. "The Sermon of Dr. Pep" begins in a protest against ham-burger for the bad conscience in its disguise of the slain beast and ends in a protest against the suicide by which a gentle humanity dis-guises its murders. Men must eat, and murder is the cost of civiliza-tion.

But that statement is merely ecstatic. Bellow's major heroes, com-pelled to live beyond the lyrical moment, confront the beast within and the human propensity to murder, and they cannot rest in their perception. They must — each of them — as well confront the moral conditions of civilization, the cost of which would seem to be precisely the self.

Each of the major protanogists is forced, like Augie, to suffer con-fusion between love and an independent fate. Not only that, he must strain to reconcile those impossible opposites. That is what the struggle for accommodation comes to. Joseph strains and fails — or he ends not quite in failure but in a desperate attempt to reacquaint himself with ordinary communal reality. Asa Leventhal, a self-enclosed, self-righteous victim, is assaulted by the imperative of brotherhood, which at the end he cannot accept. But he does reach a large idea of what it is to be exactly human. An old man in the lavatory of a movie theatre tells him that Boris Karloff is a law unto himself. One wouldn't be Boris Karloff. To be neither more nor less than human, Asa dis-covers, is to be "accountable in spite of many weaknesses," and with that discovery he achieves a tentative goodness. Augie, not hurt enough by the fate of other people, particularly fails the severe test of romantic love. The test, his affair with Thea, is most particularly rich in confusion — not only for Augie; Bellow too has groped his way through it. Thea's love is murderous. But it is real love, a way of dis-covering other people. If it is strange to Augie, then, Augie himself comes to admit, that is his own fault. The struggle for Augie is to make it less strange. And Tommy Wilhelm and Henderson, too, struggle to admit love to their freedom, to be themselves and at the same time to have a place in the human community.

Tommy Wilhelm at the last extremity of his need seizes the day and moves toward the consummation of his heart's ultimate need. But it is with *Henderson* that the consummation is first achieved and ren-dered, achieved by a Nietzschean notion of heroic self-transcendence based on freedom, a notion that has been hinted at in all the previous novels.

Despite all circumstances of oppression, despite the violence of nature and the violence of men, despite the cocky, assertive "I," despite all determinisms and despite finitude and death, the individual *is* free and free to choose. He can become better. Joseph felt that by some transcendent means human beings could distinguish themselves from brute things and he considered that the universal quest was for pure freedom, but the practical means to transcendence were not at hand. In *The Victim* the patriarch Schlossberg suggests as equal possibilities that man is "lousy and cheap" and that he has "greatness and beauty." But if those are equal possibilities, then one *can choose*. The means of transcendence are at hand. And what would one choose? "Have dignity, you understand me?" he says. "Choose dignity." But for Asa there are practical difficulties. Augie's Einhorn preaches a similar doctrine of self-transformation, as does Augie himself, in passing. And Tamkin strenuously offers Tommy Wilhelm the possibility of choice. Tommy *can* seize the day and thereby choose life. But not yet nobility. a word much favored by Bellow and meaning the coalescence of self-lessness and selfhood. The individual who would exert his freedom toward such transcendence will need great spiritual capabilities to begin with, and then hard discipline.

Henderson is the man, and, in terms of a succession of meta-morphoses, he gets such discipline.

By Bellow's own inspiration or by astonishing coincidence, Hender-son's career follows with great closeness, with only one initial deviation, that of the spirit in the first parable of *Thus Spake Zarathustra*. Says Zarathustra:

> Of three metamorphoses of the spirit I tell you: how the spirit becomes a camel; and the camel, a lion; and the lion, finally, a child.
> There is much that is difficult for the spirit, the strong reverent spirit that would bear much: but the difficult and the most difficult are what its strength demands.
> What is difficult? asks the spirit that would bear much, and kneels down like a camel wanting to be well loaded. What is most difficult, O heroes, asks the spirit that would bear much, that I may take it upon myself and exult in my strength? Is it not humbling oneself to wound one's haughtiness? Letting one's folly shine to mock one's wisdom?
> Or is it this: feeding on the acorns and grass of knowledge and, for the sake of the truth, suffering hunger in one's soul?
> Or is it this: stepping into filthy waters when they are the waters of truth, and not repulsing cold frogs and hot toads?
> Or is it this: loving those who despise us and offering a hand to the ghost that would frighten us?
>
> [*Walter Kaufmann translation*]

Henderson is not a camel — he is a Connecticut millionaire, not a Bedouin, and so without that opportunity — but he is a strenuous spirit who would bear much and who demands the extremest test of his strength. He engages the Zarathustrian burdens of humility and folly. If he does not feed on acorns and grass, he raises and identifies with pigs that do, and he suffers hunger in his soul. He does precisely, among the first of his African tribes, meet the test of frogs in the filthy waters, but without humility, and it is to his sorrow that he repulses them. And he strains to love those who despise and reject him.

Says Zarathustra:

> All these most difficult things the spirit that would bear much takes upon itself: like the camel that, burdened, speeds into the desert, thus the spirit speeds into its desert.
>
> In the loneliest desert, however, the second metamorphosis occurs: here the spirit becomes a lion who would conquer his freedom and be master in his own desert. Here he seeks out his last master: he wants to fight him and his last god; for ultimate victory he wants to fight with the great dragon.
>
> Who is the great dragon whom the spirit will no longer call lord and god? "Thou shalt" is the name of the great dragon. But the spirit of the lion says, "I will." "Thou shalt" lies in his way, sparkling like gold, an animal covered with scales; and on every scale shines a golden "thou shalt."

> My brothers, why is there a need in the spirit for the lion? Why is not the beast of burden, which renounces and is reverent, enough?
>
> To create new values — that even the lion cannot do; but the creation of freedom for oneself for new creation — that is within the power of the lion. The creation of freedom for oneself and a sacred "No" even to duty — for that, my brothers, the lion is needed. To assume the right to new values — that is the most terrifying assumption for a reverent spirit that would bear much. Verily, to him it is preying, and a matter for a beast of prey. He once loved "thou shalt" as most sacred: now he must find illusion and caprice even in the most sacred, that freedom from his love may become his prey: the lion is needed for such prey.

Henderson speeds from the meek, reverent, cow-worshipping Arnewi into the desert. There he destroys himself, body and soul, in order to become a lion, and in the very process he learns something about the possibilities of self-transformation. He learns, moreover, what it is to contain one's freedom. The lion, Dahfu tells him, is pure Being. It is entirely itself, it is all unobliging will, and, heavy with the clutter of existence, on all sides oppressed, Henderson secures from it a way of confronting the oppressing, death-dealing universe. The lion is for Henderson, and Dahfu, the intensity of the self beyond all reverence, the avatar of freedom, and Henderson, as lion, looks forward to new creation.

Says Zarathustra:

But say, my brothers, what can the child do that even the lion could not do? Why must the preying lion still become a child? The child is innocence and forgetting, a new beginning, a game, a self-propelled wheel, a first movement, a sacred "Yes." For the game of creation, my brothers, a sacred "Yes" is needed: the spirit now wills his own will, and he who had been lost to the world now conquers his own world.

Of three metamorphoses of the spirit I have told you: how the spirit became a camel; and the camel, a lion; and the lion, finally, a child.

The last of Henderson's tutelary spirits is the child he adopts on his plane back to America. The airplane makes a fueling stop and he runs with the child in his arms around the airport in Newfoundland. What, specifically, Henderson has newly found is his way back, after he had been lost to the world, to his ordinary life, but he comes back now in a new movement with a new will to creation: "I guess I felt it was my turn now to move, and so went running — leaping, leaping, pounding, and tingling over the pure white lining of the gray Arctic silence." A self-propelled wheel. And he is provided with a sacred "Yes." He has always had a "service ideal." It had been crushed, but now it has been newly invented, he will enter medical school, and his suicidal violence has been transformed to love.

Thus spake Zarathustra, and it is perhaps of note that Zarathustra at that time sojourned in the town that is called The Motley Cow.

That is not to suggest anything programmatic about *Henderson*. The novel is not a manual for living. If the Nietzschean parable is at the center of it, the parable is elaborated, indeed sportively elaborated. It is a funny book and it goes off all sorts of ways. Nor is it to suggest that *Henderson* is the summit of a mountain of thought up which Bellow has been scrabbling the years thus far of his novelist's career. Bellow, too, has been disorderly and boisterous, full of strong assertions and apothegms which have the finality only of the fullest fiction, which crack on the next turn of events and mood.

And there will be more events.

But the novels have, all this while, been going somewhere — not, of course, toward any summit at all, nor toward any solution to anything. Bellow's domain for investigation is nothing less than the bases of all moral behavior, wherein one expects no solutions except by fiat or by sermon. Fiction is only the jittery act of reaching. When the goal is sufficient, as in Bellow's fiction it is, and when in spite of jitters the reach is serious and long and one can see that it is reaching, fiction becomes crucial. As in Bellow's case it has.

☙ OLIVER EVANS

Paul Bowles and the "Natural" Man

I

THERE is a handful of living American novelists who have established enviable reputations on the strength of a very few books. There is Katherine Anne Porter; there is J. D. Salinger; there is, perhaps most importantly of all, Carson McCullers, whose first novel, *The Heart Is a Lonely Hunter,* written when the author was twenty-two, is a work of astonishing maturity — wise, compassionate, and irreproachably executed. Such writers seem, like Minerva, to have sprung full-blown from the forehead of Jupiter, by-passing the developmental stages of talents more laboriously formed.

Paul Bowles is such a novelist. *The Sheltering Sky,* published in 1949, was an impressive performance; it was followed by a collection of short stories, *The Delicate Prey* (1950), and two more novels, *Let It Come Down* (1952) and *The Spider's House* (1955). This is his complete production to date, yet it has been sufficient to place him in the very first rank of American prose artists: playwright Tennessee Williams even goes so far as to place him above Hemingway and Faulkner. However one may cavil at such a pronouncement, it is difficult to deny that the four works, taken as a whole, constitute a consistent and thoughtful statement about life: they present, in Conrad's phrase, a particular "vision of life" — always the mark of a first-rate artist.

It was apparent as early as 1945, to readers of magazines like *Partisan Review* and the now defunct *Horizon,* that a remarkable new talent had emerged — a talent which, one would have been informed if he had taken the pains to glance at the "Notes on Contributors," was as much at home in musical as in literary composition. One expected and hoped to hear more from the author of such stories as "Under the Sky" and "Pages from Cold Point." That expectation and that hope have been justified: Mr. Bowles has come a long way, both as composer and author, since 1945. Serious talent deserves serious criticism, and

Reprinted from *Critique,* III, No. 1 (Spring–Fall, 1959), 43–59, by permission of the author and the editors. Copyright © 1959 by *Critique.*

it is time that we evaluate his literary accomplishment (since that is what concerns us here) to date.

II

Bowles is an obsessionist, and his obsession may be simply stated: that psychological well-being is in inverse ratio to what is commonly known as progress, and that a highly evolved culture enjoys less peace of mind than one which is less highly evolved. This is of course a romantic attitude, going back at least as far as Rousseau by way (in English literature) of Samuel Butler, D. H. Lawrence, and E. M. Forster. Lawrence is probably Bowles's strongest single influence, and it seems curious that none of the newspaper reviewers have noted this connection: Faulkner and McCullers, with much less justification, are usually pointed to, and such unlikely and dissimilar antecedents as Henry James, Frederic Prokosch, Jean Genêt, and even Elinor Glyn have all been suggested.

It is no accident that the three novels and that fifteen of the seventeen stories in *The Delicate Prey* have a foreign setting. Nor is it true, as has sometimes been charged, that Bowles is merely indulging in a pointless exoticism, for not only are the settings foreign, they are usually primitive as well. For this reason he chooses such remote locales as a small town in the Sahara, a Colombian jungle, a river boat winding painfully through the interior of an unidentified Latin-American country. And in nearly all of his work the tension arises from a contrast between alien cultures: in a typical Bowles story, a civilized individual comes in contact with an alien environment and is defeated by it. The United States is not without primitives of its own, and Bowles could perhaps have achieved something of the same effect by going to the mountains of East Tennessee or the sheep ranches of Montana — or, for that matter, by doing a little social work in his native Manhattan. The contrast, however, would not have been so great: it is important for his purpose that the language, beliefs, and psychology of his natives be as different as possible from those of his travelers, the victims of modern civilization.

There is still another reason for Bowles's choice of remote locales. Deserts and jungles are places in which people can easily get lost, and Bowles believes that modern man, if not already lost in a spiritual and moral sense, is in serious danger of becoming so. It is symbolically fitting that his civilized traveler should suffer defeat at the hands of a nature, or of a "natural" (*i. e.* primitive) society which he has insisted upon "improving." In *The Sheltering Sky*, one is tempted to equate the Sahara with Dante's *selva selvaggia* and with Eliot's Waste Land. There is, indeed, a certain correspondence, but the difference

— and an important one — is that in Dante's poem there is no connection between the symbolic forest, which has only a malevolent aspect, and a natural one; and Eliot's Waste Land has only a negative relation to nature. Bowles's desert on the other hand, is neutral — malevolent only insofar as it is prepared to destroy those who are out of tune with nature itself, of which it is the real as well as the merely formal symbol. There is nearly always a symbolic level present in Bowles's work, and he has suffered considerable injustice at the hands of popular reviewers who have insisted upon reading him at a single level.

III

The action of Bowles's first novel, *The Sheltering Sky,* is relatively simple. The protagonists, Port and Kit Moresby, are members of New York's intelligentsia, and they have come to North Africa accompanied by a friend, or rather a hanger-on, named Tunner, a young man whose intellectual endowments, while inferior to those of the Moresbys, are in some degree compensated for by his good looks: he is handsome, we are told, in a "late Paramount way." There is tension in Port's relationship with his wife, and it is partly in the hope of redefining this relationship that the two of them have come to Africa. They are out of tune with each other, the result, Port suspects, of being out of tune with their metropolitan environment, which never really satisfied either of them. In the Sahara, he feels, they have a chance of rediscovering their love, and themselves in the process.

Port and Kit have fallen out of love, but they have preserved their respect for each other. In rebellion against this state of affairs, Kit allows herself to be loved briefly by Tunner, for whom she has no respect, and Port has an occasional commercial contact with native women. At Aïn Krorfa, a remote village in the Sahara, the Moresbys part with Tunner, who plans to rejoin them in a few days. They proceed deeper into the desert, where Port contracts typhoid and dies.

Kit joins a caravan of merchants whose two leaders rape her and share her as their mistress until they reach their destination, where the younger of the two installs her in his harem. She succeeds at last in escaping, but the strain has been too much for her and she breaks down mentally. In the meantime, at Tunner's instigation, a search for her has been organized. French authorities finally locate her and return her to Oran, where she is met by an official from whom she breaks away and disappears once more, mindless, into the Casbah.

That, on a literal level, is all there is to the story, but this is not the level with which Mr. Bowles is primarily concerned. Port and Kit have been carefully chosen for their role, the role of the doomed and civilized traveler. The highly evolved representatives of a modern urban society, it is significant, to begin with, that they are unhappy at home. Intuition tells them that their chances for happiness lie in a less complex environment and they come to the Sahara — he with his maps, for which (like the Professor in "A Distant Episode") he has a passion, she with her Mark Cross fitted case and her cosmetics. But Port's maps only lead him to his death, and Kit's case is stolen from her in the desert. He suffers physical destruction; she, mental.

Tunner is a more important character than he at first appears. Less intelligent than the Moresbys, he is also closer to Bowles's type of "natural" man (who, incidentally, is frequently handsome, which is of course symbolically appropriate). The desert does not destroy him as it does the other two. Subtlety not being his strong point, he possesses instead a healthy egotism: he is unaware of the real reason for Kit's yielding to his advances, and it never occurs to him that in retrospect she should find the experience distasteful. She, for her part, can neither love a man she cannot respect nor, as it happens, love the man she does respect — a dilemma peculiar, perhaps, to a civilized individual. Port's is a similar predicament; his encounters with the native women are ill-fated, and of the three only Tunner is untroubled where such matters are concerned. Tunner is also untroubled by any feeling of guilt at having seduced his friend's wife, but Kit's conscience does not let her off so lightly.

Kit stands midway between Port, who is completely civilized, and Tunner, who is half animal. We are told in so many words that she is torn by "the war between reason and atavism." She has a profound regard for omens, and a large part of her consciousness is devoted to the classification and interpretation of them; nevertheless, "in intellectual discussions she was always the proponent of scientific method." One somehow feels that the fault for their estrangement lies with Port, who is entirely a rational being (he understands his wife so well that he can even predict the effect certain omens will produce upon her), and it is part of the peculiar justice of the situation that Port's destruction comes first and is the more complete and final.

There is a strongly sensual side to Kit's character which Tunner, who is only half a primitive, touches but fails to release when he makes love to her. The real primitive in the story, of course, is Belqassim, the young Arab who imprisons her in his harem. Belqassim is everything that Port is not, and this relationship is more satisfactory than the one she has had with Tunner because it is not complicated by the element of respect, which (so different are she and Belqassim culturally) simply does not enter into the picture — or perhaps it would be more accurate to say that she respects him because he *is* so very different from all the men she has ever known, like a being from another planet.

Paradoxical though it may appear, Kit's series of amorous adventures with Belqassim and other natives in the latter part of the book offers her an opportunity of spiritual salvation: intuitively she realizes this, which is why she accepts these adventures with a willingness which would otherwise appear rather motiveless, since obviously she is not a nymphomaniacal type. The love of a civilized man had never been able to satisfy her (Bowles's implication is that civilized man has lost the art of making love); perhaps another kind of love can. And it does satisfy, at the same time that it destroys her. Kit's tragedy is that her experience has unfitted her for a primitive type of love, for love on a "natural" plane; her civilized background revolts, and she explodes mentally. Looked at in this light, Book III is far from being merely erotic exercise: the protagonist (and there is no question but what Kit and not Port is the main character) is undergoing an ordeal by fire, as it were, and the ordeal, painful though it is, is very much worth watching. The book is in effect a moral tragedy, presented in terms of allegory — and it is tragedy rather than pathos, for Kit does put up a struggle. Nor is the tragedy merely personal: the allegory includes all of civilized humanity, incapable of leading a purely rational existence (Port's way, the way of death) or of returning atavistically to a merely intuitive way of life, as Kit does with such heart-rending consequences.

IV

It was his second book, a collection of short stories entitled *The Delicate Prey,* that gained for Mr. Bowles the reputation of being a specialist in horror, a "pornographer of terror, a secret lover of the horror he evokes," as Leslie Fiedler put it in *Kenyon Review* (Winter, 1951, p. 170). "The whole impact of his work is his insistence on the horrible," wrote Mr. Fiedler, who went on, incredibly enough, to place Bowles in the tradition of science fiction.

There is no denying it: the stories, many of them, *are* terrible, and their horror is intensified by the manner in which they are written: they are told quietly, gently, almost tenderly, in a style as pure and as polished as any in modern English. But granting the horror, it is reasonable to inquire whether the stories are *merely* horrible — that is, whether the horror may not be essential to these intentions; and, finally, whether some beauty may not exist even in the midst of the horror.

Even in this collection, Bowles does not usually indulge in horror for its own sake; it is nearly always related, as a careful reading of the stories proves, to his central obsession — an effect through which he strives to dramatize a thesis. They are most of them highly moral tales in the sense that *The Sheltering Sky* is moral — and in the sense that Faulkner's "A Rose for Emily" is not. A few examples will show what I mean. In "A Distant Episode," an American (or European) pedant, a professor of languages, is captured by a tribe of desert bandits who cut out his tongue and retain him as a kind of performing clown: he is dressed in a suit of tin cans, made to dance, grimace and turn handsprings, and is kept in a cage like an animal. The professor reminds us at once of Port, in *The Sheltering Sky*: "He came down out of the high, flat region in the evening by bus, with two small overnight bags full of maps, sun lotions and medicines." Prim and overcivilized, he is an ideal candidate for defeat and degradation at the hands of a primitive people, and there is terrible irony in the circumstance of a linguist's losing his tongue. One reason the story seems so horrible is that the reader is not made to feel that the author sympathizes with the professor: this, however, is purely a matter of implication, not of statement nor even overt suggestion, for Mr. Bowles realizes that for his story to be effective dramatically it has to be told with the utmost objectivity. The skill with which he creates in the first few pages an atmosphere of danger and impending disasaster is remarkable, and reminds one of the beginning of *Benito Cereno*.

In another story, "Under the Sky," a Mexican peon watches the arrival at a railway station of three tourists, two women and a man: "Each one carried a leather bag covered with small squares of colored paper stuck on at different angles." Several hours later, when he has been smoking marijuana, he meets one of the women in the park and rapes her. The scene reminds us of Kit's violation in the desert: this woman exhibits a similar type of nervelessness ("Mechanically she allowed him to push her along") and her bag, like Kit's, is a pathetic symbol of the civilization which has produced her. She is another civilized traveler, doomed for disaster. The drug is introduced into the story to make it seem more credible: it is one of the few occasions where Bowles permits the realistic level to profit, perhaps, at the expense of the symbolic.

In "Pastor Dowe at Tacaté," defeat occurs without violence. In this story, a Christian missionary in a remote Latin-American outpost discovers the futility of his labors: the only way he can ensure a congregation is to entice the natives with gifts of salt and to intersperse his sermons with pieces like "Sonny Boy" and "Crazy Rhythm" played on his portable phonograph. To these they listen happily: "In this way 'Crazy Rhythm' became an integral part of Pastor Dowe's weekly service. After a few months the old record was so badly worn that he determined to play it only once at each gathering. His flock submitted to this show of economy with bad grace."

The natives are satisfied with their own deities, a beneficent one named Hachakyum, and a malevolent one named Metzabok. In an important scene near the beginning of the story, the missionary, prompted by curiosity, quizzes one of his congregation, a man named Nicolás, about these gods. Did Hachakyum, he inquires, make the world and everything in it? "No," replies Nicolás, "Hachakyum did not make everyone. He did not make you. He did not make guns or Don Jesucristo." Pastor Downe then asks, "Who made me?" and Nicolás replies, "Metzabok." It is the first time the missionary has ever heard the name. "Who is Metzabok?" he wants to know, and Nicolás answers: "Metzabok makes all things that do not belong here." Finally Pastor Dowe admits defeat, and decides to leave: "Locking his door, he proceeded to pack what personal effects he could into his smallest suitcase. His Bible and notebooks went on top with his toothbrush and atabrine tablets." The missionary is prim, squeamish, androgynous — another ideal victim for the natural man, who is here symbolized by Nicolás.

Three of the remaining stories in the collection — "Call at Corazón" (in which the honeymooning couple bear a striking resemblance to Port and Kit; as in *The Sheltering Sky,* the conflict between them is mirrored in the contrast between them and the primitive surroundings), "At Paso Rojo," and "The Echo" — are all related in some way to Bowles's dominant theme. To my mind, the least successful stories are those in which the horror does constitute an end in itself, like the title story and "Pages from Cold Point," which last, a study of homosexual incest, is a brilliant *tour de force* written in Bowles's very best manner but without any apparent root in the author's fundamental convictions: in this respect, as also in the cumulative horror of its situation and its technical perfection, it reminds us of *The Turn of the Screw.* The most pessimistic story in the book is "The Fourth Day Out from Santa Cruz," a fable with a terrible message: that it is cruelty which holds men together; it is the leveling influence, the lowest common denominator of human behavior. The story is remarkable for its delicate balancing of narrative and allegory: on both levels it is completely coherent.

v

At a first reading, Mr. Bowles's second novel, *Let It Come Down,* seems to bear only a superficial resemblance to his earlier work: the setting is still North Africa, and the protagonist is a young man just arrived from New York, but the scene of the story is Tangier, not New York, and the young man, though he bears the stamp of civilization, is no intellectual; he is, on the contrary, almost astonishingly naïve. It is true that he suffers defeat, and that it is an alien environment which defeats him, but the environment here is not a primitive one, and it is not immediately apparent how this novel is related to Mr. Bowles's theory of the superiority of the "natural" man.

The action, reduced to its simplest outline, is as follows: the young man, Dyar, leaves his job as bank teller in New York and comes to Tangier, where he has been offered a job in a tourist agency run by a man named Wilcox, whom he has known only casually. It soon develops that the agency is a blind for illegal dealings in international exchange. Little by little Dyar becomes infected by the amorality of his surroundings: he comes to serve as an agent for the Soviet government; he absconds, with the help of a young Arab named Thami, with a large sum of money which his employer has given him to exchange; finally, in a hashish delirium, he murders Thami by driving a nail into his ear as the latter lies asleep in a mountain hut to which they have retreated. There is also considerable minor complication (on a narrative level the story is more interesting than *The Sheltering Sky*) and a whole gallery of lesser characters, many of whom, like the alcoholic lesbian, Eunice Goode, are extraordinarily convincing.

Of all the characters in Bowles's fiction Dyar is the most anonymous — at the beginning, that is. His background, humdrum and effete, has made of him a completely passive individual; he is entirely without engagement, in the French sense of the word, and therefore without identity. He is a man to whom nothing has happened. All he knows is that he exists:

> Lately he had been wont to sit quietly alone in his room saying to himself that he was here. The fact kept repeating itself to him: "Here I am." There was nothing to be deduced from it; the saying of it seemed to be connected with a feeling of anaesthesia somewhere within him. He was not moved by the phenomenon; even to himself he felt supremely anonymous, and it is difficult to care very much what is happening inside a person one does not know.

Dyar does not know himself, for he has never been confronted with a real choice; his life hitherto has been one of unquestioning acceptance.

Dyar's emptiness is not merely personal; it is, the author believes, a condition common to civilized humanity, of which he is the symbol. This is implied in a conversation between Dyar and the Marquesa de Valverde:

> "You're not really alive, in some strange way. You're dead."
> "Why dead?" His deep voice was even; she imagined its inflection was hostile.
> "Oh, not dead!" she said impatiently. "Just not alive. Not really. But we're all like that, these days, I suppose. Not quite so blatantly as you, perhaps, but still . . ."
> "Ah." He was thinking: "I've got to get out of here. I've got to get going."

"We're all monsters," said Daisy with enthusiasm. "It's the Age of Monsters."

It is significant that Book III, in which this dialogue occurs, is entitled "The Age of Monsters."

In Tangier, Dyar observes, there are only winners and losers:

> If one was not a winner one was a victim, and there seemed no way to change that. No pretense was of any avail. It was not a question of looking or acting like a winner — that could be managed, although no one was taken in by it — it was a matter of conviction, of feeling like one, of knowing you belonged to the caste, of recognizing and being sure of your genius.

At this point he makes his second choice: he will be a winner, and it is this determination which involves him in treason, larceny, and, finally, in murder. He is determined to have an identity, even if it is a criminal identity.

But Dyar's attempt to establish a genuine identity miscarries. The author has deliberately diluted the morality, or rather the immorality, of Dyar's choice: thus, he does not actually supply any information to the Russians, though he agrees to; and the money with which he absconds has been entrusted to him for illegal purposes. Even the murder which he finally commits under the influence of hashish is not the result of a choice: it is an accident, and this is the final irony of the story.

It is easy to recognize the influence of French existentialism in this insistence upon the necessity for engagement, upon the importance of choice, and upon the authority of the individual in deciding ethical matters for himself; and indeed *Let It Come Down* is, ideologically considered, a singular fusion of existentialist doctrine and Bowles's particular variety of neo-romanticism. Dyar is a bona fide (though atypical) traveler, and, as such, a born "loser." He fits uneasily into the world of winners — Wilcox, the Marquesa de Valverde, even the grotesque Eunice Goode — to which he is introduced in Tangier. These are all bold, primitive types — people of action, however dubious, and I think it is reasonable to infer that they represent the type of natural man which is Dyar's opposite. It is through them, after all, that he suffers defeat, since it is at Wilcox's invitation that he has come to Tangier, and Miss Goode deliberately sets in motion the machinery which is to involve him in espionage.

Robert Gorham Davis observed in the New York *Times* that *Let It Come Down* belongs to a "well-defined literary tradition with deep psychological roots," but added: "If we try to make it mean more than that, if we take it as a serious social or philosophical novel, then it seems malign and corrupting." Philosophically viewed, however, *Let It Come Down* is not corrupting so much as it is inconclusive. The extent to which Bowles's belief in the superiority of natural man can be reconciled to existentialist doctrine is debatable: there are points of similarity, but there are also points of difference; and there are times when it is difficult to decide out of which conviction the author is writing. There is lacking here the singleness of moral purpose which distinguished the earlier book. By way of compensation, *Let It Come Down* is a more engrossing novel on a purely narrative level; and the North African background is presented with a greater realism and in more detail — one of the results, perhaps, of Mr. Bowles's increasing interest and immersion in it.

VI

The Spider's House, Mr. Bowles's latest novel, is his most overt statement of the theme which has always obsessed him. Its main characters are Amar, a youth of Fez; Stenham, an American writer who has lived in Morocco for a number of years; and Lee Veyron, a pretty young divorcée, also American, who is touring North Africa.

Amar, the hero of the story, is a real noble savage. Although he can neither read nor write, he possesses *baraka,* the gift of healing (both his father and his grandfather had been well-known healers), and is wise beyond his years, which are a mere fifteen: what he lacks in knowledge, we are told, is more than made up for by intuition. He is a strict Moslem, and the principles of the *Koran* have been thoroughly instilled in him by his father.

Stenham is an intellectual, a disappointed idealist whose background is as different from Amar's as can possibly be imagined; he is the son of New England parents of "advanced" beliefs: "Religion in his family had been an unmentionable subject, on a par with sexuality." For a year he was a member of the Communist Party, and his resulting disillusionment was such that he came to reject the concept of human equality altogether: "There could be no equality in human life," he decides, "because the human heart demanded hierarchies." This position, however, led him into a position of meaningless subjectivity "which refused existence to any reality or law but its own." He is at this point when the book opens:

He had begun to be preoccupied by an indefinable anxiety which he described to himself as a desire to be "saved." But from what? One hot day when he was taking a long walk over the hills behind Fez, he had been forced to admit to himself with amazement and horror that there was no better expression for what he feared than the very old one: eternal damnation.

Mrs. Veyron's charm is mainly physical. A believer in progress, conceived of in technological terms, she is a thoroughgoing materialist, repelled by the squalor but intrigued by the color of modern Morocco, naïvely unaware that the one could not exist without the other. She is, in short, a symbol of almost everything that Mr. Bowles detests, just as Amar symbolizes everything he admires. Knowing this, the reader might well expect to find the cards stacked against her, but a surprise is in store for him — Mr. Bowles does not do things quite so simply.

Considering the length of the book (and it is probably overlong for what it has to say), the action is extremely simple: it is primarily a novel of ideas. Stenham meets Mrs. Veyron, to whom he finds himself attracted physically although her views are anathema to him; then he meets Amar, whose simple philosophy intrigues and fascinates him. What the situation really amounts to, though it is never squarely presented as such, is that the sophisticated but superficial American woman and the primitive but profound native youth are rivals for Stenham's love. (The Arabic name *Amar* is also the infinitive form of the Spanish word for *love*.) The three of them take a trip to a mountain village where a religious festival is in progress; here Lee and Stenham have one of their fiercest quarrels, which they settle by falling into each other's arms. The story ends with their driving off together, while Amar runs after their car in his bare feet. It is a story of betrayal: the corruption of Stenham, we are made to feel, is now perfect and complete, a *fait accompli;* he has made his choice, and his "desire to be saved" will never know fulfilment.

The native uprisings in Morocco provide a dramatic background for this essentially simple narrative, and the rather complicated political issues at stake there give Mr. Bowles an excellent opportunity for defining his characters, as well as for airing his own views (which he presents as those of Stenham) on the subject. Stenham despises the French, but he despises even more the fomenters of the revolution — the local nationalist party, Istiqlal, a Communist-inspired group of terrorists whose aim is to make of Morocco a completely modern state, thereby destroying all its charm and color, the simple integrity of its people, and even the very religion in whose name it has ostensibly taken up arms. A political situation such as this is, of course, grist for Mr. Bowles's philosophical mill.

Of the three characters, Amar's emerges with the greatest clearness, though one feels that he has been oversimplified. Mr. Bowles is careful to stress the fact that he has never been to school. "In the school," Amar's father tells him, "they teach you what the world means, and once you have learned, you will always know." But Amar thinks: "Suppose the world changes? Then what would you know?" Elsewhere Amar reflects that "many of his friends had decided what the world looked like, what life was like, and they would never examine either of them again to find out whether they were right or wrong. This was because they had gone or were still going to school." And when he meets those same friends a little later on in life, we are told that "it seemed to him that they had grown to be like old men, and he did not enjoy being with them." (This, of course, is purest Transcendentalism — one is reminded immediately of Wordsworth's "Expostulation and Reply," of Thoreau, and, especially, of Whitman's "Song of Myself"; "No shutter'd room or school can commune with me, / But roughs and little children better than they.")

Amar feels much as Stenham does about the political situation, though of course he does not see in himself, as Stenham does, a symbol of that moral and religious integrity which the Istiqlal, even more than the French, seem determined to destroy. Lee, on the other hand, sides with the nationalists, and her conversations with Stenham on this matter constitute the polemical core of the novel. Stenham, as has been said, is Bowles's mouthpiece:

"When I first came here," he tells Lee shortly after their first meeting, "it was a pure country. There was music and dancing and magic every day in the streets. Now it's finished, everything. Even the religion. In a few years the whole country will be like all the other Moslem countries, just a huge European slum, full of poverty and hatred." She replies: "I think that's the point of view of an outsider, a tourist who puts picturesqueness before everything else. I'm sure if you had to live down there in one of those houses you wouldn't feel the same way at all. You'd welcome the hospitals and electric lights and buses the French have brought." This, Stenham decides, "was certainly the remark of a tourist, and an ignorant tourist, too. . . . He was sorry that it should have come from her."

Toward the end of the novel, Amar observes to Stenham that Lee is unhappy: "She's always going to be unhappy in her head, that lady." Stenham asks him, "Why? Do you know why?" and Amar replies confidently, "It's because she doesn't know anything about the world." Stenham is impressed: "He had been struck again and again by the boy's unerring judgment in separating primary factors from secondary ones."

Nevertheless, and not many pages later, Stenham (who, to do him justice, is not aware of the importance he has assumed in Amar's life) abandons him in favor of the fool's gold which Lee has to offer. The seduction, to be sure, is physical rather than intellectual, but the reader is somehow made to feel that Stenham has chosen between two distinct ways of life, and that he has chosen unwisely. And while it might appear on the surface that the outcome of *The Spider's House* reverses the typical Bowles formula in that here it is the native and not the traveler who is defeated, Stenham is the real loser: however deeply Amar may have been hurt, his virtue renders him impregnable.

The Spider's House is a frankly didactic novel, an unfavorable comparison of the materialism of the West (which Bowles somehow connects with official Christianity) to the spiritual idealism of the Mohammedan East. (The title is a quotation from the *Koran*: "The likeness of those who choose other patrons than Allah is as the likeness of the spider when she taketh unto herself a house, and lo! the frailest of all houses is the spider's house, if they but knew.") It is the sort of novel which one likes to the extent that he may happen to share the author's views: there is not much else in the book, really, since the symbolism is scarce and rather obvious and the style is dryer than in either of the earlier novels. It is in one respect rather remarkable: so far as I know, no one writing in English his hitherto explored the Arab mind quite so deeply nor so sympathetically in fiction.

VII

By now it should be apparent how Bowles's belief in the superiority of "natural" man, with its corollary that as societies evolve technologically their members become more neurotic and unhappy, underlies almost everything he has written to date: it is the mainspring of his philosophy, the subsisting obsession which furnishes him with the inspiration for his books — just as his travels and his many years of residence abroad furnish him with the material for them.

The conviction is a completely conscious one, nor is Mr. Bowles unaware of its dangers. In *The Sheltering Sky* he writes of Port:

> For years it had been one of his superstitions that reality and true perception were to be found in the conversation of the laboring classes. Even though he now saw clearly that their formulas of thought and speech are as strict and as patterned, and thus as far removed from any profound expression of truth as those of any other class, often he found himself still in the act of waiting, with the unreasonable belief that gems of wisdom might yet issue from their mouths.

It is difficult not to believe that Mr. Bowles is here voicing a doubt by which he himself must often have been assailed: there is, indeed, a temptation to identify Port with the author throughout.

It will be seen how Bowles's favorite formula, the defeat and degradation (whether moral or physical or both) of a civilized traveler in a primitive society, serves his didactic purpose. The author's typical traveler is seldom unsympathetic to this society — even the insensitive Tunner, watching the natives in Bou Noura, is impressed by their air of dignity and quiet contentment:

But there were other days when he felt less nervous, sat watching the old men walk slowly through the market, and said to himself that if he could muster that much dignity when he got to be their age he would consider that his life had been well spent. For their mien was merely a natural concomitant of inner well-being and satisfaction. Without thinking too much about it, eventually he came to the conclusion that their lives must have been worth living.

Indeed, it is precisely those characters who have some understanding of, and sympathy with, the alien environment who are defeated most crushingly by it: witness the professor in "A Distant Episode." By this irony I take it that the author means the differences which separate the two worlds are absolute and irreconcilable, and it is certainly true that as an artist Bowles has been much more concerned with the differences which separate men than with the similarities which bind them together.

In his latest novel, as I have indicated, Mr. Bowles emerges as a champion for religious orthodoxy, albeit of an exotic variety. One cannot help wondering, since the novel is concerned with salvation, if its author would concede the possibility of salvation outside the orbit of a particular dogma: *The Spider's House* does not answer this question, though it certainly poses it by implication. It is not surprising to encounter an anti-Christian bias in Bowles — the reader will remember "Pastor Dowe at Tacaté" — but there is an important difference, for in that story Bowles is writing as a sociologist concerned with the relativity of all religions to the particular needs which they serve rather than as the champion of any specific creed: Metzabok and Hachakyum are no better and no worse than the Christian deity; they are just different, like the people who worship them. It is possible that Mr. Bowles has not yet resolved this problem in his own mind, and that we may expect a more definitive attitude from him in his future work. The theme with which he has always been concerned will not bear infinite repetition — the occasional flatness of *The Spider's House* was proof of that — and it is quite conceivable that the author's didacticism will henceforth take an exclusively religious turn. But whatever it is of which Bowles writes, his is always an interesting mind, and he is the possessor of a talent which is very unique in modern English.

❧ PAUL LEVINE

Truman Capote: The Revelation of the Broken Image

THE inclusion of Truman Capote in any discussion that pretends to be at most scholarly and at least literary is usually frowned upon by the more stern-faced of our critics. The mention of his name conjures up images of a wispish, effete soul languishing on an ornate couch, emitting an ether of preciousness and very little else. The reaction to the amazing success of his early books, *Other Voices, Other Rooms* and *A Tree of Night*, has relegated Capote to the position of a clever, cute, coy, commercial, and definitely minor figure in contemporary literature, whose reputation has been built less on a facility of style than on an excellent advertising campaign. Even an earnest supporter would have to admit that Capote's stories tiptoe the tenuous line between the precious and the serious.

Yet the attacks on Capote seem more personal than literary. Critics like John Aldridge — whose essay appears in *After the Lost Generation,* a book that generally has little good to say about anyone (except Mr. Aldridge) — have blatantly confused the author's private life with his literary ability. The notion — as fantastic as any of Capote's stories — that Capote's style comes too easily is an excellent example. Not only is the banner of the tortured writer rather tattered by now but in Capote's case the charge of a "natural style" is false. His first stories — "These Walls Are Cold" and "The Shape of Things" — are written in the painfully realistic prose associated with those young writers in transition from the *Saturday Evening Post* to the *New Yorker*. Moreover, Capote is really no more precocious than a number of our outstanding writers. J. D. Salinger published his first story at twenty-one and Carson McCullers had written two novels before she was twenty-four. As with the legend surrounding Fitzgerald, critics have a difficult time discerning Capote from his work, a slight not only to the author but to the critic. Mr. Capote is no more an *enfant terrible* than Mr. Aldridge is.

Perhaps the most frequent criticism leveled at Capote's work is

Reprinted from the *Virginia Quarterly Review,* XXXIV (Autumn, 1958), 600–617, by permission of the author and the editors.

that he is limited in scope and remote from life. While it is true that Capote writes fantastic and grotesque stories, it is not necessarily true that these stories, because of their genre, must be remote from life. In many ways, Capote has chosen the most universal medium in which to present his thematic material, because the genre of the fantasy, evolving from the day dream, the fairy tale, and the tall tale, is among the oldest and most elemental of fictional forms.

While we must acknowledge Capote's admission that "style is the mirror of an artist's sensibility — more so than the *content* of his work," we must also recognize that there is no dearth of content in his work. To understand that content fully we must first posit some very elemental points, because Capote is to a great extent an erudite writer about primal things. At the heart of his writing is the dichotomy in the world between good and evil, the daylight and the nocturnal, man and nature, and between the internal and external manifestation of things. As Harry Levin has pointed out in a different context:

> This takes us back to the very beginning of things, the primal darkness, the void that God shaped by creating light and dividing night from day. That division underlies the imagery of the Bible from Genesis to the Apocalypse, and from the word of life to the shadow of death. It is what differentiates the children of light from the children of darkness in the Dead Sea Scrolls.
> . . . But all religions, in accounting for the relation of the earth to the sun and for the diurnal and seasonal cycles, seem to posit some dichotomy, such as the Yin and the Yang of the Orient or the twin paths of the Bhagavad-Gita.

The dichotomy of good and evil exists in each Capote character just as the dichotomy of daylight and nighttime exists in the aggregate of his stories. We might almost say that Capote's stories inhabit two worlds — that of the realistic, colloquial, often humorous daytime and that of the dreamlike, detached, and inverted nocturnal world. This double identity must be viewed with a double vision because Capote's stories can be interpreted either psychologically or as an expression of a spiritual or moral problem. In either case, whether the story be realistic or fantastic, the central focus is on the moment of initiation and the central character is either adolescent or innocent.

One way to distinguish the daylight from the nocturnal tales is to note the hero's position in relation to his private world and the public world. In the daylight stories the movement is out towards the world while in the darker tales the hero tends to move away from the world and in towards his inner Id or soul or imagination. In the daylight variety, there is a tension between the hero and his society which resolves itself often in a humorous and always in a creative or imaginative way. All these stories are told in the first person but none of them tries to move into the character's psyche or soul. The focus, instead, is on the surfaces, the interest and humor deriving from the situation and the action.

The realism in these daylight stories seems to evolve from Capote's early pieces, printed in *Decade Magazine*. But the warmth, humor, and ease of style lacking in these surface stories is picked up in "My Side of the Matter," which closely resembles Eudora Welty's "Why I Live at the P. O." in its colloquial use of language. This slim tale of a minor skirmish between a young, beleaguered hero and his querulous in-laws is slight in comparison to the later "Jug of Silver" and "Children on Their Birthdays." Both of these stories are markedly similar in that they are concerned with extraordinary, almost supernatural children. The hero of the first story, Appleseed, is blessed with a kind of extra-sensory power for determining the amount of money in a jar filled with silver: a power acquired from being born with a caul over his head.

Similarly, the heroine of Capote's most perfect story in the daylight genre, "Children on Their Birthdays," is a precocious child with an uncanny power. Like Cousin Lymon in Carson McCullers' *Ballad of the Sad Cafe,* Miss Bobbit comes to a new town and disrupts its whole pattern of living with her awesome brand of animal magnetism. From her first appearance, grotesquely made up like an adult and sporting a parasol, Miss Bobbit impresses as a fantastic mixture of innocence and experience, morality and pragmatism. She sings like Sophie Tucker, dances like Gypsy Rose Lee, and possesses the business acumen of a Polly Adler. Miss Bobbit doesn't go to church because she finds the odor there offensive but she adds:

"I don't want you to think I'm a heathen, Mr. C; I've had enough experience to know that there is a God and that there is a Devil. But the way to tame the Devil is not to go down there to church and listen to what a sinful mean fool he is. No, love the Devil like you do Jesus: because he is a powerful man, and will do you a good turn if he knows you trust him. He has frequently done me good turns, like at dancing school in Memphis. . . . I always called in the Devil to help me get the biggest part in our annual show. That is common sense; you see, I knew Jesus wouldn't have any truck with dancing. Now, as a matter of fact, I have called in the Devil just recently. He is the only one who can help me get out of this town. Not that I live here, not exactly. I think always about somewhere else, somewhere else where everything is dancing, like people dancing in the streets, and everything is pretty, like children on their birthdays. My precious papa said I live in the sky, but if he'd lived more in the sky he'd be rich like he wanted to be. The trouble with my papa was he did not love the Devil, he let the Devil love him. But I am very smart in that respect; I know the next best thing is very often the best."

It is necessary to distinguish here between the hero in the two worlds of day and night. Notice that the *mana*-laden child is the hero in the stories discussed so far, while this same figure becomes the shadowy antagonist in Capote's nocturnal stories. Instead, the protagonist becomes an impotent Prufrock, a character to whom things happen. Yet the relationship between the antagonist and the protagonist is ambiguous: one seems the alter ego of the other. The uncanny power in the daylight hero is a creative force — the manifestation of the imagination. In the nocturnal stories the hero is forced to come to grips with the destructive element — the power of blackness which resides in each of us. The confrontation of the psyche leads to the exposure of the constructive and destructive elements: the wish for death and the wish for life.

In Capote's nocturnal stories the movement out into the world becomes simultaneously the movement into the self. John Aldridge has compared Capote's novel *Other Voices, Other Rooms* unfavorably to Joseph Conrad's *Victory*. The comparison between the two writers is a just, almost obvious one when used in a different context. If we juxtapose Conrad's "Heart of Darkness" with any Capote twilight story, it becomes immediately apparent that the structures are the same. In Conrad's story, Marlowe moves into the heart of the dark continent at the same time he moves into the heart of his own subconscious or soul. In reality, the two movements are the same. The same idea occurs in Paul Bowles' *The Sheltering Sky,* in which two Americans move into the primitive Arab world and the primal inner world simultaneously. Similarly, each Capote nocturnal hero must face a fiendish form of *mana,* an external force, and his inner guilt. The relationship in all cases is the same: there is an inescapable fascination with the outer and inner faces of evil. The moment of initiation, the shock of recognition, comes when the hero discovers that the two are the same: the *mana* which confronted him was an external manifestation of his inner identity. The dichotomy then is not only between the two worlds but between the two faces of each world: the constructive and the destructive.

The story of initiation is the search for identity. For instance, in "Master Misery," one of Capote's favorites by his own admission, his heroine, Sylvia, is caught between the outside world represented by her insensitive girlhood friend, Estelle, and the impersonal, mechanical Santa Clauses in store windows, and the personal world of her own dreams. In an attempt to escape the outside world, Sylvia sells her dreams to the anonymous Master Misery, only to discover that she has not escaped the outer world but only lost the inner.

Sylvia is befriended by Oreilly, a used-up clown with no more dreams to sell, who squints one eye and says: "I don't believe in Jesus

Christ, but I do believe in people's souls; and I figure it this way, baby; dreams are the mind of the soul and the secret truth about us." When Oreilly leaves her with a smile to go "travelling in the blue" where *"the best old pie is whiskeyberry pie"* and not *"loveberry pie,"* Sylvia is left completely alone, having lost her dreams and her friend:

> I do not know what I want, and perhaps I shall never know, but my only wish from every star will always be another star; and truly I am not afraid, she thought. Two boys came out of a bar and stared at her; in some park some long time ago she'd seen two boys and they might be the same. Truly I am not afraid, she thought, hearing their snowy footsteps following after her; and anyway, there was nothing left to steal.

In no other nocturnal story is the reader as conscious of the tension between the individual and society. Sylvia, in attempting to escape from society, discovers that the destructive element comes from within. Master Misery is himself a bogey man that "all mothers tell their kids about": a force outside the self and yet an extension of the self. Sylvia's surrender at the end of the story is not to society but to the dark side of her soul, the destructive element which dominates when the creative imagination is exhausted. In this lies the idea that the creative imagination of the dream world is the one *thing* by which the individual is identified; the surrender of identity and of the creative force is the acquiescence to the death wish.

The differences between the lighter and darker sides of Capote's writing come out more clearly in one of his most famous stories, "Miriam." In it, an old woman, Mrs. Miller, is haunted by a striking and uncanny child who is her namesake — Miriam. The story shows how Miriam moves in and takes over Mrs. Miller's home, person, and life. The plot is similar to "Children on Their Birthdays" and "Jug of Silver": an uncanny child upsets the equilibrium of the drab routine of living. Miriam is in many ways similar to Miss Bobbit and we may almost think of her as that remarkable child's darker sister. But in "Miriam" there are some significant differences from the daylight stories, most important of which is the withdrawal from the outside world, a movement from the relationship of self to society to a confrontation of the self by the self in which Miriam becomes an uncanny device — a result of *mana* and projection. In fact, Miriam stands as the primal alter ego to Mrs. Miller: an extension of her destructive, unconscious instinct. The withdrawal from the outer world is accompanied by a complementary shift in style; the clarity and realism of "Children" is replaced by a filmy and surreal style in which Miriam's fingers "made cobweb movements over the plate, gathering the crumbs."

The hero's encounter with, and surrender to, *mana* is perhaps most richly stated in the inverted story, "The Headless Hawk," in which an extraordinary young girl, half child, half adult, innocent, experienced, demented, homicidal, naïve, and primitive, invades the sterile life of a young failure on the fringes of the art world. Vincent is "a poet who had never written poetry, a painter who had never painted, a lover who had never loved (absolutely) — someone, in short, without direction and quite headless. Oh, it wasn't that he hadn't tried — good beginnings, always, bad endings, always . . . a man in the sea, fifty miles from shore; a victim, born to be murdered, either by himself or another; an actor unemployed." Vincent falls under the spell of a demented young girl, D. J., whose painting of a headless hawk hovering over a headless body — a vivid symbol of his own disconnectedness — forces on Vincent "a note of inward recognition." Vincent takes the girl as his mistress because she recalls from his past his incurable fascination with carnival freaks and because "it was true that about those he loved there was always a little something wrong, broken." D. J. thus becomes a mirror of his own disconnected self into which he can retreat. He shuns all his old friends because he does not know how to explain his relationship with the grotesque young girl.

However, Vincent's immersion in D. J. takes a sharp turn when he discovers her obsession with a Mr. Destronelli, a shadowy figure out of her past who she is sure will kill her. When Vincent discovers her dementia he knows he must betray her in favor of his old life, just as he had betrayed his other lovers, just as "he'd betrayed himself with talents unexploited, voyages never taken, promises unfulfilled . . . why in his lovers must he always find the broken image of himself?" He soon turns her out of the house and on the same day symbolically stabs the headless hawk in her painting as he is trying to catch a butterfly. But, of course, he has not escaped her. D. J. haunts him night and day, convinced that he is Destronelli. Vincent, returned to his old world which he now finds "sterile and spurious," discovers that he is held by "a nameless disorder . . . a paralysis of time and identity." Vincent's fascination with D. J. is the fatal confrontation with Mr. Destronelli — the executioner in each of us: he sees in D. J. the grotesque reflection of his own broken image.

The heart of the matter — the heart of darkness — is revealed significantly enough in a dream that Vincent has on the night of D. J.'s eighteenth birthday. He is at a huge party with "an old man with yellow-dyed hair, powdered cheeks, kewpie-doll lips: Vincent recognizes Vincent." The old man is on Vincent's back and Vincent feels out of place until he notices that he is not alone. "He notices then that many are also saddled with malevolent semblances of themselves, outward embodiments of inner decay." The host has a headless hawk attached to his wrist drawing blood with its talons. Suddenly the host announces in a soprano voice: "Attention! The dancing will commence." Vincent finds himself dancing with a succession of old lovers.

> Again, a new partner. It is D. J., and she too has a figure barnacled to her back, an enchanting auburn-haired child; like an emblem of innocence, the child cuddles to her chest a snowball kitten. "I am heavier than I look," says the child, and the terrible voice retorts, "But I am heaviest of all." The instant their hands meet he begins to feel the weight upon him diminish; the old Vincent is fading. His feet lift off the floor, he floats upward from her embrace. The victrola grinds away loud as ever, but he is rising high, and the white receding faces gleam below like mushrooms on a dark meadow.
>
> The host releases his hawk, sends it soaring. Vincent thinks, no matter, it is a blind thing, and the wicked are safe among the blind. But the hawk wheels above him, swoops down, claws foremost; at last he knows there is to be no freedom.

The confrontation of the inner world becomes the confrontation of man's innate guilt. The dark side of the subconscious reflects not only the death instinct but the Christian sense of man's depravity. The burden that each carries becomes more than the darker alter ego: it is also the sense of original sin which each of us carries like a cross. Thus even the child is heavier than she looks; and thus Vincent cannot transcend his wickedness, even among the blind, even through love. Truly, there is to be no freedom from original sin.

The ingredients in all of Capote's nocturnal stories are present in their most striking expression, "A Tree of Night." Kay, a young college girl on her way back to her insulated environment from her uncle's funeral, is intimidated by two grotesque carnival performers: a deaf mute who plays Lazarus by being buried alive in tank towns and his one connection with the outside world, a woman made freakish by her huge head. Much against her will, Kay is coerced, almost mesmerized, into buying a worthless charm which she had previously refused to buy. Like Capote's other heroes, Kay finds herself acquiescing to an uncanny power.

> As Kay watched, the man's face seemed to change form and recede before her like a moon-shaped rock sliding downward under a surface of water. A warm laziness relaxed her. She was dimly conscious of it when the woman took away her purse, and when she gently pulled the raincoat like a shroud above her head.

On the one level the story may be read as a tawdry and ironic parable of Lazarus —

> "I am Lazarus come from the dead,
> Come back to tell you all, I shall tell you all" —
> If one, settling a pillow by her head,
>   Should say: "That is not what I meant at all;
>   That is not it, at all."

— just as Carson McCullers' novel, *The Heart Is a Lonely Hunter*, can be read as an ironic parable of Christ. But perhaps the religious significance is being overemphasized:

> [Confronted by the afflicted mute] Kay knew of what she was afraid: it was a memory, a childish memory of terrors that once, long ago, had hovered above her like haunted limbs on a tree of night. Aunts, cooks, strangers — each eager to spin a tale or teach a rhyme of spooks and death, omens, spirits, demons. And always there had been the unfailing threat of the wizard man: stay close to the house, child, else the wizard man'll snatch and eat you alive! He lived everywhere, the wizard man, and everywhere was danger. At night, in bed, hear him tapping at the window? Listen!

Fear seems the motivating emotion in these stories just as love is the motivating force in McCullers' novels. *"All our acts are acts of fear,"* remembered Walter Ranney, the hero of "Shut a Final Door," and perhaps he was right. For the wizard men and the Master Miseries are all personifications of some form of *mana,* formalized by superstition — that primitive and perhaps honest type of religious observance. At the same time, the Master Miseries and the Destronellis are not the products of our creative imagination but the very heart of darkness, the black, destructive, guilt-ridden side of our subconscious and soul. In each of these nocturnal stories, a seemingly normal but creatively bankrupt person encounters a destructive force at once outside himself and within his depths, which is so dreadful that he is utterly vanquished by fear and surrenders his very essence — his identity. The hero is drawn towards the source of power — the primal heart of darkness — and in doing so removes himself from the public world. Like Narcissus watching his reflection, Capote's hero becomes fascinated and mesmerized by his own evil alter ego. Like Jacob wrestling with the dark angel, the hero in these stories is wrestling not only with the outside world of reality but with his own personal world, losing the former while winning the latter. For the moment of defeat, of despair, of unconditional surrender, is also the moment of revelation.

What we have discovered about the two worlds of Truman Capote's short stories is equally true in his two novels. Conveniently, one novel describes each world: *The Grass Harp* seems the daylight metaphor of *Other Voices, Other Rooms.* And yet both novels exhibit a deepening of perception, a widening of scope, and an enrichening of the dense thematic material found in the stories. On the other hand, neither novel is entirely successful, whereas some of his stories — notably "Children on Their Birthdays" and "A Tree of Night" — are striking examples of their medium. Even Capote admits he is most at home in the short story.

Still, no piece of Capote's fiction has elicited as much comment, criticism, and bewilderment as the gothic and complex first novel, *Other Voices, Other Rooms*. Indeed, the dust jacket picture of the sensitive reclining face staring out from beneath boyish bangs was perhaps as great a cause for the excited confusion as anything in the book. But the difficult and fantastic remoteness of the book has been exaggerated by the mistaken identification of the hero with his exotic and precocious creator. Basically, *Other Voices* resembles Capote's twilight stories in that it concerns an adolescent's initiation into the private and inverted adult world, full of danger and evil. John Aldridge has called it essentially a search for the father and Carvel Collins has likened it to the quest for the Holy Grail: both are right. Yet Joel Knox's search for his father, which leads him from the realistic daylight of New Orleans to the fantastic twilight of Skully's Landing, can be considered as a search for identity. Joel moves from the outside world towards the personal, just as he moves from the bright afternoon heat of Noon City to the dream-like darkness of his new home — Skully's Landing.

John Aldridge has accused Capote of being metaphorical and remote, but his symbolic treatment of thematic material seems clear enough if examined in the same manner as we have examined his other stories. Like his other work, *Other Voices* can be read from either a psychological or a moral, perhaps Christian, viewpoint. Basically, Joel "was trying to locate his father, that was the long and short of it," for the discovery of his father's identity would cast some light on his own essence. But when Joel discovers the terrible truth that his father is a helpless, paralyzed invalid, he must look elsewhere for help in his search for identity. Joel stands as a stranger at Skully's Landing, poised between going further into the private world with his fascinating, witty, cynical, and homosexual cousin, Randolph, and moving out into the real world with the adolescent tomboy, Idabel. Joel's initiation can be seen as a straight-line development from the outside world of Noon City through the decadent limbo of Skully's Landing to the private, dreamlike ruins of the Cloud Hotel — and back again.

In order to tell his story, Capote has expanded the technique of metaphorical use of characterization seen in "Miriam" and "The Headless Hawk." Each character in *Other Voices* is a metaphor or alter ego of another. The tomboy, Idabel, has a twin sister, Florabel, because, as Florabel says, "the Lord always sends something bad with the good." Similarly, the dwarfish Miss Wisteria, "weeping because little boys must grow tall," is a grotesque reflection of Randolph's hopeless, homosexual quest for completion. Little Sunshine, the hermit who inhabits his own private world at the Cloud Hotel, mirrors the old Negro servant, Jesus Fever. And, finally, Joel himself is reflected in Jesus Fever's daughter, Zoo: both must reject their fathers in an effort to escape from the Landing.

Joel's first test comes when he is not allowed to meet his father. In his mind the illusions he had built around his father are confused with the reality of his father's absence. "He couldn't believe in the way things were turning out: the difference between this happening and what he'd expected was too great." With the confrontation of his father's impotence, Joel must look elsewhere for the key to his identity. Randolph offers him one possibility: the narcissistic immersion in the self.

> "They can romanticize us so, mirrors, and that is their secret: what a subtle torture it would be to destroy all the mirrors in the world: where then could we look for reassurance of our identities? I tell you, my dear, Narcissus was no egotist . . . he was merely another of us who, in our unshatterable isolation, recognized, on seeing his reflection, the one beautiful comrade, the only inseparable love. . . Poor Narcissus, possibly the only human who was ever honest on this point."

But even in the personal world Randolph cannot escape his own guilt, for "it is easy to escape daylight, but night is inevitable, and dreams are the giant cage." Like Vincent, in "The Headless Hawk," Randolph is "a victim born to be murdered, either by himself or another." He remains a broken figure hopelessly committed to, and castrated by, the destructive side of his personal vision.

Caught between a loyalty to his father and a need to escape his stultifying influence, Joel at first rejects his father for Idabel, with whom he plans to run away. But the final act of initiation — the revelation of his own guilt that smashes the tinted glasses of childhood — renders Joel powerless to escape. In leaving his father, Joel, like Zoo, is judged guilty by his father and must act as his own executioner. Both he and Zoo can never really leave the Landing; their dreams of escape from limbo are shattered. When Randolph takes Joel to the Cloud Hotel — the private world which Randolph never left — a revelation of identity comes to Joel in a flash of insight:

> (He looked into the fire, longing to see their faces as well, and the flames erupted an embryo: a veined, vacillating shape, its features

formed slowly, and even when complete stayed veiled in dazzle; his eyes burned tar-hot as he brought them nearer: tell me, tell me, who are you? are you someone I know? are you dead? are you my friend? do you love me? But the painted disembodied head remained unborn beyond its mask, and gave no clue. Are you someone I am looking for? he asked, not knowing whom he meant, but certain that for him there must be such a person, just as there was for everybody else: Randolph with his almanac, Miss Wisteria and her search by flashlight, Little Sunshine remembering other voices, other rooms, all of them remembering, or never having known. And Joel drew back. If he recognized the figure in the fire, then what ever would he find to take its place? It was easier not to know, better holding heaven in your hand like a butterfly that is not there at all.)

Unable to live in either the private or the real world, Joel makes the compromise of the artist: finding his identity by walking the tenuous line between the illusory and the tangible, between the imaginative and the real:

"I am me," Joel whooped. "I am Joel, we are the same people" . . .
And Joel realized then the truth; he saw how helpless Randolph was: more paralyzed than Mr. Sansom, more childlike than Miss Wisteria, what else could he do, once outside and alone, but describe a circle, the zero of his nothingness? Joel slipped down from the tree; he had not made the top, but it did not matter, for he knew who he was, he knew that he was strong.

Yet Joel's search for his identity contains another and perhaps more significant level of meaning. At the very beginning of the book, while riding to Skully's Landing, Joel passes a sign — a sign for him and for the reader: "The Lord Jesus is Coming! Are you ready?" But the Christ figure we meet is one we are not prepared for: the paralytic father, Mr. Sansom, who drops red tennis balls like drops of blood, an ironic, afflicted Christ similar to the deaf-mute, Singer, in Carson McCullers' *The Heart Is a Lonely Hunter*. Joel's search for his father leads to the confrontation of his innate guilt — guilt symbolized in the desertion of his father and manifested in his sudden awareness of the disparity between illusion and reality and his perception of the impossibility of escape from the Landing. His situation is mirrored by Zoo, who leaves her father's grave to escape the Landing only to find that she has taken "the wrong road" to salvation. She is crucified by assaulters just as Joel, like Christ, is condemned and abandoned by his father and crucified by surrendering to Randolph. But in the act of the crucifixion are the seeds of redemption: Joel is crucified a boy and resurrected a man.

Every Capote character is scarred permanently just as Zoo bears the marks of a razor slashing on her neck. They are all marked men, marked perhaps by original sin. Even the artist — like Joel — is afflicted: "the feeble-minded, the neurotic, the criminal, perhaps, also, the artist, have unpredictability and perverted innocence in common." But Capote's nocturnal hero remains essentially the failure. And in Randolph he has created his most fascinating and grotesque failure, who speaks for Vincent and Sylvia, Mrs. Miller and Walter Ranney, when he says:

> "But we are alone, darling child, terribly, isolated each from the other; so fierce is the world's ridicule we cannot speak or show our tenderness; for us, death is stronger than life, it pulls like a wind through the dark, all our cries burlesqued in joyless laughter; and with the garbage of loneliness stuffed down us until our guts burst bleeding green, we go screaming round the world, dying in our rented rooms, nightmare hotels, eternal homes of the transient heart."

In *The Grass Harp,* Capote again moves to the daylight style. Essentially, it is the story of a group of innocents, alienated from society because of their innocence, who move into a tree house to escape the world and discover their true selves. The theme is again the search for *true* identity. For the tree dissolves all of society's restrictions and replaces them with a beatific feeling of freedom; it is a realm where wish becomes fulfillment. The tree becomes the refuge for the outcasts from society: the saintly Dolly, the most innocent of all, who, like J. D. Salinger's misfit hero, Seymour Glass, loves people so much she hides in corners for fear of scaring them with her love. With Dolly is her constant companion, Catherine, a zany mixture of Negro and Indian, harshness and loyalty, who brings to the tree house a sense of hard-headed reality, and Collin Fenwick, the adolescent narrator, who lives with Dolly and her brutish sister, Verena. These three have left home after a quarrel over Dolly's home-remedy dropsy cure: Verena wants to mass produce it and Dolly refuses to commercialize it. They are soon joined by a retired judge, Judge Cool, whose sons feel he has outgrown his usefulness. "I sometimes imagine," he says, "all those whom I've called guilty have passed the real guilt on to me: it's partly that that makes me want once before I die to be right on the right side." The fifth party is a "tense, trigger-tempered," directionless youth, Riley Henderson, who also happens to be Collin's idol.

Like Salinger's Holden Caulfield, these five stage a "quixotic" battle against hypocrisy, materialism, and anything that takes beauty away from the world. The small revolt from society forces them to move towards the inner world of the imagination. Judge Cool sums up the whole idea nicely:

"But ah, the energy we spend hiding from one another, afraid as we are of being identified. But here we are, identified: five fools in a tree. A great piece of luck provided we know how to use it: no longer any need to worry about the picture we present — free to find out who we truly are. If we know that, no one can dislodge us; it's the uncertainty concerning themselves that makes our friends conspire to deny the differences. By scrapes and bits I've in the past surrendered myself to strangers — men who disappeared down the gangplank, got off at the next station: put together, maybe they would've made the one person in the world — but there he is with a dozen different faces moving down a hundred separate streets. This is my chance to find that man — you are him, Miss Dolly, Riley, all of you."

But this leafy retreat seems hardly the place for soul-searching; Verena soon has the authorities there to demand that they return to their homes. A pitched battle occurs between the rebels and the authorities, which, with the help of the right of creative imagination and the might of an ingenious family of gypsies, is decided in favor of the rebels. However, they do leave the tree house when Verena returns broken by the swindler of her heart and money — the bogus doctor who was to bottle the dropsy cure. Dolly returns to Verena because she is needed and the magic of the "dissolving" chinaberry tree is gone.

In the story the end of innocence is two-fold. For Collin, it is an elegiac remembrance of things past, a vicarious initiation at Dolly's own loss of innocence, and his real initiation at Dolly's death. But for Collin the act of initiation brings the discovery of love and the redemption of the identity. It now becomes clear that for Capote love is the redeeming element in life. Echoing the judge's words in an earlier part of the book, Dolly tells Collin just before her death:

"Charlie said that love is a chain of love. I hope you listened and understood him. Because when you can love one thing . . . you can love another, and that is owning, that is something to live with. You can forgive everything."

Like Carson McCullers in her story, "A Tree, A Rock, A Cloud," Capote here shows "that life is a chain of love, as nature is a chain of life." Arching over the story of Dolly and Collin and the chinaberry tree is the grass harp, a symbol of the immutable moral order, an order of the good and the imaginative which always tells a story of the lives of the people, good and bad, with and without identity, who have lived and died there. And so the search for identity comes to rest in the shock of recognition — recognition of the primacy of the natural order of the creative instinct — of love and imagination over the death wish. Both Joel and his daylight brother, Collin, have learned the same thing: the search inward for identity must eventually turn outward if it is to reflect anything but the broken image of the grotesque self.

The world was a frightening place, yes, he knew: unlasting, what could be forever? or only what it seemed? rock corrodes, rivers freeze, fruit rots; stabbed, blood of black and white bleeds alike; trained parrots tell more truth than most, and who is lonelier: the hawk or the worm? every flowering heart shrivels dry and pitted as the herb from which it bloomed, and while the old man grows spinsterish, his wife assumes a mustache; moment to moment, changing, changing, like the cars on the ferris-wheel. Grass and love are always greener; but remember Little Three Eyes? show her love and apples ripen gold, love vanquishes the Snow Queen, its presence finds the name, be it Rumpelstiltskin or merely Joel Knox: that is constant.

❧ EARL H. ROVIT

Ralph Ellison and the
American Comic Tradition

THE most obvious comment one can make about Ralph Ellison's *Invisible Man* is that it is a profoundly comic work. But the obvious is not necessarily either simple or self-explanatory, and it seems to me that the comic implications of Ellison's novel are elusive and provocative enough to warrant careful examination both in relation to the total effect of the novel itself and the American cultural pattern from which it derives. It is generally recognized that Ellison's novel is a highly conscious attempt to embody a particular kind of experience — the experience of the "outsider" (in this case, a Negro) who manages to come to some sort of temporary acceptance, and thus, definition, of his status in the universe; it is not so generally recognized that *Invisible Man* is an integral link in a cumulative chain of great American creations, bearing an unmistakable brand of kinship to such seemingly incongruous works as *The Divinity School Address, Song of Myself, Moby-Dick,* and *The Education of Henry Adams.* But the latter proposition is, I think, at least as valid as the former, and unless it is given proper recognition, a good deal of the value of the novel will be ignored.

First it should be noted that Ellison's commitment to what Henry James has termed "the American joke" has been thoroughly deliberate and undisguised. Ellison once described penetratingly the ambiguous *locus* of conflicting forces within which the American artist has had always to work: "For the ex-colonials, the declaration of an American identity meant the assumption of a mask, and it imposed not only the discipline of national self-consciousness, it gave Americans an ironic awareness of the joke that always lies between appearance and reality, between the discontinuity of social tradition and that sense of the past which clings to the mind. And perhaps even an awareness of the joke that society is man's creation, not God's." This kind of ironic awareness may contain bitterness and may even become susceptible to the

Reprinted from *Wisconsin Studies in Contemporary Literature,* I (Fall, 1960), 34–42, by permission of the author and the editors.

heavy shadow of despair, but the art which it produces has been ultimately comic. It will inevitably probe the masks of identity and value
searching relentlessly for some deeper buried reality, but it will do this
while accepting the fundamental necessity for masks and the impossibility of ever discovering an essential face beneath a mask. That is to
say, this comic stance will accept with the same triumphant gesture
both the basic absurdity of all attempts to impose meaning on the
chaos of life, and the necessary converse of this, the ultimate significance of absurdity itself.

Ellison's *Invisible Man* is comic in this sense almost in spite of its
overtly satirical interests and its excursions into the broadly farcical.
Humorous as many of its episodes are in themselves — the surreal
hysteria of the scene at the Golden Day, the hero's employment at the
Liberty Paint Company, or the expert dissection of political entangle-
ments in Harlem — these are the materials which clothe Ellison's joke
and which, in turn, suggest the shape by which the joke can be com-
prehended. The pith of Ellison's comedy reverberates on a level much
deeper than these incidents, and as in all true humor, the joke affirms
and denies simultaneously — accepts and rejects with the same uncompromising passion, leaving not a self-cancelling neutralization of momentum, but a sphere of moral conquest, a humanized cone of light
at the very heart of the heart of darkness. *Invisible Man,* as Ellison
has needlessly insisted in rebuttal to those critics who would treat the
novel as fictionalized sociology or as a dramatization of archetypal
images, is an artist's attempt to create a *form.* And fortunately Ellison
has been quite explicit in describing what he means by *form;* in specific
reference to the improvisation of the jazz-musician he suggests that
form represents "a definition of his identity: as an individual, as member of the collectivity, and as a link in the chain of tradition." But
note that each of these definitions of identity must be individually exclusive and mutually contradictory on any logical terms. Because of
its very pursuit after the uniqueness of individuality, the successful
definition of an individual must define out the possibilities of general-
ization into "collectivity" or "tradition." But here for Ellison in his
embrace of a notion of fluid amorphous identity lies the real morality
and humor in mankind's art and men's lives — neither of which have
much respect for the laws of formal logic.

At one time during the novel when Ellison's protagonist is enthusi-
astically convinced that his membership in the Brotherhood is the only
effective means to individual and social salvation, he recalls these words
from a college lecture on Stephen Dedalus: "Stephen's problem, like
ours, was not actually one of creating the uncreated conscience of his
race, but of creating the *uncreated features of his face.* Our task is
that of making ourselves individuals. The conscience of a race is the

gift of its individuals who see, evaluate, record. . . . We create the race by creating ourselves and then to our great astonishment we will have created something far more important: We will have created a culture. Why waste time creating a conscience for something that doesn't exist? For, you see, blood and skin do not think!" This is one of the most significant passages in the novel, and one which must be appreciated within the context of the total form if the subtle pressure of that form is to be adequately weighed. And this can be done only if the Prologue and the Epilogue are viewed as functional elements in the novel which set the tempo for its moral action and modulate ironically upon its emergent meanings.

The Prologue introduces the narrator in his underground hibernation musing upon the events of his life, eating vanilla ice-cream and sloe gin, listening to Louis Armstrong's recording, "What Did I Do to Be So Black and Blue?" and trying to wrest out of the confusions of his experiences some pattern of meaning and/or resilient core of identity. The next twenty-five chapters are a first-person narrative flashback which covers some twenty years of the protagonist's life ending with the beginning, the hero's descent into the underground hole. The concluding Epilogue picks up the tonal patterns of the Prologue, implies that both meaning and identity have been discovered, and dramatically forces a direct identification between the narrator and the reader. Ostensibly this is another novel of the initiation of a boy into manhood — a *Bildungsroman* in the episodic picaresque tradition. The advice of the literature teacher has been realized; the hero has created the features of his face from the malleable stuff of his experience. He who accepts himself as "invisible" has ironically achieved a concrete tangibility, while those characters in the novel who seemed to be "visible" and substantial men (Norton, Brother Jack, and even Tod Clifton) are discovered to be really "invisible" since they are self-imprisoned captives of their own capacities to see and be seen in stereotyped images. However, to read the novel in this way and to go no further is to miss the cream of the jest and the total significance of the whole form which pivots on the ironic fulcrum of the blues theme introduced in the Prologue and given resolution in the Epilogue. As in all seriously comic works the reader is left not with an answer, but with a challenging question — a question which soars beyond the novel on the unanswered notes of Armstrong's trumpet: "What did I do to be so black and blue?"

For the protagonist *is* finally and most comically *invisible* at the end of the novel; he has learned that to create the uncreated features of his face is at best a half-value, and at worst, potentially more self-destructive than not to strive after identity at all. For Ellison ours is a time when "you prepare a face to meet the faces that you meet" —

a time when we have learned to shuffle and deal our personalities with a protean dexterity that, as is characterized through Rinehart, is a wholesale exploitation of and surrender to chaos. After the narrator's fall into the coalpit he discovers that his arrogantly naive construction of personality is nothing more than the accumulated fragments in his briefcase: the high-school diploma, Bledsoe's letter, Clifton's dancing doll, Mary's bank, Brother Tarp's iron. And most ironically, even these meager artifacts — the fragments he has shored against his ruin — represent not him, but the world's variegated projections of him. The narrator learns then that his educational romance is a farcical melodrama of the most garish variety; the successive births and re-births of his life (his Caesarean delivery from college, his birth by electronics at the factory hospital, the christening by the Brotherhood) were not the organic gestations of personality that he idealized so much as they were the cold manipulations of artificial insemination. His final acceptance of his invisibility reminds us of the demand of the Zen Master: "Show me the face you had before you were born."

However, we must note also that this acceptance of invisibility, of amorphous non-identity, is far from a resignation to chaos. The pro-tagonist has successfully rebelled against the imposition of social masks whether externally (like Clifton's) or internally (like Brother Tarp's) bestowed; his is not a surrender of personality so much as a descent to a deeper level of personality where the accent is heavier on possibilities than on limitations. The 1,369 glowing light bulbs in his cellar retreat attest to the increased power and enlightenment which are positive gains from his experience, as well as to the strategic advantages of his recourse to invisibility. The literature teacher un-wittingly pointed out the flaw in his exhortation even as he declaimed it: "Blood and skin do not think!" For to think is to be as much con-cerned with analysis as it is with synthesis; the ironic mind tears radi-ant unities apart even as it forges them. Accordingly Ellison's narrator assumes the ultimate mask of facelessness and emphasizes the fluid chaos which is the secret substance of form, the dynamic interplay of possibilities which creates limitations. The narrator is backed into the blank corner where he must realize that "the mind that has conceived a plan of living must never lose sight of the chaos against which that pattern was conceived." In accepting himself as the Invisible Man he assumes the historic role which Emerson unerringly assigned to the American poet; he becomes "the world's eye" — something through which one sees, even though it cannot itself be seen.

And here it may be fruitful to investigate briefly the peculiar rela-tionship of Emerson's work to Ellison (whose middle name is pro-pitiously Waldo). In the recently published excerpt from a novel in progress, "And Hickman Arrives," Ellison has his main character

Alonzo Zuber, Daddy Hickman, make some complimentary remarks about Emerson, "a preacher . . . who knew that every tub has to sit on its own bottom." Daddy Hickman, a Negro preacher ("Better known as GOD'S TROMBONE"), is vividly characterized as a wise and shrewd virtuoso of the evangelical circuit who might not unfairly be taken as a modern-day Emerson, preaching eloquently the gospel of humanity. These facts may be significant when we remember that Emerson's work is given short shrift as rhetorical nonsense in *Invisible Man* and his name is bestowed upon a character whose minor function in the novel is to be a self-righteous hypocrite. This shift in attitude may indicate that Ellison has come to realize that there are some major affinities binding him to his famous namesake, and, more important, it may enable us to understand more clearly the remarkable consistency of the American struggle to create art and the relatively harmonious visions which these unique struggles have attained.

Superficially there would seem to be little to link the two men beyond the somewhat labored pun of their names and Ellison's awareness of the pun. The one, an ex-Unitarian minister of respectable, if modest, Yankee background, whose orotund explorations in autobiography gave fullest form to the American dream — whose public pose attained an Olympian serenity and optimistic faith which have caused him to be associated with a wide range of sentimentalities from Mary Baker Eddy to Norman Vincent Peale; the other, an Oklahoma City Negro, born in 1914, ex-Leftist propagandist and editor, who would seem to have belied the Emersonian prophecy of individualism and self-reliance by the very title of his novel, *Invisible Man.* The one, nurtured by the most classical education that America had to offer; the other, a rapt disciple of jazzmen like Charlie Christian and Jimmy Rushing who has attributed to their lyric improvisations his deepest understanding of aesthetic form. The one, white and given to the Delphic utterance; the other, black and adept in the cautery of bitter humor. But in their respective searches for identity, in their mutual concern with defining the possibilities and limitations which give form and shape to that which is human, the poet who called man "a golden impossibility" and the novelist who teaches his protagonist that life is a latent hive of infinite possibilities draw close together in their attempts to find an artistic resolution of the contrarieties of existence.

"Only he can give, who has," wrote Emerson: "he only can create, who is." Experience is the fluxional material from which these all-important values and identities are created, and Emerson's great essays are processive incantations whose ultimate function is to bring identity into being, even as they chant the fundamental fluidity of all forms spontaneously and eternally merging into other forms. When we remember that Emerson once wrote: "A believer in Unity, a seer of

Unity, I yet behold two," it may be worth a speculation that the Emerson behind the triumphant artifices of the *Essays* was not a terribly different person from the Invisible Man in the coalpit whose submersion into the lower frequencies had given him an entree to the consciousnesses of all men. This awareness of the absurdity of meaning (and potential meaningfulness of chaos) is at the heart of Emerson's delight in paradox, his seeming inconsistencies, his "dialogistic" techniques, his highly functional approach to language. "All symbols are fluxional," he declaimed; "all language is vehicular and transitive and is good for conveyance not for homestead." Thus Melville's attempted criticism of Emerson in *The Confidence Man* misses widely the mark; Emerson isn't there when the satire strikes home. Melville, who above all of Emerson's contemporaries should have known better, mistook the Olympian pasteboard mask for a reality and misread the eloquent quest for identity as a pretentious melodrama. For, as Constance Rourke recognized, Emerson is one of our most deft practitioners of the American joke, and the magnitude of his success may be measured by the continued effectiveness of his disguises after more than a hundred years.

But again we must return to the *form* of *Invisible Man* to appreciate how deeply involved Ellison's work is with the most basic American vision of reality. Although it is probably true as some critics have pointed out that the dominating metaphor of the novel — the "underground man" theme — was suggested by Dostoevsky and Richard Wright, it is for our purposes more interesting to note a similar metaphor in Hart Crane's poem, "Black Tambourine":

> The interests of a black man in a cellar
> Mark tardy judgment on the world's closed door.
> Gnats toss in the shadow of a bottle,
> And a roach spans a crevice in the floor.
>
>   *   *   *   *   *
>
> The black man, forlorn in the cellar,
> Wanders in some mid-kingdom, dark, that lies,
> Between his tambourine, stuck on the wall,
> And, in Africa, a carcass quick with flies.

Invisible Man achieves an expert evocation of that "mid-kingdom," that *demi-monde* of constant metamorphosis where good and evil, appearance and reality, pattern and chaos are continually shifting their shapes even as the eye strains to focus and the imagination to comprehend. The Kafkaesque surrealism of the novel's action, the thematic entwinement of black-white and dark-light, and the psychic distance from the plot-development which the use of the Prologue and the Epilogue achieves posit the moral center of the novel in that fluid area where experience is in the very process of being transformed into value. The narrator, the author, and the reader as well are caught in the "mid-kingdom" which seems to me to be the characteristic and unavoidable focus of American literature. For this mid-kingdom, this unutterable silence which is "zero at the bone," seems to me to be the one really inalienable birthright of being an American. Some Americans following Swedenborg named it "vastation"; others gave it no name and lamented the dearth of an American tradition within which the artist could work; at least one commissioned the sculptor, St. Gaudens, to incarnate it in a statue. One way of attempting to describe the sense of being within this mid-kingdom can be most dramatically seen in "The Castaway" chapter of *Moby-Dick* where Pip is left floundering in the boundless Pacific. And although the techniques of approaching the experience have been richly various, the experience itself, an incontrovertible sense of absolute metaphysical isolation, can be found at the core of the most vital American creations.

"American history," writes James Baldwin in *Notes of a Native Son,* is "the history of the total, and willing, alienation of entire peoples from their forebears. What is overwhelmingly clear . . . is that this history has created an entirely unprecedented people, with a unique and individual past." The alienation, of course, is more than sociological and ideological; it seeps down into the very depths whence the sureties of identity and value are wrought; and it imprisons the American in this mid-kingdom where the boundaries — the distance from the tambourine on the wall to the carcass quick with flies — cannot be measured in either years or miles. The American seeking himself — as an individual, a member of the collectivity, a link in the chain of tradition — can never discover or create that identity in fixed restrictive terms. The past is dead and yet it lives: note Ellison's use of the narrator's grandfather, the yams, the techniques of the evangelical sermon. Individuals are frozen in mute isolation, and yet communication is possible between them: the Harlem riot, the way the narrator listens to music. Ellison's novel is the unique metaphor of his own thoroughly personal experience, and yet it makes a fitting link in the chain of the American tradition.

That Ellison and his narrator are Negroes both is and is not important. From the severe standpoint of art the racial fact is negligible, although there are doubtless areas of meaning and influence in *Invisible Man* which sociological examination might fruitfully develop. From the viewpoint of cultural history, however, the racial fact is enormously provocative. It is strikingly clear that contemporary American writing, particularly the writing of fiction, is dominated by two categories of writers: members of religious and racial minorities, and writers who possess powerful regional heritages. Both groups have an instinctive leasehold within the boundaries of the "mid-kingdom"; the Negro, the Catholic, the Jew, and the Southerner share the immediate experience of living on the razor's edge of time, at the very point where traditions come into desperate conflict with the human need to adapt to change. And, of equal importance, both groups — in varying degrees — are marked out on the contemporary scene as being "different"; both groups cannot avoid the terrible problem of identity, because it is ever thrust upon them whether they like it or not. These are the conditions which in the American past have nourished our spasmodic exfoliations of significant literary activity: the great "Renaissance" of the 1840's and '50's, the Twain-James-Adams "alliance" of the late nineteenth century, the post-World War One literary florescence from which we have just begun to break away. But the Lost Generation was the last generation which could practise the necessary expatriation or "fugitivism" in which these factors — the disseverance from the past and the search for identity — could operate on non-minority or non-regional American writers. Thus Ralph Ellison — and contemporaries like Saul Bellow, Flannery O'Connor, and William Styron — are *inside* the heart of the American experience by the very virtue of their being in some way "outsiders." Like Emerson, himself a royal inhabitant of the mid-kingdom over a century ago, they are challenged to create form, or else succumb to the enveloping chaos within and without.

And the answers which they arrive at — again as with Emerson — are answers which cannot be taken out of the context of their individually achieved forms without being reduced to platitude or nonsense. Form, the creation of a radical, self-defining metaphor, is the one rational technique which human beings have developed to deal adequately with the basic irrationality of existence. The answer which *Invisible Man* gives to the unanswerable demands which life imposes on the human being has something to do with human limitation and a good deal to do with freedom; it has something to do with hatred, and a good deal more to do with love. It defines the human distance between the tambourine and the carcass and it accepts with wonder and diginity the immeasurable gift of life. The black man in the cellar transforms his isolation into elevation without denying the brute facts of existence and without losing his ironic grip on the transiency of the moment. The amorphous ambiguity of the mid-kingdom is for a timeless instant conquered and made fit for habitation. Perhaps tragedy teaches man to become divine, but before man can aspire to divinity, he must first accept completely the responsibilities and limitations of being human. The American experience, cutting away the bonds of tradition which assure man of his humanity, has not allowed a tragic art to develop. But there has developed a rich and vigorous comic tradition to which *Invisible Man* is a welcome embellishment, and it is this art which promises most as a healthy direction into the future.

❧ BERNARD DUFFEY

The Three Worlds of Jack Kerouac

IF, in the 1960's, there is still a special something called the Beat
Generation, and if it is still to be thought of as contributing to recent
fiction, then one name especially, that of Jack Kerouac, must be taken
as representative of its nature and work. The movement with which
he has been identified is now nearly twenty years old. It has to some
considerable extent merged into a broadening sea of personal restlessness. It has produced a number of poets and a widely felt area of
influence in poetry, but its one distinct achievement in fiction is marked
by Kerouac's work. The Beat Generation, as I shall note, has never
so much been an artistic as a social phenomenon, a post-war response
to post-war times, which produced some writing along the way.
Kerouac himself has been clear enough in this matter, and, whatever
the fate of the Beats or Kerouac's relation to them, he has identified
himself with their world sufficiently to make that the first and most
basic of his own three worlds.

> . . . there's nothing to get excited about. Beat comes out actually
> of old American whoopee, and it will only change a few dresses and
> pants, and make chairs useless in the living room. And pretty soon
> we'll have Beat Secretaries of State and there will be instituted new
> tinsels, in fact new reasons for malice and new reasons for virtue
> and new reasons for forgiveness.

But immediately following such light-heartedness, Kerouac falls into
an apocalyptic turn of speech.

> But yet, but yet, woe unto those who think that the Beat Generation
> means crime, delinquency, immorality . . . woe unto those who at-
> tack it on the grounds that they simply don't understand history
> and the yearning of human souls . . . woe unto those who don't
> realize that America must, will, is changing now, for the better I
> say. Woe unto those who believe in the atom bomb, who believe
> in hating mothers and fathers, who deny the most important of
> the Ten Commandments. Woe unto those (though) who don't
> believe in the unbelievable sweetness of sex love, woe unto those
> who are the standard bearers of death, woe unto those who believe
> in conflict and horror and violence and fill our books and screens
> and living-rooms with all that crap, woe in fact unto those who

175

make evil movies about the Beat Generation where innocent house-wives are raped by beatniks! Woe unto those who are the real dreary sinners that even God finds room [*sic*] to forgive . . . woe unto those who spit on the Beat Generation, the wind'll blow it back.[1]

This neo-Freudian denunciation is far from accidental to Beat living and thinking. It is the heart of much that is most revealing in the Beat Generation and in the fiction of Kerouac and the other writers of the school. The Beats have formed one more crest in the continuing wave of romantic American dissent — but with this difference. They came not to replace one political or moral scheme with another, but to deny all such systems in favor of apparent anarchy. Where Ameri-can dissenters have often made qualified or systematic negations, the Beats have made a total and immediate sweep. And then, the work of demolition accomplished, they attempt a total affirmation. Perhaps the word demolition is badly chosen. The Beats would not so much destroy society and its values as simply disaffiliate, and, once free, begin a quest for some reality, but one governed only by individual existence. It is in this search that the fiction of Jack Kerouac makes an intelligible place for itself in recent American writing.

Kerouac himself was born into a family of French-Canadian ex-traction in 1922. Through high school he lived in Lowell, Massa-chusetts — a city, to judge by his account, of glooms and wonders dominated by dark mills and shadowy mansions, and populated largely by a polyglot working class left to its own devices for living in so alien a town. It may be noted that Kerouac, like Dreiser, belongs to that small but increasing number of American novelists who come to their trade from working class and other than English speaking origins, suggesting something of the kind of penetration which American writ-ing must expect from our later nineteenth and early twentieth century immigration. Kerouac did some work at Columbia University but left without a degree and spent several years living like a compound of the vagabond characters in his own novels.

Even so scanty a sketch takes on importance in that, as it indicates a way of life, so does it indicate the foundation upon which Kerouac's fiction rests. Edgar Lee Masters, a member of an earlier dissenting generation, wrote in 1919 to Theodore Dreiser:

> What would you think about preparing a manifesto calling it the Artists' Manifesto, and get ten to twenty leading men and women to sign it, on the general subject of the state of the country?
> What I have in mind is that something should be done to coun-teract the influence and the insistent labors of these people — preachers, professors and suburban minds who are really running

[1] *Playboy,* Vol. 6, No. 6 (June, 1959), p. 79.

the country. . . . We could lay down a program with reference to liberty of speech and of the press, marriage, ethics, art, or anything else, and all other things important. Make it forthright and direct, revolutionary if that word be applicable.[2]

Kerouac's generation, however, have found their act of negation not in manifestoes against society but in act, they vote with their behavior. How much or what kind of Existentialism may be active in so total a commitment is hard to gauge, but there are similarities between the two. Negation or affirmation is unreal until it enters into and becomes life itself. To have joined the Beat Generation is to participate in the life of the Beats. The religious overtones of certain beat writing, including Kerouac's own, is genuine, not affected. The Beat Generation would settle finally for nothing less than the whole soul: whoever is not with them is against them.

In this sense, Kerouac's novels are not only about the Beat Generation but of it. They came into existence because the Beats came into existence, and this is another fact setting them apart from the generality of American dissenters. Dissent literature, where it has most truly become literature, has grown most often from the imagination and craft of individual artists turned to a concern with individual plights without much reliance on group movements. To take some names typical of earlier vanguards, Sherwood Anderson, or Ezra Pound, or James Farrell — each one stood as spokesman for his kind of individual against what he saw as the dehumanization of the twentieth century. But when all was said and done, they could achieve little identity except that of affirmation. Even Marxism in Farrell or Christianity in Eliot have led to the ultimate assertion of individual existence. But this is the point which Kerouac takes as his starting place. For, if a philosophical point may be made about a largely unphilosophical movement, the Beat Generation may be said to have all its character compressed into the radical aseity of the formula, "I am that I am." Other movements have sought to derive personal identity from sources outside the self: deity, fate, nature, family, society, ideology, history — all these have been drawn upon to support that claim to identity that man has made his own. But the Beats, I will suggest, are the most important example in America of a movement which has spread itself broadly through western life. They are Beat precisely because none of the older sources of identity hold any promise. I do not know that their feeling is right, but, in various guises it is widely shared. Jacques Maritain describes the state of mind which he thinks gave rise in the early century to the vitalistic philosophy of Henri Bergson and which remains an admirably succinct description of the prevailing mentality.

[2] Chicago, March 10, 1919. In the Theodore Dreiser Collection, University of Pennsylvania Library.

The whole effort of modern philosophy ended in mathematicism or universal mechanism and in that venerable mixture of materialism and scepticism called the scientific or positive outlook. . . . Thus, the absolute was unknowable, there was no other reality for us but phenomena, that is to say appearance and accident; the superior had its whole being and its whole reason in the inferior from which it sprang spontaneously; everything happened as though God did not exist, men had no soul, free will was an illusion incompatible with scientific determinism, and the world was one day to be taken apart by scientists like a big mechanical toy.[3]

Bergson's response was to construct a philosophy of intuition designed to bring a sense of life back into a dead world. But for the Beats, even his effort would be less than sufficient. What must be done is to *act out* the proposition, "Nevertheless, existence." And to dig whatever in existence may be, and, finally, is.

The Beats, it can be said, have had no program critical of the modern orthodoxy except to dub it "square," and if you don't quite dig that, the lengthiest explanation you are likely to get is a shrug of the shoulders. You have to intuit because intuiting is the one resource available in the face of all the arid tangles which immobilize modern man. Beat rejection is one forced by history rather than invented. For the Beat who attains it, the proper state is "cool." As nearly as this term can be translated, it means a poise centered in the self alone without regard to any circumstance, a total concentration in what the German existentialists have called the *Eigenwelt,* the world of one's self only. It is the self affirming itself in despair.

The cool Beat, what Kerouac has called the "subterranean," is most typically the user of narcotics, partly as an analgesic aid in preserving the stricken self and partly because narcosis is an assertive chemical act. If the self is so to be put at bay, then let the self be its own hunter and, finally, executor of its own sad triumph. In John Clellon Holmes' novel, *Go,* a drug addict riding on a bus thinks thus to himself:

They're disgusted because they've got to save their own egos, you see. But I haven't got one, I mean I don't care about all that anymore, so it doesn't matter to me. . . . I just accept it so as not to get hung up.

Here a man has found some kind of soul by losing it. The resemblance of this to traditional sanctity is striking in itself, and all the more so when it is compared with the reported self-denials of the less savory saints. But a great difference remains in the fact that the religious ascetic denies himself for a reality presumed to be outside himself. The Beat's final cause is himself, the recovery of existence in a world but outside an ego he has never made.

[3] *Bergsonian Philosophy and Thomism* (New York, 1955), p. 120.

Kerouac's fiction lies short of the cool to share in what he dubs the hot, an active and ceaseless effort at affirmation still stemming from the individual will but flowing through different channels.

> . . . the "hot" today is the crazy talkative shining eyed (often innocent and open hearted) nut who runs from bar to bar, pad to pad, looking for everybody, shouting, restless, lusty, trying to "make it" with the subterranean beantniks who ignore him. Most Beat generation artists belong to the hot school, naturally since that hard gemlike flame needs a little heat. In many cases, the mixture is 50–50 . . . In 1948 the "hot hipsters" were racing around in cars like in *On The Road* looking for wild bawling jazz like Willis Jackson or Lucky Thompson (the early) or Chubby Jackson's big band while the "cool hipsters" cooled it in dead silence before formal and excellent musical groups like Lennie Tristano or Miles Davis.

Kerouac explains that he himself began hot but "finally cooled it in Buddhist meditation" and has remained a mixture of the two.

I hope I have said enough to make two or three central facts clear. The Beat Generation is characterized by a way of life which can be grasped only by living it. Its nature is ineffable. At its fullest it combines a total rejection of any life governed by conventional space, time or causality with a total affirmation of the self thus exiled. It is colored by some sense of the holy or sacred, and if this can only be found in the implacable reality of narcotics, then let it there be found. It is, in a word, a late and vehement assertion of the native romantic spirit against an obdurately unromantic American ethos.

II

But what of the romantic's writing in a world where the romantic ideal has diminished almost to extinction? The form to which Kerouac has committed himself is personal narrative, one scribbled down without correction and at high speed in a quest for the same spontaneity of expression in letters as in living. His is an affirmative attitude in which wonder and delight take the largest place, but a wonder and delight always in himself, his adventures, and his friends. Too often, perhaps, the result has been a collapse into literary sentiment or authorial self-indulgence carried to a tiresome length. At his worst he is a bore, and this charge has been repeated against him over and over. He writes too much about too little and is too easily enamored of his friends, his style, and his life. We get tired of his special admiration, Neil Cassaday, who, as Dean Moriarty, dominates *On The Road,* and who is given an apotheosis as Cody Pomeray in *Visions of Cody*. Whatever Cassaday's appeal may have been gets lost in the sheer bulk of Kerouac's admiration and language. Where he is strongest, as in *The Subterraneans, Doctor Sax,* or *Lonesome Traveler,* there is a sharper evocation of character and "feel," apparently because his "spontaneous prose" has, for the time, led him away from rhapsody and into the definition of characters through action and setting.

Rhapsody, however, is the indispensable second world of Jack Kerouac. His child-men will never have a growing-up, but they will survive in their Beatness and celebrate that which has granted them survival. They are victims, sufferers from the angular world of the squares. Their cities, like those of Eliot's *Waste Land,* are unreal. A vainglorious idealism has disposed of the sacred; science has disposed of nature; and the competitive rat race has disposed of most people. Here, I think, Kerouac takes our age at a most sensitive point — the widely felt crisis of existence — and if his work suffers from sentimental self-indulgence it perhaps springs from the same cause which puffs so many of his adverse critics into a pompous self-indulgence. The advantages of joy and wit, however, remain with the author.

Although the subject does not receive extended discussion in his work, Kerouac's fiction shares with much other modern writing a relapse into the world of subjective and qualitative time. To "dig," in Beat talk, is to allow something to fill one's time-consciousness. By this means, the whole world built on event, feeling, thought, and motive in time is replaced by a world in which all these are themselves time and are the only stuff of human apprehension and of life itself. If Kerouac is an irrationalist, it is less because he opposes reason with some other faculty than because he would feel reason, given its mechanistic concept of time, to be denying itself any chance of seeing life truly. An hour is really a cluster of events, but our time-bound apprehension mistakes mensuration for reality. The latter is in events alone, and we have no choice but to base our action on immediate apprehension or intuition of events. Other considerations are in fact irrelevant.

The result is the immediacy and unrelatedness of everything. This introduces us to a world which seems strange but which is, in fact, the world we all inhabit but have been taught to ignore. Stripped of its ordering scaffold of time, in becomes, in Beat jargon, simply "it," the unnameable which exists only in its own manner and quality. In this sense, "digging" experience is not a transcendental act but a more purely aesthetic thing where, in words older than Kerouac's, not the fruit of experience but experience itself is the end. The conventional world having been dismissed for the operative and subjective illusion it is, we are rewarded by the gift of the real world, but that is a gift which is almost too much. Along with Dean Moriarty of *On The Road,* we must live by saying, "Yes, yes, yes, yes yes," no matter what happens.

"Oh man! man!" moaned Dean. "And it's not even the beginning of it — and now here we are at last going East together, we've never gone East together; Sal, think of it, we'll dig Denver together and see what everybody's doing, although that matters little to us, the point being that we know what IT is and we know TIME and we know that everything is really FINE." Then he whispered, clutching my sleeve, sweating: "Now you just dig them in front [the people driving the car]. They have worries, they're counting the miles, they're thinking about where to sleep tonight, how much money for gas, the weather, how they'll get there anyway, you see. But they need to worry and betray time with urgencies false and otherwise, purely anxious and whiny, their souls really won't be at peace unless they can latch on to an established and proven worry, and having once found it they assume facial expressions to fit and go with it, which is, you see, unhappiness, and all the time it all flies by them and they know it and that too worries them, no end."

The critical problem is not really one of who is right but of whether Moriarty does illuminate for the reader something of the reader himself and the world in which he lives. What seems not to be recognized is that Kerouac's desire to drive his fiction back to the strangeness of nature is in fact a continuing of the drive that has existed since romanticism began. True to the organic principle, the only one which literary romanticism can admit without committing suicide, Kerouac founds his style upon the substance of experience, that which stands under it and constitutes its reality. Like the Zen devotee he has sometimes thought himself to be, the Beat artist seeks to clear away the debris of convention, to discover anew the reality which pattern has come to obfuscate, and so recapture the living process of art itself.

III

Where such a discovery does, in fact, occur, Kerouac fights free of the intransitive subjectivity which weakens his lesser work to carry his reader into a discovery of art as process analogous to the discovery of nature. The reader's pleasure becomes that of seeing the work grow into its natural form rather than using it as a token by which he observes the frantic doings of the Beats or strains for sympathy with a less than Ionic rhapsody. As organic time is the essence of the writer's work, so is it of his reader's. Kerouac's third world, the process of fiction, incorporates its foundations in the Beat Generation and the privately inspired rhetoric of *On The Road* or *Visions of Cody*. But it changes these from literary objects in their own right to avenues of imaginative discovery. It is here that his theory of spontaneous prose justifies itself, perhaps in serendipity or perhaps in something a little more calculated. In conventional terms, I would suggest that his achievement is that of romantic comedy, romantic in its continued embroilment in the strangeness of nature but comic in a growing power of wry detachment from the preciousness of its subject or the author's self. But "the achievement of comedy" suggests too static an accomplishment unless the sense of "achieving" as a verb is remembered. *The Subterraneans, Doctor Sax,* or *Lonesome Traveler* are more acts than things, and their object is the literary process itself.

They are, for example, more like Sherwood Anderson's stories than like Hemingway's. My own term, "world," is misleading since we do not walk into them as we walk into the world of the Lost Generation in *The Sun Also Rises.* Rather, we watch what happens in them and, along with the author, learn as his circumstances make learning possible. Like Anderson, Kerouac is a storyteller rather than a god who stands outside his creation paring his finger nails, and much of the interest in a story told must lie in the telling; the performance of the storyteller as it runs parallel to or counterpoints the story he is telling. Kerouac has been compared to Thomas Wolfe, but there is a great difference in that direction too. Wolfe was always overwhelmed by his subject. Kerouac is fascinated by his subject, but only as subject, not as ethos or revelation. His great temptation is mannerism, and he succumbs to it sometimes. But in the tradition to which he belongs, that of Anderson or Mark Twain, mannerism is a paradoxical risk of improvised narrative. That art, in any case, must be seen for the kind of thing it is and not as a clumsy imitation of something it was never meant to be.

In a perceptive essay on Kerouac's style, Warren Tallman has found its chief influence to be that of Bop, in which jazz fights its way free of structure. The great musicians are those, like Charlie Parker, who without losing their own kind of control make their escape from original melody and rhythm into free improvisation. The performer becomes a performer-composer, a creator of new music. The Bop musician clears away the fixity of conventional pattern to discover a new reality and so recaptures the nature of music itself. His hearer, like Kerouac's reader, listens not only to a musical object but to a musical process in action.

Spontaneous prose must justify itself through such a discovery of its own nature. The author's seemingly random gyrations eventually fall into place as being the only possible way in which his discovery can present itself to his reader as discovery. In the strict sense of a battered old term, his prose is experimental, made up of trial efforts which sometimes come off and sometimes don't. As Kerouac puts it in the "Preface" to *Visions of Cody:* "My work comprises one vast book like Proust's *Remembrance of Things Past,* except that my remembrances are written on the run instead of afterwards in a sickbed."

No doubt, there is also an art of "spontaneity," as perhaps in E. E. Cummings, where the author is not really naive but sentimental, a pretend primitive. Kerouac's work, however, gives every sign, including that of its collapses, of genuine experiment and discovery. *On The Road* and *The Dharma Bums* lead, by and large, to experience which has its being apart from the writing of the stories. They are conventional but mussed up by the author's manner, still tied to the preconceived end which goes far toward determining their structure. The character of Neil Cassaday, the discipline of Zen Buddhism do not depend on having stories told about them for their existence, and the stories emerge mainly as perfervid reports. But Kerouac's blunderingly ironic discovery of his real marriage to his writing, his "constructions," in the teeth of the rival love affair, engrossing, sad, and funny, in the *Subterraneans*, or the surprised discovery of his portentous but rather vaguely allegorical comic-book hero in *Doctor Sax* that evil, as in some kinds of comedy, does away with itself, or the several discoveries of the author in *Lonesome Traveler* of railroading, or shipping-out, or spending a hermit summer as fire-watcher — all these come through to the reader as things found. Again, the problem is not that of the philosophic rightness of Kerouac's conclusions, which, in any case, are only occasionally of philosophic breadth. Rather it is the complex clarity generated by his textual progress.

In addition, there is a second level of discovery, one different from the over-all curve of the story or sketch, which occurs in the line-by-line divagations, the associations of thought and feeling as experienced so that the detail of experience becomes the object of the author's questing.

> . . . ah, loved it all, and the first night finest night, the blood, "railroading gets in yr blood" the old hogshead is yelling at me as he bounces up and down in his seat and the wind blows his striped cap visor back and the engine, like a huge beast is lurching side to side 70 miles per hour breaking all rulebook rules, zomm, zomm, were crashing through the night and out there Carmelity is coming, Jose is making her electricities mix and interrun with his and the whole earth charged with juices turns up the organo to the flower, the unfoldment, the stars bend to it, the whole world's coming as the big engine booms and balls by with the madman of the white cap California in there flossing and wow there's just no end to all this wine —[4]

Locomotive, sex, the wild engineer, his strangely white-capped fireman who merges into the white-capped California coast, the movement of the train, of the earth, and of the universe toward whatever ends they may have, all done up in endless wine — a great jumble no doubt, but one nevertheless held in control by its own context and prevented from flying off on irrelevant historical or philosophical tangents of

[4] *Lonesome Traveler* (New York, 1960), p. 83.

the kind produced in Thomas Wolfe. The specific experience itself. Kerouac leads us not into the subjectivity of his feelings finally, as does Wolfe, but into the objectivity of his writing. As the train bangs along, we hang onto our hats.

One may well argue that Jack Kerouac offers little to the philosophic future of American literature except through his identification with the disaffiliate movement. His literary contribution, however, has a distinction and a value. This may be generalized by reference to a dictum, surprisingly enough, from George Bernard Shaw: ". . . it is the business of the stage to make its figures more intelligible to themselves than they would be in real life; for by no other means can they be made intelligible to the audience." One cannot imagine Shaw and Kerouac finding much common ground for definitions of intelligibility, but both could agree to its mystical nature, as Shaw does in the preface to *St. Joan* from which his opinion is taken. For Shaw, the life is known by intelligence, its specifically generated power of knowing itself. For Kerouac it is more blindly known by accidental experience. It is tactile, felt in many bits and pieces. This kind of knowledge, like the unrationalizable knowledge one has while eating a grapefruit that one is eating a grapefruit, is Kerouac's literary medium and goal in one. It has its obvious limits, but within such limits it achieves its own literary being. This is not confined to the kind of enthusiasm which is most apparent in quotably short excerpts. It can be summed up by saying that the writer comes to a practical knowledge of himself as a writer about his experience and invites the reader to share in that particular and radical literary experience.

Leo Percepied in *The Subterraneans,* after his intense love affair, is sent away by his mistress, Mardou:

> I think you're like me — you want one love — like, men have the essence in the woman, there's an essence . . . and the man has it in his hand, but rushes off to build big constructions.

But his anguish over losing Mardou cannot blunt the rightness of her perception. He has one love. He wants "big constructions" more than he wants her and is willing to make even of their tangled and intimate passion precisely such a construction. It will become the subject of his writing and so, perhaps, be made intelligible to him.

> What'll we do? I think — now I go home, and it's all over for sure, not only now is she bored and has had enough but has pierced me with adultery of a kind, has been inconstant. . . .
> "Baby, it's up to you," is what she's actually saying, "about how many times you want to see me and all that — but I want to be independent like I say."
> And I go home having lost her love.
> And I write this book.

✿ NORMAN PODHORETZ

Norman Mailer: The Embattled Vision

NORMAN MAILER is one of the few postwar American writers in whom it is possible to detect the presence of qualities that powerfully suggest a major novelist in the making. Anyone trying to describe these qualities would be likely to dwell on Mailer's extraordinary technical skill, or on the boldness and energy of his mind, or on his readiness to try something new whenever he puts pen to paper. What seems even more remarkable, however, is that his work has responded to the largest problems of this period with a directness and an assurance that we rarely find in the novels of his contemporaries. Mailer is very much an American, but he appears to be endowed with the capacity for seeing himself as a battleground of history — a capacity that is usually associated with the French and that American writers are thought never to have. He is a man given to ideologies, a holder of extreme positions, and in this too he differs from the general run of his literary contemporaries, so many of whom have fled ideology to pursue an ideal of sensible moderation both in style and philosophy. To follow Mailer's career, therefore, is to witness a special drama of development, a drama in which the deepest consciousness of the postwar period has struggled to define itself in relation to the past, and to know itself in terms of the inescapable, ineluctable present.

Now for many people the only Mailer worth considering is Mailer the realist, and for these *The Naked and the Dead* is the only one of his three novels that matters at all. It is true, I think, that Mailer's phenomenal talent for recording the precise look and feel of things is his most impressive single gift, and there is some ground for arguing that in deserting realism he has made insufficient use of this power. But it was not by arbitrary choice that Mailer abandoned realism, any more than it was by arbitrary choice that he wrote as a realist in the first place. Far from merely being a technique selected for its suitability to the author's talents, the realism of *The Naked and the Dead* is in itself an expression of his response to a certain structure of experi-

Reprinted from *Partisan Review,* XXVI (Summer, 1959), 371–391, by permission of the author.

ence. The world of *The Naked and the Dead* is one in which a varied group of clearly defined individuals are pitted in a very direct and simple way against two allied enemies — the army and nature. Nature brings violent storms and intolerable heat, it provides jungles to be crossed and mountains to be climbed, and it also sets limits to the physical strength of the men exposed to its rigors. The army, on the other hand, is a society, tightly organized, efficiently ruled, and almost as confident of its power as nature itself. From the point of view of the individual, driven by a hunger for absolute freedom, hardly any distinction can be drawn between them. Just as nature threatens him with pain and fear and death, so the army threatens him with moral destruction, aiming finally to destroy his will altogether and reduce him to a mere servant of its own ends. To keep himself alive physically, he must be strong, resourceful, and determined; to keep himself alive spiritually, he must have enormous reserves of inner resistance.

This was an ideal situation for a writer with Mailer's natural gift of observation. Something palpable was there to describe and he described it brilliantly, down to the last quiver of a particular muscle in a man's thigh as he was climbing the face of a rock, down to the last twitch of temptation as he was saying no to an offer of promotion. The availability of a great literary tradition — a tradition which had itself developed out of just such situations in an age when society seemed as solid and substantial and unshakable as the army is in *The Naked and the Dead* — certainly helps to explain how it came about that a first novel by a young man of twenty-five should have exhibited mastery of so high an order. But there is more to the success of the best passages in *The Naked and the Dead* than a happy confrontation of talent, circumstance, and tradition. The rainstorm that descends on Anopopei shortly after the division has landed; the episode in which the platoon drags four huge guns through the muddy jungle in the black of night; the climb up Mt. Anaka — all these are so good and so moving because they are written by someone who in the deepest reaches of his being believes that the world is made up exclusively of stone walls and that life consists in a perpetual crashing of the head against them. It is as though the war provided Mailer with a never-ending succession of examples that confirmed everything he had ever felt or thought about human existence, and one can almost detect the relish with which he piled up the evidence in scene after astonishing scene.

The Naked and the Dead, however, cannot simply be read as an expression of Mailer's feelings about life in general; it also attempts to make certain specific statements about World War II, the American army, and the character of American society. In 1948 Mailer — who was shortly to become a leading figure in Henry Wallace's campaign for the Presidency — subscribed to the notion that our postwar difficulties with Russia were the sole responsibility of American capitalism. We had gone to war against Hitler not because the American ruling class was anti-fascist, but because Hitler had shown himself unwilling to play the capitalist game according to the rules, and the next step was to dispose of Russia, the only remaining obstacle on the road to total power. World War II, then, was the first phase of a more ambitious operation, while the army had been used as a laboratory of fascism, a preview of the kind of society that the American ruling class was preparing for the future. These ideas are brought into *The Naked and the Dead* in various ways. Some of them emerge from the long discussions between General Cummings (the commander of the division that has invaded the island of Anopopei) and his young aide Lt. Hearn (a rich midwesterner whose political sympathies are with the Left and whom Cummings is trying to convert to his own special brand of fascism). Another channel is supplied by the "Time Machine" flashbacks, which are there partly in order to demonstrate Mailer's contention that American society is essentially a disguised and inchoate form of the army. But it is in the main line of the plot that the politics of the novel are most heavily emphasized. The scheme of *The Naked and the Dead* is to follow a single campaign from the preparations for invasion to the mopping-up operation, and the technique is to shift back and forth between command headquarters and one small platoon in the division. This enables Mailer to observe the campaign both through the eyes of the man who is running it and in terms of the day-to-day fortunes of those who are affected in the most immediate way by his every move. The experience of the enlisted men serves throughout as an ironic commentary on the general's behavior, but the irony becomes most pronounced in the last third of the novel when Cummings decides to send a patrol to the rear of the Japanese positions for the purpose of determining the feasibility of a daring new plan that he has just conceived. This decision, prompted not by the interests of victory but by vanity and opportunism, results in the death of three men and in immeasurable misery for several others — all of it wasted. Even after the Japanese have surrendered, the patrol (which has not yet heard the news) is still being dragged up Mt. Anaka, again ostensibly in the interests of victory but really in order to further the mad ambitions of the platoon sergeant, Croft.

The army, then, is evil and the individual caught in its grip has only two basic choices: he can either submit without resistance (and eventually be led into identifying himself with his persecutors) or he can try to maintain at least a minimum of spiritual independence. To be sure, there are many degrees of submission, from Stanley's abject brown-nosing to Wilson's easy-going indifference, but only one character among the enlisted men in the book is still completely unbroken by the time we come upon them: the ex-hobo Red Valsen. As for the officers, they are all (with the exception of Hearn) willing instruments of the evil power embodied in Cummings. Like Cummings and Croft, Hearn and Valsen represent the same principle on different levels of articulation and self-consciousness: they are rebels who do what they have to do but who will not permit their minds or their feelings to be drawn into collaboration with the system. The army proves too strong even for them, however, and ultimately both men are beaten down in much the same fashion.

Mailer's intentions are thus perfectly clear. Cummings and Croft exemplify the army's ruthlessness and cruelty, its fierce purposefulness and its irresistible will to power, while Hearn and Valsen together make up a picture of the rebellious individual who, for all *his* determination and courage, is finally defeated in an unequal contest. But no sooner do we become aware of this intention than we notice that there are forces at work in the novel whose effect is to subvert the general scheme. The most insidious of these, perhaps, is Mailer's tone: *The Naked and the Dead* simply does not *sound* like a book drawing up an angry indictment, though the things it says explicitly provide plenty of ground for indignation. The tone, indeed, is rather more disinterested than partisan; it is the tone of a man whose capacity for political indignation is inhibited by a keen sense of the world as a very complicated place, not easily to be understood by grand formulas. And the strength of this sense manifests itself unmistakably in Mailer's treatment of Valsen and Hearn, who turn out to be less sympathetic than their role in the general scheme would seem to require, just as Cummings and Croft somehow develop into more admirable figures than they were ever meant to be.

Hearn, the rich Harvard graduate, and Valsen, the penniless hobo, have a great deal in common. They are both incapable of attaching themselves to anything or anyone, and they share the nihilistic belief that "everything is crapped up, everything is phony, everything curdles when you touch it." Their rebellion against the system is sterile and ineffective, for it involves nothing more than a determination to preserve their "inviolate freedom," as Hearn puts it, "from . . . the wants and sores that caught up everybody [else]." What Mailer tells us in a key passage about Hearn is also true of Valsen: "The only thing to do is to get by on style. He had said that once, lived by it in the absence of anything else. . . . The only thing that had been important was to let no one in any ultimate issue ever violate your integrity." Style without content, a vague ideal of personal integrity, a fear of attachment, and a surly nihilistic view of the world are not enough to save a man in the long run from the likes of Cummings and Croft, and certainly not enough to endow him with heroic stature — and Mailer knows it. His desperate effort to redeem Hearn toward the end comes too late and in any case lacks conviction: perhaps the weakest passage in the whole novel is the one dealing with Hearn's decision on the night before he is killed to resign his commission and take a principled stand against everything that Cummings represents.

The same desperation shows through Mailer's effort to deflate Cummings and Croft. Like Valsen and Hearn, the platoon sergeant and the general have so much in common that they seem to be the same person in two different incarnations. They are both immensely competent; they are both very brave; they are both contemptuous of weakness; they both suffer from a sexually determined hunger to dominate. Most important of all, what they are both pursuing is the dream of absolute freedom, the dream of exercising will without obstruction or limit. Man, Cummings tells Hearn, is a being "in transit between brute and God," and his deepest urge is to "achieve God." It is this urge that drives Croft to drag the platoon up Mt. Anaka, just as it provokes Cummings to feats of military brilliance. But it is also what establishes the two men as the *natural* heroes of *The Naked and the Dead*. If life is truly what *The Naked and the Dead* shows it to be — a fierce battle between the individual will and all the many things that resist it — then heroism must consist in a combination of strength, courage, drive, and stamina such as Cummings and Croft exhibit and that Hearn and Valsen conspicuously lack. Moreover, Cummings and Croft are the only characters who point to anything like an adequate response to life as we see it in the novel. They are, of course, reactionaries, but they demonstrate (as reactionaries often do) the workings of the radical spirit — which is to say that the principle of their behavior is a refusal to accept the limitations inherent in any given situation as final, a refusal stemming from the conviction that the situation itself need not be regarded as final in advance. The trouble with Hearn and Valsen is their inability to transcend the terms of the given; they know perfectly well that these terms are intolerable, yet they cannot envisage any condition other than the ones before their eyes, and therefore they are reduced to apathy, cynicism, and despair. Croft and Cummings also know that the terms are intolerable, but the knowledge acts as a stimulus to their energies and a goad to their imagination. Though the laws of nature seem to prohibit a man from climbing to the top of Mt. Anaka, Croft, who cannot bear to remain imprisoned within the boundaries of what has already been accomplished, dares to attempt the climb, while Hearn and Valsen shrug helplessly at the sight of the peaks: like liberalism itself, they lack the vision and the drive to push toward the top of the mountain. All this being the case, Mailer either had to give up his liberalism or forcibly prevent Croft and Cummings from running away with *The Naked and the Dead* altogether. Because he was not yet ready to write liberalism off and because it seemed impossible to find virtue in Cummings and Croft without also finding virtue in fascism, he had no alternative but to violate the emotional logic of his novel by destroying them as best he could. The destruction of Croft is spread thin throughout the novel, but the disposal of Cummings is only effected at the end, when Mailer contrives by a shocking twist of plot to rob him of credit for winning the campaign.

The Naked and the Dead, then, shows an exceptionally gifted young writer in the years immediately after the war discovering what he did not know he knew — that American liberalism is bankrupt because it cannot provide an answer to the challenge with which history has presented it. Not only does liberalism confine itself to the terms of the given at a time when there can be no hope of working within these terms, but it is animated by a vision of the world that neither calls forth heroic activity nor values the qualities of courage, daring, and will that make for the expansion of the human spirit. In the "absence of anything else," however, and out of his awareness that it was impossible to "get by on style" as so many intellectuals of his generation were trying to do, Mailer held on stubbornly to his liberal views, even as he was beginning to recognize that his real values tended in an anti-liberal direction. So little, indeed, did liberalism affect his deepest judgments that the most compassionate writing in *The Naked and the Dead* is devoted to the tribulations of the pathological anti-Semite Gallagher when he receives the news of his wife's death in childbirth. Fascist or no fascist, Gallagher is a violent, passionate man, and this was enough to turn the balance in his favor, just as the timidity and mediocrity of Roth, Wyman, and Brown are the decisive factors in the adverse judgment Mailer passes on them. Ultimately what Mailer was looking for — and has continued to look for — is not so much a more equitable world as a more exciting one, a world that produces men of size and a life of huge possibility, and this was nowhere to be found in the kind of liberalism to which he committed himself in the earliest phase of his literary career.

It is characteristic of Mailer — and, I believe, of the essence of his strength as a novelist — that he never pays much attention to intellectual fashion. In 1948, when everyone of any sophistication understood that Henry Wallace had been duped by the Communists, Mailer was campaigning vigorously for the Progressive party, and if this amounted to a confession of political naivete, it also exhibited a healthy reluctance on his part to be guided by the experience of others. He must always work everything out for himself and by himself, as though it were up to him to create the world anew over and over again in his own experience. He abandoned what was then being called "unreconstructed" liberalism only when he could see at first hand why it was wrong to support it, and even then he did so in his own good time and for his own special reasons. Certainly he must be the sole American example of a liberal who responded to the cold war by rushing to embrace revolutionary socialism. There was nothing "nostalgic" about Mailer's new radicalism; only a man who had been affected by Marx and Trotsky down to the very core would have been capable of writing *Barbary Shore,* and it is because he was so profoundly affected that he could blithely ignore all the good arguments against Marx and Trotsky that were in currency at the time. It would be impossible to guess from a reading of this novel that the case it constructs with such loving care had ever been challenged or refuted or in the least damaged. Nor would it be easy to guess that objective conditions played their own imperturbable part in the break-up of revolutionary socialism as an active political movement. Everything in *Barbary Shore* seems to hang on the will of the people involved, and in this sense Mailer is right to describe the book as "existentialist" in spirit.

In Marx and Trotsky, Mailer found a system that brought the courage, vision, and uncompromising determination of Cummings and Croft into the service of freedom and equality rather than class and privilege, and consequently there is no conflict between idea and feeling in *Barbary Shore* of the kind we have seen operating in *The Naked and the Dead.* But if *Barbary Shore* exhibits an almost perfect internal coherence, it also suffers from a certain straining for effect, a certain shrillness and melodramatic solemnity of tone often verging on the pretentious that contrast very sharply with the flawless pitch of *The Naked and the Dead.* The source of this trouble seems to be Mailer's unwillingness to make any use whatever of the techniques he learned to handle so well in *The Naked and the Dead* and his attempt to write in a completely new style. Here again we see him beginning from scratch, repudiating the help of his own past as vigorously as he repudiates the help of everyone else's. But there is more to Mailer's desertion of realism than that. To write realistic fiction a novelist must believe that society is what it seems to be and that it reveals the truth about itself in the personalities it throws up, the buildings it builds, the habits and manners it fosters; all the writer need do is describe these faithfully, selecting whatever details seem to him most sharply revealing and significant, and the truth will be served. But Mailer's point in *Barbary Shore* is precisely that our society is *not* what it seems to be. It seems to be prosperous, vigorous, sure of itself, and purposeful, whereas in fact it is apathetic, confused, inept, empty, and in the grip of invisible forces that it neither recognizes nor controls. To write about this society as though the truth of it lay embedded in its surface appearances would be to endow it with a solidity and substantiality that it simply does not possess. The only hope of making any sense of such a society is with reference to the invisible forces that work in and through it and that cannot be described but that can be talked about abstractly and pictured allegorically. In delineating the world of the cold war, then, what Mailer tries to do is convey a sense of the strangeness of the way things are and to evoke a feeling for the overpowering reality of the invisible forces that supply a key to this strangeness.

Since an extremely bad press and a climate unfavorable to political radicalism resulted in a tiny readership for *Barbary Shore*, let me summarize its plot briefly before making any further observations. Most of the action takes place in a rooming-house in Brooklyn Heights which turns out to be the refuge of a man calling himself McLeod, who — we eventually learn — had once been notorious throughout the world as the "Hangman of the Left Opposition." After breaking with the Communist party on the signing of the Nazi-Soviet pact, McLeod had come to the United States to work for the State Department and had subsequently run off again, this time to devote himself to a Marxist analysis of why the revolution went wrong. An FBI agent, Hollingsworth, is also living in the rooming-house under an assumed identity, and the plot centers around his efforts to recover a mysterious "little object" which had disappeared from the State Department along with McLeod. Neither Hollingsworth nor anyone else knows what the "little object" is, but he assumes that it must be worth a fortune and is planning to steal it himself once he gets it away from McLeod. The landlady, Guinevere, a former burlesque queen secretly married to McLeod, is in league with Hollingsworth, and he also has the help of a girl named Lannie Madison who had literally been driven out of her mind by the assassination of Trotsky and who hates McLeod because he is the "undertaker of the revolution." The story is told by another tenant, Michael Lovett, a would-be novelist who is a victim of total amnesia and so can remember nothing whatever of his past but who, it develops, had been almost as deeply involved in the Trotskyite movement as Lannie. In the end, Lovett decides to devote his life once again to the hopes that had been shattered for him by the wartime collapse of revolutionary socialism, and this decision makes it possible for McLeod to pass the "little object" on to him instead of surrendering it to Hollingsworth, as he had finally agreed to do. In a rather hasty climax, McLeod commits suicide, Hollingsworth runs off with Guinevere before the police arrive, and Lannie is taken into custody. Lovett is left alone with McLeod's will and the "little object," charged with the responsibility of keeping the flame of "socialist culture" alive while he waits for the apocalyptic war that is inevitably to come, hoping against hope that out of the conflagration a new opportunity may arise for realizing the goals that were betrayed in the first great revolution of this century.

Barbary Shore is obviously an allegory, but of what? Most of the reviewers in 1951 took it to be an extravagant view of McCarthyism, but McCarthyism as such is actually a negligible element in the book. Mailer's real subject is the effect on modern life of the failure of the Russian revolution, and if there is an extravagant assumption at work in *Barbary Shore,* it is that *all* our difficulties (political, spiritual, psychological, and sexual) are directly traceable to this failure. "The growth of human consciousness in this century demanded — for its expanding vitality — that a revolution be made," Mailer wrote some years later, and in this sentence, I think, we have the key to *Barbary Shore.* The Russian revolution figures here not as one important historical event among many but (in the words of Lovett) as "the greatest event in man's history," the culmination of an evolutionary process dictated by the inner necessities of the human spirit. The race, in Mailer's view, must either grow into greater possibilities or retreat into less; there can be no stagnation. But the retreat into less is not merely a matter of shrinking or cowering; it involves a disruption of the whole organism, a radical dislocation — it is a disease that infects the life of individuals no less than the behavior of nations. *Barbary Shore* is an investigation of this disease, a pathology of the modern spirit.

The two characters in the book who have been most directly affected by the failure of the revolution are Lovett and Lannie. After his first political discussion with McLeod, Lovett begins to recall his days as a member of a Trotskyite study group, and he describes them in a remarkably evocative passage:

> I was young then, and no dedication could match mine. The revolution was tomorrow, and the inevitable crises of capitalism ticked away in my mind with the certainty of a time bomb, and even then could never begin to match the ticking of my pulse. . . . For a winter and a spring I lived more intensely in the past than I could ever in the present, until the sight of a policeman on his mount became the Petrograd proletariat crawling to fame between the legs of a Cossack's horse. . . . There was never a revolution to equal it, and never a city more glorious than Petrograd.

Lovett's amnesia is the consequence of the death of this passion, and its effect has been to cut him off from everything, including his own experience. He represents the modern consciousness, and the weird unfamiliar world that we see through his eyes is in fact intended as a picture of the world we all inhabit. In Lannie, we get an image of the modern consciousness in its most violently pathological aspect. The loss of hope in her case has taken the form of guilt for having presumed to think "that there was a world we could make," and her insanity consists in a total surrender to the given — submitting herself with grim enthusiasm to the brutal handling of Hollingsworth and to the bewildered narcissism of Guinevere. This surrender constitutes insanity because the given (as Lannie herself says in an extraordinary outburst to Lovett) is a world whose nature has been most sharply revealed in the Nazi death camps. What follows from the surrender, moreover, is a frantic attempt to reinterpret the moral meaning of things: "There is neither guilt nor innocence," she tells Lovett, "but there is vigor in what we do or the lack of it," and it is in Hollingsworth and Guinevere that she imagines she sees vigor. Hollingsworth she believes to be strong and purposeful, for to her he is the embodiment of those who now rule the earth, while to the raucous, grotesque, and vulgar Guinevere she makes her sick love, calling what Guinevere symbolizes good and beautiful and begging it to discover its goodness and beauty in her eyes, just as she wants only for the powerful to discover their strength in exercising it upon her.

If Lannie and Lovett together make up a picture of the modern consciousness, Guinevere and Hollingsworth must be regarded as different aspects of the disease engendered by the failure of the revolution. Nothing could be more fantastic than the way everyone takes Guinevere to be the fulfillment of his own special desires. Her vitality, however, is only superficial, the air of abundance about her is a lie, and she lacks the wherewithal to deliver on her vast promise. Given all this, I would suggest that she figures in the allegorical scheme as an image of the life outside politics, the attempt to live by and for self, the purely private life, and that she is Mailer's comment on the sorry possibilities of such a life in America today.

Hollingsworth's role is easier to formulate, since it is described explicitly by McLeod in an analysis of the forces that make the Third World War inevitable. Today, he says, "the aim of society is no longer to keep its members alive, but quite the contrary, the question is how to dispose of them." This is "the first stage of cannibalism" in a process leading inexorably to the destruction of the world, and it expresses itself initially in the rise of a class of bureaucrats who came to power "at the very moment they are in the act of destroying themselves." Far from being strong and purposeful, then, Hollingsworth is the creature of conditions he neither controls nor comprehends and the victim of inner compulsions he neither respects nor recognizes. Sick with greed and homosexual longings, he can only find relief in outbursts of petty sadism and in the symbolic seduction of McLeod (whose crimes, Lannie declares at one point, were responsible for his very existence). Mailer, however, gives him a moment of genuine self-consciousness in which, like a character in poetic drama, he is suddenly permitted to enunciate the principle of his own being with force and conviction:

> More modesty. We ain't equipped to deal with big things. If this fellow came to me and asked my advice, I would take him aside and let him know that if he gives up the pursuits of vanity, and acts like everybody else, he'd get along better. Cause we never know what's deep down inside us . . . and it plays tricks. I don't give two cents for all your papers. A good-time Charley, that's myself, and that's why I'm smarter than the lot of you.

This is the doctrine by which the disease being investigated through Guinevere and Hollingsworth calls itself health and by which the blindness to reality that is one of its major symptoms claims the right to be known as "realism."

At the center of *Barbary Shore* stands McLeod, the incarnation of the revolutionary spirit itself. His biography amounts to a moral history of that spirit — its early achievements, its subsequent crimes, its temporary abdication, and then its agonized attempt to find new strength by a humble return to "theory." The "little object" that McLeod has stolen from the State Department is never identified, but we can be fairly confident in thinking of it as Hope or Dedication or Vision or a "coagulation" of all three — the loss of it is what accounts for the gradual and subtle derangement of the system and the possession of it by this lone individual entails the most fearful of responsibilities. Vision and hope and dedication, at any rate, are the qualities that separate McLeod from all the other characters and that finally enable him to jolt Lovett out of his stupor and to win the support of Lannie. By the rigorous terms set up in *Barbary Shore* he points to the only possible course left to the modern consciousness — which is to hold on with all its might to the "little object" while crying a plague on both your houses to the two contending powers in the cold war who are irrevocably committed to the cause of death. The heritage McLeod passes on is a feeble thing, but it means feeling for Lovett where there was apathy before and relatedness where there was absolute isolation.

What it meant for Mailer, however, was another matter entirely, since the grand heroic life he was looking for could no more be found in revolutionary socialism than in liberalism. If the one is bankrupt in drive, vision, and imagination, the other is dead in practice, frozen in outworn categories, and cut off from the living realities of the present. Several years after the appearance of *Barbary Shore* Mailer declared (in replying to Jean Malaquais' attack on his *Dissent* article

"The White Negro") that Marxism had failed in application because it was "an expression of the scientific narcissism we inherited from the nineteenth century" and motivated by "the rational mania that consciousness could stifle instinct." One might almost take this as a criticism of the cold, tense, claustrophobic brilliance of *Barbary Shore* itself; and indeed, Mailer's abandonment of revolutionary socialism in favor of the point of view he calls "Hip" was as much a repudiation of ideological thinking in general as of Marx and Trotsky in particular. Here again we have an example of the curious relation to intellectual fashion that appears to mark the movements of Mailer's mind. Just as he remained untouched by all the sophisticated arguments against "unreconstructed" liberalism that were circulating so energetically through the intellectual atmosphere of 1948 until he had discovered their truth for himself and in his own good time, so he had to go through a period of revolutionary fervor and ideological rigidity before beginning to yearn (as so many former radicals had done before him) for a breath of fresh air and a supple, open-ended point of view. Unlike the great majority of his literary contemporaries, who knew all about the deleterious effects of ideological commitment without ever having tasted the accompanying passion, Mailer was able to experience both the passion and the rigidity on his own pulses, and when he finally turned against ideology it was with the roar of a man betrayed, not with the complacency of the wise at one remove. And again — as in the case of his shift from liberalism to revolutionary socialism — he followed a wholly unexpected path in making his escape from the constrictions of ideological commitment.

In the Hipster (whom he calls the American existentialist) Mailer believes he has found an effective mode of rebellion against the terms of the given neatly combined with the flexibility and openness to life that were lacking in revolutionary socialism. In contrast to Lovett — who had nothing to do once he accepted the "little object" from McLeod but drift from one back alley to another while waiting for the apocalypse to come — the Hipster has developed a strategy for living fully and intensively in the present. He too refuses to have any truck with the world around him and he too recognizes that collective death is the goal toward which our society is moving, but he differs from Lovett in the further refusal to pin his hopes on the future. Having no future, he cares nothing for the past and therefore he is totally consigned to the fluctuating dimensions of the "enormous present." In effect, the Hipster as Mailer describes him in "The White Negro" is a man who follows out the logic of the situation in which we are all presumably caught: a man who, faced with the threat of imminent extinction and unwilling to be a party to the forces pushing toward collective death, has the courage to make a life for himself in the only way that conditions permit — by pursuing the immediate gratification of his strongest desires at every moment and by any means.

The full consequences of this new position for Mailer's work are yet to emerge, but several results have already become visible in *The Deer Park* — which, though written before "The White Negro," belongs to Mailer's Hip phase — and in the completed sections of the ambitious novel on which he is currently engaged. The most important consequence, perhaps, is that Hip, with its "burning consciousness of the present" and the "terribly charged" quality of experience it involves, has allowed Mailer to make a more intensive use of his great powers of observation than he has done since *The Naked and the Dead.* Whereas *Barbary Shore* seems to have been produced by a mind shut in upon itself and glowing with the febrile intensity of a lonely intellectual passion (it is a book such as might have been written by one of those brooding, distracted students who haunt the pages of Russian literature), *The Deer Park* exhibits a newly liberated capacity for sheer relish in the look and feel and sound of things. Mailer is now back in the world that he deserted in *Barbary Shore,* though it is by no means the same world that he evoked in *The Naked and the Dead.* What he sees in Hollywood is the image of a society that has reached the end of its historical term, a society caught between the values of an age not quite dead and those of a new era that may never crawl its way out of the womb. The defining characteristic of such a society is a blatant discrepancy between the realities of experience and the categories by which experience is still being interpreted — a discrepancy that can make simultaneously for comedy and horror. The reality is that the scruples, inhibitions, and conventions which were once effective in restraining the natural egoism of the individual no longer work very well because the values from which they drew their strength no longer command much respect. No one, however, is willing to admit this, and they all go on talking and sometimes acting as though what they "really" wanted were the things that people used to want when their basic psychological drives were still roughly in harmony with their professed values — when, that is, these values were powerful enough to create internal needs that became almost as pressing as the primary needs themselves. This situation reveals itself in every department of life, but it is in sex that its contours are most clearly defined, and therefore it is on the sexual affairs of his characters that Mailer concentrates in *The Deer Park.* What he gives us is a remarkable picture of people saddled with all the rhetoric of the monogamous while acting like some primitive tribe that has never heard of monogamy and is utterly bewildered by the moral structure on which this strange institution rests. It is a world of people who talk incessantly about being in love and craving "decent, mature relationships" but who are in fact tightly imprisoned in their own egos and who have no true interest in anything but self. For them sex has become a testing-ground of the self: they rate one another on their abilities in bed, and the reward of making love is not so much erotic satisfaction or spiritual intimacy as a sense of triumph at being considered "good." Mailer's attitude toward all this — I mean the attitude built into his tone and his emphases — is very tricky. There is an unmistakable note of shocked disapproval at many of the things he is describing, yet he insists on treating them with the respect due a major fact of experience. What follows from that respect is a highly disciplined refusal to dismiss the "decadent" narcissistic sexuality of his characters either as immoral or (what comes to the same thing) immature, either as sinful or unhealthy. It would be difficult to exaggerate the originality of this approach, for it is almost impossible to think of another serious American novelist who has even so much as attempted to study contemporary sexual life on its own terms, let alone one who has brought to the subject anything resembling Mailer's readiness to find the organizing principle, the principle of meaning, that may be implicit in these terms.

The Deer Park takes place largely in Desert d'Or, the favorite resort of the Hollywood movie colony, and it centers mainly on Charles Francis Eitel, a famous and very talented director who has been blacklisted for refusing to cooperate with a Congressional investigating committee and who, after holding out for a whole year against all the pressure to capitulate, finally collapses and gives in. This, of course, is the standard Mailer situation — the rebellious individual crushed by the powers that be — but we do not have to read very far into the novel before we realize that Mailer's view of the nature of the conflict has changed considerably since *The Naked and the Dead*. Hearn and Valsen were defeated in a contest against a hopelessly strong adversary; it is not, however, the strength of his adversaries that defeats Eitel. The two producers Teppis and Munshin are formidable enough in their own way but they are also — what Cummings and Croft could never be — figures of comedy and objects of ridicule. For the first time in Mailer, then, victory over the system has become possible to those who can see through it and who are sufficiently brave to act on what they see. Eitel, a sensitive and intelligent man, understands the secret of the system quite as well as the two characters in the novel who succeed in overcoming it — the narrator Sergius and the diabolical young pimp Marion Faye — but he fails because he lacks the courage to disregard "all the power of good manners, good morals, the fear of germs, and the sense of sin," and to turn himself into a complete and ruthless egoist.

Sergius and Marion are thus the natural heroes of the world of *The Deer Park,* as Cummings and Croft were the natural heroes of

The Naked and the Dead, and since Mailer is aware of this, there is no need for him to wrench our sympathies in a direction that the novel itself refuses to support. He does, however, make several positive assertions about Sergius and Marion that are as unwarranted aesthetically as the negative assertions made in *The Naked and the Dead* about Cummings and Croft. It is impossible, for example, to believe that the Sergius we see moving around in *The Deer Park* could ever have developed into the author of this novel.[1] Not only is he simpleminded, unimaginative, affected, and basically sentimentatal, but (what is perhaps more to the point) utterly dismissing in his view of other people. When Eitel, who has been his good friend, finally capitulates to Teppis and Munshin and the Committee, Sergius cuts him off brutally — he has failed and is therefore entitled to no further consideration. There is no question that this is the final judgment Mailer himself passes on Eitel, but it is only a final judgment and it is qualified and complicated by the rich, full picture we get of the process that brought Eitel to the painfully sorry pass in which we see him in the last chapter of the novel. Now it is hard to credit that the man who could respond so insensitively to his friend's failure would ever have been able to summon up the subtlety and the insight to understand how a failure of this sort comes about. Nor could such a man conceivably have produced the account of Eitel's affair with Elena, where every nuance in the progress of a vastly complicated relationship is registered with a delicacy and a precision that recall Proust himself. He would also have been incapable of the brilliant comic portraits of Munshin and Teppis, which are so good precisely because they are *not* dismissing — Mailer devastates the two producers while allowing them their full due. Nothing we see of Sergius in the novel could explain how he might have come to compose the marvellous letter of self-justification that the drunken Elena sends to Eitel after she has gone to live with Marion — that letter in which a girl who has been universally snubbed and patronized because of her social crudity suddenly bursts forth with astonishing power as a woman of feeling and perception.

But if Sergius could not conceivably be the author of *The Deer Park,* Eitel very easily could; what Mailer has done here is to endow Sergius with Eitel's sensibility, just as he tries to endow Marion's nihilism with grandiose theological significance. The reason, I think, can be found in "The White Negro," where Mailer tells us that the nihilism of the Hipster is really a creative force. In Hip "incompatibles have come

[1] To forestall the obvious objection, I ought to explain that Sergius's role as narrator is comparable not to Nick Carraway's in *The Great Gatsby* but to Marcel's in Proust. Moreover, he is an active character in the story, one of whose purposes is to explain why he rather than Eitel must be considered the true artist.

to bed, the inner life and the violent life, the orgy and the dream of love, the desire to murder and the desire to create." Yet the curious thing is that the Hipster who "lives out, acts out, follows the close call of his instinct as far as he dares," who is the herald of a revolution moving "backward toward being and the secrets of human energy," and whose subversiveness takes the form of a constant pursuit of immediate gratification — the curious thing is that this "adventurer" of the night is deeply suspicious of feeling and mortally afraid of passion. The nihilism of Marion Faye, for example, amounts to a rebellion *against* feeling, a kind of Nietzschean repudiation of his "civilized" or Christian self. Everything he does is done precisely because it is repugnant to him, and he believes that "there is no pleasure greater than that obtained from a conquered repugnance." He is not naturally cruel and therefore he forces himself to be hideously cruel; he is not naturally vicious and therefore he cultivates the vices with the grimness of a hermit scourging himself in the desert. Similarly with Sergius, who bends all his efforts toward the perfection of a style based on the suppression of spontaneous feeling: above all he wants to be *cool*.

The irony is that with Sergius and Marion we are back again to Hearn — and he is still trying to get by on style and an ideal of personal integrity. It is much the same style and derives from much the same source (the unavailability of radical political solutions), but in the rank atmosphere of cold-war stalemate it has grown and matured and begun to mistake itself for a portentously weighty philosophy. At the time of the Korean war, when the apocalypse seemed about to descend at any moment, Hearn (who had been killed off in *The Naked and the Dead* before his newly formed resolve to throw off his surly nihilism could be tested) reappeared in *Barbary Shore* split into the amnesiac Lovett and the madwoman Lannie. The loss of the political faith that would have sustained him in the 30's was now seen by Mailer as worse than simply a sign of spiritual inadequacy — it was a sickness of the mind and a disease of the soul. But his brave attempt to recapture that faith proved to be only a dramatic gesture in the face of a dramatic situation; when the situation lost its drama and settled into the dull round of aimless anxiety that marked the Eisenhower years, the gesture lost its air of glory, as all apocalyptic gestures inevitably do when the apocalypse itself takes too long in coming. Under these circumstances, Mailer turned back to the old Hearn and began to cast about for hidden resources of creativity where before he had seen only the emptiness of mere style, and for stature where before he had perceived only a well-intentioned mediocrity. In identifying himself finally with Hearn, he has in effect acknowledged his kinship to the intellectuals of his own generation — that generation of whose failings he has always been the most intransigent critic and whose qualities he has always tried so hard to extirpate from his own character. His espousal of Hip indicates that he is still trying — for what else is Hip as he defines it but a means of turning away in despair (as most of his contemporaries have done) from the problems of the world and focusing all one's attention on the problems of the self without admitting that this must automatically entail a shrinking of horizons, a contraction of the sense of possibility, a loss of imaginative freedom?

One can only sympathize with Mailer's latest effort to maintain a sense of huge possibility, even if one is totally out of sympathy with some of the doctrines he has recently been preaching. In my opinion, his great mistake is to attribute direction and purpose to the Hipster (and I think that the weakness of Sergius and Marion as imaginative creations indicates that the novelist in Mailer is once again resisting the commands of the theoretician). Hipsterism, it seems to me, is a symptom and not a significant protest, a spasmodic rather than an organized response. The Hipster is the product of a culture (exemplified beautifully in the Hollywood of *The Deer Park*) whose official values no longer carry any moral authority, and he reacts to the hypocrisy, the lying, and the self-deception that have contaminated the American air during the cold-war period by withdrawing into a private world of his own where everything, including language, is stripped down to what he considers the reliable essentials. To this extent, his response to the America of Eisenhower bears a certain resemblance to Hemingway's response to the America of Woodrow Wilson. As many critics have pointed out, Hemingway's prose was generated by the wish to liberate language from the fine lying rhetoric in which Wilsonian idealism had cloaked the horrid realities of the First World War; like the personal style Hemingway elaborated in his stories — the code of courage and craft in the face of a constantly threatening universe — the prose style itself was the expression of an effort to establish a truth of human experience that would be proof against the distorting encrustations of "culture" and "civilization," a truth (as it were) of the state of nature, a truth at rock-bottom. But the difference between Hemingway and the Hipster is the difference between mastering a bad situation and being victimized by it, between exercising intelligence, sensibility, and discipline in order to overcome the rot of history and seizing upon the rot of history as an excuse for resigning from the painful responsibility to exercise the mind at all.

If it is true that Mailer has been reading things into Hip that are simply not there — and just those things that Hip would need to satisfy his demand for size and importance and a sense of huge possibility — then we can be fairly certain that sooner or later his restless imagination will light out for some other territory. Indeed, he has already shown signs of an impulse to drop his original emphasis on the political significance of Hip in favor of what he takes to be its theological implications. The idea, apparently, is that God is "no longer" omnipotent and therefore needs the help of man to fulfill the "enormous destiny" with which He has been charged (by whom Mailer does not say). Here is how he put it spontaneously to an interviewer:

> . . . I think that the particular God we can conceive of is a god whose relationship to the universe we cannot divine; that is, how enormous He is in the scheme of the universe we can't begin to say. But almost certainly, He is not all-powerful; He exists as a warring element in a divided universe, and we are a part — perhaps the most important part — of His great expression, His enormous destiny; perhaps He is trying to impose upon the universe His conception of being against other conceptions of being very much opposed to His. Maybe we are in a sense the seed, the seed-carriers, the voyagers, the explorers, the embodiment of that embattled vision; maybe we are engaged in a heroic activity, and not a mean one. . . .

The attraction of this astonishing collection of ancient Christian heresies for Mailer comes out explicitly a little later in the interview:

> This involves new moral complexities which I feel are far more interesting than anything the novel has gotten into yet. It opens the possibility that the novel, along with many other art forms, may be growing into something larger rather than something smaller, and the sickness of our times for me has been just this damn thing that everything has been getting smaller and smaller and less and less important, that the romantic spirit has dried up. . . . We're all getting so mean and small and petty and ridiculous, and we all live under the threat of extermination. . . .

We get some notion of what Mailer means by these "new moral complexities" from the prologue to his novel-in-progress which was published in the Fall 1958 issue of *Partisan Review* under the title "Advertisements for Myself on the Way Out." The reader, he announces, must be prepared "for a dissection of the extreme, the obscene and the unsayable" in this "tale of heroes and villains, murderers and suicide, orgy-masters, perverts, and passionate lovers," and it is abundantly clear that the exploration of these "mysteries" is to be made without the help of any traditional moral assumptions. Murder is not necessarily to be regarded as evil, perversion is not necessarily to be considered perverse, suicide is not necessarily to be looked upon as an act of simple self-destruction, and so on. We can now only wait to see what comes of all this, and Mailer being so unpredictable a writer, the one safe guess we can make is that it will turn out to be very different from what many readers of "Advertisements" have assumed — very different and very much more exciting than most of the fiction that is being produced by most of the other novelists of his sorely beleaguered generation.

❧ BEN SIEGEL

Victims in Motion:
Bernard Malamud's Sad and Bitter Clowns

SINCE 1952 Bernard Malamud has published three novels and a collection of short stories. Each is a moral critique, an attempt to explore and reveal the melancholic state of the human condition, its basic — even banal — realities. Having undertaken this Socratic search into the human soul, Malamud's favorite vantage point is the dark prison of the self. From there he looks out upon a somber, cramped, and joyless world in which failure and calamity are daily staples. Thus if such literary compeers as Saul Bellow, Philip Roth, and Herbert Gold create active participants in a prosperous society, Malamud does not. His sad and bitter clowns are outsiders. Most are urban Jews — a few tradition-bound, the majority secularized. But all — Jews and non-Jews alike — are uncertain, unlucky, and unloved.

Malamud does not view modern society as blameless for man's tragic plight, but neither does he consider anyone the mere passive victim of social cruelty or neglect. His people embody their own self-destructive demons. If they are social misfits, it is primarily of their own doing. They are incompetent or unworldly, or both. Like Miller's Willy Loman, they can't stand success; they finally must destroy it.

In *The Natural* (1952), Malamud's only non-Jewish novel, both Roy Hobbs and society contribute to his ultimate tragedy. Roy had emerged from the backlands with a champion's physical co-ordination, a childlike innocence, and the unshakable conviction he would be "the best there ever was" in baseball. Roy pays the price of his humanity. For his *hybris* the gods administer the first blow: they send a tantalizing but demented young temptress who promises him sex but instead fires a silver bullet into his intestines. But much more traumatic than near-death for the young athlete is his glimpse of the chasm between his heroic self-image and actual moral flabbiness.

Seventeen years pass before Roy again reaches the major leagues. Years of wandering and defeat spur him to superhuman feats, but

Reprinted from *Northwest Review,* v (Spring, 1962), 69–80, by permission of the author.

present again is a sexual temptress to hasten his fall; present also are
the temptations that have outlasted Rome: bribe money, succulent
foods, the crowd's tyrannical adulation. Malamud knows his baseball
folklore and makes the diamond exciting, even important, skilfully
attributing to Roy some of its most memorable historical moments.
But baseball is not Malamud's prime concern. He is interested primarily in the comi-tragic paradoxes of modern existence, particularly
as these paradoxes reveal the progressive corruption of a basically
honest professional athlete. But to add depth and breadth to his essentially simple narrative, he follows the mythological trail blazed by
James Joyce through twentieth-century literature. Malamud's particular guides, however, are Jessie Weston and T. S. Eliot and their
handling of the Holy Grail motif in *From Ritual to Romance* and *The
Waste Land*. Hence Roy Hobbs becomes not only Shoeless Joe Jackson
but Achilles in his tent and Sir Percival in vain pursuit of the Holy
Grail. And his team, the New York Knights, is managed by Pop
Fisher, who not only suffers from a skin ailment, but bemoans continually the "dry season" and the woeful state of his "club."

Wielding his lightning-scorched bat, Roy lifts the Knights into pen-
nant contention, but his success and happiness are short-lived. To the
sin of pride he has added gluttony, and his health fails. Only then does
he half-heartedly agree to throw the crucial game — changing his mind
when it is too late. As newspaper headlines shout his disgrace, Roy
stands in the street and weeps. A newsboy then sobs the immortal
words (supposedly leveled at Joe Jackson of the Chicago "Black Sox") :
"Say it ain't true, Roy." Suffering has taught him not only "to want
the right things" but the difficulty of being a "hero" in a society that
demands its knights resist the fruits those of weaker flesh hasten to
enjoy.

Overpraised at publication, *The Natural* has since been undeservedly
devalued. (Hemingway's *The Old Man and the Sea* offers an obvious
parallel.) Actually, its true literary worth falls about midway between
past and present critical judgments. For if its symbolism and language
are frequently strained, both are handled more effectively than some
recent critics (several of whom obviously haven't bothered even to
read it) have realized. And if the characters consistently are more
metaphor than flesh and blood, they never lose completely their human
connections. In any event, Roy Hobbs serves as archetype for all of
Malamud's small heroes, who — like their larger Greek and Shake-
spearean counterparts — fall victim to a tragic flaw aggravated by
misfortune.

Malamud's last three books deal primarily with contemporary Jewish life and represent the most consistent — if not the most "realistic"
— recent attempt to blend the traditional Yiddish folktale with the

modern American scene and its values. Malamud most resembles such Yiddish masters as I. L. Peretz, Mocher Seforim, and Sholem Aleichem in his concern for morality and ethics rather than aesthetics. Like them, his central subject is ambivalent, unpredictable human nature. And where many contemporary American-Jewish novelists search "for the human being in the Jew, Malamud (like his Yiddish predecessors) seeks the Jew in the human being. "All men are Jews," he has declared, and he attempts to raise the alienated Jew's deep personal suffering to the level of universality.

Malamud's second novel, *The Assistant* (1957), is a parable of atonement and conversion reversing the familiar assimilation story: beginning with a sinful act, it traces the painful expiation. His Jews are not "good" in the traditional sense; few, in fact, reveal any concern for Judaism as a coherent body of doctrine. They share only a communal sensitivity to persecution and suffering. Ritual and custom are for Malamud mere surface trimmings; all that matters is the human heart — that is, man's essential dignity and responsibility to his fellows in a grim, inhuman world.

Roy Hobbs's tragic ineptness and ill-fortune are paralleled by Frank Alpine, a shabby, broken-nosed Italian wanderer from the West who is as uncertain of his identity as the most alienated Jew. With an accomplice Frank robs Morris Bober, an honest but inept grocer whose only "talent" is for poverty. But Frank is a thief haunted by childhood stories of St. Francis of Assisi, whom he resembles in name and appearance. Frank reappears shortly after the robbery seeking to undo his crime, and begs the bewildered grocer to let him work for nothing. When Bober refuses, Frank descends to a living death in the Bober cellar. Only when Bober has a heart attack is Frank able to don the grocer's apron and rejuvenate the dying business.

Frank longs to confess his current past and begin a clean future. But he is afraid of losing what little he now has attained. Nor is he ready for redemption. For despite his sincere repentance, Frank cannot resist stealing from Bober and lusting after the grocer's lonely daughter, Helen. And he is plagued by the certainty that eventually he will cause his own undoing: "Sooner or later everything I think is worth having gets away from me. . . . Just when it looks like I am going to get it I make some kind of a stupid move, and everything . . . blows up in my face."

Nor can Frank shake past prejudices, experiencing self-repugnance for living so close to Jews in such ugly, confined quarters. Only a Jew can imprison himself like this, he thinks. "That's what they live for, to suffer." Yet if the Jews get on his nerves, they also arouse in him a gnawing curiosity. Frank asks Bober why he neither goes to synagogue nor adheres to the dietary laws. Bober replies he is concerned only "to do what is right, to be honest, to be good." But the dissatisfied clerk then inquires why "the Jews suffer so damn much?" and is shaken by Bober's reply: "I suffer for you."

Inevitably, Bober catches Frank stealing and fires him. Hoping to win sympathy, the latter blurts his part in the robbery, but this Bober had guessed. Frank also spoils his chances with Helen — who was beginning to return his love — when he loses self-control and rapes her. Driven from the Bober home, Frank is cut off from his only means of expiation. But he is able to return when Bober dies of pneumonia. And as a rabbi drones platitudes over her father's body, Helen Bober's thoughts underscore Malamud's recurrent theme: "He made himself a victim. He could, with a little more courage, have been more than he was."

But if dead and a recognized failure, Bober continues to shape the lives he left behind. Frank determines not only to win redemption by taking Bober's place, but to rewin Helen "with discipline and love." He reopens the store and falls into Bober's routine, even to wearing his clothes. Between customers Frank reads the Bible and thinks often of St. Francis. In the spring he has himself circumcised: "The pain enraged and inspired him. After Passover he became a Jew."

Doctrine plays little part in Frank's conversion; Judaism merely provides him with a practical means of enduring the suffering necessary for salvation. As Christian-Jew, Frank Alpine becomes Everyman, exemplifying the fundamental unity of man's spiritual needs. For Malamud, religion's function is to convey the essentials of the "good heart"; he has little sympathy either for the ghetto-minded Jew or parochial Christian.

If *The Natural* has been downgraded undeservedly, *The Assistant*'s obvious moral values and rejection of the parochial have caused it consistently to be overrated. Admittedly, Malamud achieves considerable dramatic effect by implication, compression, and suggestion. But in his eagerness to develop his themes of moral indebtedness and responsibility, he describes rather than explains his characters' deeper and darker emotions. His people never are more than ritual figures in a deterministic morality play. Yet *The Assistant* undeniably remains a probing and disturbing study of modern man's social and spiritual confusion.

As much cannot be said, however, for any of Malamud's shorter tales. He is not a major short-story writer. The same impatience to develop idea rather than character is all the more evident in the thirteen wry, ironic vignettes comprising *The Magic Barrel,* which won the 1959 National Book Award for fiction. Despite his award, Malamud is here more entertainer than explorer. However, he does avoid the cliché of the Jewish social-protest and "hot-pastrami" writers, and despite some obvious plot and character indebtedness to the Yiddish storytellers, he does fashion his own vernacular. For example, where Mendele and Aleichem's prose conveys the slow, deliberate tempo of the European *shtetl* — or small town, Malamud's idiom is terse, rapid, and urban. It is a Hemingwayesque Yiddish-English mannered and highly stylized. Yet the bitterly ironic Yiddish undertone remains.

But if his tales catch eye and ear, they only occasionally arrest heart and mind. Disbelief is seldom suspended, for always there are the ingenious symbols, the picturesque (even grotesque) characters, and the quick, mildly shocking conclusions: two men kissing, two death-chants for the living, several victor-victim reversals, a Negro-Jewish angel, and innumerable flashes of self-revelation. If on occasion these endings actually illuminate the truth behind the masks, more often they leave the reader slightly dazzled and bemused.

Yet even the most disappointing tales remain strangely haunting segments of human experience. "The First Seven Years," moreover, not only recasts the Jacob-Rachel story but reveals the early stirrings of *The Assistant*. Feld, a prosperous shoemaker, is appalled to discover that Sobel, his homely refugee assistant, wants to marry his attractive teenage daughter. Feld is cruel, insulting — and then filled with sudden pity for this sad, bookish man who had missed Hitler's incinerators only to fall in love with an American girl half his age. Sensing the match is inevitable and that his dreams of a better life for his daughter are best forgotten, Feld requests only that his assistant not ask for her hand until she is twenty-one. Sobel is content.

A somewhat similar shock of recognition is experienced by Gruber, the greedy, unfeeling landlord of "The Mourners." Having failed repeatedly to dispossess an elderly tenant from a tenement room, the landlord bursts in to find the old man sitting on the floor moaning. The latter is bewailing his own misdeeds, but the guilt-stricken Gruber interprets the chant as a prayer for the dead. In fact, he decides the old man is mourning for him — for his lost compassion and humanity. Seizing a bedsheet for a prayer-shawl, the abashed Gruber sinks down beside the old man to mourn for himself. The old man's probable surprise at this sudden act of contrition is exceeded only by that of the unprepared reader.

But if one Malamud character wins the right to remain, several others overcome the inner forces imprisoning them in their rooms. Mitka, the unsuccessful novelist of "The Girl of My Dreams," sulks in his room because of repeated failure. But a published short-story by one "Madeline Thorne" fires his interest, and he forces a meeting with the reluctant writer. His resultant disappointment is crushing: "Madeline" is lonely, pathetic, middle-aged. And her name is Olga.

His dream girl, like all his dreams, had fragmented, disappeared. He will go back and "entomb himself forever." But Olga feeds and counsels him, assures him "character" is what counts. Mitka pities her, himself, the world. When she leaves, Mitka discovers the crushed, defeated Olga has awakened something in him. Now, whatever his fate, he will meet it in the world.

At that, Mitka's chances for success are better than those of George Stoyonovich, the lost, uneducated youth of "A Summer's Reading." Unable to find a job George, too, hides, in his room. To placate his hardworking sister and curious neighbors, George lets slip that he plans a summer reading a library list of one hundred books. He then is able to walk the neighborhood feeling the silent but approving glances. In a few weeks, however, sister and neighbors begin to doubt. George returns to isolation, but admiration and respect have proved heady wines. One fall evening George runs to the library, counts off a hundred titles and sits down to read. George's failure is inevitable, and the reader is left to ponder its possible ramifications.

But if Malamud returns repeatedly to man's frightened need for success and status, he is no less interested in the mocking irony of human ingratitude. The human animal, as Malamud sees him, neither understands nor appreciates kindness. In "The Prison" that is the candy store bestowed on him by his father-in-law, Tommy Castelli finds life intolerably dull. His one interesting customer is a homely ten-year-old who constantly steals candy. Tommy doesn't know how to help her. When his wife catches the little girl stealing, Tommy defends her. Yet as the frightened child is being led to punishment, she repays Tommy's kindness by sticking out her tongue at him. Obviously, kindness or generosity makes man vulnerable and ashamed.

And in the strangely disembodied tale he calls "Take Pity," Malamud illustrates that selfishness can engender cruelty. Rosen, an ex-coffee salesman, had led a sickly and lonely existence; now he is in a post-mortal state. In life he had attempted to help a friend's widow and two children, asking nothing in return. But the widow, with obvious dislike, had rejected his generous offers. Stubbornly determined to "give" her something, Rosen had willed her his possessions and turned on the gas. Now she stands beneath his window with upraised arms and "haunted, beseeching eyes." However, Rosen, who has given all he has to give, shouts insults at her, orders her home.

Another who misses his chance to pay a debt is tenement janitor Willy Schlegal in "The Bill." Willy runs up a needless bill of eighty-three dollars at the Panessas' dark little grocery and then switches to the self-service market. Obsessed by guilt, he develops a hatred for the elderly Panessas. When a letter from Mrs. Panessa pleads for ten dollars for her sick husband, Willy hides in the cellar. But the next day he pawns his overcoat and runs back with the money — only to discover the grocer emerging in a coffin. Willy's sinking heart informs him he will never rid himself of his debt. (Only in his later form as Frank Alpine will he achieve expiation.)

Money, of course, need not change hands to scar a friendship or man's inner being. In "The Loan," Lieb the baker and his wife, Bessie, are approached by his estranged friend Kobotsky. He needs money for his sick wife. For Lieb their past friendship is not dead; he is willing. Bessie is not. They, too, she argues, are elderly and sick. A heated debate follows. Kobotsky tells them not to fight: he has lied. His wife has been dead five years; the money is for an overdue headstone. Bessie remains adamant, and Kobotsky is forced to leave empty-handed. Their now-famous parting slices deep into the memory: the two elderly men "embraced and sighed over their lost youth. They pressed mouths together and parted forever." Each again has learned that life's recurrent crises have no "solution" — at least on this earth.

Malamud, however, does hold out the possibility of occasional divine assistance — provided one believes. For much faith is needed to recognize the incongruous shapes of God's possible messengers. In "Angel Levine," for instance, the Job-like Manischevitz is guilty of being man and Jew. A once-prosperous tailor but now a pitiable failure, he is told his dying wife can be saved only by his recognizing a Negro with the unlikely name of Alexander Levine as "a bona-fide angel of God." The tailor's orthodox mind boggles at the seeming irreverence of "a black Jew and angel to boot." But if he rails against God and disavows his previous beliefs, he is forced ultimately to track Levine to a Harlem bar and proclaim him a Jewish emissary from on high. Returning home the tailor finds his wife hale and hearty. Overwhelmed, he blurts the punchline to a score of Yiddish jokes: "A wonderful thing, Fanny. . . . Believe me, there are Jews everywhere." Malamud thus affirms not only the possible presence of God's spirit "in all things" but joins Norman Mailer and Leslie Fiedler in the attempt to say something meaningful about Negro-Jewish relations.

But if Malamud's Jews are not quite "everywhere," a few of them do make it to Italy, that perennial fount of sophistication and self-knowledge for fictional Americans. There Henry Levin, the pretentious hero of "The Lady of the Lake," learns the consequences of moral cowardice and self-denial. When Henry inherits some money, he heads for Europe seeking romance. In the process he changes his name to (what else?) Henry R. Freeman. On an Italian island estate he falls in love with a dark-eyed beauty he believes to be of an aristocratic Italian family. To her pointed question, the unbelievably dense Henry three times denies his Jewishness (strangely enough no cock crows). Only then does she reveal herself as the caretaker's daughter and a Buchenwald survivor. And as she treasures her tragic past, she declares she will marry only a Jew. Henry then quickly admits his Jewishness but embraces "only moonlit stone," for she has fled into the mists. And if Henry Levin-Freeman is a clear Semitic descendant of Henry James's naive pilgrims, his exotic Jewess is obviously out of Shakespeare by way of Scott.

"Behold the Key" presents another American innocent abroad. Carl Schneider, a young graduate student in Italian studies, is in Rome with wife and children and needs an apartment. He quickly discovers there is much to Italian life not found in books. A shabby rental agent leads him on a picaresque journey through Rome's "apartment" life until the ideal place is found. But the key is held by the owner's discarded lover, who demands a bribe. Carl refuses so un-American a gesture, and is plummeted into a mesh of intrigues and arguments. When entrance to the apartment finally is gained, the weary pilgrims discover the spiteful lover has ruined the interior. As Carl bravely proclaims his undaunted love for Italy, the angry lover appears to hurl the key at his fellow Italian — who adroitly ducks. It strikes Carl on the forehead, leaving "a mark he could not rub out." So if his failure to grasp the Latin character has stirred hatred between brother Italians, Carl now has a key to the enigma marked on his flesh.

A more permanently scarifying experience is Arthur Fidelman's in "The Last Mohican." Having failed as a painter, Fidelman has come to Rome to write a critical study of Giotto. He carries one extra suit and his opening chapter. But his first hello seals his fate. He is spotted as an easy mark by a skeleton in knickers, one Shimon Susskind. The crafty, voracious Susskind — whose single redeeming feature is a compulsion to survive — follows Fidelman everywhere; insisting that he too "knows" Giotto, he demands an equal share of the American's meager money and clothes. When Fidelman gives him four dollars, Susskind asks: "If four, then why not five?" He shrugs off insults and threats and makes his victim feel guilty at every meal. When the desperate American demands why he should feel "responsible" for him, his tormentor coolly replies: "Because you are a man. Because you are a Jew."

Susskind repays Fidelman's kindness by destroying his manuscript. "I did you a favor," he tells the enraged visitor. "The words were there but the spirit was missing." During the grotesque pursuit that follows, Fidelman has a "triumphant insight." He shouts to the fleeing spectre, "Susskind, come back. . . . All is forgiven." Apparently Susskind's insight is even deeper — he keeps running. But if nothing else, Fidelman, through suffering and loss, has gained wisdom. Heaven's agents come in strange shapes indeed.

Malamud's title story, "The Magic Barrel," underscores again the impossibility of rejecting the demands of the flesh. Nearing graduation Leo Finkle, an ascetic, scholarly rabbinical student, decides to acquire a wife. He calls in a marriage broker, Pinye Salzman, who promises the timid Leo results from the photographs and information cards he keeps in a barrel.

For Leo, looking for a wife proves a soul-shattering experience. One prospect asks how he became "enamored of God," and the future rabbi unconsciously blurts: "I came to God not because I loved Him, but because I did not." But he guiltily consoles himself that he is a Jew and that a Jew suffers — and if he was imperfect, his ideal was not. And he feels this new self-knowledge will help him find a bride.

But his hopes fade; most of Salzman's protographed faces bear the marks of defeat. Yet the final one, a face of sadness, regret, and evil, touches his heart. If Salzman is delighted at the prospect of a commission, he is horrified at Leo's choice. Her picture was a mistake, he protests. The girl is wild, "like an animal. Like a dog. For her to be poor was a sin. This is why to me she is dead now. . . . This is my baby, my Stella, she should burn in hell." Leo is adamant. This girl will understand — perhaps even love — him. Yet when the old man finally agrees, Leo suspects a well-laid trap.

Stella, appropriately enough, awaits him under a street lamp. As Leo rushes toward her, he notes her eyes ". . . are filled with desperate innocence," and he pictures in her "his own redemption." Around the corner the old marriage broker leans against the wall to chant the prayer for the dead. But what has died may be Salzman's honesty, Leo's innocence, or Stella's guilty youth: all merit lamentation. What is clearer is Malamud's reluctance to give up on anyone. Each being is unique, responsible, imperfect, and redeemable. No one is beyond redemption, and in most instances love is the surest means of attaining it.

If in *The Magic Barrel* Malamud fluctuates uncertainly between realism and allegory, he remains essentially a moralist. His persistent theme here is the almost frightening consequences of the human encounter. Those whose lives entangle our own, no matter how lightly, he reiterates, alter irrevocably our and their lives. None is ever the same, and this implies the moral obligation of love, or at least concern, toward one another.

Several critics (most recently Philip Roth, in *Commentary*) have criticized Malamud for his concentration upon the small, innocuous "private life" to the total neglect of controversial public issues. But Malamud's latest novel, *A New Life* (1961), indicates a definite broadening of his social horizon. Not only is it a penetrating satire of the academic life lived at many American colleges, but its hero is

Malamud's first to share the social indignation of the angry and mis-guided proletarian prophets who filled Jewish novels during the Thirties. Seymour Levin, also, is a spiritual wanderer, having severed his Judaic roots and values. He, too, is driven by love and lust, duty and selfishness, and — beneath his waywardness and self-indulgence — by a painfully stern morality. Moreover, Malamud adds to his novel's "realism" by unabashedly settling a series of old and deeply personal scores, for the characters clearly are drawn from his own teaching experiences.

Yet basically *A New Life* repeats Malamud's belief that the human struggle is one of few successes and many failures but that the important thing is to endure. It stresses also that the past is never buried but rises always to poison the present.

Seymour Levin fits easily into the Malamud pattern. For if Frank Alpine, as lonely western Christian, journeyed east to be transfigured and absorbed by the small but unified Jewish world there, Levin merely travels from east to west. There, in the equally isolated Northwest college community of Eastchester, his beard, black fedora, and Yiddish inflection mark him "outsider." But his failure to gain acceptance is due to other reasons. Levin lacks both the Wandering Jew's passive underdog psychosis and Alpine's Christian patience and humility. He cannot remain a spectator to crimes against the liberal spirit. Nor is he the comic *shlemiel* of Yiddish literature, as some critics would have it; rather, he is close to the traditional *shlimazel*: the ill-starred blun-derer who can expect the worst return for the best intentions, evil for every kindness, punishment for every misdeed. For him to sin is to get caught. And Levin quickly proceeds to do both.

He has come to Cascadia College in search of integrity, rebirth, continuity, "a new life." He is determined to be a good English in-structor, to forget an unhappy childhood, and to live down a series of alcoholic failures. To his pent-up urban spirit the Northwest's vistas present a new world. Like a famous namesake, Tolstoy's Konstantine Levin, he finds the mountains, air, woods, and streams overwhelming. At first he is exultant and hopeful, but his "new life" soon proves little different from what it was. He wanders the streets alone. Reaching out for friendship, he receives only friendliness. He envies the stu-dents their youth, good looks, and futures, as well as their sense of belonging. And as had Frank Alpine, he lives in constant fear of not being able to master his inner compulsions.

His work, however, provides his most crushing disappointments. Cascadia College graduates engineers and farmers. The few literature courses are reserved for others; he teaches only composition. The students are interested only in passing grades, while his colleagues — reacting to social pressures and physical setting — long since have lost intellectual curiosity and integrity. Moreover, Levin is compared repeatedly to one Leo Duffy, a "disagreeable radical" who two years earlier had been dismissed for unorthodox behavior. Although he promises himself not to repeat Duffy's errors, he finds himself occupying Duffy's office and reliving his predecessor's ill-fated existence. Excruciatingly lonely, he yields to sexual temptations, becoming involved finally with his departmental chairman's wife — Duffy's ex-mistress. Yet he can't enjoy his stolen fruits; in addition to his fear of being caught, he is plagued by conscience. For despite having discarded his Judaic heritage, he remains a descendant of Israel's priestly Levites. Hence his shame is intense and spirit-shattering; every sin causes a "pure Levin reaction, for every pleasure, pain."

He shares also the Levitical need to fight misuse of the human spirit and written word. Zealous to impart knowledge to his students, to teach them "what's for sale in a commercial society, and what had better not be," he overdoes it, breeding only incomprehension and dissension among students and faculty. Increasingly frustrated at his failures to establish his ethical standards at the college, he resorts to his opponents' tactics: deceit, connivance, and blackmail.

The final scene is pure Malamud in its symbolism, irony, and pathos. Discharged and beardless, Levin heads south in a second-hand car, crushingly aware his search for integrity and happiness has produced mainly guilt and failure. Not only has he relived Leo Duffy's experiences, but he carries with him a woman he no longer loves and her adopted children. She, however, is pregnant, so Levin has, in a sense, found his "new life." If he has mitigated loneliness at some cost to his identity (his child will be but half-Jewish), he actually has gained a partial Malamud victory. In other words, Levin has begun his transformation into Everyman.

A New Life is Malamud's best effort. Plot and background develop more slowly, characters are more fully realized. His sad, eager, little people are neither villains nor paragons; they stand revealed as frightened, love-starved human beings entangled in their own motives, weaknesses, and emotions. But if Malamud here has written his best novel to date, he still could have produced an even better one. He occasionally gives vent to a self-conscious virtuosity which results in lengthy, brittle, and pseudo-poetic ruminations. If dazzled, the reader also is distracted. Also distracting are Malamud's repeated efforts to impose physical nature upon his urban outsider and his essentially urban problems. His Levin is not Tolstoy's, and the pastoral theme so integral to *Anna Karenina* here seems forced and extraneous.

Still, Malamud's technical skills are undeniable. He has an inspired eye and ear for the revealing gesture or word. When under control, as it is during most of *A New Life,* his language is spare, imaginative, and lyrical. If his characters often are left without illusions, they are never completely crushed or dehumanized. If his works are near-achievements rather than major accomplishments, they reveal always an ironic yet compassionate insight into the dark dilemma that is modern life. Surely few of us today can afford to ignore such assistance.

✻ IHAB H. HASSAN

Carson McCullers: The Alchemy of Love and Aesthetics of Pain

> *Un Ange, imprudent voyageur*
> *Qu'a tenté l'amour du difforme,*
> *Au fond d'un cauchemar énorme.*
>
> BAUDELAIRE

SINCE the publication of *The Heart Is a Lonely Hunter* in 1940, when its author was only twenty-three years old, Carson McCullers has been recognized as one of the most likely talents in the South. The next decade, which remains the most productive of her career, saw her established as an important writer who brought strange and artful gifts of sensibility to the contemporary novel. The strangeness, however, reminded some readers of Poe's artifices, and it persuaded them to discredit her fiction as simply Gothic. The judgment at best is hasty. It is true that Mrs. McCullers lacks the scope, strength, and fury of Faulkner, lacks his dark apprehension of the Southern past and his profound insight into the American wilderness, symbols both of our guilt and innocence. And it is also true that Mrs. McCullers, hypnotized as she seems to be by the burning point where love and pain secretly meet, forgoes a certain richness of surface which, let us say, Eudora Welty seldom misses. Still, the Gothic element, the personal principle in Mrs. McCullers' work, excludes none of the larger aspects of the Southern tradition to which it belongs. In his recent introduction to *Great Tales of the Deep South*, Malcolm Cowley has summarized well these aspects of the Southern literary mind: a mind preeminently aware of custom and ceremony yet deeply responsive to the elemental nature of existence, a mind anxious to preserve the sense of place and time, of family and community, of folk life and, above all, of oral discourse. Its basic assumption seems to be, as Robert B. Heilman has noted in *Southern Renascence,* that "The concrete evi-

Reprinted from *Radical Innocence* by Ihab Hassan, by permission of Princeton University Press. Copyright © 1961 by Princeton University Press. This essay first appeared in *Modern Fiction Studies,* v (Winter, 1959–60), 311–326.

dence of the human being is that he does not change much, that he may actually be harmed by the material phenomena usually implied by *progress,* and that in any case his liability to moral difficulty remains constant." Formal and conservative, oriented at once towards the personal and the mythic, therefore symbolic, the Southern imagination seems determined to capture man in his very essence. Hence its marked anti-existential bias — "in the *ethos* of Jefferson and Yoknapatawpha, the essence of man lies in being, not in having or doing," John Maclachlan has said of Faulkner's country *(Southern Renascence).*

It is precisely within the framework of these assumptions that the Gothic imagination of Carson McCullers operates. Yet being Gothic, which is to say Protestant — for the Gothic may be conceived as a latent reaction to the Catholic hierarchy under God — being both Protestant and Gothic, her imagination derives its peculiar force from a transcendental idea of spiritual loneliness. The relevance of that idea to the work of Carson McCullers has been demonstrated by Oliver Evans in his fine essay in *New World Writing 1.* Our business must remain less specialized; it must encompass the whole spectacle of love and pain which constitutes her fiction, and in which the idea of spiritual isolation comes repeatedly to focus. For so broad a view, some provisional clarifications are necessary.

To say that Mrs. McCullers has a Gothic penchant is but to note, and note superficially, her interest in the grotesque, the freakish, and the incongruous. Such qualities, to be sure, exert a large influence on the contemporary imagination. There is another sense, however, in which the Gothic element may be defined more pertinently. The Gothic insists on spiritualization, the spiritualization of matter itself, and it insists on subjectivism. We have it from Erwin Panofsky that "Late Gothic art broke up into a variety of styles" reflecting the ideological developments of the Middle Ages; these developments were "unified by a subjectivism" which extended from the visual arts to the political sphere *(Gothic Architecture and Scholasticism).* The Gothic impulse is also transcendental: it reaches out in a piercing line to the sky. The distinction Allen Tate has made, in *The Forlorn Demon,* between the symbolic and the angelic imagination is here apposite. The first, like Dante's, is catholic: "It never begins at the top; it carries the bottom along with it, however high it may climb." The second, like Poe's, is both Gothic and Protestant: in a transcendental effort of the will, "it declares itself independent of the human situation in the quest of essential knowledge." It should not be difficult to see how the mysticism of Suso and Eckhart, the idea of prayer in Luther, the experience of spiritual horror without sensible correlative in Poe, and the Gothic nightmare of alienation in the fiction of Carson McCullers fall into a sombre sequence.

Protestant as the fundamentalist tradition of the South may be, and Gothic as its experience of guilt and tragedy is likely to appear, it is the peculiar stamp of subjectivism, wistful and bizarre, that emerges like a watermark on every page Mrs. McCullers has written. Such introversion, we are accustomed to say, is a result of the disjunction between the self and the world which contemporary life has magnified. The point is sharply made by Nathanael West, a past master of the grotesque, through one of the characters in *Miss Lonelyhearts* who says, "The trouble with him, the trouble with all of us, is that we have no outer life, only an inner one, and that by necessity."

The necessity is the wheel, the cross, to which the characters of Carson McCullers are bound, and often bound without hope of remittance. Yet it is only fair to add that her attitude is more complex than I imply. There is, of course, one sense in which Mrs. McCullers can be said to celebrate the lonely and the outcast, the frail children of the earth, those, like Singer in her first novel, who have in their face "something gentle and Jewish, the knowledge of one who belongs to a race that is oppressed." Adolescents and freaks are her rueful heroes because the first are as yet uninitiated and the latter are forever unacceptable; both do not belong, and in both physical incompleteness is the source of a qualitative, a spiritual difference. And lonely as her characters are, encased as they are in their teeming dreams, most private of human expressions, their actions usually serve only to intensify their solitude. Their situation is, as Oliver Evans has noted, "not so much a comment on the futility of communication as it is on the undesirability of it." But there is still another sense, deeper and more significant, in which Carson McCullers can be said to underscore the inadequacy of subjectivism. The integrity of her vision depends on her guiding insight into the hopelessness of our predicament, caught as we are between dissipation of the self in a mass society — what Ortega called immersion in the Other — and dissipation of the world leading to madness or hermeticism. For the novelist, who is compelled by the exigencies of his form to negotiate continually between the self and the world, the dilemma is an everlasting challenge.

The challenge of form is the measure of insight; the formal tension between the self and the world in the novel corresponds to the thematic juxtaposition of the power of love and the presence of pain in the vision of Carson McCullers. It is in *The Ballad of the Sad Café* that the doctrine of love, implicit in all her fiction, is most clearly enunciated. The passage deserves extensive quotation:

> First of all, love is a joint experience between two persons — but the fact that it is a joint experience does not mean that it is a similar experience to the two people involved. There are the lover and the beloved, but these two come from different countries. Often the beloved is only a stimulus for all the stored up love which has lain

quiet within the lover for a long time hitherto. And somehow every lover knows this. He feels in his soul that his love is a solitary thing. He comes to know a new strange loneliness and it is this knowledge that makes him suffer. . . . Let it be added that this lover . . . can be man, woman, child, or indeed any human creature on this earth.

Now, the beloved can also be of any description. The most outlandish people can be the stimulus of love. . . . Therefore, the value and quality of any love is determined solely by the lover himself.

It is for this reason that most of us would rather love than be loved. . . . And the curt truth is that, in a deep secret way, the state of being beloved is intolerable to many. The beloved fears and hates the lover. . . .

Here are some consequences of this remarkable statement: To love is to suffer, to intensify one's loneliness. Love needs no reciprocation; its quality is determined solely by the lover; and its object can be as "outlandish" as the world may offer. Hence the grotesque nature of the objects of love in Carson McCullers' fiction: hunchbacks, deaf mutes, weddings, clouds. Hence also the de-sexualization of love since the love relation, often incongruous, does not admit of sexual communion. "By nature all people are both sexes," Mrs. McCullers says. "So that marriage and the bed is not all by any means." Singer, Brannon, Penderton, Amelia, and the men-women freaks who appear in her fiction are all bi-sexual, which is to say a-sexual. Then, too, without reciprocity, love becomes a crazy whirligig, the object of one love becoming the subject of another — witness Macy, Amelia, Lymon, Macy, in *The Ballad of the Sad Café*. Finally, love as a pure attitude of the lover towards *any* object seems to be beyond Protestantism and to arrogate for itself the powers of God. As Tate put it with regard to Poe, man as "angelic delegate of God" is empowered to perform His functions: "not only is every man his own God, every man *is* God."

The Protestant element in disembodied love is as obvious as the Gothic element in the uncouth objects which love must choose. But by far the most startling consequence of Mrs. McCullers' idea of love is its avowal of pain, of *death* itself. It would seem that love, in intensifying the lover's pain, in precluding communion, and in electing outlandish recipients, seeks its own impediments. A revealing parallel is suggested by Denis de Rougemont in his book, *Love in the Western World*. De Rougemont argues that certain types of love which seek continually to defeat their end mask the fearful powers of the death wish. Boundless Eros, or transcendental Love, "despises Venus even when in the throes of sensuality," and whether it manifests itself in Courtly Love or Manichaean mysticism, it "intensifies our desires only to offer them up in sacrifice." Its real end is death.

The omnipresence of pain in the work of Carson McCullers, the spectacle of a love forever seeking its own denial, leads us to a similar conclusion. The single affirmative note is sounded almost accidentally, and it is sounded by those who simply endure: Portia and Brannon in Carson McCullers' first novel, by members of the chain gang in her last story. "Radiance" and "darkness," "ecstasy" and "fright" — these are the words with which the two works end, words that defy resolution.

II

The Heart Is a Lonely Hunter, 1940, the first of Mrs. McCullers' books and the longest, anticipates in many ways the power and ambiguities of her achievement. Despite its disconsolate title, the novel finds a way of acknowledging the social realities of its time. Its events hark back to the economic distress of the thirties and reverberate with the distant echoes of Nazi tyranny, and its spirit shudders with the "strangled South." But it is from the singular relation of the characters to one another that the book takes its shape. What makes the relations singular, literally, is that they are all centripetal: all the the characters are singly drawn towards one man, the deaf-mute, Singer, who stands bewilderedly at the center. The novel's structure is broken up to convey the sense of "mutual isolation"; each person remains in a padded cubicle, victimized by the very dreams which nourish his dignity.

There is Biff Brannon, quietly observing the scene from behind his restaurant counter, a lonely man capable of strange, ambivalent feelings of tenderness — towards his dead wife, Alice, towards the adolescent girl, Mick Kelly, towards the revolutionary, Jake Blount. Brannon is forever waiting, forever asking the impossible question: Why? We shall have occasion to see more of him later. There is Jake Blount, the uncouth Marxist, violent and rootless, forever crying out "you dumb bastards" to all the world, forever dreaming of himself as a wanderer among crowds, carrying on his shoulders a great burden which he can never put down. There is Benedict Copeland, the Negro doctor, forever smoldering with the fire of the oppressed, and bound by a harsh concept of dignity to a life of labor. He is proud like Faulkner's Lucas Beauchamp and as intransigent, but less wise in his attachment to an abstract idea of justice. Alienated even from his family, he can assent to but never allow himself to understand his daughter, Portia, when she says: "Us talk like our own Mama and her peoples and their peoples before them. You think out everything in your brain. While us rather talk from something in our hearts that has been there for a long time." Through Copeland and Blount, the novel gains its force of social reference; the idea of fascism abroad is constantly played off against that of racism at home. Yet it is only fair to add that neither Copeland nor Blount is permitted to present his simplistic view of social evil unqualified — in their rare meetings, reformers both, they can only testify to their discord. But it is probably Mick's story of negative initiation to the world that imparts to the book its pathos. Searching at once for privacy and recognition, she moves outwards from a musical core in the "quiet, secret night" of her being. We see her revert momentarily to childhood in a decorously adolescent party; grope towards an adult understanding of her broken father; suddenly confront the experience of sexual knowledge; and finally, assuming too early a financial duty incommensurate with her dream of fulfilment, we see her settle down to a life of drudgery in a Woolworth store. Her "initiation," which leads to a dead end, is complete, and it is attended by the bitter feeling that she has been somehow cheated. "Only nobody had cheated her. So there was nobody to take it out on."

Singer, of course, appears as the focus of repose in a circle of sad, tormented, and lonely people. He becomes the town legend, its hero, confessor, and enigma. "Each man described the mute as he wished him to be." He asks nothing, listens endlessly to what he cannot hear. To him flock all who would unburden themselves: their desperation requires no fuller response than a mute can offer, and their Protestant confessions need only a deaf confessor. He is sought, as Brannon puts it, "because in some men it is in them to give up everything personal at some time, before it ferments and poisons — throw it to some human being or some idea. They have to. In some men it is in them — The text is 'All men seek for Thee.' " At times he appears to take upon himself the mystery of things, playing the role of an unwilling Christ for men whom, in the end, he is powerless to redeem. In the spiritual hierarchy of the novel, Singer's position is clearly defined in his own dream:

> Out of the blackness of sleep a dream is formed. There were dull yellow lanterns lighting up a dark flight of stone steps. Antonapoulos kneeled at the top of these steps. He was naked and he fumbled with something that he held above his head and gazed at it as though in prayer. He himself knelt halfway down the steps. He was naked and cold and he could not take his eyes from Antonapoulos and the thing he held above him. Behind him on the ground he felt the one with the moustache [Blount] and the girl [Mick] and the black man [Copeland] and the last one [Brannon]. They knelt naked and he felt their eyes on him. And behind them were the uncounted crowds of kneeling people in the darkness. His own hands were huge windmills and he stared fascinated at the unknown thing that Antonapoulos held.

What the novel makes abundantly clear is that the charisma of Singer does not simply derive from his receptivity to the sorrows of others, nor from his own affliction and forbearance, but mainly from the fact that he alone in the novel is a *lover,* he alone loves. The object of his love is a cretin, a deaf-mute, Antonapoulos, who appears in the preceding passage sanctified, and who elsewhere appears "sitting motionless in his bright, rich garments . . . like some wise king from a legend," but who is in the end simply Man, the Unlovable Creature, redeemable only by an impossible Lover.

The meeting of the various characters in Singer's room, late in the novel, is a focal point in its development. Hitherto, each character has been impelled to seek the mute by a sense of his own desperation; when they all meet together at last, their jarring interests, their spite and suspicion, fling them further apart. Together at last, they represent a society, not of communion, but of collective isolation. The ironic void at the center of the novel is made evident when Singer, after the death of his Greek friend, commits suicide, precipitating a debacle in the lives which surround him. (Only in this sense can the novel be seen as "an ironic parable of fascism," a description of the work which seems to have encrusted itself like a barnacle in the standard reference works on contemporary authors.)

It is at this point that our attention is drawn back to Biff Brannon, with whom the novel opens and also closes. In Brannon we are asked to entertain an image of clumsy endurance, a will for right action which no excess of hate or suffering or disenchantment can wholly suspend. And we recognize that his final vision, though its promise falls short of redemption, is somehow more central than Singer's and more viable:

> For in a swift radiance of illumination he saw a glimpse of human struggle and of valor. Of the endless fluid passage of humanity through endless time. And of those who — one word — love. His soul expanded. But for a moment only. For in him he felt a warning, a shaft of terror. Between the two worlds he was suspended . . . he was suspended between radiance and darkness. Between bitter irony and faith. Sharply he turned away.

The presence of pain, the failure of initiation, the betrayal of love, and the horror of solitude — these somehow define the tragic confrontation with reality which Mrs. McCullers chooses for her characters. But the tragic confrontation, in this novel much more than in the later works, retains a certain ambiguity, a kind of elusiveness, which the form is incapable of bringing to account. The failure of form can be clarified, I think, with reference to a statement Mark Schorer has made in *Society and Self in the Novel:* "The novel must find a form that will hold together in some firm nexus of structure the individual human being and the social being . . . for it is in the connection, in the structural nexus, of the self-responsible individual and the socially related individual that the moral springs of action lie. . . ." *The Heart Is a Lonely Hunter* is addressed to some wide social and religious issues, and it is at the same time deeply concerned with the secret issues of the soul. Yet the nexus between the soft private thing and the world of pogroms and economic exploitation is never firmly established, just as the nexus between Singer's love for the Greek and the Christian idea of redemption is never made convincing. The metaphor of the freak as sacrificial hero cannot hold the novel together, and neither can the style, which vacillates between a perception of things as they are and a feeling of things as they are hoped to be.

III

Reflections in a Golden Eye, 1941, is a starker tale. It shares with Mrs. McCullers' best work, *The Ballad of the Sad Café,* the atmosphere of primitive terror, "that Sense of The Awful which is the desperate black root of nearly all significant modern art, from the *Guernica* of Picasso to the cartoons of Charles Addams," as Tennessee Williams, who ought to know, has put it in his Introduction to the book. It also shares with *The Ballad* the laconic form of a fable, just as her earlier novel shares with *The Member of the Wedding* a certain density of social specification and an underlying mood of ineffable sadness. The novelette renders a world of stealthy, chaotic feelings in a lapidary style, poetic through the precision of its implications; the grotesque aberrations of the characters involved are reflected in a cold and steady mirror of which the disquieting symbol is a peacock's eye. "A peacock of ghastly green. With one immense golden eye. And in it these reflections of something tiny and . . . grotesque" — in these words, Anacleto, the Filipino servant, playfully describes a sinister vision to his ailing mistress. But the Golden Eye only reflects; it does not see. The various personages move towards an inexorable fate, which is itself a product of their instinctual necessities, in a manner reminiscent of Paul Bowles' somnambulist creations.

The novelette is set in a Southern army camp. The action, which contrasts in its growing violence with the monotony of the camp, covers little more than a month. In the austere words of the author, the participants are "two officers, a soldier, two women, a Filipino, and a horse." A savage, improbable relation soon develops between Private Ellgee Williams and Captain Weldon Penderton, and in developing it energizes the whole story. Williams is a silent twenty-year-old animal who remains to the end an enigma. His sudden actions — whether he buys a cow, declares his faith in the Lord, kills a man, enlists in the army, rides a horse naked in the sun, or steals in every night to watch the Captain's voluptuous wife, Lenora, sleep in her bed, unconscious of his feral presence — all remain equally unaccountable in logical, moral, and, perhaps, even dramatic terms. But the motives of Williams' antagonist take on a more subtle color. Captain Penderton — who, incidentally, wears a truss, and is at once a savant and a kleptomaniac — shows a "sad penchant for becoming enamored of his wife's lovers"; and he is also both a coward and a masochist. The polarity of the two men is obvious. It is further magnified, or rather distorted, by a network of unstable relations. Leonora, sensual and obtuse, takes Major Morris Langdon for her lover, a bluff, thoughtless man whom the Captain greatly admires — till Williams comes on the scene. The Major's wife, Alison, is a suffering, neurotic woman. Ever since the death of her malformed baby — it *would* be malformed! — she can attach herself to no one except the festive Anacleto, an Ariel to Williams' Caliban, who shares with his mistress a world of tender phantasies. And in the middle stands the brilliant, powerful horse of Leonora, Firebird.

The horse may stand as an embodiment of instincts and the military camp as an image of social regimentation. Between the two, men must somehow mediate. This is the predicament on which Captain Penderton reflects: "You mean . . . that any fulfilment obtained at the expense of normalcy is wrong, and should not be allowed to bring happiness. In short, it is better, because it is morally honorable, for the square peg to keep scraping about the round hole rather than to discover and use the unorthodox square that would fit it?" The unorthodox square! This is one way of mediation. But Mrs. McCullers implies that there is another, the way of love, of *relation*. In the book all relations fail: the relation of man to man and man to woman, of man to environment and woman to child. All communication is blocked, vitiated, or restricted to the inarticulate moment which witnesses Private Williams riding a horse naked in the sun or watching Leonora sleep in a dark room. Love, dispensing with its object, reaches the dead end of Protestant isolation.

Technically, of course, the book has more firmness than its predecessor. The style can light on a fraction of huge time, while the mind is both shocked and sensitized beyond speech. The skillful structure makes good use of flashbacks, developing the action without halts, and maintaining a certain overlapping in the narrative — hints dropped and picked up again — so that suspense and revelation keep in step. And Mrs. McCullers finds the right if lurid gesture for each character — the Captain abandoning himself voluptuously to a mad ride on

Firebird, Alison cutting off her nipples with garden shears, etc. Yet the novel remains somehow inert, brutish. In the peacock's golden eye the dreadful existence of each person goes unredeemed. As the novel shifts its focus from one character to another — it is a portrait gallery — no "lucid consciousness" emerges to interpret or qualify the whole. Only Alison, who has the gift of partial insight, can do so, though she is herself blind to what touches her most closely. And the violent denouement of the *novella,* which neither she nor Anacleto is present to interpret, confirms our prevailing sense of barrenness. Yet it is not the presence of "underlying dreadfulness," as Tennessee Williams has put it in his gallant defense of the book, to which one objects; it is rather the absence of life. A comparison with Lawrence's "St. Mawr" and "The Prussian Officer," or even Faulkner's *Sanctuary,* makes it clear that Carson McCullers is not primitivist. She can recognize the forms which primitive impulses take, but she cannot always render the sense of joy and defiance that the best primitivists irradiate. Her work, haunted by the need to suffer, lacks the energy that redeems suffering.

IV

In *The Member of the Wedding,* 1946, Carson McCullers exhibits the kind of formal unity which her first novel lacks. There is also a smarting sense of life in the work, a profound sense of change, and a quality of intense groping which the behavior of the central characters seeks continually to incarnate. The story is primarily that of Frankie Addams, a motherless, twelve-year-old girl engaged in a romance with the world. The agonies of growth, the search for identity, the paradoxical desire to escape, to experience, to belong, suddenly converge on Frankie on the occasion of her brother's wedding, which becomes the intolerable symbol of all her longings and the focus of her perverse misunderstanding of the adult world.

Like Mick Kelly, Frankie is first of all animated by the desire to escape: escape boredom, escape her identity, escape the South itself. Her life, like the dream she relates to a fortune teller, is a door slowly opening on nowhere. "You going, but you don't know where. That don't make no sense to me," Berenice, the Negro cook, expostulates. Yet Frankie dimly knows what she is escaping *from.* It is partly the familiar scene of lazy buzzards, rotten gray shacks, and lonesome cotton fields she watches on her bitter return from the wedding. It is also an accident of identity that Berenice recognizes as inescapable. "We all of us somehow caught," Berenice says. "We born this way or that way and don't know why. But we caught anyway. . . . And maybe we wants to widen and bust free. But no matter what we do we still caught." And when John Henry, Frankie's six-year-old cousin, asks in his child's voice, "Why?" Berenice can only answer, "Because I am black. . . . Because I am colored. Everybody is caught one way or another." Frankie, however, cannot reconcile herself to the condition of "being caught." She is still propelled *towards* experience, still obsessed by images of the "spinning world" which riddle the novel in response to her romantic imagination, to her need of giving substance to her dreams. Images of the world, the same that in *Antony and Cleopatra* betrayed the expense of love, betoken here the promise of initiation.

Yet it is characteristic of initiation in the modern world that its course must be oblique and its rewards ambivalent. Mrs. McCullers' treatment of the traditional theme of sexual initiation is to the point. The sexual impulse, as we might have been led to expect, is diffused through the novel; it acts as a faint, persistent scratching on Frankie's consciousness; and it is never really understood. Nowhere do we perceive Frankie's insight into sexual experience or confront the action which gives form to that insight. This is not to say that sexual initiation is the central theme of the novel. It is not. The point is simply that initiation no longer requires the commitment of action, the definition of choice, or the confirmation of self-knowledge. Frankie's dominant mode of coming to terms with the world is *feeling,* and her prime mode of acquiring experience is *dreaming.* She dreams of participating in the war as a Marine, of traveling round the world with the bridal pair; she likes to pretend that she is a Mexican or a Hollywood star. Against the wiles of her phantasies, even Berenice is powerless.

But the animating center of the novel, the unifying force in Frankie's character, is of course her wish to belong. "She belonged to no club and was a member of nothing in the world." If she dreams inordinately, it is because her dreams confirm her in the illusion that she is enlarging her experience and also permit her to believe that she is at one with the world. Thus, the blood she wants to donate to the Red Cross is not simply a modest token of heroism; it would flow "in the veins of Australians and Fighting French and Chinese, all over the world, and it would be as though she were close kin to all these people." The urgent need to belong comes to focus in the ritual of the wedding. Frankie, in search of we-hood, says of her brother and his bride, "they are the we of me"; and Berenice, with her customary shrewdness, quickly sees that Frankie has "fallen in love" with the wedding, that, in fact, she is determined to walk down the aisle between the bridal pair. But after the wedding, what then? "We will have thousands of friends, thousands and thousands and thousands of friends. We will belong to so many clubs that we can't even keep track of all of them," Frankie gloats. If the novel accords to the idea of the wedding so much significance, it is because the ceremony happens to satisfy all of Frankie's needs in that particular August of her life.

Formally the novel is divided into three parts, each taking its character from the role which Frankie assumes. We see her first as Frankie Addams, the tomboy, bored and restive. "Until the April of that year, and all the years of her life before, she had been like other people." Her actual world is defined by the kitchen which she shares with Berenice and John Henry. "The three of them sat at the kitchen table, saying the same things over and over, so that by August the words began to rhyme with each other and sound strange." The transformations begin when Frankie suddenly decides to become a member of the wedding: "Her heart divided like two wings." In the next section of the novel we see Frankie as the new, exotic personality, F. Jasmine, who is all pride and anticipation. Her flirtation with a soldier, her lengthy conversations with Berenice on the subject of love, and her lone wanderings through the town reflect the mood of will-fulness which is the prelude to disenchantment. It is in the last part of the novel that disenchantment sets in. Mrs. McCullers beautifully disposes of the wedding itself in a few lines and devotes the rest of the book to convert the initial bitterness of, not Frankie or F. Jasmine, but Frances now, to a final affirmation of youth's resilience. Frances, entitled at last to her full name, outgrows the humiliation of her first defeat. Unlike Mick Kelly, she moves beyond the acrid feeling that the world has cheated her. And with the heedlessness of youth she takes up new friends and other illusions, remotely conscious of the death of John Henry and the separation from Berenice. There is change; there is no knowledge or confirmation. Guilt and anxiety are equally forgotten. As the identity of Frankie changes from part to part, so do her images of "the spinning world," now fractured, now whole; and the seasons, keeping richly in step, change from spring to fall.

The style of the novel presents the blossoming of human feelings no less aptly than it presents the varying moods of nature. But it is a style of confession, or rather of manifestation, sensitive to the sudden epiphanies of our daily life. It is not dramatic despite the inimitable tang and humor of its dialogue, and despite the plasticity of character which allowed the novel to be made into a highly successful play.

What drama the novel contains, it draws from the juxtaposition of three characters to one another — not from their interactions. Thus is Frankie caught between the innocence of John Henry and the experience of Berenice. Berenice is indeed the rock on which the novel rests. She calls to mind both Portia and Brannon, and calls forth a quality of existence as wholesome as our daily bread and as enduring.

To all of Frankie's wild dreams, she stands as a silent modifier — for she is too wise to rebuke. With three husbands behind her and a fourth in the offing, she speaks as one who has known love and experienced loneliness. Her understanding of life is as tragic, in a Chekovian sense, as Frankie's misunderstanding is pathetic. Without her, the tortured sensitivity of Frankie — a sensitivity, after all, which has no correlative but the wistfulness of puberty — would seem pointless and contrived. But between innocence and experience only illusions can lie. And the illusions of Frankie disguise the hopes of all mankind.

v

It is interesting that the least and the most successful of Mrs. McCullers' works, *Reflections in a Golden Eye* and *The Ballad of the Sad Café,* 1951, should strike us as variations on the same fictional genre. There is a statement by Frank O'Connor which serves to clarify the genre, and serves also to put both works in a nice relation to the tradition of the novel. "If Jane Austen were writing *Pride and Prejudice* in the modern way," O'Connor says in *The Mirror in the Roadway,* "the hero would never need to reveal his arrogance by all those subtle touches which Jane Austen analyzed. He would have been satisfied with a peacock on the lawn, and Elizabeth Bennet would have ultimately wrung its neck. . . . The main thing is that the character would be represented by an image corresponding to the author's view of his principal obsession or the author's view of his part in a poetic phantasmagoria. Either way, his character and role are determined, and his part in the story is more metaphorical than real." The characters of *The Ballad of the Sad Café* are both metaphors and grotesques (grotesques almost in Anderson's sense); the plot moves in the familiar pattern of a whirligig spinning out the impossible intricacies of love and pain; and the style, unconscious of its power, transforms this eccentric tale into something as universal as the old ballads about love and dread, revenge and madness.

The decayed house of Miss Amelia, its porch half painted, its shuttered windows boarded, appears in the first scene of the story and in its last. The house, edifice to love betrayed, to loneliness irrevocable, stands in a small, dreary Southern town — "The winters . . . are short and raw, the summers white with glare and fiery hot." From behind its shutters the strange face of Miss Amelia occasionally peers, a face "sexless and white, with two gray crossed eyes which are turned inward so sharply that they seem to be exchanging with each other one long secret gaze of grief." Firmly and with a sense of finality the narrative unfolds in retrospect before it comes to pause once again, at the end, on the same scene; the Gothic touches never seem out of place, so strong is the feeling of mystery and doom.

The story itself is simple. Miss Amelia, "a powerful blunderbuss of a person, more than six feet tall," owns the only store in town. At the age of nineteen, she is courted by a strong, darkly handsome loom fixer, Marvin Macy, with an "evil reputation" — he is supposed to carry around the dried, salted ear of a man he killed in a razor fight. Under the spell of love, Macy reforms temporarily, and Miss Amelia marries him in her slow absent way. But the marriage, which is never consummated, lasts only a few days; Miss Amelia, despite all of Macy's pitiful protestations, beats him out of bed, and subsequently out of the house, after despoiling him of his possessions. Macy vanishes to lead a violent criminal life in other counties. Some years after, Lymon, the hunchback, appears at the doorstep of Miss Amelia, a tired and forlorn figure, seeking shelter, timidly claiming the rights of a dubious kinship. Lymon touches a hidden chord in Miss Amelia's character, touches in her a formless instinct, neither wholly feminine nor altogether maternal. She takes him in; he becomes Cousin Lymon; and the miraculous transformation in her life, of which the new café is evidence, induces a comparable transformation in the town. For Miss Amelia had ceased to be alone and ceased to find herself the beloved: she has suddenly become the lover, with all the "pain, perplexity, and uncertain joy" which attend that condition. Cousin Lymon thrives on her affections; alternately sour and saucy, mischievous and coy, he soon becomes the natural center of the café. But quick as Lymon is to respond in his egocentric fashion to any external interest, and much though he may be pampered by Amelia, he must secretly wilt, as Mrs. McCullers would have it, until *he* can find an object for *his* love. The object is ironically provided by the sinister return of Macy, recently out of the penitentiary and bent on vengeance. The hunchback becomes immediately, outrageously, attached to Macy; he follows him around like a crippled mongrel, wiggling his ears, a figure of humble and obscene subjugation. And so the wheel has come full circle. Macy can torture Miss Amelia through the hunchback almost at will. The tension rises to an intolerable pitch, the showdown is preordained.

The showdown is a marvelous and frightening scene, a grim wrestling match between the tigerish Macy and the lumbering Amazon, Miss Amelia. It takes place by tacit consent on Ground Hog Day in the café, is witnessed by the whole town, and is presided over by Lymon, who stands watch on the counter, an unholy trophy of man's eternal struggle with Evil, with Death itself, which is the negation of Love. And just as Amelia is about to win the day, Lymon alights screaming and clawing on her back, to give the victory, after all, to

Macy. Lymon and Macy go off together after wrecking the café, wrecking the town really, and wrecking Amelia. Miss Amelia immures herself; the town resumes its sleep of death. "There is absolutely nothing to do in the town. Walk around the millpond, stand kicking at a rotten stump, figure out what you can do with the old wagon wheel by the side of the road near the church. The soul rots with boredom. You might as well go down to the Forks Falls Highway and listen to the chain gang." Yes, the chain gang. It is the envoy of the ballad, its hidden refrain: "The voices are dark in the golden glare, the music intricately blended, both somber and joyful. . . . It is music that causes the heart to broaden and the listener to grow cold with ecstasy and fright. . . ." Unlike Pascal, who saw in the image of a chain gang "looking at each other sorrowfully and without hope" a parable of the human condition, Mrs. McCullers manages to summon, in the song of "twelve mortal men," the indestructible joy of endurance and transcendent pain.

The novelette sets a high standard of performance for Mrs. Mc-Cullers and gives authority to a certain Gothic vision, at once quaint and elemental, stark and involuted, which writers like Truman Capote and Tennessee Williams have been inclined to explore. What the novelette does not set forth is a new conception of the irrefragable conflict between the selfhood of man and the otherness of reality, between private need and communal fulfilment. Hints of man's buried life, here as elsewhere in Mrs. McCullers' work, flash darkly to the surface. There is Miss Amelia's whiskey, for instance, which has the power to reveal the "secret truth in a man's heart," and which goes a long way towards creating the convivial fellowship of the café, creating the sense of pride and openness and ceremony: "There, for a few hours at least, the deep bitter knowing that you are not worth much in this world could be laid low." But good whiskey alone is not enough; the broad sense of community in the café springs from a more personal source — Miss Amelia's love for the hunchback. It is a love, of course, that remains wholly de-sexualized; as the town puts it, there is no "conjunction of the flesh" between Amelia and Lymon. For love, it seems, must remain beyond sexual reach, un-tainted by casual gratification or instinctive need.

Few readers will deplore that Mrs. McCullers' image of love is not touched by the Corneillian attributes of reasonableness and high-soul-fulness — the age requires another image, less rational, perhaps, and more grotesque. But many readers will regret that no one in the novelette seems to have full access to his experience, to have any ultimate or even provisional understanding of it. In a sense, the work denies the possibility of *recognition,* and denies, therefore, the dramatic equivalent of illumination. It is the envoy, the style of anonymous celebration and immitigable sadness, that raises the work to the condition of a haunting performance. The style of pretended ballad reticence and naïveté, of folk motifs and stark tragedy, of augurs and foreshadowing, of incremental repetition and telescoped action — the enfabled style seems to incarnate the very spirit of story-telling whose medium, as Thomas Mann has said, "is language in and for itself, language itself."

VI

Since 1951 Carson McCullers has been publishing short stories only. (She is known, however, to be at work on a novel, entitled *Clock Without Hands,* "about good and evil," as the author puts it, "preju-dice and the affirmation of the dignity of life.") The themes of Mrs. McCullers' stories are familiar to readers of her novels, their manner far less distinguished — too often they seem nerveless, contrived. But her deficiencies in the short form remind us only more acutely of her mastery in the intermediate scope of the novelette. Against "the beautiful and blest *nouvelle,*" as Henry James called it, one can hardly cavil. It is a genre as eminently suited to the intense, lyrical gifts of contemporary writers as it is to the quick, nervous appre-hension of American experience. The predilection of Mrs. McCullers for the genre, however, defines for us once again the subjective em-phasis of her imagination. For the scope of the novelette, unlike that of the full novel, allows the characters to elude the repeated assaults of reality, and it does not always force them to convert their wishes into action.

It is upon the unconverted and inconvertible wish, as it seeks expression in love and suffering, that the imagination of Carson McCullers has fastened. In so doing she has given unique and perhaps lasting forms to an impulse that has reigned supreme in modern lit-erature, that very impulse which Trilling named the Opposing Self and characterized as having an "intense and adverse imagination of the culture in which it has being." And if in its modern adversity the imagination of Mrs. McCullers has focused on man's aloneness and sought the ambience of his decay, it has done so less in the spirit of Poe than in that of Poe's admirer, Baudelaire, to whom "fright" and "ecstasy" were household words.

❧ MELVIN J. FRIEDMAN

Flannery O'Connor: Another Legend in Southern Fiction

GORE VIDAL has recently recalled to us with some nostalgia the period when Carson McCullers "was *the* young writer." Reviewing *Clock Without Hands* for *The Reporter* for September 28, 1961, Mr. Vidal seems to feel that we have lost something very special during the twenty-one years which separate *The Heart Is a Lonely Hunter* from Carson McCullers' latest novel.

> She was an American legend from the beginning, which is to say that her fame was as much a creation of publicity as of talent. The publicity was the work of those fashion magazines where a dish of black-eyed peas can be made to seem the roe of some rare fish, photographed by Avedon; yet McCullers' dreaming androgynous face, looking out at us from glossy pages, in its ikon elegance subtly confounded the chic of the lingerie ads all about her.
> Unlike too many other "legends," her talent was as real as her face. . . . Her prose was chaste and severe and realistic in its working out of narrative. (p. 50)

This could have been written with similar appropriateness about Flannery O'Connor. In a certain sense Flannery O'Connor has replaced Carson McCullers as the image of the young writer; although her face is perhaps more rounded and less "dreaming androgynous" than her older contemporary, she still manages a talent "as real as her face" and a prose which is both "chaste and severe." She is the darling of *Kenyon Review* and *Sewanee Review* on the one hand, of *Commonweal* and *Catholic World* on the other. She has proved agreeable to most of the literary and quasi-literary factions which pass judgment on contemporary literature. She has failed to please only the most rigidly party-line Catholics who find her brand of Catholicism not orthodox enough and the most "textual" literary critics who find her language too bare and her experiments with structure not eccentric enough. The reviews of her three books have been overwhelmingly favorable

Reprinted from the *English Journal,* LI (April, 1962), 233–243, by permission of the author and the National Council of Teachers of English.

with critics as distinguished as Caroline Gordon, Granville Hicks, Louis D. Rubin, and R. W. B. Lewis passing sympathetic judgment.

Flannery O'Connor was born in Savannah in 1925 and now lives near Milledgeville, Georgia. Except for a creative writing session at the University of Iowa she has spent most of her thirty-six years in her native Georgia. She has shown the same devotion to birthplace as so many other southern writers. The settings of her stories and novels are either Georgia or Tennessee, often backwoods or rural areas. She has never tried to superimpose on these settings a mythical or ritualistic importance; she seems to have no interest in creating a Yoknapatawpha County or a Port Warwick (the city which recurs in Styron's fiction) as a symbolical southern landscape. She seems content to write about the region she knows best in its own "southern gothic" terms with a disarming modesty unknown in most writers of similar reputation.

One phase of this modesty is reflected in her unwillingness to make pronouncements about her craft. Granville Hicks asked her to contribute to his 1957 symposium on the future of the novel, *The Living Novel* (Macmillan). Hers is the only essay in the collection which does not speak *ex cathedra* about how a novel is or should be written and why it is a dynamic form. (All of the contributors are practising novelists and their remarks usually reveal the self-confidence and assurance of successful craftsmen who are certain the novel has a future because they are still writing fiction.) She credits a good deal of her success as a novelist to the region she comes from ("It's generally suggested that the Southern writer has some advantage here.") and to her position as a practising Catholic ("It affects his writing primarily by guaranteeing his respect for mystery."). Her most telling statements in this essay link the novelist's plight with spiritual and moral purpose:

> In the greatest fiction, the writer's moral sense coincides with his dramatic sense, and I see no way for it to do this unless his moral judgment is part of the very act of seeing, and he is free to use it. I have heard it said that belief in Christian dogma is a hindrance to the writer, but I myself have found nothing further from the truth. (p. 161)

This essay, ambiguously called "The Fiction Writer and His Country," is interesting not only for what it does not say about the craft of novel-writing — ascribing the novelist's gifts to what resembles divine intervention — but also for the suggestion of certain elements which commentators have been quick to find in her fiction. Words like "grotesque," "redemption," and "violence" appear with astonishing regularity. Miss O'Connor insists on a delicacy "for the grotesque, for the perverse, and for the unacceptable" in the kind of fiction she writes. This would seem to be paradoxical until one examines her novels and short stories, which abound in sordidness and poverty and yet maintain a delicate aesthetic balance on the side of gentility and religious affirmation. /

In an essay Flannery O'Connor wrote in the March 30, 1957 issue of *America* we get a similar notion that the practising Catholic and the creative writer can be temperate bedfellows. In this article, "The Church and the Fiction Writer" (another title which sounds too much like a sermon), she asks for humility in the writer — a quality which she more than amply possesses. She resolves again the seeming difficulty about being a religious writer with a clever turn of phrase: "When people have told me that because I am a Catholic, I cannot be an artist, I have had to reply, ruefully, that because I am a Catholic I cannot afford to be less than an artist." She ends on a positive note with her usual affirmative tone: "If we intend to encourage Catholic fiction writers, we must convince those coming along that the Church does not restrict their freedom to be artists but ensures it (the restrictions of art are another matter)."

The only other sampling of essay writing we have from her pen is the charming piece which appeared in the September 1961 *Holiday,* "Living With a Peacock." On the surface this seems to be nothing more than a pleasant digression on the art of peacock raising, a favorite hobby of Flannery O'Connor. A closer reading reveals an oblique glance at the artistic process — perhaps not consciously intended. A statement like the following could easily be applied to characters in her fiction: "Those that withstand illnesses and predators (the hawk, the fox, and the opossum) over the winter seem impossible to destroy, except by violence." One should especially notice the word "violence" which is so essential a part of her literary vocabulary. It becomes clear after a while that raising peacocks is almost an addendum to her fictional practises.

All of this convinces us that everything with Flannery O'Connor is related to her career as a writer. Her place (the South), her religion (Catholicism), her hobby (peacock raising) reinforce her stories and novels at every turn. One can even attach the three words most appropriate to her fiction to each: "grotesque" to the South; "redemption" to Catholicism; and "violence" to peacock raising. All of these qualities, however, spring from the humility which she asks for the creative writer. This virtue is everywhere in evidence in her infrequent interviews and in her appearance as part of a panel discussion.

When Herbert Gold set down the views on writing of the various contributors to his anthology *Fiction of the Fifties,* the shortest statement by far was made by Flannery O'Connor. Hers was the refreshingly uncomplicated remark that it is difficult to write in any age; her comment had the double virtue of reading like an apothegm and destroying the notion which Gold's anthology intended to convey that fiction writing was quite different in the Fifties from what it had been at any other period. The interviews which appeared in the June 12, 1955 *New York Times Book Review* and in the Fall 1960 issue of *Censer* had the same virtues of brevity and good sense.

On October 28, 1960, Flannery O'Connor was called on to participate in a panel discussion on recent southern writers at Wesleyan College, Macon, Georgia. She was in the good company of two established southern writers, Katherine Anne Porter and Caroline Gordon, of a younger southern writer, Madison Jones, and of the principal commentator on recent southern writing, Louis D. Rubin. Her quantitative contribution was slight indeed. She allowed Katherine Anne Porter and Caroline Gordon the long, anecdotal digressions. When called upon to contribute comments about her own working habits or fictional problems she was content with something as unpretentious and self-effacing as "I sit there before the typewriter for three hours every day and if anything comes I am there waiting to receive it" or "I really didn't know what a symbol was until I started reading about them. It seemed I was going to have to know about them if I was going to be a respectable literary person. Now I have the notion that a symbol is sort of like the engine in a story and I usually discover as I write something in the story that is taking on more and more meaning so that as I go along, before long, that something is turning or working the story." The latter may sound too consciously homespun but it is fairly typical of her refusal to enlist the aid of critical jargon when setting down an artistic notion.

It is not surprising, then, that her fiction should be filled with the same modesty and self-effacement. In a sense, the most revealing statement she has made about her techniques as a story and novel writer is found in her essay about peacocks: "I intend to stand firm and let the peacocks multiply, for I am sure that, in the end, the last word will be theirs." Indeed the last word is always that of one of her characters as Flannery O'Connor manages in each of her successive works to (in Joyce's words) "refine herself out of existence."

A Flannery O'Connor story or novel is always the slowly paced, leisurely uncovering of a series of unusual people and circumstances. She seems always intent on at first disenchanting us — mainly through a systematic puncturing of the myth of southern gallantry and gentility — and then restoring our confidence when she has forced us to view her world on her own terms. She forces us to go through a complete Cartesian purgation; our minds are cleansed of all previous notions. When we have forgotten the other books we have read, we can then allow for the existence of her Hazel Motes (*Wise Blood*), her Rayber (*The Violent Bear It Away*), and her "The Misfit" ("A Good Man Is Hard to Find"). We almost willingly "suspend disbelief" in the face of impossible happenings to unlikely people. This is part of what we must go through when we read most fiction writers. But never have I felt the compulsion to reject everything and start over again that I feel with Flannery O'Connor.

This is all the more curious because the demands she makes are not in the direction of new techniques or startling dislocations of structure. Her novels and stories are in every sense traditionally constructed and make no use of the experimental suggestions of a Joyce, a Proust, a Faulkner, or even a Styron. Her work is usually completely faithful to chronology, with no attempt at reproducing an atmosphere of psychological time. In short, her fiction bears no relation whatever to the so-called "art novel."

Where Flannery O'Connor is most unlike her contemporaries is in her almost Dickensian devotion to oddities of character. While so many recent novelists have begged for anonymity in their notion of character — a letter of the alphabet or a strange pun like Watt often suffice as names — Flannery O'Connor insists on precise and detailed delineation. Her creatures are usually rounded personalities, believable if only on their own terms. Caroline Gordon has already made this point abundantly clear: "In Miss O'Connor's vision of modern man — a vision not limited to Southern rural humanity — all her characters are 'displaced persons,' not merely the people in the story of that name. They are 'off center,' out of place. . . ."[1] This does not mean that they are "outsiders" in Colin Wilson's sense or "absurd" men in Albert Camus' sense. They are not introspective types who brood about metaphysical problems, nor are they very concerned with the existentialist notion of self-identification. They go about their business in a workaday manner, but it is the "business" which is usually unorthodox or, in Caroline Gordon's words, "off center." Flannery O'Connor's characters are almost all fanatics, suffering from what we might diagnose as an acute sense of dislocation of place.

Almost everywhere in her fiction some person is trying to fulfill a mission in unfamiliar surroundings. The mission is usually self-imposed and the role assumed is invariably self-appointed. Hazel Motes is on a train at the beginning of *Wise Blood*, Flannery O'Connor's first novel, in the act of leaving his native Eastrod, Tennessee, on his way to Taulkinham. He has decided to reject the traditional Jesus figure and preach a new "Church of Christ Without Christ." He has

[1] Caroline Gordon, "Flannery O'Connor's *Wise Blood*," *Critique*, II, 2, 1958, p. 9.

first to go through the ritual of dislocation before he can fulfill the terms of his prophecy, thus leaving a known area to travel to an unknown one. The prophecy and dislocation end in disaster and death. The same formula may explain Mr. Head's and Nelson's trip to Atlanta in "The Artificial Nigger." The grandfather and grandson return home after a hectic and cathartic day in the big city realizing that the mission was to no end. The Guizacs' sojourn on the McIntyre farm in "The Displaced Person" ends in disaster for all concerned; Polish immigrants fail to transplant their Catholicism and old-world morality to the Bible Belt South. Finally, Tarwater, in *The Violent Bear It Away,* does not successfully carry the prophecy of his great-uncle to the big city in an attempt to convert his remaining relatives; he too returns to his native Powderhead after a succession of failures.

The transplantation-prophecy-return motif is as old as the Greeks. We find it in Homer. But more important, we find it in most of the contemporary Southern School. William Styron's characters often leave their native surroundings with a prophetic urge to renew themselves; they either return unsuccessfully like Mr. Head, Nelson, and Tarwater, or die horribly like Hazel Motes or Mr. Guizac. In the first category we would place Cass Kinsolving of *Set This House on Fire* and Captain Mannix of *The Long March;* in the second Peyton Loftis of *Lie Down in Darkness* and Mason Flagg of *Set This House on Fire.* The theme also recurs in Faulkner and Carson McCullers. But nowhere is it as strenuously present as in the fiction of Flannery O'Connor. One feels that her entire notion of character depends on the fictional creature's leaving his native habitat with an evangelical urge and then returning in defeat or else dying in defeat. The peculiarities and oddities seem a part of the whole plan; the working out of a mythical situation in modern terms forces the odd behavior and credos of a group of people who are often ironical counterparts of classically defined heroes.

It is probably safest to leave this kind of interpretation as a marginal suggestion. Flannery O'Connor is no believer in mythical parallels and certainly offers no outward concern with archetypal patterns in her fiction. One cannot insist often enough that she depends on traditional procedures to the almost complete exclusion of experimentation. It is probably no accident, however, that the motif which we have discovered running through almost all her writing is of great antiquity — Homerically conventional.

To look more closely at her fiction, one finds her publishing stories as early as 1946 in the prestige "little magazines." Some of these like "The Geranium" (*Accent,* 1946), "Greenleaf" (*Kenyon Review,* 1956), "A View of the Woods" (*Partisan Review,* 1957), and "Comforts of Home" (*Kenyon Review*, 1960) have not been collected.[2] She has occasionally published stories in *Mademoiselle* and *Harper's Bazaar* but has generally favored the smaller circulation journals, with *Partisan Review, Kenyon Review, Sewanee Review,* and *New World Writing* as her preferred outlets. To my knowledge, she has never published in the *New Yorker*, which distinguishes her in a curious way from most of the other successful story writers of our generation; even John O'Hara has recently been willing to forget the snobbery and cultishness of the *New Yorker* in favor of its wide and distinguished circulation.

Parts of her two novels, *Wise Blood* and *The Violent Bear It Away*, also appeared separately in magazines before they were recast as sections of longer works. Essential changes were generally made during the transference. The most intriguing instance was when "You Can't Be Any Poorer Than Dead" (*New World Writing*, 8, 1955) was reshaped to become the first chapter of *The Violent Bear It Away*.[3] This easy rhythm of writing shorter fiction and then, on occasions, reshaping it slightly to suit the needs of a novel and, on others, allowing it to remain intact gives one the impression (and this has frequently been said before about her) that she is essentially a story writer who has twice strayed into the novel form.

With that in mind it is probably best to look first at her short stories. Her first published story "The Geranium" sets the tone for the transplantation and dislocation of place theme. Old Dudley has been forced to leave his accustomed southern setting in favor of the squalor and confinement of New York City. His one pleasure is watching through his window, with studied interest, a neighbor's geranium plant during the long periods of the day. By the end of the story he has been deprived of this single diversion and understands, with so many other Flannery O'Connor characters, how stifling displacement can be. He is a part of that southern diaspora who has experienced the bitter taste of exile. Flannery O'Connor's unpretentious style is already noticeable in this early story.

> He shuffled to the chair by the window and sank down in it. His throat was going to pop. His throat was going to pop on account of a nigger — a damn nigger that patted him on the back and called him "old timer." Him that knew such as that couldn't be. Him that had come from a good place. A good place. A place where

---

[2] "Greenleaf" won first prize in the O. Henry Awards of 1957 and is also included in the Martha Foley collection for that year. "A View of the Woods" is in the Martha Foley volume for 1958.

[3] For details on this see Sumner J. Ferris, "The Outside and the Inside: Flannery O'Connor's *The Violent Bear It Away*," *Critique*, II, 2, 1960, p. 19.

> such as that couldn't be. His eyes felt strange in their sockets. They were swelling in them and in a minute there wouldn't be any room left for them there. He was trapped in this place where niggers could call you "old timer." He wouldn't be trapped. He wouldn't be. He rolled his head on the back of the chair to stretch his neck that was too full.

Although the entire passage is in the third person, some of it is detached narrative, the rest the characteristic manner of Old Dudley. The first two sentences, with their grammatical and syntactical regularity, are the words of the omniscient author. In the third sentence we already feel the pressure of Dudley's mind which takes over entirely in the ungrammatical and incomplete fourth through seventh sentences. The rhythm starts again in the eighth sentence with almost exactly the same pattern of objective narrative turning into Dudley's idiom. Flannery O'Connor in this passage avoids the more experimental possibilities of stream-of-consciousness fiction, as she does everywhere else in her work, but does try to approximate the workings of the characters' minds if only through the indirect third person.

A much later story, "Greenleaf" has quite a different setting from "The Geranium" but the story-telling techniques remain the same and the characters have the same sense of righteous indignation as Old Dudley. "Greenleaf" is, however, a more characteristic part of the O'Connor canon than "The Geranium." The "southern gothic" tone is more authentically felt and the ingredients of revivalism and violence are now a functional part of the narrative. Mrs. Greenleaf has a curious avocation which she calls "prayer healing."

> Every day she cut all the morbid stories out of the newspaper — the accounts of women who had been raped and criminals who had escaped and children who had been burned and of train wrecks and plane crashes and the divorces of movie stars. She took these to the woods and dug a hole and buried them and then she fell on the ground over them and mumbled and groaned for an hour or so, moving her huge arms back and forth under her and out again and finally just lying down flat and, Mrs. May suspected, going to sleep in the dirt.

The story moves slowly until the very end when it erupts in sudden and unexpected violence. The ending clearly favors the "grotesque" as it turns on a simple but rather dreadful stroke of irony.

Flannery O'Connor's most recent stories seem to depend more on obviously disturbed types. There is considerable introspection in stories like "The Enduring Chill" and "The Comforts of Home." The first of these reads almost like a Southern caricature of late Salinger. There are the Salinger overtones of Buddhist orientalism, of the impending nervous breakdown. Flannery O'Connor manages to get inside the mind of Asbury who suffers from the spiritual irresolution of so many of the Glass clan. The final words of the story cast a mood of religious terror:

> Asbury blanched and the last film of illusion was torn as if by a whirlwind from his eyes. He saw that for the rest of his days, frail, racked, but enduring, he would live in the face of a purifying terror. A feeble cry, a last impossible protest escaped him. But the Holy Ghost, emblazoned in ice instead of fire, continued, implacable, to descend.

"The Comforts of Home" exploits irony as tellingly as anything else in her fiction. The title, the character relationships, the style itself depend heavily on ironical juxtapositions. The "psychopathic personality" of the girl, who is the unwilling and inactive protagonist of the story, is not quite advanced enough for the asylum; her nymphomaniac tendencies, on the other hand, do not quite suit her for the ways of southern gentility. This is all explained in an appropriately ironical passage which has some of the cleverest turns of phrase in all of Flannery O'Connor:

> The lawyer found that the story of the repeated atrocities was for the most part untrue, but when he explained to her that the girl was a psychopathic personality, not insane enough for the asylum . . . not stable enough for society, Thomas's mother was more deeply affected than ever. The girl readily admitted that her story was untrue on account of her being a congenital liar; she lied, she said, because she was insecure. She had passed through the hands of several psychiatrists who had put the finishing touches to her education. She knew there was no hope for her. In the presence of such an affliction as this, his mother seemed bowed down by some painful mystery that nothing would make endurable but a redoubling of effort. To his annoyance, she appeared to look on *him* with compassion, as if her hazy charity no longer made distinctions.

"Hazy charity" heightens the effect which has been steadily built up in the passage; it is well placed in the final sentence to underscore the irony, the same kind of irony which Katherine Anne Porter achieves with a phrase like "sour gloom."

Most of Flannery O'Connor's other stories are found in the 1955 collection, *A Good Man Is Hard to Find*. The ten stories in this volume have fairly similar southern settings and exploit the problems of violence, redemption, and grotesquerie which have always obsessed her. *A Good Man Is Hard to Find*, however, lacks the essential unity and organization of another book of stories which it occasionally resembles, *Winesburg, Ohio*. Flannery O'Connor's "grotesques" seem to have gone through the same kind of disturbing experiences as Sherwood Anderson's characters. Most of them have had classical "moments of illumination" which have revealed special "truths" to them; it was the truths, as Sherwood Anderson would say, which made them grotesques.

Hulga's artificial leg in "Good Country People," The Misfit's misplaced Jesus complex in "A Good Man Is Hard to Find," Bevel's need for baptism in "The River," Ruby's fear of pregnancy in "A Stroke of Good Fortune" have made them all, in Flaubert's words, *"grotesques tristes."* Almost every critic who has written about Flannery O'Connor has suggested the presence of grotesques surrounded by a gothic eeriness. Very few of the characters in *A Good Man Is Hard to Find* are free from this charge. But Flannery O'Connor is always patient enough to explain the source of the moral, physical, or spiritual discomfort and has a way of building her story upon it. Her prime concern, as we mentioned earlier, seems to be with oddity of character but always within the demands of narrative expression.

As a good example of all this, we might take "Good Country People." Flannery O'Connor introduces us to Hulga's infirmity on the first page. She is careful to surround her with two other women, Mrs. Hopewell, her mother, and Mrs. Freeman, "a good country person." In a way, the grossness and insensitivity of these two women clash with the hypersensitivity of Hulga; without their presence in the story we could not appreciate her aloneness and frustration. Flannery O'Connor persists in referring to three things about Hulga which have a way of recurring like leitmotives: her artificial leg, the symbolical change of her name from Joy to Hulga, and her Ph.D.[4] When the Bible salesman appears and makes ready his seduction of the young lady, we have been aesthetically prepared for what is to happen. The "grotesque" scene in the barn when the salesman makes off with the artificial leg and mockingly shows his irreverence does not shock the reader who has already been warned of impending ironical twists and turns by an elaborate series of clues.

Thus the grotesqueness and oddity of character are not suspended in a vacuum. Flannery O'Connor painstakingly prepares us for all her effects. In a fictional world where everyone is some kind of prophet one is prepared for false Bible salesmen making off with artificial legs which belong to female Ph.D.'s. The delicate moral balance on which all the stories in *A Good Man Is Hard to Find* are built is similarly understandable. We tend to suspend disbelief in the presence of a young boy who cannot get enough of baptism ("The River"), of a

---

[4] Name changing was used also in "The River" when Bevel forced his new identity on Mrs. Connin, thus denying his parents the name they gave him. His "conversion" proceeded with less calculation than Hulga's.

murderer who likens himself to Jesus ("A Good Man Is Hard to Find"), of a 104-year-old Civil War veteran who drops dead on a graduation platform watching his sixty-two-year-old granddaughter receive a bachelor's degree ("A Late Encounter With the Enemy"), or of a tramp with a philosophical turn who abandons a deaf mute he has just married in a roadside restaurant ("The Life You Save May Be Your Own"). Prose paraphrase does no justice to Flannery O'Connor's plots and characters. She convinces us of things which are quite outside our experience through means which require considerable aesthetic reorientation.

Her first novel *Wise Blood* (1952) is not the apparent success of *A Good Man Is Hard to Find*. Flannery O'Connor's talents seem to lie so clearly in the direction of short fiction that we should not be surprised that her first attempt at the longer form should be episodic and fragmentary. Four of the fourteen chapters were earlier published separately, which reinforces the sense of short stories being strung together to form a novel. The first edition, published by Harcourt, Brace, in fact leaves blank pages between chapters almost begging that we come to a complete end-stop before proceeding to the next division.

Nathanael West and Franz Kafka are the writers most often suggested as inspirations for *Wise Blood*. Hazel Motes, the central figure of the novel, has the crusading zeal of a Miss Lonelyhearts and the blind steadfastness of a Kafka hero; but it is probably unwise to carry the connection further. When he arrives in Taulkinham to preach the gospel of the Church of Christ Without Christ he receives his redemption and purification in a way which seems unorthodox: he frequents the bed of a well-known prostitute whose address he found on a lavatory wall. This establishes the tone of unconventional prophecy and evangelism which runs through the novel. Hazel Motes meets a succession of false religionists and we are intended to measure the sincerity of his convictions against the hypocrisy of theirs. One of these figures, Asa Hawks, has pretended to blind himself to enhance his career as an itinerant beggar. Another, Hoover Shoats, has made a profitable career of espousing new religions: "You watch out, friend. I'm going to run you out of business. I can get my own new jesus and I can get Prophets for peanuts, you hear?" A third, Enoch Emery (blessed with the hereditary faculty of "wise blood"), steals a shriveled-up mummy from a museum to oblige Hazel Motes with a new jesus for his religion. Hazel makes his way through this corrupt universe of false prophets to advance the sincere cause of his new cult. When he realizes that all has failed he blinds himself with quicklime and proceeds to subject himself to every variety of torture (like a latter day Oedipus, as one critic has suggested). In accustomed fashion for

Flannery O'Connor's characters, Hazel Motes has had his moments of religious feeling and violence. He has experienced a series of surrealistic horrors and has worked out his destiny in terms of the rigid transplantation-prophecy-return (death) pattern. There is one observer of all this action who supplies the final irony to Hazel Motes' "achievement." This is his landlady who represents the common sense of the unenlightened and uninitiated; Flannery O'Connor is fond of giving this type the final say:

> The landlady sat there for a while longer. She was not a woman who felt more violence in one word than in another; she took every word at its face value but all the faces were the same. Still, instead of blinding herself, if she had felt that bad, she would have killed herself and she wondered why anybody wouldn't do that. She would simply have put her head in an oven or maybe have given herself too many painless sleeping pills and that would have been that. Perhaps Mr. Motes was only being ugly, for what possible reason could a person have for wanting to destroy their sight? A woman like her, who was so clear-sighted, could never stand to be blind. If she had to be blind she would rather be dead. It occurred to her suddenly that when she was dead she would be blind too. She stared in front of her intensely, facing this for the first time. She recalled the phrase, "eternal death," that preachers used, but she cleared it out of her mind immediately, with no more change of expression than the cat. She was not religious or morbid, for which every day she thanked her stars. She would credit a person who had that streak with anything, though, and Mr. Motes had it or he wouldn't be a preacher. He might put lime in his eyes and she wouldn't doubt it a bit, because they were all, if the truth was only known, a little bit off in their heads. What possible reason could a sane person have for wanting to not enjoy himself any more?
> She certainly couldn't say.

One notices how this passage shifts from objective narrative to the landlady's idiom. The change probably occurs in the third sentence. The irony of the second sentence is the one didactic attempt on the part of the narrator to ridicule the landlady. From then on Flannery O'Connor allows the landlady herself to complete the caricatured portrait of Bible Belt morality.

Hazel Motes and the other oddly named eccentrics[5] in *Wise Blood*

---

[5] R. W. B. Lewis' review of *Wise Blood* in *Hudson Review* (Spring, 1953) comes closest to explaining the significance of the names: "The characters seem to be grotesque variations on each other, as even their names suggest: Hazel Motes, Hoover Shoats, Asa Hawks — names uttered antiphonally, in dying echoes, by persons just out of range of each others' voices; like the washerwomen in *Finnegans Wake*." (p. 150) With the obsession that our contemporaries have — very often in the direction of rendering the characters anonymous — Flannery O'Connor is almost unique in dwelling on the suggestive value of names.

seem quite without precedents until one recalls again the Sherwood Anderson of *Winesburg, Ohio*. A possible model for Motes' Church of Christ Without Christ could be Dr. Parcival's strange crucifixion notion: everyone is Christ and we are all crucified. At least the sense of violence and metaphysical grotesqueness attached to each are vintage fanaticism.

The Violent Bear It Away (1960) is a much better novel. Unlike *Wise Blood* it is more than a tightly knit collection of stories. It is the best example in Flannery O'Connor's work of the tranplantation-prophecy-return motif; in fact, the novel is divided into three parts which correspond neatly to the three phases. In the first section, Tarwater prepares to leave home, after the death of his great-uncle, to join his uncle Rayber. The long middle section is the strange working out of the prophecy which ends in Tarwater's baptism-drowning of Rayber's idiot son, Bishop. The final section is the return to Powderhead. The picaresque element in the novel has already been suggested, but more important probably is the *bildungsroman* aspect. Tarwater is another authentically American boy, in the tradition of Huck Finn and the young Ike McCaslin, who goes through a typically American initiation before he can become a man. His "education" and character formation are intimately linked to Flannery O'Connor's South, which Arthur Mizener has characterized as "a breeding ground for prophets." Tarwater's confused attempts at converting Rayber and baptising Bishop can easily be likened to Ike McCaslin's ambivalent feelings about the bear hunt in Faulkner's "The Bear" or more cautiously to Huck's uncertainty about Jim's destiny in Twain's novel. In each case the spiritual resolution which turns the boy into a man is crucial.

The link with Faulkner has already been pointed out by several reviewers of *The Violent Bear It Away*. Vivian Mercier writing in the *Hudson Review* (Autumn 1960) has said that "all the characters are Faulknerian grotesques, including the idiot's atheist father." Louis D. Rubin had earlier pointed out similarities between the Bundrens of *As I Lay Dying* and Flannery O'Connor's characters in the Autumn 1955 issue of the *Sewanee Review*. It can be pointed out convincingly, I think, that the burial complications in *The Violent Bear It Away* are at least related to the funeral procession in *As I Lay Dying*. Tarwater's great-uncle had insisted that he be given Christian burial rites. Tarwater, prompted by a voice which follows him around almost like his conscience in reverse, decides to set fire to the house which contains the great-uncle's corpse. Upon his return to Powderhead in the third part of the novel, he discovers that despite his efforts the uncle was granted proper burial through the unexpected intervention of a Negro, Buford. In a curious way the novel gains a kind of structure through the repeated references to the burial in much the same way that *As I*

Lay Dying is constructed about the journey to Jefferson with the corpse of Addie Bundren. In both novels there is also an elaborate series of observers who pass judgment on the proceedings and form a *consensus gentium* to counterbalance the eccentricities of the participants in the action. Tarwater's behavior is viewed with some surprise by a salesman who offers him a ride on his way to Rayber's house. A truck driver serves a similar function as Tarwater makes his way back to Powderhead. Another observer, Buford, is waiting for him there to condemn him for failing to give his great-uncle Christian burial. We get this balance between the "grotesques" and the workaday world which Flannery O'Connor failed to give us convincingly in *Wise Blood*.

We notice also in *The Violent Bear It Away* what P. Albert Duhamel has called "a 'violent' view of reality." This seems also to be unmistakably Faulknerian. Faulkner's novels rarely harbor false prophets but they are almost always filled with every variety of violence: suicide, rape, lynching. Tarwater's pyromania beautifully suits him for an elite position in Yoknapatawpha County.

Lest we carry the Faulkner parallel too far, we should make clear that Flannery O'Connor has learned nothing from Faulkner's prolix style, from his experiments with structure and technique, from his frequent use of the devices of stream-of-consciousness fiction. Her chaste, unimposing sentences, her fairly strict chronological narratives, her refusal to tamper with consciousness place her at the other extreme from the Faulkner of *As I Lay Dying, The Sound and the Fury, Absalom, Absalom!,* and "The Bear." The third person is scrupulously maintained even in a passage which tries to cope with Tarwater's mind as seriously as the following:

> The boy did not intend to go to the schoolteacher's until daylight and when he went he intended to make it plain that he had not come to be beholden or to be studied for a schoolteacher magazine. He began trying to remember the schoolteacher's face so that he could stare him down in his mind before he actually faced him. He felt that the more he could recall about him, the less advantage the new uncle would have over him. The face had not been one that held together in his mind, though he remembered the sloping jaw and the black-rimmed glasses. What he could not picture were the eyes behind the glasses. He had no memory of them and there was every kind of contradiction in the rubble of his great-uncle's descriptions. Sometimes the old man had said the nephew's eyes were black and sometimes brown. The boy kept trying to find eyes that fit mouth, nose that fit chin, but every time he thought he had a face put together, it fell apart and he had to begin on a new one. It was as if the schoolteacher, like the devil, could take on any look that suited him.

Tarwater, in an interesting bit of speculation, tries to fit together from memory the diverse parts of his Uncle Rayber's (the schoolteacher) face. We get a revealing glimpse into the boy's mind. We can only expect, however, that Faulkner would have handled the interior monologue differently.

Even *The Violent Bear It Away,* Flannery O'Connor's most ambitious work to date, is not very helpful in suggesting the future course of her work. She has thus far remained oblivious to almost all the literary fads of her contemporaries; whether she can continue to be so free from influence is difficult to say. It is fairly certain, however, that she will continue to be free from such judgments as that implied in Gore Vidal's exclamation of despair in his recent review of *Clock Without Hands:* "Southern writing — we have had such a lot of it in the last thirty years!"

❧ PAUL HERR

The Small, Sad World of James Purdy

WITH the publication of *Malcolm* (1959), James Purdy has left no
doubt that he is a writer of integrity with a voice of his own. In
America today, when most novels seem to be hurriedly manufactured
with standardized patterns and interchangeable paragraphs, Purdy's
work stands out as something of a rarity. He also has a highly personal
vision of his own — bitter, ironic, and grotesque. Perhaps it is this
combination of qualities that reminds us of Nathanael West. In two
short novels, *Miss Lonelyhearts* and *The Day of the Locust*, West
revealed more of the inner rot of the America of his day than several
shelves of the naturalistic "political" novels produced by his more popular contemporaries. Similarly, Purdy, in *Color of Darkness* (1957)
and in *Malcolm*, has said more in fewer words about the hunger and
horror of our fragmented, business-cheapened life today than a whole
chorus of best-selling, grey-flanneled voices from Irwin Shaw to Herman Wouk.

Much of Purdy's unusual achievement is made possible by his flat,
bald style. It is precise and deceptively simple. He uses few of the
rhetorical devices available to him in English; he is even sparing of
adjectives and adverbs. In *Malcolm* especially his prose is terse, almost naked, sometimes matter-of-fact, dry. His individual voice comes
through in a strange twist of a phrase here, an odd choice of a word
there, and in a peculiar tension that vibrates from even his least tightly
structured paragraphs.

Purdy's vision of the world is equally exclusive. His characters
move on a stage as barren and starkly lighted as that of Samuel Beckett.
The sociological backdrop is barely suggested, and the customary props
of psychological motivation are most conspicuous by their absence.
Purdy's people have little or no past. We never learn how they came
to be what they are; they simply *are*. The objects they use, the streets
they walk upon, the houses they inhabit, even the clothes they wear
seem to have no immediate or organic relationship to these people.
They are cut off from the physical world. And they are even isolated

Reprinted from the *Chicago Review*, XIV, No. 3 (Autumn–Winter, 1960),
19–25, by permission of the author and the *Chicago Review*.

from themselves in that they raise only the most superficial questions when faced by a crucial decision.

This is not to say, however, that these people are not real; they are — very much so — in a strangely moving if grotesque way. For we see them so clearly defined in such a hard, fine light, as we can never hope to see the people we know in a thing-cluttered world in which each person is a function of his job, what he owns, and what he feels other people want him to be. Like Ionesco, he makes "specialists" of his characters: they speak clichés of clichés; blandness is driven to the point of intensity; and the most gratuitous of acts becomes suddenly a commonplace.

James Purdy has created a world of his own. When an artist does this, even to a limited degree, much of what the average intelligent reader calls life will by necessity be excluded; for only by rigorous exclusion and distortion can such a vision become both personalized and free of the person of the artist. This is the essential paradox of art. The world of James Purdy is small and sad. It excludes much that even a sympathetic reader, keenly aware of the pain and rubbish of our life today, would find essential. It is as if Isaac Babel cut from *Red Century* those few passages in which, often only by suggestion, he permits his characters to reveal (against a backdrop of general terror in which individuals become fantastic in their inhumanity) the ghostly image of all the love we have known.

The size of the world a writer creates is not in itself significant. In *Finnegans Wake,* James Joyce took Man's dreaming life as his province; sleep is a big world. While in *Magic Mountain,* Thomas Mann took a few neurotic characters in one sanatorium atop one mountain and transformed these materials into a vision of all of Europe writhing with the illness of World War I. The large world can be highly personalized, as is that of Joyce, inhabited by most of the people he had ever known well. The point is this: is this world true? *True* is also a big world, like sleep which it closely resembles at times. And we shall closely examine it in terms of our private nightmares.

II

The plot of *Malcolm* is simple in that, like a clean and carefully calculated billiard shot, the path of the cue ball (Malcolm, the fifteen year old protagonist) can be easily observed. At the beginning of the novel we find Malcolm "wedded" to The Bench (in this case a park bench opposite the plush hotel in which he lives on his vanished father's money). Like many red-blooded American boys (and all cue balls) he has not yet been put into the game; he is "waiting," he says, "for his father." Mr. Cox, an astrologer (concerned with the abstract relationships of spherical objects in the sky at precise moments), is the cue that shoots him into motion. Cox supplies "addresses" (contacts with other balls), direction in the sense that something must be *done* (motion). "Give yourself up to things," he advises. And Malcolm does precisely this; he becomes as passive as any thing. He bounces about from ball to ball, from wall to wall, and ends up in statis (death).

Plot in the traditional sense is not crucial to a discussion of Purdy's intent or achievement in *Malcolm*. He is doing a lot more than telling a simple story; although he does this too and does it very well. What is crucial is Purdy's treatment of his characters, the way they relate to life and to each other, and what they are supposed to mean. By this latter implication I do not wish to suggest that *Malcolm* is a philosophical or symbolic novel. (The dust jacket announces that it is a "Comic Novel," but I trust the author is not guilty of this absurdity.) What I mean is that Purdy's people signify (mean) more than their surface actions and words relate to us. Unlike the traditional naturalistic novel which explores *ad nauseam* the psychological and sociological origins of its characters and upon this data bases its conclusions (and, one might add, with this chalk draws us neat pictures), *Malcolm* invites us to the heresy of poetry. We are asked to get acquainted with the people and draw our own conclusions about them. We are invited to *participate;* seldom today in America is a reader treated with this old world deference.

Malcolm is the central character. He is a strange fifteen year old boy. His father, with whom he had traveled much before the novel began, has vanished. Dead, alive, on the lam? No one knows. Malcolm is waiting for the return of his father. Indeed, everything he does during the action of the novel is a kind of marking time (*killing* time) until this great day. He has been waiting on The Bench across the street from a hotel in which he lives. Mr. Cox, the astrologer, eventually sends him into The Game (Life); like most neurotic coaches, he can't bear to see even mediocre material forever wedded to The Bench. He suggests that Malcolm forget about his father, as does everyone else he meets. Malcolm is willing to try to "do something." He accepts the addresses Mr. Cox offers. But Malcolm has only one desire — to find his father. And he has but one worry — the money left him by his father is rapidly running out. About Malcolm's mother we learn nothing; perhaps he did not have one? We can only assume that Purdy considered this detail irrelevant, or wished us to draw a conclusion from its understatement. (We shall consider this problem in a different context.)

Malcolm might as well have remained on The Bench. He does not act; he is acted upon. He is used, but never touched in a way that summons life and change. His hair grows white (due to an accident), but he dies at the close of the novel much the same as we discovered him — a passive child. Everyone he meets in one way or another wishes to manipulate him (as a "thing"). His feelings are thin and very brief. When confronted by even mild emotion in another person, he escapes the scene by dozing off. Only when his father is attacked does he respond "white with terror, and trembling all over." And these attacks are verbal. Words, words, words. So is Malcolm's response. The only action he ever threatens is to return to his room in the hotel where he is waited on hand and foot by paid servants.

Most of the people who meet Malcolm think him a little stupid. He has all sorts of difficulties establishing rapport. Usually he is tactless: he asks a midget if he is a midget; he comments on the color of Negroes. He is a child, uncivilized and passive and boorish. Then why are these people drawn to him, why do they wish to become his friend, adopt him, marry him? Perhaps because, being the perfect American consumer, he offers nothing save the urge to be *sold*. Here is a virgin Market. He only needs a little "preparing." So all are patient, all are helpful. The only exception is Estel Blanc.

Blanc is the first address Cox gives Malcolm. Blanc is a Negro mortician. He entertains Malcolm graciously, looks at his teeth, pronounces him an "infant," and tells him to "come back in twenty years." Dying, Malcolm yells, "It's *not* twenty years!" (This quote is also the title of the last chapter of the novel.) Is Estel Blanc (white star?) intended as a symbol of Death? He is the only character in the novel who without qualification rejects Malcolm totally on first encounter. Malcolm finds something strange in his "darkness." Madame Girard, a later address of Mr. Cox, is said to fear Blanc "more than anybody else."

This is as close as Purdy comes to the manufacture of a nice, pat symbol. But even in this case, Estel Blanc is first of all presented as a person. If an effort were made to reduce Blanc to a symbol of Death, a lot of his characterization would stick out very awkwardly. None of Purdy's characters in *Malcolm* can be reduced to this level of pawn in a purely intellectual game. This is where Purdy reveals again his artistry: he does not give us a tidy little picture; he suggests meanings and leaves it to the reader to supply the final details. Like a good poem, the novel has several levels of meaning.

III

Malcolm is a novel that invites interpretation in the worst sense of the word; those critics with a proclivity for systematizing and a weakness for pedantry will search for a firmly structured allegory, and they will find it. For it is characteristic of such critics that they inevitably find what they are looking for, even when it is not there. As I have suggested above, this "discovery" would do violence to what I feel is Purdy's intent. Some of his characters — perhaps all the chief ones — possess symbolic value to a greater or lesser degree, but these values are not firmly fixed in a purely allegorical structure. *Malcolm,* like any imaginative work of art, means first of all what it *is.*

We can get at part of this meaning by examining Purdy's attitude toward his characters. Like the good objective artist characterized by James Joyce, Purdy stands back from his characters, very calm, cool, paring his finger nails. One can almost see him prodding them in the chest so they will move farther away from him. He doesn't want to be kind to them, or to be identified with them. He makes such a point of this detachment that it comes very close to becoming the opposite. Just before a rubber band snaps it sings. Purdy sings. With his spare, objective prose he sings of no love.

He sings of a world in which there is no passion. The men of this world have no use for women, the women no use for men. No relationship is deeply meaningful, no mating is really worth the effort. All is greyness, confusion, pointless loss, frustration. Hope is a fifteen year old boy waiting on a bench for his father to return.

Purdy, by rigidly excluding all love from his world (or satirizing it or making it grotesque), seems to be saying that this is precisely what is lacking in America today. If this is his point, he is making it the hard way. As suggested above, a writer who creates a world of his own must exclude much of what exists in reality. But it is doubtful if the most basic of human drives can be excluded and the novel not suffer from this lack. Such an exclusion deprives the writer of his greatest source of power to catch and hold the reader's attention and sympathy. Also, as in the case of *Malcolm,* it brings sharply into question the intent behind this exclusion. Purdy may be saying that love is lacking or distorted in America today; he may not. It may be that, as a writer, he is reacting violently to the treacle of Romantic Love oozing from the fiction of our mass media (and more than a few Little Magazines). If so, he is confusing sentimentality with passion. The mass media, too, exclude all passion.

In this connection we must consider another curious exclusion. So much attention is given to Malcolm's "search" for his father that the reader almost forgets that the boy must have had a mother. She is not mentioned. Most competent observers of American life today, even the not-so-competent disciples of St. Luce, deplore the predominance of Mother in our society. Father, they say, is most conspicuous by his absence. (In this, the symbolism involved in Malcolm's missing father, whether intentional or not, is most accurate.) But Mother, bless her ever-loving heart, is always there. So much so, in fact, that

Madison Avenue seldom if ever composes an ad that is not intended to appeal directly or indirectly to Mother. But there are no mothers in *Malcolm* . . . only adults with no children and a motherless child.

In one of the most powerful stories of *Color of Darkness,* "Why Can't They Tell You Why?", Purdy has given us a vivid portrait of Mother. The central figure is a little boy who secretly pores over photographs of his missing father. The mother, in an hysterical attempt to destroy this father image, burns the photographs in front of the little boy. This boy, his terror and anguish turning into rage, is reduced to the state of an animal, hissing at her, "while from his mouth black thick strings of something slipped out, as though he had spewed out the heart of his grief." Here is Mother with a vengeance!

In *Malcolm* all man and woman relationships are presented as painful or absurd. Marriage is a kind of hell. Kermit (a midget) and Laureen (a whore) marry before the novel begins. We discover them fighting; they separate. Mr. and Mrs. Girard do not get along; they, too, separate. Malcolm marries Melba because she insists (we suspect he would have married any other female who insisted), and his death, we are told, is hastened because she wears him out in bed. There is no suggestion of passion in this mating, no tenderness of man for woman — only a kind of mechanical grinding down of one person by another. If this is sex, it is of the insect variety.

Upon occasion Purdy's people become angry, but they do not hate with passion. They call each other names. And the greater their anger, the more frequently do these names suggest sexual perversion. Cox is called "an old pederast" several times by different people. Malcolm's wife, Melba, exasperated by his persistent search for his father, says, "Blow your father." Such direct references to homosexuality are frequent in the novel, and they are all gratuitous.

Neither in terms of structure nor characterization is homosexuality as a theme made pertinent to *Malcolm,* but in this peevish namecalling he underscores a problem raised by those exclusions delineated above. The homosexual world is one lacking that which is lacking in the world of *Malcolm* — the only significant difference is the absence of Mother, and this absence is so total that it becomes a kind of presence. Father is *there* (absent in both the literal and the Freudian sense); heterosexual love is not there; and all relationships are reduced to *addresses* supplied by "an old pederast."

To exclude so much that is vital to the novel and to intrude a theme (homosexuality) that seems irrelevant, is to invite misinterpretation. This is the major weakness of *Malcolm.* The fine writer excludes to make that which he includes more significant. He calls his shots.

Purdy is without doubt a serious and significant writer. He has created a world of his own. It is a small, sad world, but it is also very close to an accurate image of life in America today.

J. D. Salinger's Seventy-eight Bananas

Six years have passed since the publication of J. D. Salinger's single novel, *The Catcher in the Rye,* yet the author still retains his transfixing influence on the very young writer. The guileless "It killed me, it really did" idiom has enraptured hundreds of imitators during this time, and the imprint of Salinger's hero, Holden Caulfield, the boy who left fencing foils on the subway and wound up on a psychiatrist's couch, has engrafted itself so indelibly on the separate imaginations that young heroes by the scores have been spawned in his image.

Yet Salinger remains undignified by any very close attention to his work. On the one hand, he has been regarded as innocuously sentimental (John Aldridge says so); on the other he has been found insufferably crude (one large Western university, for example, fired an instructor for using *The Catcher in the Rye* in a freshman literature class). Still, he has not been conscientiously rejected so much as he has been righteously ignored.

This neglect is unfortunate for at least two reasons. First of all, and perhaps less important, Salinger has, in a measure, revived the dormant art of dialect in American fiction. His ear has detected innumerable idiomatic expressions that were simply unrecorded before. And with this gift he has been able to reach a level of readers that Mark Twain, for example, was able to reach. Unlike others who have made the attempt to transcribe distinctive speech patterns, Salinger has succeeded, as few beyond Twain have, in making his characters something more than cracker-barrel philosophers or, worse, good-natured boobs.

But this achievement is somewhat self-evident. I prefer to justify Salinger on a second basis: namely, the coherence of his particular vision of the world. This is essentially the vision of his heroes — of Holden Caulfield, Seymour Glass, Teddy, Franny, Daumier Smith, and the rest. The important question in Salinger is why these intelligent, highly sensitive, affectionate beings fight curious, gruelling battles, leaderless and causeless, in a world they never made.

Reprinted from the *Chicago Review,* XI, No. 4 (Winter, 1958), 3–19, by permission of the author and the *Chicago Review.*

In simple terms, they are a family of non-conformists and Salinger documents their brotherhood by presenting several of them as brothers and sisters in "Franny," "Raise High the Roofbeam, Carpenters," and "Zooey," his most recent stories. However, this is not traditional non-conformity. Logically, the enemy of the non-conformist is society or some oppressive segment of society; and in the recent tradition from Sinclair Lewis's Arrowsmith and Hemingway's Frederick Henry right down to Ayn Rand's Howard Roark, the non-conformist hero is constantly threatened by external forces which seek to inhibit and to destroy him. With the Salinger hero, however, the conflict is never so cleanly drawn. Holden does not leave the fencing team's foils on the subway because of any direct external pressure, nor does he flunk out of Pencey and the other schools because of unreasonable demands made on him. Holden knows this as well as anybody. He is a victim not so much of society as of his own spiritual illness.

Salinger has spent much of his career seeking a cure for this illness; however, before we examine that search, we need a somewhat more precise definition of the illness. Perhaps it is best described in his second to last story, "Raise High the Roofbeam, Carpenters," a work which amplifies and explains the first of the *Nine Stories,* "A Perfect Day for Bananafish." The earlier story describes the last few hours in the life of Seymour Glass and is a brief, impersonally told, and slightly obscure work. The later story, seven or eight times as long, tells of Seymour's wedding day some years before his death. Its main scene is a long interlude in a taxicab in which Seymour is discussed by several interested parties, including his brother Buddy. It concludes with sections from Seymour's personal journal, material designed to explain why he leaves his bride at the altar, and to suggest why he kills himself after several years of marriage. Without "Carpenters" the suicide which closes "Bananafish" appears motivated chiefly by Seymour's inability to put up with his bourgeois wife. With "Carpenters," however, we see Seymour as a man not deprived of, but rather surfeited with, the joy of life. Salinger's sole excuse for Seymour's desperate social irresponsibility is this same curious surfeit of sensation.

We learn, for example, in the course of "Carpenters," that Seymour does not show up for his wedding because he is too "happy," or as he puts it in his journal, he is "too keyed up . . . to be with people." The nature of this happiness is further illuminated through the use of a boyhood experience of Seymour's: at the age of twelve he threw a stone at a young girl, scarring her for life. Seymour's brother, the narrator, explains the incident this way:

> We were up at the Lake. Seymour had written to Charlotte, inviting her to come and visit us, and her mother finally let her. What

happened was, she sat down in the middle of our driveway one morning to pet Boo Boo's cat, and Seymour threw a stone at her. He was twelve. That's all there was to it. He threw it at her because she looked so beautiful sitting there in the middle of the driveway with Boo Boo's cat. Everybody knew that, for God's sake — me, Charlotte, Boo Boo, Walker, Walt, the whole family.

Seymour's own understanding of his malady is a more poetic one. He writes in his journal:

If or when I do start going to an analyst, I hope to God he has the foresight to let a dermatologist sit in on the consultation. A hand specialist. I have scars on my hands from touching certain people. Once, in the park, when Franny was still in the carriage, I put my hand on the downy pate of her head and left it there too long. Another time, at Loew's Seventy-second Street, with Zooey during a spooky movie. He was about six or seven, and he went under the seat to avoid watching a scary scene. I put my hand on his head. Certain heads, certain colors and textures of human hair leave permanent marks on me. Other things too. Charlotte once ran away from me outside the studio, and I grabbed her dress to stop her, to keep her near me. A yellow cotton dress I loved because it was too long for her. I still have a lemon-yellow mark on the palm of my right hand. Oh, God, if I'm anything by a clinical name, I'm a kind of paranoiac in reverse. I suspect people of plotting to make me happy.

The "skin disease" which Seymour sees himself afflicted with in 1942 apparently becomes worse. By 1948, the date of his suicide, the "lemon-yellow marks" have attained weight and shape; he has become mortally ill.

During the course of his interlude with the little girl on the beach in "A Perfect Day for Bananafish," he says to her:

"You just keep your eyes open for any bananafish. This is a perfect day for bananafish."
"I don't see any," Sybil said.
"That's understandable. Their habits are very peculiar. . . . They lead a very tragic life. . . . You know what they do, Sybil?"
She shook her head.
"Well, they swim into a hole where there's a lot of bananas. They're very ordinary-looking fish when they swim *in*. But once they get in, they behave like pigs. Why I've known some bananafish to swim into a banana hole and eat as many as seventy-eight bananas. . . . Naturally after that they're so fat they can't get out of the hole again. Can't fit through the door."
. . . "What happens to them?"
. . . "Well, I hate to tell you, Sybil. They die."
"Why?" asked Sybil.
"Well, they get banana fever. It's a terrible disease."

In other words, Seymour, a bananafish himself, has become so glutted with sensation that he cannot swim out into society again. It is his own banana fever, not his wife who is at fault, or his mother-in-law. If they are stupid and insensitive, "Carpenters" shows them also to be without malice, and hence basically as inculpable for the bananafish's condition as is the Matron of Honor, who represents the whole level-headed society in criticizing Seymour for his peccadilloes.

In general, the bananafish diagnosis applies to all the Salinger invalids. Holden Caulfield's trouble, for example, is not that he hates, or that he fears, or, as Aldridge suggests, that he has no goals — but rather that he has no capacity to purge his sensations. He is blown up like a balloon, or like a bananafish, with his memories. He says at the very end of the novel: "About all I know is, I sort of *miss* everybody I told about. Even old Stradlater and Ackley, for instance. I think I even miss that goddam Maurice. It's funny. . . ." Thus, with the good things he remembers like Allie, his dead brother, and like Jane, the girl who kept her kings in the back row, he retains the bad things as well — until nothing is either good or bad after a point, but simply retained and cherished as a part of himself, submerging him with the sheer weight of the accumulated burden.

The important word in the passage quoted above is "miss." What is unbearable is not that some people are bad, but that experience is fleeting. Everything must be retained. The image Holden has for himself of being "the catcher in the rye" is the perfect metaphor for this objective. He wants to guard the children from falling off the edge of the rye field; likewise he tries to guard each experience from falling into oblivion. With this perspective he fails to discriminate between "important" and "unimportant" experiences to determine which to retain and which to reject — and the bananafish becomes the more bloated and uncomfortable. The "perfect day" is the day when the bananafish is able to end all his suffering by killing himself.

II

In going back, we find the bananafish in embryo even in Salinger's very early stories. Most of those which appeared in *The Saturday Evening Post* and *Collier's* during the war years are rather standard pieces about GI's which the magazines were full of then. But what is distinctive about them perhaps is a particular undertone of very imminent tragedy: the moment imperiled by what is to come. Even the glimpses of life we get away from the front are fraught with a fragile sense of impermanence. Everything is in a state of flux. There is no arrested moment.

The hero of three of these stories is John (Babe) Gladwaller. For the most part, Babe is a Hemingway soldier who suffers in silence.

Occasionally, however, there are clues of self-torment in the character, traits which are to become the hallmark of the Salinger heroes in the late stories. In "The Last Day of the Last Furlough," Babe speaks of a girl he loves. "The more unrequited my love for her becomes," (he says), "the longer I love her, the oftener I whip out my dumb heart like crazy X-ray pictures, the greater the urge to trace the bruises."

"The Stranger" closes with Babe's little sister jumping off the curb into the street as Babe walks beside her. "Why was it such a beautiful thing to see?" he asks, as if with an urge to fight the feeling for its very largeness. In *Catcher,* the same situation is echoed in Phoebe's carousel ride. Holden says of it, "I felt so damn happy all of a sudden, the way old Phoebe kept going around and around. I was damn near bawling. I felt so damn happy, if you want to know the truth. I don't know why. It was just that she looked so damn *nice,* the way she kept going around and around, in her blue coat and all. God, I wish you could've been there."

The Babe Gladwaller stories therefore foreshadow what is to become the chief concern in Salinger's fiction, but they remain unfocused. The war is still an irrelevant part of them — irrelevant because it was too easy to blame the war for the hero's state of mind, when probably Babe Gladwaller had an incipient case of banana fever. It took Salinger some years to define Babe's feelings as a disease, to recognize, in other words, that so-called normal people were not affected with these strange symptoms of chronic hyper-sensitivity and sense of loss.

With the publication of his stories in *The New Yorker,* beginning with "A Perfect Day for Bananafish," he makes his first inroads into understanding. In "Bananafish," his awareness that his hero is "diseased" is still intuitive, I think. Although the "bananafish" metaphor is brilliant in itself, the insight is somewhat neutralized by Salinger's apparent blame of the wife and the mother-in-law for Seymour's suicide. The two women are, at any rate, mercilessly satirized in the telephone conversation through the mother-in-law's constant interruption of the impassioned discussion of Seymour's perilous mental health with questions like "How's your blue coat?" and "How's your ballerina?" As a result, Seymour seems as clear a victim of an external force, namely, the bourgeois matriarchy, as Babe Gladwaller was of "the war." When the important bananafish symbol arrives later in the story, it is impossible to do much with it. There is no demonstrated connection between society's insensitivity and Seymour's zaniness.

The problem recurs again in the next story, "Uncle Wiggily in Connecticut," but not without growing evidence that Salinger is ready to resist the easy answer that the bourgeoisie and/or the war is responsible for the bananafish's condition. Here, for example, it is quite clear that it is Eloise Wengler's tormenting memories of her lost lover, Walter, that make her unable to swim out of the cave into her proper place in Exurbia. Although "the war" is a factor in her despair since her lover is killed in it, he dies not in battle but in an "absurd" camp accident; likewise, her militantly bourgeois husband may contribute to her unhappiness, but she is allowed to repay him in kind. No mere victim of society, Eloise is a bitch, not only with her husband, but with her daughter and her maid as well. She takes the revenges of an invalid.

This story contains the first clear explanation of banana fever: it is the sense of what is missing that causes the suffering. Here, the lover's death brings the loss. Death, of course, is the most primitive way of making loss concrete; it is the villain of the war stories and it is still the villain here. In "Uncle Wiggily," however, we have Salinger's first sign of awareness that this sense of loss ought to be overcome, the first sign, in other words, that remembering too much is a bad thing. Eloise, for example, resents her daughter's habit of inventing invisible playmates, Mickey Mickeranno and Jimmy Jimmereeno, to take to bed with her at night. Unconsciously, Eloise knows that Walter, her lost lover, is as invisible as Ramona's boyfriends. She forces Ramona to move into the middle of the bed to prevent her daughter from lying with an invisible lover, as she has had to lie with one in the years since Walter's death. She knows the consequences: her bitchiness.

These "consequences" show that Salinger was not yet willing to settle completely for a story about somebody with banana fever. In the war, he learned that actions not only had social causes but also social consequences, so he must indicate that Eloise's unhappiness affects others. In this way he absolved himself from having written an isolated, clinical report about one of the hyper-sensitive.

III

After "Uncle Wiggily," the desire to blame somebody or something generally vanishes. No longer was the evil out there somewhere; rather it was a microbe within us. We were not oppressed; we were sick.

The stories of Salinger's middle period, from "Uncle Wiggily" to "Franny," are stories of the search for relief. Having evidently rejected impulsive suicide as a cure ("A Perfect Day for Bananafish") and having seen the futility of trying to forget ("Uncle Wiggily in Connecticut"), Salinger alternately considered the following remedies: sublimation in art ("The Laughing Man"), the barefaced denial of pain ("Pretty Mouth and Green My Eyes"), the love and understanding of parents ("Down at the Dinghy"), the love and understanding of children ("For Esmé" and *The Catcher in the Rye*), psychiatry (*The Catcher in the Rye*), a mystic vision ("De Daumier-Smith's Blue Period"), a mystic faith ("Teddy"), and a mystic slogan ("Franny"). It is interesting to note that each of the remedies seems to furnish at least a temporary restoration of balance for the protagonist.

In "For Esmé — with Love and Squalor" we have an interesting development in the record of the bananafish: Salinger allows himself his first *explicit* statement of what is wrong with his heroes. Actually, he allows Dostoievski to make the statement for him; "Dear God, life is hell . . . Fathers and Teachers, I ponder, what is hell? I maintain it is the suffering of being unable to love." Although Dostoievski's lament probably does not accurately describe Sergeant X's condition, nor that of Salinger's other heroes for that matter, most of whom love too much; still the God that the Sergeant requires is clearly a God of redemption, not of justice. What the bananafish needed was to be saved; where justice lay was no longer certain.

This can be seen even more sharply in *The Catcher in the Rye,* which appeared shortly after "Esmé," but which had taken ten years to complete. It is possible to trace how Holden's need for redemption grew in these years. The bright Holden-Phoebe relationship, for example, was undoubtedly conceived early. Not only does it follow closely the Babe-Mattie relationship of the Gladwaller stories, but the framework of the first bedroom scene between Holden and Phoebe appears in an early *Collier's* story called "I'm Crazy," in which Holden Caulfield is first introduced as a character. Later, part of the skating rink episode with Sally appeared in *The New Yorker*. In these early versions, it is hard to see Holden as much more than brash and irrepressible. *The Catcher* makes him both a kinder and a sicker person, no longer just a boy with half his hair gray. The final chapter in the rest home, as well as the long and important scene with Mr. Antolini, must have been written late in the ten years.

In Antolini, the bananafish faces the demand for an agonizing judgment. Antolini has represented for Holden the last bastion of moral conscience; that is, Holden has called on Antolini in this crucial moment in his progress because Antolini "finally picked up that boy that jumped out of the window . . . He didn't even give a damn if his coat got all bloody." This is a moral value to Holden. Also, Antolini shares Holden's sentiments about D.B.'s sellout to Hollywood. When Holden arrives at Antolini's, however, he finds his teacher half high and obviously married to a woman he does not love. Holden is bored with him and disappointed in him. His disappointment increases to revulsion when he awakens during the night to find Antolini "petting me or patting me on the goddam head." Terrified, he leaves at once. But the next morning, in thinking it over, he says, ". . . I wondered if just maybe I was wrong about thinking he was making a flitty pass at me.

I wondered if maybe he just liked to pat guys on the head when they're asleep. I mean how can you tell about that stuff for sure? You can't."

What Holden refuses to do, in effect, is to make an ultimate judgment on Mr. Antolini. The result is that the bananafish, having abandoned the emotional outlet of condemnation, grows more and more frustrated, a consequence of the acceptance of a purely esthetic frame of reference (i.e., "This seems ugly to me" or "This seems beautiful to me"). Note Holden's plaintive comment on Phoebe's last carousel ride: "It was just that she looked so damn *nice* going around and around in her blue coat and all." No absolute value can be assigned.

IV

The five stories published since *The Catcher in the Rye* ("De Daumier-Smith's Blue Period," "Teddy," "Franny," "Raise High the Roofbeam, Carpenters" and "Zooey") explore a solution for the bananafish, first, in terms of union with God and, finally, in terms of re-union with society.

The stories demonstrate that although the bananafish is incapacitated by the weight of his experience, he is also afflicted with a psychological conflict between the desire to participate in and the need to withdraw from society. He is a non-conformist, but a paralyzed one, unlike Arrowsmith, for example, who was moving full-tilt toward a private goal, or Huckleberry Finn, who was making his precipitate escape away from society, unwilling to be captured. The Salinger hero, on the other hand, is carried along in the currents of his own psyche, neither toward nor away from anything. He drifts in a course more or less parallel to that of society, alternately tempted and repelled, half inclined to participate, and half inclined to withdraw.

In "De Daumier-Smith's Blue Period," the miracle regeneration of "For Esmé" recurs, this time in terms of a frankly mystical Experience. Salinger himself, only half ironically, uses the capital "e" to describe it, perhaps to indicate that it takes a momentary union with God in order to achieve a real insight into a man's relationship with his fellows.

The reconciliation to the idea of participation without illusion is pushed to fantastic new extremes in "Teddy," in some ways Salinger's most unexpected story. In "Teddy," reconciliation becomes Oriental resignation. The transition from the personal mysticism to the formal Eastern self-immolation which Teddy practices does not occur, however, without certain schizophrenic symptoms in both the form of the story and in its main character. It is the only one of Salinger's stories that is utterly incredible, and yet he goes to his usual pains to document its reality.

What Teddy, this ten-year-old Buddha, has achieved in Salinger's bargain with the East is, of course, invulnerability, the persistent wish of all bananafish. The knowledge that De Daumier-Smith comes to by hard Experience, Teddy is granted early through revelation. He then withdraws, as all great religious figures have, to be better able to participate. In Teddy's case, he removes himself from the boorish concerns of a society represented by his father and sister in order that he may be invulnerable to the malice of his father and sister, and be able to do good in return. He writes in his diary, for example: "See if you can find daddy's army dog tags and wear them whenever possible. It won't kill you and he will like it."

The recent publication of "Franny" revived the dilemma of participation or withdrawal. Here, the Zen-Buddhist material is not as well integrated on a story level as in "Teddy," since Franny merely wishes to believe in a way of living of the validity of which Teddy has had satisfactory mystic revelation. But because the tension is more psychological in "Franny," and because God is sought this side of oblivion, it is a more touching story.

In the main scene in the restaurant with her boyfriend, Franny is graphically split between the desire to withdraw and the need to participate. She has arrived to spend the weekend with Lane, already apprehensive that she will find the kind of insensitivity she has found in him many times before. She would like to be the good-time girl that Lane wants, but this time she cannot bear his egocentricity, his counterfeit participation in the world. She retreats to the stall in the Ladies' Room to weep for him and for all the others, one presumes, who, like Lane, are devoted to the Flaubertian view of society, that mean focus on personal vanity, which so offends Franny. Franny, a bananafish, sees all the beautiful possibilities instead, and she suffers for it. She tries to communicate with him again, finally withdraws once more and falls insensible to the ground. Her courage, however, has touched something in the boy at last. After her final collapse, he is kind to her, half understanding, but she ends making her final whispered appeal to God.

Pity for the bananafish ends with "Franny." The function of Salinger's two most recent stories, both long, didactic, and largely unsymmetrical, is to restore the stature of the bananafish. In "Raise High the Roofbeam, Carpenters," he removes the shame from the disease by showing Seymour Glass as a superior man. In "Zooey," he shows that reconciliation with society is possible if the bananafish, with courage, practices the act of Christian love.

"Raise High the Roofbeam, Carpenters" affirms the bananafish in spite of the fact that the reader knows that Seymour Glass is to end as Teddy did, embracing death. Its very title, first of all, is a paean for the bridegroom, a singularly appropriate symbol for all the Salinger heroes, who are young people, people uninitiated, unconsummated, unassimilated. The story thus is a celebration of experiences, rather than a dirge for them. Moreover, it celebrates for the first time, the sensitivity of the hero, making perhaps a final surrender of the author's identification with the hero and a beginning of appreciation for him. If Seymour is a sick man, he is also a big man and that becomes an important thing here.

While the story explains the suicide of Seymour in "Bananafish," it also makes that suicide seem a little irrelevant. It is Seymour's life, his unique way of looking at things that concerns Salinger here, and although he is obliged to mention the subsequent death of Seymour early in the story, he refers to it simply as "death," rather than suicide. For a change, the remark seems incidental, rather than a calculated understatement, the device Salinger consistently uses when he talks about what touches him particularly.

Concerned with Seymour's life rather than his death, Salinger is at last able to expose the bananafish here. Banana fever no longer seems the shame that it did in "Pretty Mouth," "The Laughing Man," "For Esmé," and in "A Perfect Day for Bananafish" itself where Seymour can express himself only to a little girl, and ambiguously at that. The secretly prying eyes of others he is unable to bear. Witness the curious scene on the elevator when he accuses a woman in the car of staring at his feet. This happens less than a minute before he puts a bullet through his head.

In "Raise High the Roofbeam, Carpenters," the frank advocacy of Seymour enables Salinger to transcend the limits of the tight pseudo-poetic structure which hamstrings so much of modern short fiction. Because the story is partisan, it must be analytic as well as metaphoric. No longer deceived into thinking his characters are prey to simple grief or to bourgeois insensitivity, rather than to beauty, he is able to expose them at last. The loosening of form, which begins with "Esmé," culminates with Seymour's throwing the stone at Charlotte, the affirmation of the effort for expression and communication even at the expense of exposure and pain.

Finally, it takes Zooey, in the story which bears his name, to communicate the new awareness and to act upon it. The redeeming union with the divine is the same as union with society, Zooey believes. If Buddy remains unreconstructable, Zooey, the youngest Glass son, comes to recognize that to be a deaf-mute in a high silk hat or a catcher in the rye is not the privilege of many.

Essentially, Zooey is a man of action. Appropriately enough, his profession is acting. Although he does not care much for a great deal of the world, he participates in it. He performs in television scripts which he detests; he meets people for lunch he does not like; he argues with his mother; he challenges his sister; he even dares to deface the shrine of the long-dead Seymour. In none of these things is he remotely self-immolating or contemplative, in the manner of Teddy; in none of them does he seek an "affinity." It is suggested that it is because Zooey alone among the Glasses has "forgiven" Seymour for his suicide that he is enabled to take a more involving and distinctly Western view of society. Zooey's final advice to his sister Franny, who has had aspirations to the stage, is: "The only thing you can do now, the only *relig*ious thing you can do, is *act*. Act for God, if you want to — be *God's* actress, if you want to. What could be prettier? You can at least try to, if you want to — there's nothing wrong in *try*ing."

Action then is the remedy here, and although remedies come and go in Salinger, it is perhaps most important because when action becomes an end in itself, it becomes possible to distinguish again between the deed and the doer. Zooey remonstrates with Franny about it: ". . . what I don't like — and what I don't think either Seymour or Buddy would like *either,* as a matter of fact — is the way you talk about all these people. I mean you don't just despise what they represent — you despise them. It's too damn personal, Franny. I mean it." Zooey's aim is to recognize that principles exist by which men live; and that without action, things are neither good nor bad. Principles vanish. The bananafish's mind is full of still photographs; action thaws these photographs; action again makes judgments possible. It forestalls the rapt contemplation of moments that have no meaning to others and which tend to isolate each individual in his own picture gallery. To transcend the particular for the sake of the general is to overcome the paralyzed moment for the sake of the principle which animates it.

Although this is a new step for Salinger, one must observe that throughout the story, he keeps Buddy's opinion in abeyance. In the speech quoted above, Zooey suggests that Buddy and Seymour agree with him about the distinction between the deed and the doer. But the shadow of Buddy and Seymour would suggest otherwise. Zooey's consent to participate is as much rebellion from as it is practice of the way of life of his older brothers. As a matter of cold fact, principles have always gotten in the way for the bananafish because principles, ideas, systems are too far away from life as the bananafish lives it. That is why every participation in the social system has turned out to be counterfeit in the end.

v

Where Salinger fits in the mainstream of American fiction remains uncertain. As I have noted earlier, his is not what is ordinarily termed social fiction, except insofar as all novels and short stories must concern themselves with the fabric of human relations. The "disease" which I have discussed at length is innate, not social, and society's reaction to it hardly affects its virulence. If anything, society is a palliative force. Occasionally, a hero like De Daumier-Smith becomes infected with the health of the society. For those who remain in the sanitarium, the remedies are many, but the truly sick seldom recover. Like Camille, they cough their way through their eternal confinement — not brave, but sometimes witty invalids, hating the disease that Salinger has diagnosed, even as Fitzgerald had diagnosed Gatsby's.

Call the disease Illusion or Delusion, Salinger stands, in regard to the nature of his insight, as close to Fitzgerald as he does to any American author. Both are concerned with the effect of the immaculate moment on men. These moments are so complete in themselves that better balanced heroes could assimilate them as the minor esthetic experiences which the "well adjusted" know them to be. Fitzgerald has always emphasized the ideational attraction. That the response of Gatsby to Daisy, of Avery to Rosalind, of Dick Diver to Nicole, and of Anthony West to Gloria is hardly sexual at all has been generally recognized. Attraction arises out of a conceptual ideal that some men have, the kind that Goethe's Werther had over a century earlier, and that Salinger's heroes were to have a generation later.

Salinger, in resisting the dominant trend of determinism in American fiction during the last fifty years, has simply succeeded a little better than Fitzgerald in isolating the hero's response by keeping the "passion" as remote from sexual connotation as possible. Where the object of delight is found in women, these women are often little girls or nuns, and what is admired is sexless in essence, some capacity for charity or candor, sensitivity or simplicity. Fitzgerald's heroes, on the other hand, usually confused glamor with beauty. To this extent, they were far more conditioned by a particular social climate than Salinger's are. If, however, they mistook Duessa for Una more often than not, it was not because they were especially at fault, but because the ideal had been corrupted by the Zeitgeist. One is compelled to feel that Fitzgerald would have been as sympathetic to Gatsby as Goethe was to Werther and as Salinger is to Seymour Glass if only Daisy Buchanan had been less obviously phony.

Fitzgerald moralizes because Daisy is a social by-product. Salinger, in his best work, does not because he sees that the terrible fascination with other human beings is apart from any good-ness or bad-ness in society as a whole or in particular individuals. This attitude places him at a little distance from Fitzgerald, and, of course, at a great distance from other American writers who have handled "fatal fascination" with traditional Puritanism, assuming that what was fascinating was necessarily either voluptuous or evil or both. Authors from Hawthorne and Poe all the way down to Faulkner are victims of this fallacy, but Salinger is not.

For this reason, Goethe's Werther (whom Salinger himself mentions in "The Girl I Knew") seems to be a more likely forebear of the bananafish than anybody in our own literature. Werther was distracted by what was fair. Plain enough. So was Tristan. And in modern German fiction, so is Thomas Mann's Aschenbach in "Death in Venice." In each case, there is an effort to estheticize the passion, that is, to idealize its object, to see it perhaps for the purposes of the story as the hero sees it. This is Romantic, of course, and with the concomitant additions of irony, peculiarly German-Romantic — a habit of mind which many regard as archaically self-indulgent.

A part of Thomas Mann's subject matter — disease and the non-conformist, as treated in "Death in Venice," "Tonio Kröger," "Little Herr Friedemann," and in much of *The Magic Mountain* and *Buddenbrooks* — is the whole of Salinger's. Both explore the non-conformist's ambivalent attitudes toward bourgeois society. Stylistically both write with wit, with a gift for the well-turned phrase and a lack of timorousness about didacticism. Allowing that Salinger has neither the intellect nor the creative energy of Mann, it seems reasonable to suppose he could benefit from the security of a form and a tradition more sympathetic to his genius than our own: for all his fidelity to the native idiom and the native scene, Salinger, like his characters, is himself hardly more than a "visitor in this garden of enamel urinals."

❦ DAVID L. STEVENSON

William Styron and the Fiction of the Fifties

I

WILLIAM STYRON, brilliantly in his first work of fiction, *Lie Down in Darkness* (1951), and somewhat opaquely in his very recent *Set This House on Fire* (1960),[1] writes the peculiarly bleak, uncomforting, largely a-social novel of the fifties. In company with such contemporary writers as Norman Mailer, Herbert Gold, Saul Bellow, George P. Elliott, and J. D. Salinger, he has given us the moral bewilderment and the unfocussed anxiety haunting some of the most serious minds of his World War II generation. And he has pushed his explorations of the nature and meaning of human value, in an existential world, to the point where the essential act of staying alive is itself at stake, is the central question of his novels. His created characters — Peyton Loftis in *Lie Down in Darkness* and Cass Kinsolving in *Set This House on Fire* — do not isolate themselves by private and catastrophic actions, after the fashion of an Othello, from a world which, otherwise, would have made existence possible and enjoyable for them. It is rather, for Styron's characters, that *being* as opposed to *non-being* is resolved out of the times and events of their lives by a contest between a moribund moral imagination and a sheer animal instinct for survival.

At the surface level of narrative event, Styron's first novel, *Lie Down in Darkness,* was a richly detailed portrait of the unresolvable emotional chaos which defined the between-the-wars marriage of Milton Loftis and his wife Helen. Against an upper-middle-class, Southern background of country-club dances and drinking, Episcopalian moral conformity, and Negro primitive Christianity, the Helen Loftis of the novel clings with pathological, maternal devotion to the mentally retarded, crippled daughter Maudie, and her husband, Milton Loftis, over-indulges, in his half-sick role of father, the bright, seductive daughter Peyton. The central focus of the novel, however, is the

Reprinted from *Critique,* III, No. 3 (Summer, 1960), 47–58, by permission of the author and the editors. Copyright © 1960 by *Critique.*

[1] I omit from my discussion Styron's novelette, *The Long March* (1952), a well-executed piece of documentary fiction in conventional narrative form.

suicide of Peyton herself, after the collapse of her own disastrous marriage. Perhaps in part the victim of her parents' unmitigated and fascinated hatred of each other, Peyton Loftis is shown to be more essentially the victim of the driving moral disorientation of the generation which came to maturity after World War II. It is not that Peyton actively sets out to destroy her own desire to live. It is rather that, for her, existence or death can be decided by no act of affirmation that can be isolated from the tumbled events of her life. The desperate moment of her suicide, I think, is almost wholly a question as to when the welling up in her of pure instinct for survival will cease.

Lie Down in Darkness was the first important post-war novel to demonstrate, both by its rather loose, episodic, unsynthesized structure, and by its assumptions concerning the nature of human reality and human value, that the novel, as novel, had undergone an actual and a verifiable metamorphosis,[2] that if it were to be taken seriously, it had to be viewed as having outgrown its old form and content as they had been set by the giants of the twenties and the thirties. Its first critics were, on the whole, favorably impressed by the quality of the writing it displayed, though the new "existential" atmosphere and tone of *Lie Down in Darkness* seems to have been puzzling to them.

Maxwell Geismar, for example, found the novel "practically perfect." He also noted, in praise of Styron's use of the visual, that "we are *at* all these ghastly parties, ceremonials, and festivals of a middle-class business society." And yet he could conclude of a book whose basic involvement was with the flight of coherency in our time, that it was "simply a domestic tragedy" (*Saturday Review,* September 15, 1951). The commentator for *Time* magazine, in his own inimitably patronizing way, perhaps recognized the essential attitudes of the novel toward the human condition more clearly than Geismar when he described Styron as "one more recruit for the dread-despair-and-decay camp of U. S. letters" (September 19, 1951).

Lie Down in Darkness seemed to me when I first read it (and as I have re-read it a number of times since) to be almost in a class by itself in its power to create characters caught in the mood of a generation, hovering, in its daily lives, between a drugged conventionality, a faceless and soulless identification with the formalized pleasures of a class, and a terror of the meaninglessness of existence. And I think *Lie Down in Darkness* contains one of the most stunning passages in contemporary fiction, in Peyton Loftis's Joyce-like internal monologue as she strips herself to what she calls "this lovely shell" of her naked body, and plunges out the window to her death on the street below. But neither this novel nor those of Styron's most alert, most dedicated

[2] As I have tried to demonstrate in "Fiction's Unfamiliar Face," *Nation* (November 1, 1958).

contemporaries have yet been generally accepted for the distinct triumphs they are, unlike and quite different from the triumphs of the novels of the twenty-five years between the wars. And an Arthur Mizener, for example, though he is willing to grant *Lie Down in Darkness* "real power," still insists (perhaps with the more tightly written, the more obvious content of a *Great Gatsby* in mind) that it loses stature by a "certain factitious solemnity about The Meaning of It All" (New York *Times Book Review,* June 5, 1960).

Styron's second major work of fiction, his recently published *Set This House on Fire,* is more explicitly and didactically contrived as an existential novel than was *Lie Down in Darkness.* It is written with a highly sensitive, clear control of language, but it remains somehow static, and oddly ineffective by comparison. *Set This House on Fire* opens with a prefatory, two-page quotation from a John Donne sermon, ascribing the fevers which rage through the human body and set it, as a house, on fire, and the horrors which seize the human soul as God's violent way of shaking a man, of tormenting him, into a sense of spiritual being, of spiritual existence. The narrative itself is largely the account of two men who, until the book's end, fiercely resist the existential implications and meanings of the fevers and the terrors of body and soul by which *they* are shaken. One of them, Mason Flagg, is a bright, rich American playboy, viewed for the longest stretches of the novel as the lavish host to other rich Americans, in a rented palace in Southern Italy. He is presented as wholly unable to live in his own person, and existing only vicariously by using other people: a series of women sexually, men as flatterers and toadies. The other of the two men, Cass Kinsolving, is Flagg's principal fool and jester for most of the novel. He is an uneducated, not very bright, would-be painter who submits to incredible public indignities and indecencies from Flagg in exchange for the alcohol which will keep him perpetually sodden. The point of view in the novel, the character through whose mind we appraise the anguished lives of Flagg and Kinsolving, is Peter Leverett, a young post-war American on the loose, spending a last weekend in Italy, where he is witness to Flagg's eventual murder by Cass, and the latter's redemption back into the world of being.

Taken page by page, the quality of writing in Styron's new novel is very high. I cite as one example this skillful capture in words of the special tone and mood of a Sunday in New York:

> The slow, late awakening in the midst of a city suddenly and preposterously still, the coffee cups and the mountainous tons of newspapers, the sense of indolence and boredom. . . . It is a time of real torpor, but a time too of a vague yet unfaltering itch and uneasiness . . . because in this most public of cities one's privacy is momentarily enforced and those old questions *What am I doing?*

Where am I going? are insistent in a way they could never be on a Monday. (7)

I cite as another example the quick, easy grace with which Styron gives the reader a generalized sense of what it would be like to be driving a small, open car through the Italian summer night:

> My headlights kindled fire in the long lanes of poplars, the under-bellies of their leaves a treasure of rustling silver, and in sleeping villages with Latin-book names — Aprilia and Pontinia — as white and as hushed as sepulchers. . . . Above me bright stars wheeled across the heavens, but south in the open country all was black as death . . . stretching out on all sides into infinite darkness. (25)

And yet for all the page-by-page brilliantly sketched detail of the book, and for all one's wishing that it might have been Styron's *Crime and Punishment,* his *Set This House on Fire* is truly and surprisingly a novel *manqué.* And its defect is not in the formal structure of the narrative, I think, nor in its insistently philosophical presentation of its subject matter. The book is, to be sure, curiously organized as a series of teasing and tentative minor revelations, a series of slow steps around, rather than toward, the central revelation of the action: Flagg's rape of a young Italian girl and Kinsolving's killing him, in retaliation. Moreover, Peter Leverett, as observer and source of the point of view, constantly avoids thinking about this central event, and thereby keeps us from really seeing it clearly until the very end of the novel. As Donald Malcolm commented somewhat truculently of this aspect of the book, in his *New Yorker* review, "Styron manages the unusual feat of stimulating the reader's curiosity without ever really arousing his interest" (June 4, 1960).

Set This House on Fire has also seemed to some of its immediate critics too self-consciously, too exclusively, Cass Kinsolving's existential *Angstgeschrei.* Mizener speaks of the novel's "fashionable meta-physical trimmings," and feels that the sharply observed material of the book "is solemnly hopped up." Cass, perhaps, is too often made to comment too obviously on his own flights from everyday reality. We follow him through one after another of his drunken debaucheries, and then hear his spiritual retching, his complaints of being "sick as a dog inside my soul" and unable to figure out "where that sickness came from." And the novel ends on an almost homiletic note, with Cass's Sartre-like explanation of his sudden flight from the confines of burning lunacy into ecstatic existence:

> . . . As for being and nothingness, the one thing I did know was that to choose between them was simply to choose being, not for the sake of being, or even the love of being . . . but in the hope of

being what I could be for a time. This would be an ecstasy. (500–501)

As I see it, however, the basic defect of the novel, and a defect which keeps the whole of *Set This House on Fire* from achieving the stature one could wish for it, is that its materials are everywhere "un-novelized." The special distinction of fiction, its essential difference from other kinds of writing, is that it cuts itself off from the actual reality it is imitating, and exists separately, as a self-contained microcosm. At its highest moments, indeed, it can seem even *more* real than actual fact. The odd difficulty in *Set This House on Fire* is that the individual scenes, the individual characterizations, accumulate, but they remain inert, they do not achieve their potential content. It is as if the imaginative materials of the book had been held too long or too lovingly in the mind of the writer, and had taken on a significance for him that he takes for granted and fails to project in his writing. They do not cross over into the house of fiction.

Gross examples of this kind of thing are scattered throughout the whole book. In its early pages, for instance, the teller of the story, Peter Leverett, gives in maddening detail a conversation with his father in which the latter attacks the Eisenhower administration. This was meant, one might guess, to suggest the flight of sense, of intelligibility, in the outside political world which we all inhabit, in order to make clear that this was the special moment in time during which Cass Kinsolving was making his own private and personal flight from coherence. But this conversation, as it occurs in the novel, merely seems strange and inconsequential. Similar in effect, I think, is the sudden, and fictionally un-assimilative appearance of a Reverend Dr. Irvin Franklin Bell at the beginning of Mason Flagg's raffish party of Hollywood celebrities (during which Flagg rapes his servant girl). Bell, his "cheeks plumped up in a sickly, illicit smile" at the goings on, is a sort of parodic sketch of a Norman Vincent Peale, a character as out of place at Flagg's orgy as a drunken stagehand stumbling across the scene as Desdemona is being smothered. Other gross examples of the un-novelized materials floating about in *Set This House on Fire* would, I think, include most of Leverett's thoughts about himself, and especially about his various love affairs. This material was no doubt meant to characterize Leverett for us. But as it is incorporated into the novel, it achieves the nonsignificance for the reader of the sudden and embarrassingly personal revelations of a rather casual acquaintance.

Much more destructive than these examples, however, is the curiously un-novelized dialogue. It attempts to maintain a driving momentum and vitality by maintaining separable and interestingly individualized speaking voices for its two principal characters, Mason Flagg and Cass Kinsolving. This voice separation is attained, however, at the cost of fictional reality. Flagg is given a language of self-mocking sentimentality, painfully uninteresting, that grates on one's ears as if heard not within but outside the novel. As an example, the character Peter Leverett is almost always "Petesy" or "Dollbaby" to Flagg. And Flagg describes his own divorce: "Weep, weep for Mason and Celia, Peter, we've gone to Splitsville." Cass Kinsolving, equally grating, speaks the half-grammatical language of a "natural" man driven frantic; and he is also heard outside the novel. He repeats the word "bleeding" so many times that one begins to wince as one turns the page ("I'll pop you in the bleeding mouth"). He is also made to speak with a kind of half-witted sense of the value of tonal emphasis, painful to follow for the many pages of the novel, and suggested on the printed page by putting one or two of his words, per paragraph, in italics ("They forced me, *drug* me there — do you understand what I mean?").

It is difficult for me to accept *Set This House on Fire* as a defective novel, in part no doubt because of the power and the brilliance of *Lie Down in Darkness*. But one needs to keep one's perspective in such things. One remembers that Norman Mailer, after creating *The Naked and the Dead,* has stumbled through much un-novelized fiction, from *Barbary Shore* to *Advertisements for Myself.* Salinger's two most recent *New Yorker* pieces on members of his Glass family are in the same category. And there are (for me, at any rate) many bad, unfictionalized moments in Bellow's *The Adventures of Augie March* which even the loose, picaresque formula of the book fails to sustain. Archibald MacLeish has given us an un-dramatized *J.B.,* and even Shakespeare, at the height of his career, was capable, one may care to remember, of *Timon of Athens.* The failure of *Set This House on Fire* was described with xenophobic, though cheerful, insolence by the reviewer for *Time* as the failure to remain patriotically within the confines of Western moral tradition: "Styron's images of evil . . . are vivid but despairingly un-Christian and even un-Greek in their fatalism" (June 6, 1960). The failure to me is the honorable one of a powerful writer's inability to shake loose a wholly created thing, or entity, from the rich materials with which he has chosen to become involved.

II

Even though his second novel is never, I think, fully realized, it is important to observe of Styron that both *Lie Down in Darkness* and his recent *Set This House on Fire* have helped define the nature of the new and major serious fiction of his generation. It is important because there has been an uneasy and insistent disappointment with this fiction, expressed both in such official organs of our culture as *Time,* and by such reputable critics as a Mizener or an Alfred Kazin. And the disappointment seems to come, in part at least, from an unwillingness to accept the substance of this new fiction in the main stream of American writing today as a valid — or perhaps only as an endurable — reflection of our post-war life.

By contrast, the much smaller efforts of competing and minor coterie writing in America of the post-war years (the novel of meticulously cultivated emotional debilitation) has actually fared somewhat better with the critics. The most distinguishing trait of this fiction has been that its perceptual impulses are easily named, and strike only through the thin, surface layer of subject matter. Truman Capote's *Other Voices, Other Rooms,* Tennessee Williams' *The Roman Spring of Mrs. Stone,* and Mary McCarthy's *The Company She Keeps* can serve as examples. They are neatly designed, truly "fictionalized" novels, and a pleasure to read. But the chief perceptual gratification which they give us is a view of our own uncomfortable knowledge of the obsessive sexuality of our time leering out at us from the actions of their characters. Such fiction is easily admired for its skill, but it only stirs our minds enough to keep the concept of fiction as a way of perception, a way of deep communing between writer and reader, alive and faintly breathing.

Styron's kind of novel, on the other hand, has been preoccupied with the emotionally marginal lives of men and women clinging to existence, or letting go of it, outside the warm, platitudinous American world of the advertised dream. It has concerned itself with the deepest private strivings, the deepest private agonies, of men and women (Styron's Peyton Loftis and Cass Kinsolving, Saul Bellow's Tommy Wilhelm in *Seize the Day,* Norman Mailer's Sam and Eleanor in *The Man Who Studied Yoga,* Herbert Gold's Burr Fuller in *The Optimist,* George P. Elliott's Jackie in *Parktilden Village,* perhaps Salinger's Holden Caulfield in *The Catcher in the Rye*) living by a raw, naked sensibility, unsupported either by a definable personal philosophy or by the codes and admonitions of institutionalized culture or religion. And the mortal despair which floats just below the surface of the major fiction of the past decade, of which Styron's work is a significant part, has been its richest communication.

The serious critics of this main stream of American writing since World War II, out of timidity in confronting its substance, perhaps, have tended to argue that the new writers, merely as writers, have failed to come up to the hopes and expectations set by their immediate predecessors, writing between the two wars. John W. Aldridge, for example, called his largely adverse account of the first showing of the post-war fiction, *After the Lost Generation* (1951). And in commenting on Gore Vidal's *The City and the Pillar,* Aldridge remarked that the novel was full of "some stuff" which the writer could not "bring to light and objectify." In back of this judgment was the implication that there had been a serious falling off in some absolute quality of American writing; that the fiction of the fifties was off to a bad start, and had almost consciously set a level of achievement for itself considerably below that established by the best of our writers of the twenties and thirties.

It is only fair to note that Aldridge has not stood alone. The new and serious fiction of the decade following the publication of *After the Lost Generation* has not been met by an especially receptive or understanding criticism, one truly conscious of a peculiarly unstable world of event and disintegrating value with which the contemporary writer must cope, a world wholly lacking the comparatively simple moral insights confronting a Sinclair Lewis or a Hemingway. Leslie Fiedler, for example, greets the most characteristic efforts of the new writers with elegant excoriations.[3] Alfred Kazin, one of the most respected of critics, writing in *Harper's* for October, 1959, finds Norman Mailer, in *The Deer Park,* sharing with Paul Bowles, in *The Sheltering Sky,* the "same essential atmosphere of paralysis, of numbness that results when people feel themselves to be lost in the pursuit of compulsion." Kazin describes Salinger as "competent and interesting," but lacking in strength. He labels Herbert Gold's style, in *The Man Who Was Not With It,* as "falsely robust." And he complains in general of "the dimness, the shadowiness, the flatness, the paltriness, in so many of the reputable novelists" of the fifties. Even Granville Hicks, who in his weekly reports in the *Saturday Review* is the most consistent admirer of this present generation of novelists, does not really attempt to define the direction or the nature of their work. He is content to write praise in avuncular generalities. He will risk telling us that Saul Bellow, in his recent novel *Henderson the Rain King,* is writing with "wisdom and power." But Hicks remains too reluctant a witness for the new novel to make explicit what the wisdom is, and where the power.

It is no doubt true, for reasons of our cultural history, that the major fiction published in America between the two wars by such dominant figures as Sinclair Lewis, Dos Passos, Fitzgerald, Hemingway, and Steinbeck, created its own immediate self-justification in a way impossible to the serious novel today. It was able to leave its first readers with an acute sense that without it they would have been

---

[3] See his article, "Some Footnotes on the Fiction of 1956," *The Reporter* (December 13, 1956).

tangibly impoverished in some difficult-to-define, but deeply felt, awareness of themselves, of their generation, of the contours of the reality of their age. This earlier fiction was immensely concerned with evaluating the basic and shifting social and personal codes and values its audience still clung to, with the ways in which its members sought, and often failed to find, an interesting or at least an endurable mode of existence in their particular culture. This fiction was not, in any very limiting sense, didactic. But such novels as Lewis's *Main Street* and *Babbitt,* Dos Passos' *U.S.A.* trilogy, Fitzgerald's *The Great Gatsby,* Hemingway's *A Farewell to Arms* and *For Whom the Bell Tolls,* Steinbeck's *In Dubious Battle* and *Grapes of Wrath,* were all "sociological" in their concerns, if one may use the word rather lightly. And they were all written for an audience which remembered a stable and an apparently purposeful world.

The new Styron, Bellow, Gold novel of our time, because of the Stygian chaos and old night in which it must be written, excludes the morally or philosophically shy from its audience. Perhaps it has failed to capture the admiration of its critics, and the sizable audience devoted to the fiction of the twenties and thirties, because it has not been tempted (or able, now) to encompass the substantial areas of human experience which the very titles *Main Street* and *U.S.A.* suggest. It has not tried to create the large, usable social images of American life of these earlier works, whereby a post-World War I generation of American readers, eager for instruction, anxious to lose a provincial morality, a political, theological, and cultural innocence, was led into a new maturity. The names of the characters in our present-day fiction have not become a part of the national language after the fashion of a Babbitt, a Robert Jordan, the Joads, to act as the symbols for our way of looking at a world.

How well this new American fiction has been written is still a matter of subjective opinion on the part of individual members of its audience. At the level of language I would argue that today's serious novel is certainly as good as that written by the old giants of the between-the-wars. A Paul Bowles or a Truman Capote as examples of coterie writing, a Styron, a Mailer, as representative of fiction in the main stream of serious writing, certainly has as sharp, as sensitive, as intelligent a control of words as had ever a Dos Passos, a Steinbeck, a Hemingway. But if one turns to the substance of the new major fiction of the fifties, one has to observe that it has made reader and critic alike uncomfortable in a new way. It is not the discomfort of a Lewis, a Cather, a Hemingway which provoked us to unburden ourselves of an outworn, small-town esthetics and a frayed, puritan morality. It is rather the discomfort of provoking in us a deeply-rooted sense of the possible meaninglessness of existence, of making us aware of characters (Peyton Loftis, Cass Kinsolving) more neurotic than we are who may seem to be (alas!) a heightening and mirroring of our own worst moments.

We can now concede that the brief quarter-century of American writing which produced *Main Street, The Grapes of Wrath, For Whom the Bell Tolls,* has become our history. We might also risk admitting that the new fiction of our post-war generation has attempted to commune with its readers at a deeper and less purely sociological level. A Styron, in his successful *Lie Down in Darkness,* evokes a world of complex, half-conscious perceptions, feelings, attitudes concerning the meaning of love and sex. He uncovers our most profound awareness of the fragile nature of the dogmatic and institutionalized values of our culture when ultimate questions of being and non-being are involved. His novels, like those of his major contemporaries, are attempts at communicating, ways of apprehending, some bitter sense of the flight of moral congruity in our age. With Bellow's character Henderson, in his *Henderson the Rain King,* with his insatiable *cupiditas,* his exuberant, aimless, witless "I want, I want," and with Styron's Peyton Loftis with her intolerable longing for nothingness, we find merely the complementary extremes of the characters of our new fiction: all of them as rudderless and adrift in the unknowable condition of existence as a Hamlet or a Lear.

That this sort of novel has been written at all is a tribute to the high seriousness, and the willingness to take a risk, of our young writers. Most of our society, no doubt, thinks itself little impoverished by its ignorance of this major fiction of the past decade. And I would agree that to the casual reader of novels of light intent, a novel by a Styron which attempts to communicate the deeply relevant in the human condition must seem of slight importance. But to the truly serious reader, concerned with fiction's role in one's leading the examined life, it must seem, in Tillich's way of putting such things, that these new novels of the fifties are, for the most part, not metaphysically hopped-up, but genuinely concerned with the ultimate and the unconditional. Peyton Loftis, as she evaluates her life before ending it, Tommy Wilhelm, in Bellow's *Seize the Day,* as he weeps through the funeral of a man he has never known, Burr Fuller, in Gold's *The Optimist,* who, like Cass Kinsolving, decides finally to accept being as a kind of ecstasy, are all gratifications of our most deeply rooted perceptions of the nature of the human condition: moments of being surrounded by the terror and the allure of the timeless dark. Our new generation of literary artists has abandoned social man for the unconditioned in man. Their novels may seem only small and partial illuminations to their critics. But it is both fascinating and reassuring, I think, to have even their partial illuminations of the unconditional elements in man constantly flickering in the high winds.

BIBLIOGRAPHY

I. OVERVIEWS

Books

ALDRIDGE, JOHN W. *After the Lost Generation.* New York: McGraw-Hill Book Company, 1951. Deals with the writers who came to prominence concurrently with World War II. See Aldridge's "What Became of Our Postwar Hopes?" (listed below, under "Articles") for follow-up comments.

ALDRIDGE, JOHN W. *In Search of Heresy.* New York: McGraw-Hill Book Company, 1956. "The absence of an active alternative to conformism is attested to . . . by the emptiness of some of the recent novels" — by Bellow, Salinger, Styron, McCullers, among others.

ANGOFF, ALLAN, ed. *American Writing Today.* New York: New York University Press, 1957. A collection of essays originally printed in the *London Times Literary Supplement* in 1954.

BLOTNER, JOSEPH L. *The Political Novel* (Doubleday Short Studies in Political Science). Garden City, N.Y.: Doubleday & Company, 1955. Brief survey, including Ellison, Mailer, and Irwin Shaw.

BONE, ROBERT A. *The Negro Novel in America.* New Haven, Conn.: Yale University Press, 1958.

COWLEY, MALCOLM. *The Literary Situation.* New York: The Viking Press, 1954. The chapter entitled "The 'New' Fiction: A Tidy Room in Bedlam" is critical of recent fiction's tendency to accept "life" uncritically.

FIEDLER, LESLIE A. *Love and Death in the American Novel.* New York: Criterion Books, 1960. American literature from 1789 to the present shown as incapable of presenting sexual matters in an adult manner, and in consequence excessively preoccupied with death.

FULLER, EDMUND. *Man in Modern Fiction.* New York: Random House, 1958. Essays on contemporary literature, highly critical of its tendency toward presenting "a corrupted and debased image of man."

GEISMAR, MAXWELL. *American Moderns.* New York: Hill and Wang, 1958. Includes essays on Salinger, Bellow, Jones, Styron, and Griffin.

275

HASSAN, IHAB H. *Radical Innocence*. Princeton, N. J.: Princeton University Press, 1961. For a brief essay-outline of this book, see Hassan's "The Character of Post-War Fiction in America," in the present collection.

HICKS, GRANVILLE, ed. *The Living Novel*. New York: The Macmillan Company, 1957. A collection of essays about form and content in the work of such novelists as Bellow, Ellison, Gold, Harris, Morris, O'Connor.

HOFFMAN, FREDERICK J. *The Modern Novel in America*. Chicago: Henry Regnery Company, 1951. The final section, "The Last Ten Years," looks briefly at some of the early efforts of writers like Bellow and Bowles.

HUGHES, CARL M. *The Negro Novelist*. New York: The Citadel Press, 1954.

KAZIN, ALFRED. *Contemporaries*. Boston: Little, Brown and Company, 1962. Survey approach, with occasional critical comments about some of the writers considered here: Styron, Mailer, Bellow et al.

LIPTON, LAWRENCE. *The Holy Barbarians*. New York: Julian Messner, 1959. A discussion of the San Francisco Beats.

LUDWIG, JACK. *Recent American Novelists* (University of Minnesota Pamphlets, No. 22). Minneapolis: University of Minnesota Press, 1962. A brief (37 pages) essay followed by a useful bibliography of the novels.

McCORMICK, JOHN. *Catastrophe and Imagination*. London: Longmans, Green, 1955. Discusses the profound effects of political catastrophe, especially war, on art. Survey approach; includes Bellow and Mailer.

PARKINSON, THOMAS, ed. *A Casebook on the Beat*. New York: Thomas Y. Crowell Company, 1961. A solid collection of primary and secondary source materials.

SPILLER, ROBERT E., ed. *A Time of Harvest*. New York: Hill and Wang, 1962. Essays on American literature, 1910–1960; includes the essay by R. W. B. Lewis listed below, under "Articles."

WATTS, ALAN W. *Beat Zen, Square Zen, and Zen*. San Francisco: City Lights Books, 1959. Draws distinctions between the three in terms of legitimacy and illegitimacy. (See also the essay by Stephen Mahoney listed below, under "Articles.")

Articles

ALDRIDGE, JOHN W. "What Became of Our Postwar Hopes?", *New York Times Book Review*, July 29, 1962, pp. 1, 24. Asserts that very few of the writers who showed promise immediately after

World War II have delivered; Mailer, Capote, Vidal, Jones have been supplanted by Bellow, Baldwin, Malamud, Salinger, Purdy, Roth.

ARROWSMITH, WILLIAM. "Literature and the Uses of Anxiety," *Western Humanities Review*, x (Autumn, 1956), 325–335. Good on *angst*, with references to Bellow and McCullers.

BALDANZA, FRANK. "Plato in Dixie," *Georgia Review*, xii (Summer, 1958), 151–167. McCullers, Capote, and Platonism.

BALDWIN, JAMES. "As Much Truth as One Can Bear," *New York Times Book Review*, January 14, 1962, pp. 1, 38. The writer must write about the world as it is, as he knows it; the recent writer must go farther than his elders went in terms of realism or truth.

BALDWIN, JAMES. "The Black Boy Looks at the White Boy," *Esquire*, LV (May, 1961), 102–106. Reply to Mailer's "The White Negro"; denial, in effect, of Mailer's thesis that Negro and hipster are motivated alike.

BALDWIN, JAMES. "The New Lost Generation," *Esquire*, LVI (July, 1961), 113–115. The American expatriate leaves in order to find — to become — himself.

BARRETT, WILLIAM. "American Fiction and American Values," *Partisan Review*, XVIII (November–December, 1951), 681–690. In current fiction, affirmative values are found in lower-class characters; educated middle-class characters are nihilistic.

"THE 'BEAT' GENERATION," *Current Affairs Bulletin,* December 7, 1959, pp. 35–48. A descriptive, largely uncritical, account in an Australian publication.

BELLOW, SAUL. "Facts That Put Fancy to Flight," *New York Times Book Review,* February 11, 1962, pp. 1, 28. American readers — and writers — are enamored of "real" facts; hence, the journalistic novel. But "truth" transcends the factual; it grows out of the novelist's sensitivity and excitement in face of the facts.

BERGLER, EDMUND. "Writers of Half-Talent," *American Imago,* XIV (Summer, 1957), 155–164. Psychoanalytical examination of the novels; asserts that Augie March is not a well-realized character, since he is too passive to have had his adventures.

BESSIE, SIMON MICHAEL. "American Writing Today: A Publisher's Viewpoint," *Virginia Quarterly Review*, XXXIV (Winter, 1958), 1–17. Concludes that writing today seems to be going nowhere, hence achieves nothing.

BITTNER, WILLIAM. "Kilroy Is Here," *New Republic,* February 10, 1958, pp. 17–18. New writers investigate the problems involved in remaining civilized in a barbaric society.

BITTNER, WILLIAM. "The Literary Underground," *Nation,* September 22, 1956, pp. 247–249. "The main theme of current American fiction is the quest for personal identity.

BOURJAILY, VANCE. "No More Apologies," *Discovery,* No. 2 (August, 1953), pp. 186–190. New York: Pocket Books, 1953. The recent novelist can and will stand on his own merits; no longer will invidious comparisons humiliate him.

BROOKS, CLEANTH. "Regionalism in American Literature," *Journal of Southern History,* XXVI (February, 1960), 35–43. The Southern literary renaissance is said to be part of the Southern rise to prominence as the subject of literature.

BRUSTEIN, ROBERT. "America's New Culture Hero: Feelings without Words," *Commentary,* XXV (February, 1958), 123–129. On the inarticulate heroes in America's entertainment media. Little about the novel, but a suggestive essay.

BURDICK, EUGENE. "The Innocent Nihilists Adrift in Squaresville," *Reporter,* April 3, 1958, pp. 30–33.

BUTLER, FRANK A. "On the Beat Nature of Beat," *American Scholar,* XXX (Winter, 1961), 79–82. Primarily on verse, and brief, but a solid, resounding attack.

CARPENTER, FREDERICK I. "The Adolescent in American Fiction," *English Journal,* XLVI (September, 1957), 313–319. Novels about adolescence do not necessarily denote adolescence in the authors. Some are mature and wise: Salinger, McCullers, Jessamyn West.

CHAMBERS, CLARKE A. "The Belief in Progress in 20th Century America," *Journal of the History of Ideas,* XIX (April, 1958), 197–227. Not concerned with recent writers, but a good background study of an important idea.

CURLEY, THOMAS F. "Quarrel with Time in American Fiction," *American Scholar,* XXIX (Autumn, 1960), 552–560. Review of *Advertisements for Myself, Breakfast at Tiffany's, The Spider's House, Giovanni's Room, Set This House on Fire.*

EBLE, KENNETH E. "The Individual at Mid-Twentieth Century: A Symposium. America's Lonely Writers," *Western Humanities Review,* XII (Autumn, 1958), 350–357. Today's writer is more isolated than ever, despite — or because of — the fact that he writes for a mass audience.

EHNMARK, ANDERS. "Rebels in American Literature," *Western Review,* XXIII (Autumn, 1958), 43–56. Descriptive, largely uncritical report by a Swedish newspaperman.

FEINSTEIN, HERBERT. "Contemporary American Fiction: Harvey Swados and Leslie Fiedler," *Wisconsin Studies in Contemporary Literature,* II (Winter, 1961), 79–98. Interviews with Swados and Fiedler concerning writers they consider important.

FREDERICK, JOHN T. "Fiction of the Second World War," *College English,* XVII (January, 1956), 197–204. War novelists never got beneath the surface meaning of the war.

FROHOCK, W. M. "It's Hard to See beyond the Hudson," *New York Times Book Review,* June 24, 1962, pp. 1, 32–33. In the absence of any real American literary community, American literature has been concerned with cultural diversity, American criticism with ideology, to the critical neglect of many good novels.

GEISMAR, MAXWELL. "Naturalism Yesterday and Today," *College English,* XV (January, 1954), 195–200. Algren, Mailer, Jones, Styron, Griffin cited as naturalistic novelists.

GLICKSBERG, CHARLES I. "The Theme of Alienation in the American Jewish Novel," *Reconstructionist,* XXII (November, 1957), 8–13.

GOLD, HERBERT. "Truth and Falsity in the Novel," *Hudson Review,* VIII (Autumn, 1955), 410–422. "Truth" grows out of "a thickness of feeling, a richness of time and change, and . . . a high valuation of human life." Gold as a "scholarly" critic.

GUÉRARD, ALBERT J. "The Ivory Tower and the Dust Bowl," *New World Writing,* No. 3 (May, 1953), pp. 344–356. New York: New American Library, 1953. The novelist is naturally subversive and rejects the division of the world into black and white. The recent novel, depressing and demoralizing, does reflect its world as the social-critical novels have done.

HASSAN, IHAB H. "The Idea of Adolescence in American Fiction," *American Quarterly,* X (Fall, 1958), 312–324. The cult of adolescence results from novelists' preoccupation with the theme of innocence vs. experience.

HASSAN, IHAB H. "Love in the Modern American Novel: Expense of Spirit and Waste of Shame," *Western Humanities Review,* XIV (Spring, 1960), 149–161. The dehumanization of sex and the desexualization of love in the novel reflect "the state and nature of the American soul."

HASSAN, IHAB H. "The Victim: Images of Evil in Recent American Fiction," *College English,* XXI (December, 1959), 140–146. "The figure of the victim remains at the center of the contemporary vision of evil." He purges society of sin by accepting society's punishment.

HAWKES, JOHN, D. J. HUGHES, and IHAB H. HASSAN. "Symposium: Fiction Today," *Massachusetts Review,* III (Summer, 1962), 784–797. Examinations of contemporary novels from the points of view of experimentation, characterization, and thematic existentialism.

HAZEL, ROBERT. "The Novelist's View," *Shenandoah,* X (Winter, 1959), 25–31. Part of a symposium. The novelist must learn to accept alienation instead of fighting it. He can learn from the poet.

HUGHES, CATHARINE. "A World of Outcasts," *Commonweal,* October 13, 1961, pp. 73–75.

HYMAN, STANLEY E. "Some Trends in the Novel," *College English,* XX (October, 1958), 1–9. Three "unattractive trends": self-parody by the novelists; homosexuality as a theme; the un-novel or "pseudo-fictions."

HYMAN, STANLEY E., and RALPH ELLISON. "The Negro Writer in America: An Exchange," *Partisan Review,* XXV (Spring, 1958), 197–222. Discussion of the extent to which archetypes from Negro folklore have been used in recent novels by Negroes.

HYNES, SAM. "The Beat and the Angry," *Commonweal,* September 5, 1958, pp. 559–561.

JACOBSON, DAN. "America's 'Angry Young Men': How Rebellious Are the San Francisco Rebels?", *Commentary,* XXIV (December, 1957), 475–479.

KEROUAC, JACK. "Beatific: On the Origins of a Generation," *Encounter,* XIII (August, 1959), 57–61.

KNOX, GEORGE. "The Negro Novelist's Sensibility and the Outsider Theme," *Western Humanities Review,* XI (Spring, 1957), 137–148.

LANGBAUM, ROBERT. "This Literary Generation," *American Scholar,* XXV (Winter, 1955–1956), 87–94.

LEHAN, RICHARD. "Camus' American Affinities," *Symposium,* XIII (Fall, 1959), 255–270. Though primary emphasis in this essay is on Hemingway and Faulkner, there is a good deal on Bellow and Bowles.

LEWIS, R. W. B. "Recent Fiction: Picaro and Pilgrims," in *A Time of Harvest,* ed. Robert E. Spiller. New York: Hill and Wang, 1962. Sees American literature of the '50s as picaresque, individualistic. Very good on *Augie March* and *Malcolm* — and on *Advertisements for Myself.*

LIBRA. "Ladders to Heaven: Novelists and Critics," *New World Writing,* No. 4 (October, 1953), pp. 303–316. New York: New American Library, 1953. Novelists have rejected authority in their search for truth; the serious critics have invoked it in theirs. Attacks Cowley and Aldridge primarily.

LIPTON, LAWRENCE. "Disaffiliation and the Art of Poverty," *Chicago Review,* X (Spring, 1956), 53–79. Poverty is the result of artistic integrity, of refusal to accept or defend society's values. Algren, Bellow, Ellison.

LIPTON, LAWRENCE. "The New Nonconformism," *Nation,* November 5, 1955, pp. 388–390. Good as an early general evaluation — but far too brief.

MACLEAN, HUGH. "Conservatism in Modern American Fiction," *College English,* XV (March, 1954), 315–325. Conservatism is the belief that man exists within a divine scheme having Purpose and Design. Chiefly on Faulkner, Fitzgerald, and Marquand, but with a section on Salinger.

MAHONEY, STEPHEN. "The Prevalence of Zen," *Nation,* November 1,

1958, pp. 311–315. The essay gets its impetus from Mahoney's acquaintance with Alan Watts; see Watts's *Beat Zen, Square Zen, and Zen,* cited above under "Books."

MARCUS, STEVEN. "The Novel Again," *Partisan Review,* XXIX (Spring, 1962), 171–195. The contemporary novel is all form, no ideas; novelistic prose is increasingly poetic. Malamud is the sole American writer treated at length.

MCNAMARA, EUGENE. "The Post-Modern American Novel," *Queen's Quarterly,* LXIX (Summer, 1962), 265–275. William Gaddis, John Griffin, William Styron, and James Purdy are the truly original recent novelists.

MUELLER, GUSTAV E. "Philosophy in the 20th Century American Novel," *Journal of Aesthetics and Art Criticism,* XVI (January, 1958), 471–481. The recent novel is critical of pragmatism, Christianity, capitalism, equalitarianism, and transcendentalism.

MUNRO, THOMAS. "The Failure Story: A Study of Contemporary Pessimism," *Journal of Aesthetics and Art Criticism,* XVII (December, 1958), 143–168. Discusses novels dealing with failure and defeat, but deals only briefly with recent writers.

NYE, RUSSEL B. "The Modern Quest," *Progressive,* XXIV (October, 1960), 46–50. The search for identity and relationship in a fluid world.

NYE, RUSSEL B. "Old Guard and Avant Garde," *Voices,* II (1961), 24–28. "There are a number of talented young people writing today, producing a number of very good — and possibly a few very important — novels." Comparisons make little sense; on their own terms, Bowles, Malamud, Salinger, Bourjaily et al. are the equals of Hemingway and Faulkner.

O'CONNOR, WILLIAM VAN. "The Grotesque in Modern American Fiction," *College English,* XX (April, 1959), 342–346. Literature of the grotesque is in reaction against bourgeois complacency. McCullers, O'Connor, Capote, Algren.

PODHORETZ, NORMAN. "The New Nihilism and the Novel," *Partisan Review,* XXV (Winter, 1958), 576–590. There is a hunger on all sides for "something extreme, fervent, affirmative, and sweeping." Neither radicalism nor religion satisfies it.

ROBERTS, JOHN G. "The 'Frisco Beat," *Mainstream,* XI (July, 1958), 11–26.

ROSS, BASIL. "California's Young Writers Angry and Otherwise," *Library Journal,* June 15, 1958, pp. 1850–1854.

ROTH, PHILIP. "Writing American Fiction," *Commentary,* XXXI (March, 1961), 223–233. "The American writer in the middle of the 20th century has his hands full in trying to understand, and then describe, and then make credible, much of the American reality. It stupefies, it sickens, it infuriates. . . ." Salinger, Bellow, Gold, Malamud, among others.

RYAN, RICHARD. "Of the Beat Generation and Us," *Catholic World,* CLXXXVII (August, 1958), 343–348.

SCOTT, JAMES F. "Beat Literature and the American Teen Cult," *American Quarterly,* XIV (Summer, 1962), 150–160. ". . . the Beats have brought only the sensibility of an adolescent to bear upon a problem which requires the courage and mental stamina of a man."

SHAPIRO, KARL. "Why Out-Russia Russia?", *New Republic,* June 9, 1958, pp. 10–12.

SMITH, HUGH L., JR. "Jazz in the American Novel," *English Journal,* XLVII (November, 1958), 467–478. Through expressions of respect for jazz, the novelists express a belief in the worth of the individual and in his powers of creation.

SOLOTAROFF, THEODORE. "All That Cellar-Deep Jazz," *Commentary,* XXXII (October, 1961), 317–324. A comparison of Henry Miller and Seymour Krim as partly a review of Krim's *Views of a Near-sighted Cannoneer.* But in showing Miller's influence, Solotaroff says a great deal about contemporary Beatism and hipsterism.

STEVENSON, DAVID L. "Fiction's Unfamiliar Face," *Nation,* November 1, 1958, pp. 307–309. The irritating unfamiliarity of contemporary fiction results from its structure: intensity of a series of moments rather than a progression of events.

STEVENSON, DAVID L. "The Lost Audience," *Nation,* August 2, 1958, pp. 58–59. Recent novels lack sociological significance.

WALDMEIR, JOSEPH J. "Novelists of Two Wars," *Nation,* November 1, 1958, pp. 304–307. The World War II novel is ideologically affirmative.

WARD, JOHN W. "Individualism Today," *Yale Review,* XLIX (Spring, 1960), 380–392. Unlike Emerson and Thoreau, who criticized society in the name of individualism, writers today need and seek a society which will nourish the individual.

WEBER, EUGEN. "The Anti-Utopia of the Twentieth Century," *South Atlantic Quarterly,* LVIII (Summer, 1959), 440–447. In 1945 *Animal Farm* opened a new series of attacks on Utopian dreams. A thoughtful background essay.

"What's Wrong with the American Novel?" (a forum discussion including Styron, Jean Stafford, and Ralph Ellison), *American Scholar,* XXIV (Autumn, 1955), 464–503. Excellent exchange of ideas and opinions concerning American literature generally.

WIDMER, KINGSLEY. "The American Road: The Contemporary Novel," *University of Kansas City Review,* XXVI (Summer, 1960), 309–317. The road has always appeared as a "lyric image of American yearning." Bellow, Malamud, Kerouac, Salinger, Algren, Gold all utilize the road image or metaphor.

WIDMER, KINGSLEY. "The Literary Rebel," *Centennial Review,* VI (Spring, 1962), 182–201. A rather slick treatment of rebellion, with references to Kerouac, Burroughs, Mailer, Salinger, Ginsberg. Mostly on Beats.

WIDMER, KINGSLEY. "Poetic Naturalism in the Contemporary Novel," *Partisan Review,* XXVI (Summer, 1959), 467–472. "The strange fusion of raw actuality and lyrical adoration" insistently recurs in American fiction; Malamud, Bellow, Algren.

WILLIAMS, RAYMOND. "Realism and the Contemporary Novel," *Partisan Review,* XXVI (Spring, 1959), 200–213. Problems of the individual in society are treated realistically in recent literature, rather than romantically or naturalistically.

II. ON INDIVIDUAL NOVELISTS

Nelson Algren

GEISMAR, MAXWELL. "Nelson Algren: The Iron Sanctuary," *College English,* XIV (March, 1953), 311–315.

LIPTON, LAWRENCE. "A Voyeur's View of the Wild Side," *Chicago Review,* X (Winter, 1957), 4–14.

James Baldwin

JACOBSON, DAN. "James Baldwin as Spokesman," *Commentary,* XXXII (December, 1961), 497–502.

Saul Bellow

CHASE, RICHARD. "The Adventures of Saul Bellow," *Commentary,* XXVII (April, 1959), 323–330.

EISINGER, CHESTER E. "Saul Bellow: Love and Identity," *Accent,* XVIII, No. 3 (Summer, 1958), 179–203.

FIEDLER, LESLIE A. "Saul Bellow," *Prairie Schooner,* XXXI (Summer, 1957), 103–110.

FREEDMAN, RALPH. "Saul Bellow: The Illusion of Environment," *Wisconsin Studies in Contemporary Literature,* I (Winter, 1960), 50–65.

GOLDBERG, GERALD JAY. "Life's Customer, Augie March," *Critique,* III (Summer, 1960), 15–27.

HASSAN, IHAB H. "Saul Bellow: Five Faces of a Hero," *Critique,* III (Summer, 1960), 28–36.

HUGHES, D. J. "Reality and the Hero: *Lolita* and *Henderson the Rain King,*" *Modern Fiction Studies,* VI (Winter, 1960–1961), 345–364.

LEVENSON, J. C. "Bellow's Dangling Men," *Critique,* III (Summer, 1960), 3–14.

LEVINE, PAUL. "Saul Bellow: The Affirmation of the Philosophical Fool," *Perspective,* X (Winter, 1959), 163–176.

OPDAHL, KEITH. "The Crab and the Butterfly: Themes of Saul Bellow." Unpublished doctoral dissertation, Department of English, University of Illinois, 1961.

QUINTON, ANTHONY. "The Adventures of Saul Bellow," *London Magazine,* VI (December, 1959), 55–59.

REUBEN, FRANK. "Saul Bellow: The Evolution of a Contemporary Novelist," *Western Review,* XVIII (Winter, 1954), 101–112.

ROSS, THEODORE J. "Notes on Saul Bellow," *Chicago Jewish Forum,* XVIII (Fall, 1959), 21–27.

SCHNEIDER, HAROLD W. "Two Bibliographies: Saul Bellow, William Styron," *Critique,* III (Summer, 1960), 71–91.

Vance Bourjaily

DIENSTFREY, HARRIS. "The Novels of Vance Bourjaily," *Commentary,* XXXI (April, 1961), 360–363.

Truman Capote

BUCCO, MARTIC. "Truman Capote and the Country below the Surface," *Four Quarters,* VII (1957), 22–25.

COLLINS, CARVEL. "Other Voices," *American Scholar,* XXV (Winter, 1955–1956), 108–116.

HASSAN, IHAB H. "The Daydream of Nightmare and Narcissus," *Wisconsin Studies in Contemporary Literature,* I (Spring–Summer, 1960), 5–21.

Herbert Gold

SEIDEN, MELVIN. "Characters and Ideas: The Modern Novel," *Nation,* April 25, 1959, pp. 387–392.

Jack Kerouac

ASKEW, MELVIN W. "Quests, Cars, and Kerouac," *University of Kansas City Review,* XXVIII (Spring, 1962), 231–240.

CHAMPNEY, FREEMAN. "Beat-up or Beatific," *Antioch Review,* XIX (Spring, 1959), 114–121.

GOLD, HERBERT. "Hip, Cool, Beat — and Frantic," *Nation,* November 16, 1957, pp. 349–355.

TALLMAN, WARREN. "Kerouac's Sound," *Evergreen Review* IV (January–February, 1960), 153–169.

Norman Mailer

DeMott, Benjamin. "An Unprofessional Eye: Docket No. 15883," *American Scholar*, xxx (Spring, 1961), 232–237.

Glicksberg, Charles I. "Norman Mailer: The Angry Young Novelist in America," *Wisconsin Studies in Contemporary Literature*, i (Winter, 1960), 25–34.

Glicksberg, Charles I. "Sex in Contemporary Literature," *Colorado Quarterly*, ix (Winter, 1961), 277–287.

Goldstone, Herbert. "The Novels of Norman Mailer," *English Journal*, xlv (March, 1956), 113–121.

Hoffman, Frederick J. "Norman Mailer and the Revolt of the Ego: Some Observations on Recent American Literature," *Wisconsin Studies in Contemporary Literature*, i (Fall, 1960), 5–12.

Krim, Seymour. "A Hungry Mental Lion," *Evergreen Review*, iv (January–February, 1960), 178–185.

Schroder, George A. "Norman Mailer and the Despair of Defiance," *Yale Review*, li (Winter, 1962), 267–280.

Bernard Malamud

Elman, Richard J. "Malamud on Campus," *Commonweal*, October 27, 1961, 114–115.

Rovit, Earl H. "Bernard Malamud and the Jewish Literary Tradition," *Critique*, iii (Winter-Spring, 1960), 3–10.

Carson McCullers

Durham, Frank. "God and No God in *The Heart Is a Lonely Hunter*," *South Atlantic Quarterly*, lvi (Fall, 1956), 494–499.

Evans, Oliver. "The Achievement of Carson McCullers," *English Journal*, li (May, 1962), 301–308.

Folk, Barbara N. "The Sad Sweet Music of Carson McCullers," *Georgia Review*, xvi (Spring, 1962), 202–209.

Kohler, Dayton. "Carson McCullers: Variations on a Theme," *College English*, xiii (October, 1951), 1–8.

McPherson, Hugo. "Carson McCullers: Lonely Huntress," *Tamarack Review*, xi (Spring, 1959), 28–40.

Vickery, John B. "Carson McCullers: A Map of Love," *Wisconsin Studies in Contemporary Literature*, i (Winter, 1960), 13–24.

Wright Morris

Baumbach, Jonathan. "Wake before Bomb: *Ceremony in Lone Tree*," *Critique*, iv (Winter, 1961–1962), 56–71.

Booth, Wayne, C. "The Two Worlds in the Fiction of Wright Morris," *Sewanee Review*, lxv (Summer, 1957), 375–399.

CARPENTER, FREDERICK I. "Wright Morris and the Territory Ahead," *College English,* XXI (December, 1959), 147–156.

HUNT, JOHN W., JR. "The Journey Back: The Early Novels of Wright Morris," *Critique,* V (Spring–Summer, 1962), 41–60.

LINDEN, STANTON J., and DAVID MADDEN. "A Wright Morris Bibliography," *Critique,* IV (Winter, 1961–1962), 77–87.

Madden, David. "The Great Plains in the Novels of Wright Morris," *Critique,* IV (Winter, 1961–1962), 5–23.

MADDEN, DAVID. "The Hero and the Witness in Wright Morris' Field of Vision," *Prairie Schooner,* XXXIV (Fall, 1960), 263–278.

TRACHTENBURG, ALAN. "The Craft of Vision," *Critique,* IV (Winter, 1961–1962), 41–55.

WATERMAN, ARTHUR E. "The Novels of Wright Morris: An Escape from Nostalgia," *Critique,* IV (Winter, 1961–1962), 24–40.

Flannery O'Connor

FERRIS, SUMNER J. "The Outside and the Inside: Flannery O'Connor's *The Violent Bear It Away,*" *Critique,* III (Winter–Spring, 1960), 11–19.

GORDON, CAROLINE. "Flannery O'Connor's *Wise Blood,*" *Critique,* II (Fall, 1958), 3–10.

HART, JANE. "Strange Earth: The Stories of Flannery O'Connor," *Georgia Review,* XII (Summer, 1958), 215–222.

HAWKES, JOHN. "Flannery O'Connor's Devil," *Sewanee Review,* LXX (Summer, 1962), 395–407.

McCOWN, ROBERT, S.J. "Flannery O'Connor and the Reality of Sin," *Catholic World,* CLXXXVIII (January, 1959), 285–291.

MEADOR, MARGARET. "Flannery O'Connor: Literary Witch," *Colorado Quarterly,* X (Spring, 1962), 377–386.

QUINN, SISTER M. BERNETTA. "View from a Rock: The Fiction of Flannery O'Connor and J. F. Powers," *Critique,* II (Fall, 1958), 19–27.

RUBIN, LOUIS D., JR. "Flannery O'Connor: A Note on Literary Fashions," *Critique,* II (Fall, 1958), 11–18.

WEDGE, GEORGE F. "Two Bibliographies: Flannery O'Connor, J. F. Powers," *Critique,* II (Fall, 1958), 59–70.

Philip Roth

LANDIS, JOSEPH C. "The Sadness of Philip Roth," *Massachusetts Review,* III (Winter, 1962), 259–268.

SOLOTAROFF, THEODORE. "Philip Roth and the Jewish Moralists," *Chicago Review,* XIII (Winter, 1959), 87–99.

J. D. Salinger

BRANCH, EDGAR. "Mark Twain and J. D. Salinger: A Study in Literary Continuity," *American Quarterly,* IX (Summer, 1957), 144–158.

BRYAN, J. E. "The Fat Lady and the Chicken Sandwich," *College English,* XXIII (December, 1961), 216–217.

COSTELLO, DONALD P. "The Language of *The Catcher in the Rye,*" *American Speech,* XXXIV (October, 1959), 172–181.

DAVIS, TOM. "J. D. Salinger: A Checklist," *Papers of the Bibliographical Society of America,* LIII (1959), 69–71.

GILES, BARBARA. "The Lonely War of J. D. Salinger," *Mainstream,* XII (February, 1959), 2–13.

GREEN, MARTIN. "Amis and Salinger: The Latitude of Private Conscience," *Chicago Review,* XI (Winter, 1958), 20–25.

GWYNN, FREDERICK L., and JOSEPH L. BLOTNER. *The Fiction of J. D. Salinger.* Pittsburgh, Pa.: University of Pittsburgh Press, 1958.

HASSAN, IHAB H. "Rare Quixotic Gesture: The Fiction of J. D. Salinger," *Western Review,* XXI (Summer, 1957), 261–280.

HEISERMAN, ARTHUR, and JAMES E. MILLER, JR. "J. D. Salinger: Some Crazy Cliff," *Western Humanities Review,* X (Spring, 1956), 129–137.

KAPLAN, CHARLES. "Holden and Huck: The Odysseys of Youth," *College English,* XVIII (November, 1956), 76–80.

KAZIN, ALFRED. "J. D. Salinger: 'Everybody's Favorite,' " *Atlantic Monthly,* CCVIII (August, 1961), 27–31.

KEGEL, CHARLES H. "Incommunicability in Salinger's *Catcher in the Rye,*" *Western Humanities Review,* XI (Spring, 1957), 188–190.

LEVINE, PAUL. "J. D. Salinger: The Development of the Misfit Hero," *Twentieth Century Literature,* IV (October, 1958), 92–99.

McCARTHY, MARY. "J. D. Salinger's Closed Circuit," *Harper's,* CCXXV (October, 1962), 46–48.

MIZENER, ARTHUR. "The Love Song of J. D. Salinger," *Harper's,* CCXVIII (February, 1959), 83–90.

OLDSEY, BERNARD. "The Movies in the Rye," *College English,* XXIII (December, 1961), 209–215.

SENG, PETER J. "The Fallen Idol: The Immature World of Holden Caulfield," *College English,* XXIII (December, 1961), 203–209.

STEINER, GEORGE. "The Salinger Industry," *Nation,* November 14, 1959, pp. 360–363.

STRAUCH, CARL F. "Kings in the Back Row: Meaning through Structure — A Reading of Salinger's *The Catcher in the Rye,*" *Wisconsin Studies in Contemporary Literature,* II (Winter, 1961), 5–30.

WAKEFIELD, DAN. "Salinger and the Search for Love," *New World Writing,* No. 14 (December, 1958), pp. 68–85. New York: New American Library, 1958.

WIEGAND, WILLIAM. "The Knighthood of J. D. Salinger," *New Republic,* October 19, 1959, pp. 19–21.

Jean Stafford

VICKERY, OLGA W. "The Novels of Jean Stafford," *Critique,* V (Spring–Summer, 1962), 14–26.

William Styron

BENSON, ALICE R. "Techniques in the Twentieth-Century Novel for Relating the Particular to the Universal: *Set This House on Fire,*" *Publications of the Michigan Academy of Science, Arts, and Letters,* XLVII (1962), 387–394.

DAVIS, ROBERT GORHAM. "Styron and the Students," *Critique,* III (Summer, 1960), 37–46.

FENTON, CHARLES A. "William Styron and the Age of the Slob," *Southern Atlantic Quarterly,* LIX (Autumn, 1960), 469–476.

FOSTER, RICHARD. "An Orgy of Commerce: William Styron's *Set This House on Fire,*" *Critique,* III (Summer, 1960), 59–70.

FRIEDMAN, MELVIN J. "William Styron: An Interim Appraisal," *English Journal,* L (March, 1961), 149–158, 192.

LAWSON, JOHN H. "Styron: Darkness and Fire in the Modern Novel," *Mainstream,* XIII (October, 1960), 9–18.

McNAMARA, EUGENE. "William Styron's *Long March:* Absurdity and Authority," *Western Humanities Review,* XV (Summer, 1961), 267–272.

SCHNEIDER, HAROLD W. "Two Bibliographies: Saul Bellow, William Styron," *Critique* III (Summer, 1960), 71–91.

John Updike

WARD, J. A. "John Updike's Fiction," *Critique,* V (Spring–Summer, 1962), 27–40.

III. BIBLIOGRAPHY AND REFERENCE

COWLEY, MALCOLM, ed. *Writers at Work: The "Paris Review" Interviews.* New York: The Viking Press, 1958.

JONES, HOWARD MUMFORD. *Guide to American Literature and Its Backgrounds since 1890.* Cambridge, Mass.: Harvard University Press, 1959.

LEARY, LEWIS. *Articles on American Literature, 1900–1950.* Durham, N. C.: Duke University Press, 1954.

LEARY, LEWIS, ed. *Contemporary Literary Scholarship.* Champaign, Ill.: National Council of Teachers of English, 1958.

LEVINE, PAUL. "American Bards and Liberal Reviewers," *Partisan Review,* XV (Spring, 1962), 91–109.

WARFEL, HARRY R. *American Novelists of Today.* New York: American Book Company, 1950.

NOTES ON THE CONTRIBUTORS

BERNARD DUFFEY is Professor of English at Michigan State University. He is the author of *Chicago Renaissance in American Letters* and of many articles on American literature and criticism, and is editor of *Modern American Literature*.

OLIVER EVANS has published widely on contemporary literature. He is the author of *Young Man with a Screwdriver*, a collection of poems; *New Orleans*, a descriptive study; and a translation of Machiavelli's *Clizia*. He is Assistant Professor of English at San Fernando Valley State College.

LESLIE A. FIEDLER is Professor of English at Montana State University and author of books of criticism and fiction, including a novel, *The Second Stone*.

WOLFGANG B. FLEISCHMANN is Associate Professor of Comparative Literature in the Graduate Institute of the Liberal Arts, Emory University. His research interests and publications concern the impact of the Graeco-Roman classics upon modern European literatures, the theory of poetic translation, and various aspects of contemporary literature.

MELVIN J. FRIEDMAN is Associate Professor of English and Comparative Literature at the University of Maryland. He has published articles on various contemporary writers, including Samuel Beckett, William Styron, and Flannery O'Connor.

EDMUND FULLER teaches at Kent School in Connecticut. He has published two novels, numerous reviews and articles, and *Man in Modern Fiction*, a collection of critical essays concerned with contemporary American writing.

HERBERT GOLD is a well-known novelist and short-story writer who has published extensive criticism of contemporary literature.

IHAB H. HASSAN is Professor of English at Wesleyan University in Connecticut. He has published numerous articles and reviews and is the author of *Radical Innocence*, a study of contemporary American fiction.

PAUL HERR's articles and short stories have appeared in *Chicago Review, Contact, december,* and other journals. He has published two novels, *Journey Not to End* and *The Amnesiacs*. He teaches English at Indiana University.

IRVING HOWE, Professor of English at Stanford, is the author of *Politics and the Novel, William Faulkner: A Critical Study,* and other books.

ALFRED KAZIN is the author of many books and articles on American literature, including *Contemporaries,* published in 1962.

MARCUS KLEIN is Assistant Professor of English at Barnard College.

RICHARD LEHAN is Assistant Professor of English at U.C.L.A. He has published widely on American and French fiction.

PAUL LEVINE, now at Harvard, has published articles and reviews in several journals.

NORMAN PODHORETZ is Editor of *Commentary* and contributor to many other magazines.

EARL H. ROVIT, who teaches English at the University of Louisville, is the author of *Herald to Chaos* (1960) and the forthcoming volume on Ernest Hemingway in the Twayne U. S. Authors Series.

BEN SIEGEL is Head of Language Arts at the California State Polytechnic College (Pomona) and an associate editor of *Recall* magazine.

DAVID STEVENSON is Professor of English and Coordinator of Graduate Studies, Western Reserve University; author of *The Love-Game Comedy;* editor, with Herbert Gold, of *Stories of Modern America.* He has published many critical articles and reviews of American fiction.

JOSEPH J. WALDMEIR teaches American Thought at Michigan State University. He has published numerous articles on contemporary literature.

WILLIAM WIEGAND teaches English at San Francisco State College. He has published two novels, *The Treatment Man* (1959) and *At Last, Mr. Tolliver* (1950), and is the author of numerous reviews and critical articles.

3-104